The Apocalypse

The Perennial Revelation of Jesus Christ

by

Eugenio Corsini

Translated & Edited by

Francis J. Moloney, S.D.B.

WIPF & STOCK · Eugene, Oregon

ABOUT THE AUTHOR:

Eugenio Corsini is the Professor of Ancient Christian Literature at the University of Turin. He has studied at the University of Turin; the Sorbonne, Paris; and the Pontifical Biblical Institute, Rome, and he has a long list of important publications in the area of the early Fathers of the Church. His interest in the Apocalypse is long-standing, and it was precisely his study of its use in the earliest Fathers and the acts of the Martyrs which made him question the usual "eschatological" method of interpreting the document.

ABOUT THE TRANSLATOR & EDITOR:

Francis J. Moloney, S.D.B., is an internationally renowned Johannine scholar. He teaches at Salesian Theological College, Australia, and he has lectured extensively. His books include *The Johannine Son of Man; The Word Became Flesh; Disciples and Prophets;* and *A Chance to Love: Poverty—Chastity—Obedience*.

Wipf and Stock Publishers
199 W 8th Ave, Suite 3
Eugene, OR 97401

The Apocalypse
The Perennial Revelation of Jesus Christ
By Corsini, Eugenio and Moloney, Francis J., SDB
Copyright©1983 by Corsini, Eugenio
ISBN 13: 978-1-5326-6604-9
Publication date 3/18/2019
Previously published by Michael Glazier, 1983

FOREWORD TO THE
2019 REPRINT EDITION

EUGENIO CORSINI (1925-2018) WAS Professor of Early Christian Literature at the University of Turin. In 1980, his interests in very early Christianity led him to publish a provocative interpretation of the Book of the Apocalypse, with the Italian title *Apocalisse prima e dopo* (Turin: Società Editrice Internazionale, 1980). As a young scholar, with an interest in the Johannine literature, I found his interpretation fascinating. Corsini argued that the almost universal use of Jewish and Christian apocalyptic literature as a paradigm for the interpretation of the biblical Apocalypse ignored the fact that the victory of God in and through the death and resurrection of Jesus Christ is proclaimed from the first to the last pages of the book (see, for example, Apoc 1:5-6; 5:1-14; 8:1; 11:15-18; 16:17-21; 19:4-8; 21:6). The Apocalypse did not ask persecuted Christians at the end of the first century to persevere in suffering, assured that God will ultimately destroy all evil forces; it proclaimed that the victory over evil had already been won. Indeed, the victory of the slain and risen Lamb has been with us "from the foundation of the world" (see 5:6; 13:8).

The cover created for this reprint is representative of the widespread Eastern Christian iconographic theme of the Anastasis portraying the risen Jesus' *descensio ad inferos* ("descent into hell" or "harrowing of hell"), raising Adam and Eve into life by taking their hands and leading them upward. Old Testament kings and prophets look on. Although the artistic tradition is associated with the temporal, indicating what happened in the silence of Holy Saturday (see 8:1), it can also be interpreted as an indication of the transtemporal saving effects of Jesus' death and resurrection "from the foundation of the world" (13:8).

The book that follows, *The Apocalypse: The Perennial Revelation of Jesus Christ*, was my edited translation of Corsini's original Italian, first published in English in 1983 (Good News Studies 5 [Wilmington: Michael Glazier, 1983]). The goal of my translation was to make available in English a challenging study, written in a language rarely consulted by mainstream New Testament scholars. To my disappointment, although the book was commercially very successful, it made no impact upon English or European scholarship. Craig R. Koester's outstanding recent commentary upon Revelation (*Revelation*, Anchor Yale Bible 38A [New Haven: Yale University Press, 2014]) does not even list Corsini's work in his 53 pages of general bibliography.

By the 1990's, given its almost total neglect, I accepted that Corsini's suggestions must have been unacceptable to scholarship at large, and thus no longer pursued his line of interpretation. However, in the early stages of my direction of a doctoral dissertation on the hymnic material in the Apocalypse in 2012, I asked the candidate to read a cross-section of major commentaries to "get the feel" of the document itself, and classical and contemporary commentary upon it. He returned to me overwhelmed by the potential of Corsini's reading of the text. By this stage, Professor Corsini himself had decided to return to his earlier research, publishing a further study entitled "The Apocalypse of Jesus Christ according to John" (*Apocalisse di Gesù Cristo secondo Giovanni*, Sestante [Turin: Società Editrice Internazionale, 2002]). I took the occasion to read this further study, and was once again impressed by the somewhat maverick but challenging interpretation of the most puzzling of New Testament books.

I did not agree with everything that Corsini had proposed, and was concerned by his lack of attention to the traditional early Christian expectation of the final action of God in the second coming of Christ (see especially 22:20). In the meantime, Apocalypse studies were moving away from the traditional endtime interpretative paradigm. For example, Leonard Thomson argued that the Christians of Asia lived quite peacefully within the Roman Empire (Leonard L. Thompson, *The Book of Revelation. Apocalypse and Empire* [New York: Oxford University Press, 1990]), and Steven Friesen's archeological study of the presence of Imperial Cults in Asia suggested that, however important the Cults may have been, the Apocalypse should not be regarded as a Christian response to their practice (Steven J. Friesen, *Imperial Cults and the Apocalypse of John. Reading Revelation in the Ruins* [New York: Oxford University Press, 2001]). My interest was piqued to such an extent that I began to plan my own reading of the Book of the Apocalypse.

It remained only a plan until a significant USA publishing house approached me, requesting a monograph on a New Testament book or theme. Some years ago, therefore, I began my research that has produced *The Apocalypse of John. An Alternative Commentary* (Grand Rapids: Baker Academic, 2020). However distant from my original interaction with Professor Corsini's work in 1983, his interpretation, repeated with great clarity and detail in 2002, undergirds my recent study. This is especially true of his strong focus upon the famous "sevens" within the Apocalypse (churches, seals, trumpets, and bowls) as the determining elements in grasping the document's overall literary structure. This structure provides the "skeleton" that shapes the flesh of an eventual interpretation.

Understandably, my translation of 1983, *The Apocalypse. The Perennial Revelation of Jesus Christ*, has long been out of print. It is occasionally available online, but at exorbitant prices. In the light of my recent study of the Apocalypse, referring continually to that foundational study and Corsini's further work of 2002, that has never been translated, I approached Al Ullman, Reprint Acquisitions and Custom Reprinting Coordinator at Wipf & Stock (Eugene: OR), suggesting that it be reprinted, and once be made widely available. I am delighted that Wipf & Stock, an admirable and adventurous trail-blazer among contemporary biblical and theological publishers, has provided easy and affordable access to the study reprinted here. It certainly serves as a companion-volume to my more recent volume. But it is more than that. As I have indicated above, it was the seed-bed for my "alternative approach," and deserves close attention on its own right. I thank Wipf & Stock for making that possible.

Francis J. Moloney, SDB, AM, FAHA
Catholic Theological College
University of Divinity
Melbourne, Victoria. AUSTRALIA

CONTENTS

Foreword by Francis J. Moloney SDB 1
Translator's Preface 7
Introduction 11
THE PROLOGUE (1:1-8) 64
THE SEVEN LETTERS TO THE CHURCHES
   (1:9—3:22) 80
   Structure and General Theme................... 80
   The Introduction to the Seven Letters (1:9-20) 83
   The "Letters" to the Churches of Asia Minor
     (chs. 2-3).................................. 95
THE SEVEN SEALS (4:1—8:1) 118
   Structure and General Theme................... 118
   The Introduction to the Seven Seals
     (4:1—5:14) 121
   The First Four Seals: the Creation and the Fall
     of Man (6:1-8) 137
   The Fifth Seal: The Salvation of the Just Ones in
     the Old Economy (6:9-11) 148
   The Sixth Seal: The Two Moments of the Divine
     Salvific Intervention (6:12—7:17) 155
   The Seventh Seal: The End of the Old Economy
     (8:1)...................................... 161
THE SEVEN TRUMPETS (8:2—11:19) 164
   Structure and General Theme................... 164
   The Introduction to the Seven Trumpets
     (8:2-6) 171
   The First Four Trumpets: The Fall of the
     Angels (8:7-13) 174
   The Fifth Trumpet (The First "Woe"): The Fall
     of Man (9:1-12) 178

    The Sixth Trumpet (The Second "Woe"): The
    Value and Limitations of the Old Economy
    (9:13—11:14) 181
    The Seventh Trumpet (The Third "Woe"): The
    Fulfilment of the "Mystery of God"
    (11:15-19) 201

THE SEVEN BOWLS (12:1—22:5) 206
    Structure and General Theme 206
    The Preface to the "Seven" of the Bowls: The
    First Two "Signs" (chs. 12-14) 211
        The Creation and the Fall of Man (ch. 12) ... 211
        The Corruption of Political and Religious
            Authority (ch. 13) 225
        The First Divine Salvific Intervention (The
            Old Economy) as an Announcing and a
            Prefiguring of the Second (The Death of
            Christ) (ch. 14) 255
    The Seven Bowls: The Third "Sign"
    (15:1—22:5) 279
        The Pouring out of the Bowls: The Death
            of Christ as Judgment upon the
            Consequences of the Original Fall
            (chs. 15-16) 279
        The Death of Christ as Judgment upon
            History: The Destruction of Babylon
            (17:1—19:10) 313
        The Death of Christ as the Definitive
            Destruction of all Evil Powers
            (19:11—20:15) 347
        The Death of Christ as the Basis for the
            Gathering of the Chosen Ones in the
            Messianic Kingdom (Heavenly
            Jerusalem (21:1—22:5) 385

THE EPILOGUE (22:6-21) 411

Bibliography 424

TRANSLATOR'S PREFACE

I first heard Prof. Eugenio Corsini's startling approach to the Apocalypse at a Patristic Congress held in the Salesian Pontifical University in April, 1978 (see the summary in E. Corsini, "L'Apocalisse di Giovanni nella Catechesi Patristica," *Salesianum* 41 [1979] 419). Some twelve months later, again in Rome, I was directed by Fr. Egidio Vigano, the Rector Major of the Salesian Congregation, to a book which he had just received in a pre-publication stage from the Turin publishers, Società Editrice Internazionale. The book was a work of E. Corsini, *Apocalisse prima e dopo*. Fr. Vigano, aware of my interest in matters Johannine, claimed that he had found the work startlingly refreshing and logical in its approach to this most difficult of New Testament documents. I was able to purchase a copy just as I was leaving Europe, at the end of 1980.

In 1981 I researched and taught a course on the Apocalypse at Catholic Theological College, Melbourne, Australia. The more I read, the more it struck me that Corsini had uncovered something surprisingly unique in the area of New Testament scholarship, where many of us tend to go on repeating the same old things in different ways. Whatever its worth, I felt that it needed more exposure than it was likely to receive in its Italian form. I began to write a course which quarried ideas from his book, yet attempted to keep in touch with the wider spectrum of other contemporary scholarship on the Apocalypse. Although I tried throughout my course of lectures to present the wider spectrum of current scholarly discussion of the document, it soon became apparent that Corsini's contribution would stand or fall on its own merits and faults. It is so unique that it cannot be "integrated" into contemporary scholarship.

I completed my course greatly enriched and armed with a very large typescript which had been painstakingly produced from reams of my handwritten notes by my sister, Mrs. Pauline Cullen. As always, I am most grateful to Pauline for her usual care and support. Only when I had the whole typescript on my desk did it occur to me that I was now in a position to present Corsini's work to an English-speaking public. Too few of us devote sufficient time and attention to Italian and Spanish biblical scholarship, as we are so fascinated by the Germans and (to a lesser extent) by the French. After initial contacts with the publishers and Prof. Corsini, I found that I still had a mammoth task ahead of me: the further "translation" of my schematic, edited and hurriedly written lecture notes into a faithful rendition of Prof. Corsini's book. At this stage I had the good fortune to obtain the assistance of Sr. Mary Philip, R.S.M., of the Convent of Mary of Mercy, Ballarat East, Victoria. A person of considerable experience and literary talent in her own right, she devoted herself to the thankless task of correcting my already-corrected version of my sister's typescript! I am sure that there are still difficult passages and turns of phrase that reflect an Italian original, but Sister Mary Philip's enthusiastic yet exacting contribution to this project makes Prof. Corsini, myself and future readers her debtors.

The major part of the translation which follows is a fairly close rendition of the original. The main feature of the editing process has been an attempt to show a greater economy of words than is sometimes possible in Italian, but necessary in English.

It is not for me to indicate the contents of this extraordinary book. The reader must discover that, and I am afraid that a "spot check" of interesting passages will do less than justice to the work. It gains momentum and increases in its credibility as the overall argument unfolds. Corsini would argue that the Apocalypse itself works in the same way! I would like simply to indicate that there were two aspects of the work which I found most helpful.

a) It explains a great number of *internal* difficulties which the Apocalypse has always presented: structure, unity, coherent argument, its use of the Old Testament, symbols and symbolic language, and even some difficult textual problems (see his treatment of Apoc 5:7; 13:8 and 20:10). Most recent commentators would probably claim that they have also done this. Corsini has explained *all* the difficulties of the Apocalypse by detaching them from the eschatological interpretation that is so common, and gathering them *all* around a single argument: the perennial revelation of Jesus Christ.

b) Despite the many recent attempts to provide a commentary which shows that John was a pastor, I have always been left wondering if we can rightly call the Apocalypse a *Christian* document. Is it really Christian to ask a suffering Church to live in the hope that in the end all will be well? What of the death and resurrection of Jesus of Nazareth which the rest of the New Testament authors believe has *already* created a newness and a fulness of life? Corsini attempts to show that the Apocalypse is a profound meditation upon the Old Testament witness to the Cross and Resurrection as the fulfilment of Jesus' messiahship, and that the new Jerusalem, the new heavens and the new earth are not a description of how things will be at the end of time, but a portrait of the present reality of the Church, "freed from our sins by his blood,...a kingdom of priests to his God and Father" (Apoc 1:5-6). If his attempt is successful, then he has restored the Apocalypse to an important place in *Christian* literature.

There are two practical matters which must be mentioned at this stage. The reader will notice that I have inserted sections of the text of the Apocalypse immediately before the reflections upon them. Any system which enables the reader to have the text continually before him is useful, but I have also followed this practice because it was part of the design of the original Italian work. The English version of this book, however, loses one of the great achievements of the original: Eugenio Corsini's translation of the Greek text. I have simply followed the Revised Standard Version throughout, except where the commentary forced a different version in 4:9-10; 5:7; 6:8; 13:8 and 20:10. In those places I have made my own translation. Finally, this is not a full-scale commentary upon the Apocalypse, despite its length. It is rather a biblical-theological meditation based on an assiduous use of the text itself, in an attempt to catch the mind of an inspired author whom we shall, for the sake of clarity and simplicity, continue to call "John."

This translation has been done so that scholarship may eventually come to a decision on the interpretation which follows. I do hope that my work, fitted into the breathing spaces allowed by a very active ministry, makes that decision possible for a wider group of scholars. I have already mentioned the contribution made to this translation by Sister Mary Philip, R.S.M. I would like to conclude this preface by sharing a reflection which she sent to me as she finished her final instalment: "This interpretation reveals that the Apocalypse is really a summing up of the biblical writings – a kind of triumphal climax. I Tim 1:9 (in the Jerusalem Bible translation) strikes me as a summary of all that John is saying:

> 'God has saved us and called us to be holy – not because of anything we ourselves have done, but for his own purpose and by his own grace. This grace has already been granted to us, in Christ Jesus, before the beginning of time.'"

Francis J. Moloney, S.D.B.
Salesian Theological College
Oakleigh
Victoria 3166
Easter Sunday, 1982.

INTRODUCTION

The work which follows is not intended to be a commentary upon the Apocalypse. There have been many such commentaries, reaching back into the earliest times of the Christian era. Some, especially during the Middle Ages, have been quite spectacular in their ingeniousness. Our modern era has seen a series of fine commentaries, applying all the criteria of a historical-philological analysis to this difficult book. Outstanding examples of this approach have been the commentaries of Bousset, Zahn, Charles, Allo and Lohmeyer. Quite frankly, I believe that it would be presumptuous to think that I could do better than they have already done. What I have attempted to do here is to provide a continuous reading of the text, trying to show, especially through the links which can be made with the Old Testament tradition, the coherent and unified argument of the whole work. I will insist upon the unity of the structure and theology of the Apocalypse as it stands. The reader will find that, despite my admiration for and debt to the older commentaries, I have introduced something quite new to the interpretation of the Apocalypse. It appears to me that the work is certainly about the coming of Jesus Christ, but not his coming at the end of time. The "coming" which stands at the centre of the argument of the Apocalypse has been going on through the whole of history, beginning with the creation of the world, and reaching its culmination in the great "event" (Greek: *kairos*) of the historical coming of Jesus Christ, especially in his death and resurrection.

If this is the case, then obviously the usual questions of "introduction" (author, date of composition, unity of the work, its relationship with the rest of the New Testament) acquire a new significance. I will briefly consider some of these, not only because they have a certain importance for our interpretation of the text, but also because it is precisely in the many and lengthy discussions of these matters, which have gone on for centuries, that one can see that many conclusions are reached because of presuppositions which need to be re-examined.

The Author

The Apocalypse is one of the few New Testament writings which carry the name of its author: John (see 1:1, 4, 9; 21:2; 22:8). Ancient tradition almost unanimously identified this "John" with the beloved disciple of Jesus, the author of other New Testament documents: the Fourth Gospel and the three Johannine letters. There were a few dissenting voices, but they could not have been many as Eusebius, who had his own reasons for listening to negative views on the book, can only mention two: the Roman Priest Gaius (beginning of the 3rd Century) and the Bishop of Alexandria, Dionysius (middle of the 3rd Century). The former attributed the Apocalypse to an obscure heretic called Cerinthus, a founder of a sect called Ebionites, paraphrased as "the poor of Christ." The latter, however, took a clearly argued position that at Ephesus there was another "John," not the Apostle, and he suggested that this John could be the author of our New Testament book. We also know that Marcion refused to accept the Apocalypse because it was too closely linked to and in favour of the Old Testament.

As one can see, these opinions come rather later, and they are few. We do not know Gaius' sources for his argument that Cerinthus was the author of the Apocalypse, but we do know that his opinion grew within the context of polemics. Gaius refused to accept the apostolic origins of all the so-called "Johannine" writings in a struggle against the Montanists who used them as their basis for a "new prophecy" which spoke of an ongoing and general revelation. Dionysius did not take any final position himself. He simply limited himself to indicate that there were problems with the tradition. He also insisted upon the obscurity and incomprehensibility of the work, but he did not deny that it was inspired. His main contribution was to show the linguistic and stylistic contrasts which existed between the Apocalypse and the other Johannine literature. In this way he ended by simply raising questions.

What is clear in Dionysius, however, is his opposition to millenarianism, a belief in a temporal and material final rule of Christ. It appears that such beliefs, at least at that time, were based upon a certain reading of the Apocalypse. Dionysius himself indicates that he was arguing against a unified tradition in support of the apostolic origin of the book.

The same position can be found in Eusebius who, in his *Ecclesiastical History*, gave a list of the various positions taken in the discussion on the authorship of the Apocalypse. Eusebius was even more explicit in his attribution of the book to another John, called by Papias John "the presbyter." However, he had no trouble with the inspired nature of the work, and he used it often, without hesitation or reserve. Nevertheless, Eusebius also had certain difficulties, and again they appear to have arisen from his struggle against millenarianism. He was deeply involved in this question, as it also infringed upon his political positions. Millenarianism, with its waiting for the final rule of Christ, tended to detract from the Christian empire of Constantine, rendering it also a part of the old order, a part of the wicked and passing era, destined to be totally destroyed. This did not suit Eusebius at all, as he was an enthusiastic supporter of the new situation initiated by Constantine.

As one can see, the authorship problem has a rather late origin, and is closely linked with questions of doctrine and politics which strongly influenced the positions taken.

Nevertheless, the position of Eusebius formulates the real issues very well: John the Apostle or John "the presbyter"? Similarity or dissimilarity, as regards both form and content, between the Apocalypse and the other Johannine writings? A millenarian text or not? Nowadays the question of the exact author seems to have lost its importance, even though most still look towards John the Apostle. This question, of course, is also closely related to that of the date of composition and the unity of the work, but again it is often the presuppositions which the scholars have about the significance of the text which colours their decisions.

The Date of Composition

Irenaeus (second half of the 2nd Century) is our earliest witness in this matter. According to him, the Apostle John wrote the Apocalypse towards the end of the reign of the Emperor Domitian who was murdered in 96 A.D. Eusebius is more precise, and records that it was written in "the fourteenth year" of Domitian, which would mean 94-95 A.D. This is not, however, the only date we have. In antiquity there were several other suggestions: the reign of Claudius (41-54 A.D.), Nero (54-68), Trajan (98-117). The indication that John is a prisoner on the island of Patmos (see 1:9ff) complicates the matter further. Some (like Vittorinus of Pettau, Eusebius, Jerome) situate this event under the rule of Domitian, but according to Tertullian (beginning of the 3rd Century) it would have happened under Nero, immediately after John's persecution in Rome. There is a further ancient opinion (Epiphanius of Salamis) which places it in the period of Claudius.

Opinion among modern scholars is divided. The majority accept the date under Domitian. Very few support the suggestion that it was written under Claudius or Trajan, but some would claim that it followed the persecutions of Nero (65-68 A.D.), during the reign of Vespasian (69-79 A.D.). Generally speaking, these conclusions are not based upon the witness of the ancient testimonies, but upon hints which the scholars find within the text itself. This, of course, means that there will necessarily be a certain amount of subjectivity in such decisions.

One example of such a tendency is the famous explanation of the seven heads of the beast as "seven kings" (see 17:10-11). Starting with this datum, one can then begin to count the Roman emperors, beginning with Julius Caesar or Augustus and making a decision about whether or not one includes the three emperors who came and went in the year that separated Nero and Vespasian (Galba, Otho and Vitellius). One can see that there are already difficulties involved, but the whole system is based upon the conviction that the seven heads of the beast are symbols of seven Roman emperors. I will attempt to show that this is not the case.

Another important factor in the dating of the work is its association with persecution and death for religious motives (see, for example, 6:9; 7:14). This explains why there is such a concentration upon the period of Nero or Domitian, two emperors which Christian tradition has presented as great persecutors of the Christian faith. This is based upon the presupposition, never questioned, that John not only refers to the persecution of Christians, but that the emperors themselves were taking up a conscious stance against Christianity itself. This latter idea only came to the Christians at a much later date.

The same sort of difficulty can be raised concerning other direct identifications made by modern scholars between references in the Apocalypse and certain personalities from antiquity. One of these is the reference to the legend of Nero "redivivus." According to this legend, the emperor escaped death and fled to the Parthians. From there he eventually would return at the head of an army to destroy Rome. This is used to explain John's reference to the beast "who was, and is not, and is to ascend from the bottomless pit" (see 17:8; 11:7) and to the beast who was mortally wounded, but healed (13:3).

Here there is a certain simplicity in the acceptance of this reference as the key to the passage, and an unwillingness to ask seriously if John, even if he knew the legend, would have made it the key to the understanding of one of the major arguments of his book. This would make of him a man who was primarily interested in the temporal and political aspects of history. This has to be proved, and it really does appear to be in direct opposition to the tenor of the whole work, which seems to be motivated by a conviction that the whole of history has its sense and purpose – not in politics and time – but in its being understood as a history of salvation, centred upon the gradual revelation of the divine salvific plan in the "revelation of Jesus Christ" (see 1:1).

This does not mean that the Apocalypse makes no reference to its contemporary history, but perhaps such references should be interpreted in a different way than is customary. Such reference is to be entirely subordinated to the major theme of the work: the perennial revelation of Jesus Christ. The references of ch. 17 can be seen in this way. As we will see later, John is symbolically describing the immediate historical prelude to the great "event" of the death of Christ: a diabolic alliance between two corrupt powers, the political and the religious authorities, Roman imperial authority and the Jewish synagogue. The reference to the terrible war which breaks out between the beast and the prostitute (see 17:16) is not a reference to Nero's destruction of Rome, but to the Jewish revolt against Rome which led to the destruction of Jerusalem in 70 A.D. The message is profound: the two powers (Rome and Judaism) which united for the death of Jesus, were finally locked in a disgusting and deadly conflict between themselves. The question is not, ultimately, about the material destruction of the powers, but about their spiritual destruction, because of the death of Jesus.

If we grant that this is the meaning of the passage, we can conclude that the Apocalypse must be dated after 70 A.D., but we must insist that while the events are clearly behind the message, they must never be brought into the front of the discussion. The events are merely used to throw into light the ultimate victory won in the death and resurrection of Jesus. The destruction described is not a material destruction. It is the spiritual destruction and ruin of corrupt political and religious authority.

The Unity of the Book

Certain presuppositions about the internal structure of the work, both as regards its content and sequence, have also been rife. It is fascinating to notice that while we have a textual tradition in the text of the Apocalypse which is almost without serious uncertainties, this same book has been subject to a whole series of suggestions about its original order. Probably more than any other New Testament documents, the text of the Apocalypse has been taken apart, reordered, delved into for the rediscovery of original sources, Jewish and Christian, studied as the product of a double or a triple redaction, etc., etc. All of this, of course, is an indication of the difficulty which contemporary scholars have in making sense of the document as it stands. Yet, as I mentioned above, those responsible for the original textual traditions seemed to have no such difficulty! The problem seems to lie with our era.

The interpretation which I am about to offer, even though it takes into consideration all the critical work which has been done, begins with the conviction that the text has to be understood as it stands. It is our task to seek the internal logic and development of the text without rewriting it to suit our own purposes. To alter the sequence of passages and to correct the logic of a book may make our task easier, but it is precisely in this exercise that we run the risk of losing touch with what the original author wished to communicate. Hopefully, the study which follows will indicate that such reworking of the text is not necessary.

The Reading of the "Apocalypse"

One of the difficulties which has arisen from the tendency to see the Apocalypse as a collection of "pieces" is that great symbols and figures tend to take on a character of their own. They thus lose their function within the overall reading of the whole book: the four horsemen, the seventh seal, the one hundred and forty-four thousand marked ones, the woman clothed with the sun, the great prostitute, the dragon, the reign of a thousand years, the spouse of the Lamb, the heavenly Jerusalem, and many others. Unfortunately, this happens not only in the popular use of the book, but also in some theological and liturgical usage. This is not a recent phenomenon. One could cite the use which Irenaeus made of the symbols of the four living creatures from ch. 4 as representations of the four Evangelists, or the widespread use of ch. 20 (see 20:4ff.) in the millenarian discussions. This latter use of the Apocalypse is important. Did millenarianism come into Christianity simply through a misuse of the imagery of ch. 20? Maybe these millenarian ideas crept into Christianity through other influences, quite independent of the Apocalypse. If this is the case, then in ch. 20 the author may well be using those ideas for his own ends? We will have to give this matter serious consideration, as it touches upon some important issues. It is not merely a question of what the Apocalypse said *then*, but a question of whether or not the Apocalypse is directly responsible for the many forms of millenarianism which still exist in Christianity to this day, many of them irrational, and some even leading to violence. Because it is generally accepted that all such movements *do* have their origins somewhere in the background of the Apocalypse, the work is often regarded suspiciously. Because this is the case, we must seriously ask whether this is really the meaning of the Apocalypse.

That answer will have to be given when we come to a consideration of the major texts which have been used. For the moment it is possible to notice a few important elements which will point us towards our eventual answer to this problem. Contrary to general opinion, the connection between the Apocalypse and the origins of millenarianism is difficult to establish. From Dionysius and Eusebius one can see that various millenarian groups were using the documents for their beliefs, but neither of these men indicate to us just what they think of the seriousness of this use of the Apocalypse for such beliefs. Both indicate that they find the book difficult, and question its apostolic origins. Yet, as I have already mentioned, Dionysius defends the inspired nature of the work, and Eusebius regularly uses it as Sacred Scripture in his writings.

Before them the priest Gaius had no hesitation: Cerinthus argued for millenarianism on the basis of the Apocalypse, but he had written the document himself. For Gaius, the document was certainly millenarian. There are other early Fathers of the Church who agreed with him: Justin, Irenaeus, Hippolytus and Lactantius. All this only proves that millenarianism existed within Christianity, and that its proponents were using the Apocalypse in their speculations. It does not prove that it is derived from the Apocalypse. We must be careful in our use of Dionysius and Eusebius. Even the information which is passed on to us through Irenaeus and Eusebius that Papias, the Bishop of Hierapolis in Phrygia, was one of the first followers of millenarianism does not indicate that there was any direct connection between his beliefs and the Apocalypse. We only know that he was a disciple of John (who for Irenaeus was the Apostle), but it is not even indicated that he knew of the Apocalypse.

There is a further consideration. Before Dionysius and Eusebius millenarianist beliefs were not shared by everyone. Yet the Apocalypse was widely known and used. In fact, some of the most serious opponents of millenarianism use it and comment upon it: Theophilus of Antioch, Clement of Alexandria, Origen, the various acts of the martyrs, and especially the *Martyrdom of Perpetua and Felicity*. This indicates, at least, that there was a current interpretation of the Apocalypse (which would have included ch. 20) which was not millenarianist. It appears that the evidence from antiquity on the relationship between the origins of millenarianism and the Apocalypse is not at all clear, and cannot be decided one way or the other. One can only say that in the heart of early Christianity there were millenarian groups which used the Apocalypse. However, there were also non-millenarian groups who used it. The same can be said for our contemporary situation. One thing, however, is clear. In the earlier period, before the intervention of Eusebius, the whole discussion went on without any interest in politics as the answer. After Eusebius this entered as it was closely tied up with the Christian empire established by Constantine. Thus, we can claim that in the pre-Constantinian era there was a use of the Apocalypse by the millenarianists which changed direction at a later stage. In the earlier period their applications of the text to their positions did not shake the confidence of those who did not accept millenarianism. Obviously, this latter group must have been able to show that the millenarian use of the text was a misreading of ch. 20.

The intervention of Eusebius was decisive. His argument against millenarianism, often inspired by political concerns, was much sharper and aggressive than that of his predecessors. His fears lay in the fact that he may not have been able to overcome the millenarian interpretation of the text, and this was accentuated by the decidedly anti-Roman direction that the interpretation of the document was now taking, after the great persecutions of the 3rd Century. The book was clearly an embarrassment to him, as it was also to Dionysius. However, as we have already said, neither ever came to condemn it.

It must be recognised, however, that the major problem for the subsequent interpretation of the Apocalypse was not this question of its contact with the origins of millenarianism. Eusebius' intervention created a situation which made the readers begin to ask just what was the significance of the reign of a thousand years. One only has to glance at ch. 20 of Augustine's *City of God*. It is almost entirely taken up with commentary upon ch. 20 of the Apocalypse, almost as if the rest of the document did not exist. Subsequent interpretation has gone along the same lines. This concentration upon the description of the end of time has brought with it a series of further problems. It has contributed greatly to the tendency to simply look at events and personalities out of their context, as I have already mentioned. This all began with the tendency to read the passages upon the reign of a thousand years as if they did not belong to an immediate context, and the immediate context to a whole book. Then followed the tendency to look for eschatological messages and images at every turn, causing the profound contributions which John has made upon God, Christology and Church to fade in importance. The Apocalypse came to be judged as a "prophecy" of the end of time, a foreseeing and a prediction of what will happen in the future.

Apocalypse and Prophecy

It is taken for granted that when John speaks of his work as "prophecy" (1:3.22; 7:18) and places himself in the category of "prophet" (19:10; 22:9) that he must be referring to the future. But what does he really mean? The analysis of the various prophetic *situations* described by him through the book (1:9ff; 4:1ff; 10:4ff, etc.) shows that he is using the term just as it was used of the Old Testament prophets: prophecy is an activity of the Spirit of God among men, in which a man is given the power and authority to receive the word, the divine revelation and charged to communicate it to others.

The function of the prophetic movement in Israel was not primarily to speak about future events. This is an unfortunate misunderstanding, and the common application of the word 'prophet' in contemporary society to one who utters dire threats about the future focuses its attention on a secondary aspect of the function of the prophets in Israel. Above all, the prophets were men who were entirely taken up with their loyalty to the covenant. The presence of Yahweh and his command were like a fire burning within them (see Jer 20:9). Ultimately, they are best described as lovers, men who are so entirely taken up with the overpowering presence of the Lordship of Yahweh that they are deeply hurt when they see Yahweh's people living in division, adoring false gods, behaving 'like all the nations,' alienated from one another, and from their unique God. In this situation they can do no other than burst forth into criticism of this situation, both by the quality of their lives and by their fierce and courageous preaching. In the light of criticism and rebuke, Amos can only reply that he is not his own master. He has been 'taken' by the Lord, and so must announce his word, cost what it may: "I am no prophet, nor a prophet's son; but I am a herdsmen, and a dresser of sycamore trees, and Yahweh took me from following the flock, and Yahweh said to me, 'Go prophesy to my people Israel'" (Amos 7:14-15).

Their function is to call Israel back to the original covenant love which was established between Yahweh and his people at Sinai. Thus, the prophet looks back to the period of original faithfulness. He looks back to the laws that were set up for the keeping of the covenant, and he criticises the unfaithfulness of his present situation in the light of the law, and in the light of that original faithfulness. The oracles telling of future blessings or of future punishment are merely the final guarantee that this prophet is, in fact, announcing God's word, and not his own:

> "And if you say in your heart, 'How may we know the word which the Lord has not spoken?' – when a prophet speaks in the name of the Lord, if the word does not come to pass or come true, that is a word which the Lord has not spoken; the prophet has spoken it presumptuously, you need not be afraid of him" (Deut 18:21-2).

Thus, the function of the biblical prophet was to act as a continual thorn in the side of the established Israel, to remind the establishment of Israel continually why she was established originally: to live in covenant love with her unique God, Yahweh, and at peace with one another (see, for example, Amos 2:6-16, where the prophet speaks out against the division and avarice of Israel).

As we proceed we will see how John used the Old Testament Biblical tradition. For the moment, my insistence that he does go back to that tradition needs consideration. I have already indicated that telling about the future was not the primary function of a prophet. Even the false prophets could do that (see Exod 22:18; Deut 18:10-12). Prophecy is directed towards the purity of the nation in the present, especially its purity of doctrine about God and its practice of cult. Such prophecy does not depend upon telling the future but upon its being based upon the authority of God, whose word and will the prophet communicates (see Is 8:18-22).

As the will of God is all powerful, it cannot simply be translated into words, but it becomes works, deeds, facts. These are the "signs" of his will. In this way, everything that exists and everything that happens, the creation of the world and the events of history are "signs" of God, manifestations of his will.

A prophet is one who, through the inspiration of the Spirit of God, succeeds in reading and interpreting these "signs," and in drawing from them the warnings, the advice, the promises and the threats which God issues by means of such "signs."

Often the divine message is communicated to the prophet, and from him to others in an indirect fashion, as visions, symbolic gestures, allegories and parables. The contents of these symbolic forms sometimes refer to the future, but more frequently they refer to the past. In both cases it is always "prophecy." The vision of the bones (see Ezek 37:1ff) and of the reconstructed Temple (Ezek 40:1ff) expressed a certainty about the future rebirth and restoration of Israel. But the parable of the two sisters (Ezek 23:1ff) is an allegory upon the past history of the two Hebrew kingdoms of Judah; that of the six men clothed in linen who entered Jerusalem (Ezek 9, 1ff) indicates the destruction of the city of Nabuchadnezzar, an event long past. This is always prophecy, insofar as it is always a reading and an interpretation of the "signs" wrought by Yahweh and the manifestation of his will through them: a will to punish unfaithfulness, guilt, injustice; a will to save his people after having subjected them to trial.

The Apocalypse and Apocalyptic

Apocalyptic literature is closely associated with an "end-time" messianism, the liberation of a suffering people from domination, announced by strange and wonderful signs. The Book of Daniel is the Old Testament example of this genre. It is interesting to notice that after the destruction of Judaism in 70, Jewish apocalyptic dies, producing only two further examples (Apocalypse of Baruch and IV Esdras, both post 70 A.D.). The literature of this genre which is produced in these post 70 A.D. years are Christian Apocalypses. These Apocalypses concentrate their attention on the final return of Jesus to destroy all evil.

Does the Apocalypse of John belong to this group? A close comparison between the two types of document show that there is much in common – signs, angels, etc., but these are severely limited in the Apocalypse insofar as they are totally subordinated to a role of *mediation*. They mediate a message which reveals Jesus Christ. Again we find that the use of signs and angels in the Apocalypse is much more closely related to the Old Testament use of these *mediations* than the fantastic speculations of some of the other Christian Apocalypses (e.g. the Apocalypse of Peter, the fifth and sixth Books of Esra, etc.).

There can be no doubt that there is much that is apocalyptic, but there is an *intended use*, in my opinion, of the apocalyptic genre which seriously betrays that genre. All of the Christian Apocalypses concentrate their attention on the *second coming* of Christ. As I have already argued, the Apocalypse is concerned with the *first coming*, and especially in the climactic and culminating event of his death and resurrection. This claim, of course, can only be substantiated by a careful study of the text. Only in the light of this first coming is the Christian, at *present* living the victory of that first coming, told to wait for the *second coming*. The Apocalypse is not a denial of the value of the present, as we wait for the future; it is a call to Christians to accept the challenge of life lived between the now and the not yet.

What sort of prophecy, therefore, are we dealing with – an

apocalyptic or a messianic prophecy? When one looks at the use John makes of the Old Testament, one is struck that there is no single use of either the traditional messianic texts, or the traditional apocalyptic texts. It has often been noticed that there is a wide-ranging use of both Old Testament texts and themes:

— Genesis story of the temptation and fall
— The Hebrew Exodus and the accompanying events
— The Temple and Jewish cult

These are continually recurring themes which have nothing to do with the Messiah or apocalyptic hopes in the Old Testament. Is it possible that the Apocalypse is not only about the second coming of Christ, but also about the bringing to fulfilment and perfection man's fallen state, the Exodus of God's chosen people, Temple and cult?

As I have already said several times, the Apocalypse is dominated by the figure of the Lamb, a clear symbol of the death of Jesus – also a symbol coming from the biblical tradition and from ancient Jewish cult (scapegoat; passover lamb?). The allegory of the marriage of the Lamb and his Bride, however, which is a clear reference to the application of the fruits of the redemption, appears only in ch. 21, almost at the end of the book. Does this mean that the fruits of the redemption are available only at the end of time, in the second coming?

Notice that what is said by the allegory of ch. 21 does not refer to some secondary aspect of the fruits of redemption, but to the very heart of it: in the marriage, the new Jerusalem comes down from heaven (21:9), and it consists in the fact that, from that moment on, God and the Lamb dwell among men, in the new City founded from above. This means that the marriage of the Lamb brings the liberation of mankind from sin, the restoration of a relationship of friendship with God, the establishment of a new cult, and the communication of a new life – eternal life.

According to the eschatological interpretation of the Apocalypse, all of this is part of the second coming. Many exegetes (beginnning with Augustine) have seen this difficulty, and have tried to draw back into history some of these "effects of the redemption," but once you claim that chs. 21-22 are to be understood as chronologically *after* the reign of a thousand years referred to in ch. 20, then all such attempts are forced, as the events of chs. 21-22 must be read as coming *after* the second judgment, at the end of time.

There are other serious problems which arise. According to 20:4-5, the only people who come to "life" are those who have been martyred – all other dead are excluded. This is sometimes explained by saying that only the martyrs enjoy the thousand years of life, while the others must wait, but even this suggestion goes contrary to any interpretation of the rest of the New Testament, especially the Fourth Gospel, which speaks of a realised eschatology: people are "alive" from the moment when they make their decision, in faith, for Christ. There must be a better solution to this problem.

One of the central reasons for the interpretation that the book is about the final vindication of the suffering christian community comes from John's regular use of the term "martyr," from the Greek *martus* and his regular use of the term *marturia* – "witness." It is important, however, to see the reason why they are described as "marturoi." It is always because of "their *testimony* to Jesus and for the word of God" (see, for example, 20:4, 6, 9). This has been traditionally taken to mean that they are Christian martyrs, slain for their faith in Christ; the book is totally concerned with a context of persecution, where people are dying for Christ. We must be careful, however, that the use of the Greek word *marturia* is only secondarily applied to this experience. Its primary meaning (as in John's Gospel) is *witness*. The application to the Christian experience under persecution is only *secondary*, a term applied to a special kind of witnessing.

A careful reading of the text will show that this is *not* the experience of the *martures* of the Apocalypse. It is not that Satan and his two agents, the two beasts, cause *marturia*. It works the other way. The marturia *precedes* this persecution, and in fact, causes it. The just ones are persecuted *because they render testimony to the word of God and to*

Jesus. It is interesting to notice that the author, John, regards himself as a *martus*, but he is certainly still alive.

He regards himself as a *martus* rendering testimony and witness to Jesus, just as do the other "witnesses" (*martures*) in the rest of the book (see 1:2, 9) – "on account of the work of God and the testimony to Jesus." If ever John wishes to speak of someone who is actually slain, he says so explicitly (see 6:9 and 20:4).

What, then, is this witness to God and to Jesus? The expression "the word of God" is clearly a reference to the commandments of God, as John himself tells us (see 12:17; 14:12).

12:17 "On those who keep the commandments of God and bear testimony to Jesus."
14:12 "Those who keep the commandments of God and the faith of Jesus."

To give witness to the Law, the commandments of God, means to observe them, live by them.

What then is meant by "bear testimony (marturia) to Jesus"? Obviously, it means to confess, proclaim one's own faith in him, in his divine nature, in his coming as Messiah, liberator and saviour. This has led scholars to see this as a reference to the Christian martyrs. I do not, however, believe that this is the case. In ch. 19 the "witness to Jesus" is explicitly identified with "the Spirit of prophecy."

19:10: "I am a fellow servant with you and your brethren who hold the testimony of Jesus. Worship God for *the testimony of Jesus is the spirit of prophecy.*"

This is said to John by his accompanying angel, whom John has tried to adore by falling to the ground. So the angel is also "*a testimony* to Jesus" – a martyr who suffered death for his faith in Jesus? This is an impossible interpretation. Given, therefore, the identity as "witness to Jesus" of John and the angel, and its explanation as having the spirit of prophecy, the expression must refer to the role of exercising the gift of prophecy. In other words "to render testimony to Jesus" does *not* mean to die for him, but it means to exercise the gift of prophecy, to announce and proclaim his coming and the significance of his salvific work.

This sort of prophecy can certainly be exercised *after* his historical presence among us. According to the words of Peter, using the prophet Joel in his Pentecost speech, the Spirit of God is communicated to all those who believe in Jesus:

> "I will pour out my spirit on all flesh, and your sons and daughters shall prophesy, and your young men shall see visions, and your old men shall dream dreams, Yea, and on my menservants and my maidservants in those days I will pour out my spirit; and they shall prophesy" (Acts 2:16-18).

Clearly, this will be done by all Christians in so far as their very presence, their quality of life, their actions and their words, announce and bear witness to the effects and the fruit of the coming of Christ.

Quite clearly this has nothing to do with the final coming of Christ. The quality of the life of the believers is the presence of the gift of the spirit of prophecy (see Acts 2:4: "And they were all filled with the Holy Spirit and began to speak in other tongues, as the Spirit gave them utterance" – and 4:31: "And when they had prayed the place in which they were gathered was shaken; and they were all filled with the Holy Spirit and spoke the word of God with boldness"). This is clearly *witness* to the *first coming* of Jesus. The same concept is conveyed by Paul when he writes to the Corinthian community of their variety of charisms:

> "But if all prophesy and an unbeliever or outsider enters, he is convicted by all, he is called to account by all, the secrets of his heart are disclosed; and so, falling on his face, he will worship God and declare that God is really among you." (I Cor 14:24-25).

This has nothing to do with the prediction of the future, but a luminous, visible witnessing to the presence of God among us, which calls into question the lives of the people who come to see this prophecy.

We can, therefore, still speak of "prophecy," in perfect accord with the concept of prophecy which we saw in the Old Testament, as a "giving witness to Jesus," to the effects among us of the first coming of Jesus. So this is an important New Testament meaning of prophecy, but John adds a further dimension. He believes (as a great deal of New Testament theological reflection quite correctly believes) that the historical coming, the death and the resurrection of Jesus was only the culminating and concluding moment of a revelation of God which had its beginning at the act of creation. In this way, there is a "witnessing to Jesus" which comes before his historical coming. This coming, to the mind of the early Church, looking back through history with glasses coloured by the resurrection of Jesus and the presence of his Spirit, could be seen in many events of this history of mankind. It was especially present, however, in the revelation of the Word of God in the Old Testament, in the Law and in the Prophets.

In my opinion, this is the "witness," the *marturia*, which is referred to by the terms "word of God" and "witness to Jesus" which can then be further defined as the Law and the Prophets, i.e., the Sacred Scriptures of the Old Testament. According to John, the Scriptures had a double role to play:
1. To affirm the existence of a one and only God, creator and Lord of the universe, to whom is due the exclusive homage of every creature.
2. To transmit the promise, and to renew continually that promise of the coming of a Messiah and Saviour.

The two are really one and the same thing, because to observe "the word of God," i.e., his commandments (the Law) means also to keep alive one's faith in the promise which he has made, to wait for it with hope and fidelity.

The Scriptures are also "prophecy" of the coming of Jesus, not only in so far as they contain messianic promises, but also because everything written there (for a Christian like John) can only be illuminated and fully understood in the light of Jesus. Therefore, the Old Testament is "witness to Jesus" in so far as Jesus himself, in his earthly coming, could look back and show that he had been promised there. The Old Testament and his fulfilment of it were the ultimate guarantee of his authority. The Fourth Gospel spells this concept out very well in 5:39:

> "You search the Scriptures, because you think that in them you have eternal life; and it is they that bear witness to me."

However, it is not only John the Evangelist who has this concept:

> Luke 24:27: "And beginning with Moses and all the prophets, he interpreted to them in all the scriptures the things concerning himself."

The list could go on, but see this as the central idea in all the discourses in Acts (for example Acts 13:27); I Pet 1:10-11; Matt 17:1-8; Mk 2:2-9 (The presence of Moses [the Law] and Elijah [Prophets] giving witness to him at the transfiguration). We will see that the Apocalypse picks up this use of Moses and Elijah as an allegorical reference to Law and Prophets in 11:3ff, in the famous episode of the "two witnesses" – generally taken as referring to two Christian martyrs, but then causing all sorts of problems in its further interpretation in the rest of the chapter. I hope to show that the interpretation of the two witnesses as Moses and Elijah makes perfect sense of the whole chapter. All in all, the Apocalypse is a coherent and thoroughgoing application of a basic idea of the whole of the New Testament in relation to the Old Testament.

The two "witnesses" of ch. 11 are witnesses of the Old Testament to Jesus, the Law and the Prophets. They are slain because of this witness – because of the word of God and the witness to Jesus. After three and a half days they receive life again, a spirit of life given from above which makes them rise to their feet and they are assumed into heaven (11:11-12). Death and a God-given resurrection.

Notice that this is *exactly* what happens to those who are slain in the sixth seal for the same two reasons (see 6:9-11) and also after the thousand years (see 20:4-6). This has always been a problem. Are only the slain Christian martyrs saved? If we are to read the Apocalypse in the traditional way, such an interpretation is inevitable. But if, in each of these cases, the reference is to the holy and faithful ones of the Old Law, of the old economy, then the problem is solved. They are the just ones and the prophets of the Old Testament, who were slain for having observed the Word of God, thereby giving witness to the coming of the Messiah, i.e., Jesus Christ (see also 17:6; 11:8; 18:24). Again we have a further spelling out of a New Testament theme. Especially eloquent is Matt 23:29-38.

This is the explanation of "why only them?" Before Christ, they are the ones who are raised up and saved (20:5), but after the coming of Christ, all the people who believe in him receive a royalty and a priesthood, the divine life – already in history (see 1:6; 5:9-10; 7:9-12). The holy ones of old had this divine life only after death. That is the point, as John sees it. The problem of the holy ones of old (esp. John the Baptist) worried the early Church. John gives this answer – and it may have even been the *death* of the Baptist – on account of "the word of God" and his "witness to Jesus," which provided John the Seer with his theology. Those who, like the Lamb himself, but before him, are slain, already have a share in the life which the slaying of that lamb has provided, as John's community knows it.

The Apocalypse and the Old Testament

From what we have just seen, it is clear that John's relationship and interest in the Old Testament is profound and it is important to him. It appears that John wishes to show that Jesus brings to perfection and fulfilment the whole of the Old Testament. His source, as we will see, is *exclusively* the Old Testament, but, he uses the Old Testament in a special way. He never just "lifts out" a section of the Old Testament and uses it word for word. He adds to it, changes it, uses it for his own purpose. For example, the four living beings who surround the throne of God in 4:6 are called "four living creatures," and they clearly are taken from the idea of the four cherubim who carry the carriage of Yahweh in Ezekiel 1:5ff. However, they are different: six wings, instead of four, four different descriptions, while in Ezekiel they are all the same. The list could go on: the serpent in ch. 12 from Genesis, but with seven heads and ten horns, the description of the Ancient of Days on the throne in Daniel (Dan 7:9ff) is there – but used differently. These we will see on our way through the book, but it is clear that John is deliberately taking the Old Testament as his source, and *deliberately* re-interpreting it. There are never direct citations, but the source, now *changed* because of Jesus Christ, is always the Old Testament.

One of the great differences, of course, is that while the Old Testament is about the history of the people of Israel, Jesus Christ has now made it the history of the whole of mankind. This leads John into a powerful criticism of any hopes or desires for the establishment of a political messiahship. The prophets were already critical of this. Jesus takes it even further with his concept of a suffering Son of man, and John is openly hostile to the idea of the establishment of a glorious Hebrew Kingdom. He is interested only in the tradition of a spiritual Judaism, which can be applied to all peoples. Any attempt to construct a worldly power which hopes to be the ultimate answer to man's hopes is severely criticised as beast, dragon, etc. Here it is that the references to Rome will enter. For John, however, it is not only Rome; it is also the Jewish people who, because of their political conniving, put to death (in collusion with Rome) the real answer to man's hopes. Thus the slain lamb is at the centre as the answer.

All other attempts to allure man will ultimately fall victim to his wrath. The greatest irony is that John takes the very scriptures of the Jews to show that their worldly hopes, their worldly cult which had become an end in itself was not faithful to their own Book: the story of the slain Lamb is! It is because of this use of the Old Testament in a *new* way that the old images are taken and given a fuller symbolic meaning, difficult for us to read, but clear to John, as he re-reads the old story in a new way. These symbols, as we shall see, all have their roots in the Old Testament, but are given something "new" in John's re-reading. This newness is created by the "newness" set up by the event of Jesus.

The Apocalypse is not, as is commonly held, the description of the second coming of Christ, using random selections from the biblical literature, especially the prophetic and "apocalyptic" elements. It is a precise exegesis of central "prophetic" situations and symbols taken from the Old Testament traditions, in the wide sense (Scriptures, legislation, cult), to throw into evidence the "witness" which such traditions give to the historical coming of Christ, to the nature and the significance of his mission. This exegesis does not transfer the content of the symbolic to the purely logical and rational. John's exegesis works directly on the symbols, using them, modifying them, and in this way transforming their significance.

However, the choice of "prophetic" elements from the Old Testament tradition is in no way by chance or improvised. Looking beyond the apparent mass of citations and allusions it is possible to identify certain blocks of material around which all the others seem to gather in a mysterious but ordered fashion. Even these central blocks of material are linked one to another by a bond which comes from their belonging to the overarching unity of the biblical tradition itself.

Dominating all of this, almost as the basic substructure of the whole book, is the messianic vision of the coming of the Son of man upon the clouds of heaven from the book of Daniel. For John this is the messianic prophecy *par excellence*. He understands it as the foretelling of the supreme moment of the "revelation of Jesus Christ," his death in which the "mystery of God" is brought to its fulfilment. Interwoven with this are other major passages: first, the Hebrew Exodus with all the wonders which both preceded (the ten plagues) and followed it (crossing of the Red Sea, the desert experience, the Covenant of Sinai). Secondly, there is another theme, less clear, formed by continual reference to the tragic events of the end of the kingdom of Judah: the destruction of Jerusalem and of the Temple of Nabuchadnezzar. This aspect is less clear because upon the memory of this "end," profanation and destruction which took place centuries before on a *material* plane, the author superimposes a troubling allusion to the "end," profanation and destruction which have taken place very recently, with the death of Christ. This "end," however, took place on a *spiritual* plane and has irremediable consequences.

Even more shadowy, but still there, is a consistent reference to *Genesis* and the events of Eden: creation, temptation and punishment of the first human couple. It is here that John shows himself to be more influenced by non-biblical speculations: the rebellion of a group of angels, a battle between the wicked and the faithful angels, the driving of Satan from heaven, and other elements. Even here, however, there is still little in common between John and the other "apocalyptic" authors. Even though he uses these traditions, he always attempts to lead them back to the biblical story.

Finally there is a block of material which carries the echoes of Israel's hopes for rebirth and the reconstruction of the Temple. This material comes, largely, from the post-exilic prophets. Naturally, John sees in these the foretelling, not of the rebirth of Israel, but of the whole of humanity, freed from diabolic oppression, of the new Jerusalem coming from heaven, of the new spiritual Temple, of the new cult in spirit and in truth.

Secular History, Hebrew History and the History of Salvation

In the intertwining of the themes which make up the various biblical allusions, it is not difficult to trace the line of a history of salvation. The author takes from it the moments which, in his opinion, are the basic moments in the long journey which runs from the creation and the fall of man to the new creation and the redemption which took place in the historical coming of Jesus Christ. The historical thread which John has in mind is basically that which emerges from the Old Testament. Initially, there is a sort of compendium of universal history (contained in *Genesis*), after which there is an almost exclusive attention given to the experiences of the Hebrew people: the vocation of Abraham, slavery, liberation from Egypt, and so on until the great moments of Hebrew rule, its dissolution, destruction, deportation and exile, the return and the attempts to restore Israel's greatness.

Although, as I have claimed, John depends basically upon this scheme, it is possible to notice some most interesting variations. In the Bible, the telling of the story of the origins and man's primitive history has the function of a prologue. It shows that right from the beginning of history the Hebrew people were a distinct people, chosen by God from among all the others and given a privileged mission and destiny. Great attention is paid to the minute and even private events of the people and events of that period. For John, however, there is clearly an attempt to go beyond this particularism, to see the universal value of human history as such. This is so because the whole of humanity, and not only the Hebrew people, is the object of the divine salvific plan, and thus of the redemption wrought by Jesus Christ (see 5:9; 7:9; etc.).

Because of this, there is a repeated insistence upon the original events, the creation and the fall, which involved the whole of humanity. Certainly, John does not totally ignore the story of the remarkable beginnings of the Hebrew people. In fact, he goes even further than other New Testament authors to stress the unique value of those events within the history of salvation. He devotes great attention to the permanent elements already found in those events which continue into the new reality brought by Jesus Christ, the relationship between the old and the new people of God, the old and the new covenant. In this way, the contribution of the Apocalypse, more than any other New Testament document, has been decisive in the early Church's struggle against a gnostic tendency to deny the value of the Old Testament traditions, as can be seen in the work of Irenaeus, Theophilus of Antioch and Origen. It is also interesting to note that the gnostic Marcion refused to consider the Apocalypse, as it was too tied to Old Testament traditions.

Spiritual Judaism

There is one aspect of the Old Testament vision which John absolutely refuses to accept: the particularist and exclusive character of its understanding of Judaism, which leads to nationalism with all its consequences. First among these, the one considered most serious by John, is the interpretation of all the messianic and prophetic promises in a political and temporal fashion. Against this tendency, which he regarded as a deviation from the authentic meaning of the divine message contained in the biblical revelation, his reaction is constant, and at times rather harsh.

He stresses the universal character of the divine salvific plan and thus of the promise of freedom made by God to mankind after the fall. The Hebrews had been the ones entrusted with this promise, almost because of a rear-guard action from God himself before the success of the diabolic attack upon humanity, which had its beginnings in Eden. Nevertheless, the promise itself was not for them alone. The liberator would come for the whole of humanity. Far too often Judaism, having forgotten the universal and spiritual value of the promise, had sought to keep this promise to itself, and to subject it to its own hopes and earthly controls.

Because of this, God had punished Israel continually, to the point where he allowed her enemies to destroy her. This is a concept which John has from the great prophetic tradition of the Old Testament. Here he is even more radical. He has no appreciation of the glorious memories of the Hebrew kingdom. He makes one allusion to the splendour of the reign of Solomon (2:19), but he runs on immediately to recall the terrible idolatry which spread among the people from the royal palace (2:20ff). The hope and the expectation of the return to the promised land and the reconstruction of the Temple which fired the hearts of the prophets and the psalmists of the post-exilic period are taken up by John, but transferred directly to refer to the foundation of the New Jerusalem by Jesus Christ. He pays absolutely no attention to the historical attempts to reconstruct political Israel on the exiles' return to Palestine, and there is no reference to any of the figures or the literature of that period. It is as if, for John, the history of the Hebrew people came to an end with the tragic day of Meggido when the good king Josiah was overcome and slain by the Pharaoh's forces, and with the destruction of Jerusalem and its Temple at the hands of Nabuchadnezzar. These are the events which he uses continually as the Old Testament's prefiguring of that other tragic event, the death of Jesus Christ in which, according to John, a corrupt and worldly Judaism came to its spiritual end.

The history of Judaism which interests John is her spiritual history, that which is found in the "witnessing," through words and deeds, of the saints and the prophets of the Old Testament, who have observed the Law and nourished the hope of the coming of the liberator. It is to this form of Judaism that John, probably more than any other author in the New Testament, renders praise. This, in fact, explains his radical condemnation of that other form of Judaism, that which longs for glory and temporal power, corrupting its true nature through monstrous collusions with the powerful people of this world to such a point that it is no longer capable of recognising that Jesus Christ is the Messiah.

This form of Judaism is refused and condemned with a violence which is paralleled only by certain expressions from the Fourth Gospel. The Jews, who have refused Jesus, are no longer worthy to bear the name. By claiming it they "lie" because they are, in fact "a synagogue of Satan" (see 3:9; 2:9). Jerusalem, where the two witnesses were slain and "where their Lord was crucified" is no longer the "holy city." It has become, on a spiritual plane, "Sodom and Egypt" (see

11:8). And, as I will attempt to show later, it is Jerusalem who is represented by the famous symbol of the great prostitute in ch. 17.

Nevertheless, there is perhaps no other New Testament writing which stresses the vital continuity between Judaism and Christianity with such force and conviction. In the vision of Patmos, which not only inaugurates the vision, but which in some ways profoundly summarises the whole of the Apocalypse, Jesus Christ appears to John in the middle of seven golden lampstands (1:13), and shortly afterwards he is described as: "He...who walks among the seven golden lampstands" (2:1). The meaning of the vision is clear: Jesus Christ comes from Judaism. Without that precedent, both his person and the significance of his messianic work would be incomprehensible. It is not just chance that leads John to describe the splendour and the perfection of the new Jerusalem, an allegory of the wonderful fruits of redemption, in terms which come from the Jewish biblical tradition.

Perhaps it would be better not to speak of the book as being anti-Jewish but rather as a profound continuation of the ancient prophetic tradition where opposition to and denunciation of injustice, corruption, worldliness of cult and life-style is no less bitter and violent. One could almost say that John's polemic against Judaism, in contrast to other writers from the early Church, is still working from *within* Judaism. When he denies the Jews the right to call themselves such, it is understood that the Christians now have that right. According to John, they are the true heirs to that spiritual Judaism which was both kept and proclaimed by the saints and the prophets, the "witnesses" of old.

Of course, the object of the polemic between John and his fellow Jews is no longer a reform of cult and way of life, as it was for the ancient prophets. It is now a more disconcerting matter: a belief that Jesus Christ is the promised and expected Messiah, that his messianic action took place in his salvific death, and that his kingdom is a spiritual kingdom. These were extremely difficult truths to accept for the Jews of a certain mentality. Nevertheless, John never ceases in his insistence that these truths form the very heart of the message of the Scriptures which the Jews themselves accept and use. Refusing them by not accepting Jesus Christ, the Jews have lost the possibility of understanding the scriptures themselves. The revelation of God, their proud possession, is now silent for them, and it has been transferred, along with Jesus Christ, to the whole of humanity which does accept him (see 10:11). Here, in the new ecclesial community, spiritual Judaism lives on: the seven lampstands, as Jesus Christ solemnly announces to John, have become the seven Churches (see 1:20).

Prophecy and Exegesis: Symbolism, Allegory, Typology

The continuity between the old and the new economy is guaranteed by the presence of Jesus Christ in both, even though in different measure and fashion, they are both "revelations of Jesus Christ." If John speaks repeatedly of a conclusion, an end to the old economy as a basic presupposition for the beginning of the new, that must be understood, on the one hand, as an effect of the blindness of those who consciously shut their eyes so as not to see fulfilment and continuation; on the other hand as a substantial modification of the content of the old economy as it moves into the new, through its fulfilment. The old was announcement, preparation, prefiguration; while the new is perfection, fulfilment and reality.

We are thus dealing with a continuity which involves a radical change. This conviction has profoundly influenced John's method of dealing with the Old Testament. This has not been given sufficient attention by commentators, as they seem to find no order or purpose in his use of the Old Testament. We speak often of John's use of symbolism, allegory, metaphoric language, use of imagination and various other techniques when we examine his use of scripture. We do not pay sufficient attention to the fact that for us, such techniques indicate a basic contrast between the thing signified and the word which is used to signify it. This comes to us from a Greek way of thinking (especially from Platonism) which distinguishes between sense experience and intellectual experience, between the bodily and the spiritual, a distinction not known by the biblical mind.

Unfortunately, Christian biblical exegesis is dominated by the Hellenistic distinction, introduced largely by the work of Origen and then widespread through medieval exegesis. Nevertheless, there have been some who have recognised that the exegesis of the Old Testament practised in the early Church was "typological." This means that it was based on the presupposition that the whole of the Old Testament was a prefiguring, a "type" (in the sense of the Greek *tupos*), of Jesus Christ and his salvific work.

This is fundamental for a correct understanding of the method of biblical interpretation used by John in the Apocalypse. Given the continuity which he sees between the two testaments, however, his "typology" is rather special, somewhat different from the few examples which we find elsewhere in the New Testament (see, for example, I Cor 10:1-5). John's use of typology is more closely linked to the original Old Testament data, be it historical or doctrinal. Those deeds, rites, visions, and the Law already had great value in themselves, even though they were incomplete: they were already concrete and real signs of a first divine salvific intervention, as yet, partial and provisional.

We must keep this in mind when we speak of the symbols, allegories and images of the Apocalypse. We may use this language as long as we see that what we are describing by means of them is a recalling, and an intentional use of sacred scripture. Another consideration must be added. That material which we call "symbolic" is more than just biblical. Given the idea of continuity which is so important to the mind of John, each symbol preserves in itself its own original meaning. In fact, it is precisely upon the permanency of the original meaning that John plays when introducing the variations which serve to modify it.

This means that when John recalls any section of scripture through a particular form of allusion, he presupposes that the original passage and its meaning are already present in the minds of his readers. When, for example, he says "Son of man" he is convinced that, on the one hand, this is sufficient to recall the vision from Daniel and that, on the other, it will be understood as a reference to the coming of the Messiah. When he speaks of a series of four horses with different colours, he presupposes that his public not only had the vision of Zechariah in mind, but also the way in which these figures were usually interpreted.

The permanence of the original meaning, the biblical significance of the symbols used by John, is another basic point for a correct reading of the Apocalypse. This is true not only for the relationship between the symbols and their place of origin, Sacred Scripture, but also for the relationships between these various symbols within the book itself, as they appear and re-appear.

Let us take, for example, the symbol of the "woman" which appears in ch. 12. We will examine its biblical origin below. What must be noticed is that the same symbol appears elsewhere in the Apocalypse, especially in ch. 17 (the great prostitute), and in ch. 21 (the spouse, the woman of the Lamb). As well as this, she is found in close contact with other symbols: a woman "in heaven"; a woman "in the wilderness"; a woman "who comes down from heaven." Even though it may appear to be a paradox, it is clear that the basic meaning of the symbol never changes. The only thing that changes is its contact with other symbols and different contexts. The same thing could be said of another famous symbol, the "book," as we shall see below (see chs. 5 and 10).

The list could go on, as this method is applied, without fail, to all the symbols of the Apocalypse. This indicates that the preservation of the original meaning of the symbols, and the modification of this meaning through differing situations and contexts constitutes a real "law of exegesis" which John is applying as he uses the Old Testament. It is so important to John that he still applies it to those rare symbols which do not have their origin in the Bible. For example, he uses the symbol of "stars." There is an identifiable link between stars, comets, heavenly bodies in general and angelic beings in the Bible, but it is not as strong as John would like. For one reason or another he places on the lips of Jesus himself an explanation of a "stars-angels" symbol (see 1:20). From that moment on, the meaning of the symbol never changes. Later, when John speaks of flaming heavenly bodies which are cast down from heaven (see 8:6ff) we know that he is speaking of the fall of the angels. Thus also the fall of the angels is behind the fall to earth of a third of the stars who are struck by the tail of the dragon (see 12:4).

A lack of appreciation of this basic rule for John's use of the Old Testament has led to a widespread impression that he uses the symbols of the Bible without any logic or purpose. It has also allowed each interpreter to go on his way, understanding each symbol as he best saw fit, often pulling it out of its overall context within the logical development of the whole book.

Symbolic Numbers

What has just been said of the biblical symbols in the Apocalypse also applies to John's other difficult and well-known use of symbols: his use of symbolic numbers. The book is full of them. A very great deal of his message is communicated through this difficult but expressive genre. We must also remark that John was convinced that as far as his use of numbers was concerned, he was basing himself upon an element which had its roots in the Old Testament Scriptures. It is pointless, for a correct interpretation of the Apocalypse, to search through the gnostic, astrological, mysterious or kabbalistic use of numbers. This may indeed be the background for some of the Old Testament's use of numbers, but all of John's use of numbers goes back to the Old Testament, and to the meanings those numbers had there.

The number seven was already firmly fixed in the biblical tradition as an indication of totality, fulfilled and already in itself. At the beginnings of this speculation stand the seven days of creation which, according to Genesis, saw the fulfilment of creation.

It was probably from this fact that there developed further speculation about the duration of world history (seven days = seven thousand years), and, consequently, calculations concerning the coming of the Messiah and the inauguration of his kingdom, fixed respectively at the end of the sixth and the beginning of the seventh millennium. These speculations were common in John's time, and he shows a great familiarity with them as he uses them for his own ends.

In every case, however, he is primarily concerned to relate these speculations to the solid basis of the authentic biblical tradition. He is able to use the speculation about the "cosmic week" which was common in apocalyptic writings, but the meaning of the number seven, in so far as it is linked to the messianic coming, was fixed with much more authority, for John, in the prophecy which is fundamental for the correct understanding of the Apocalypse.

It is used by John in many ways, but especially through his use of symbolic numbers. The enigmatic presentation of the dragon with seven heads and ten horns is probably an example ($7 \times 10 = 70$). There is certainly a reference to it in symbolic indications of time: "one thousand, two hundred and sixty days" (see 11:3; 12:6), "forty two months" (see 11:2; 13:5), "a time and times and half a time" (see 12:14), "three and a half days" (see 11:11). They are, in fact, the equivalent of the three and a half years which correspond to each of the "half weeks" into which Daniel had divided the final seventy weeks of years.

In the Bible (especially in Ezekiel, Daniel and Zechariah) John found the meaning of the number four already fixed as a number intimately linked with an indication of the whole world (four points of the compass, four winds) and of its history (four world empires). He also found that the meaning of the number twelve was fixed (the twelve tribes of Israel), the number three, in some way linked with the divinity (the three "angels" who appear to Abraham); the number six was also linked with the earth, and especially with man.

Certainly, even these numbers were subject to even further speculation. For example, particular importance is given to those numbers which result from sums or products of other numbers which were already significant in themselves. The perfection of the number twelve is explained by the fact that it is the product of four (the cosmic number) and three (a number which indicates the divinity or something of an angelic nature). A distinction is made between perfect numbers (even) and imperfect numbers (uneven). Ten and multiples of ten are considered as an indication of an indefinite and not yet perfected reality.

John shows that he is able to handle all these speculations. It has been a difficulty and a shame that commentators have not always been aware of this. For example, there would not have been all the difficulty over the reign of a thousand years if it had been noticed that the number was the indication of something not yet defined, and therefore imperfect. The number ten is imperfect, and indicates that the horns of the dragon and of the beast represent an indefinite series of wicked earthly rulers. The number seven would not be confused with perfection, if one realised that it indicates only totality. On the other hand, there would be a more careful inquiry into certain particulars. For example, into the fact that the "seven" of the seals and the "seven" of the bowls are clearly made up of two distinct groups, formed respectively by four and three elements. Far from indicating perfection, the four "sevens" of the Apocalypse (letters, seals, trumpets and bowls) all finish with an indication of the annihilation, the destruction of something.

We can, therefore, notice that the same rules of exegesis apply to both the biblical symbols and the symbolic numbers. John begins from a profound truth which he presupposes is known by his audience: these matters have their value and their guarantee from the Bible itself. Basing himself upon that accepted value, he goes ahead to work with his symbols, modifying them and transforming them for the purposes of his own message.

The "Apocalypse" and the New Testament

The relationship between the Apocalypse and the Old Testament, seen without presuppositions and forgetting all contrived schemes and patterns, is really quite different from what is generally supposed. In fact, a correct understanding of this relationship could show that the Apocalypse is not what is generally agreed. It is quite different in structure and meaning. In fact it is not an "apocalyptic" text which uses the Old Testament to foresee and describe in anticipation the meaning and circumstances of the second coming of Christ. Instead, the use of the ancient scriptures which is found in the Apocalypse is clearly to illustrate and to deepen the meaning of his first coming as an act of redemption, the putting into action of the divine salvific plan.

All this necessarily changes quite seriously the approach which one must adopt in examining the relationship between the Apocalypse and the rest of the New Testament. Here, evidently, we are not considering John's possible use of other New Testament documents, but rather the question of John's similarity or dissimilarity with various doctrinal positions in the other New Testament writings. Unfortunately, given the widespread conviction that the Apocalypse is a prediction of the second coming of Christ, the consideration of its relationship with the rest of the New Testament is always rather limited, as comparisons are drawn only with eschatological passages: the "apocalyptic" passages from Paul, the "apocalyptic" discourse of Jesus, and various other passages of this nature in the rest of the New Testament. The result of this sort of research is that the preoccupation is to see how the fully-developed eschatology of the Apocalypse is harmonious with the eschatological point of view of the other New Testament documents.

Before this major concern, other possible points of contact have become less important, or have simply not been considered. Without pretending to offer an extensive or exhaustive study of such a wide-ranging question, I would like nevertheless to offer a few suggestions, even if it were only to show that once we have removed the prejudices about the eschatological and apocalyptic nature of the document, then all sorts of further enriching possibilities open up which need further investigation.

The Pauline Letters

Paul is certainly, among all the authors of the New Testament, the most outstanding and authoritative witness to the early Church's waiting for the return of Christ, commonly called the parousia. It is most explicit and central in the two letters to the Thessalonians (see I Thess 4:13-5:11; II Thess 2:1-12). These letters are considered not only the oldest of the Pauline letters, but probably the oldest literature in the New Testament. In the first part of the two letters Paul shows that he not only believes in the parousia, but he thinks that it is near at hand, to the extent that he still hopes to be alive to experience that event (see I Thess 4:15). This hope, as all have noticed, fades in Paul as time passes. Already at the conclusion of the same letter, he insists that the parousia cannot be foretold, and that it will come suddenly. In the Second Letter to the Thessalonians, he attempts to play down in his readers the fervour over the return of Christ, arguing that it is not imminent (see II Thess 2:1ff).

In this letter, to explain the delay of the parousia, Paul refers to certain details which indicate his own particular "apocalyptic." He claims that before the return of Christ there should be an "apostasy," a revelation of the "man of iniquity" (II Thess 2:3). However, this revelation is impossible for the moment, according to Paul, because of the presence of a mysterious obstacle. Only when this is removed will it be possible for the man of iniquity to reveal himself, to be destroyed when Jesus Christ himself returns. Nevertheless, before being destroyed, this personality will succeed in bringing many to spiritual ruin through miracles and signs which he will perform with the aid of Satan (see II Thess 2:3-12).

After the two letters to the Thessalonians Paul seems to

draw away from his hope of an imminent return and even from the idea of the parousia. It is still present in the first of the two letters written to the Christian community at Corinth. Now, however, the stress is upon the importance of the way of life to be lived during the time of waiting, which seems to stretch out further and further into the future; on the organisation of the community which is beginning to confuse the future life with the life they are living now. The liturgical assembly, the Eucharistic meal and baptism all become the centre of interest for Paul. These things are now seen as a manifestation of "being in Christ" which will be perfected, of course, at the parousia, with the resurrection of the flesh (see I Cor 15:35-52). They are already in Paul, however, more than just a "manifestation." They already imply a real participation in the death and resurrection of Christ.

This gradual change of eschatological perspective becomes even more evident in the letters which come from the final period of Paul's activity. He becomes more and more concerned over the meaning of the Spirit, belonging to the body of Christ. The idea that comes to the fore is that the basic benefits of the messianic reign: the gift of the Spirit, the resurrection to a new life of a divine nature, are already realised. Writing to the Christians of Colossae and Ephesus (we are in the geographical region of the Apocalypse!) he affirms that the baptised have already died and risen with Christ (see Col 2:12; 3:1), and are even seated with him in the heavenly places (see Eph 2:5-6).

We need not discuss to what extent Paul's thought went through an evolution between the Thessalonian correspondence (about 50 A.D.) and the Letters from Prison (about 61-63). The questions which arise from a comparison with the Apocalypse are different. The first is, in what way does Paul's description of the eschatological events correspond to the descriptions of the Apocalypse? Despite attempts to make them agree, they have very little in common. Where in the Apocalypse is there any mention of "apostasy" as a sign of the coming of the parousia? Paul goes on to describe the figure of an adversary of Christ who seems to have human characteristics even though he receives his powers from Satan. This is the starting point for the development of a personal anti-Christ in later literature. There is none of this in the Apocalypse. There the adversary is clearly Satan who makes use of two historic agents, the two beasts who represent two abstract entities: corrupt political and religious authority, not human personalities. Yet more: where in the Apocalypse can one find the enigmatic obstacle which prevents the appearance of the adversary?

There is a further important question. How is one to explain the wild presence of an eschatological hope in the Apocalypse (a text which is much later than the Pauline letters), after having seen that Paul's interest in the question steadily declines? This question becomes even more interesting when we notice that Paul shows least concern for these matters precisely in the letters written to Churches in Asia, among which the Apocalypse seems to have grown. If the Apocalypse is to be understood as an eschatological document, then it must be read as a reaction to Paul.

If, however, we read the Apocalypse as a "prophecy" which refers to the first coming of Jesus Christ, that is, as a meditation upon the significance of that coming and an illustration of the historical and spiritual events which preceded and prepared for it, not only do the presumed contrasts between Paul and the Apocalypse fall away, but the two points of view can be seen as being closely linked by a harmonious and coherent line of developing thought.

Seeing the issues in this fashion, we can notice how the Christology of the Apocalypse, with Jesus Christ as the centre of the cosmos and of history, is the continuation and development of points raised already in the two Pauline letters to the Colossians and the Ephesians. There is a further common problem: that of the angels. From the two Pauline writings one can see a concern over the spreading of angel-speculations within the Christian community. It seems to be leading to an angel-cult. Paul's reaction to this teaching is stern. He speaks out against it by affirming the absolute superiority of Christ both on the level of his being and his function: he is divine by nature, and he is the one and only mediator between God and the world. The sacrifice of the cross has taken from the angels all mediating functions. In fact, claims Paul, all authority has been taken from them, and they have been subjected to Christ in his triumph over death (see Col 2:15).

The problem of the relationship between the angels and Jesus Christ seems to have been serious at the origins of Christianity. It is found often in the Pauline letters, even outside the letters to Ephesus and Colossae. It is also central to the Letter to the Hebrews. This document also attempts to demonstrate the superiority of Christ over the angels, and it does so on the basis of a richly biblical documentation. This detail also indicates that there was a link between the angel speculations and Judaism, or at least Judaizing tendencies.

If there had not been the prejudice over an eschatological interpretation, it would not have been difficult to see that the relationship between the angels and Jesus Christ is also fundamental to the Apocalypse. The issue here is that of mediation, the mediation of revelation and in cult. John throws this into relief right from the very first lines of the prologue, speaking of the "revelation of Jesus Christ" which is transmitted from Jesus Christ to John through an angel (see 1:1). This is generally seen as an angel interpreter, as is common in many apocryphal apocalyptic texts. But John has a wider and more important problem in mind, that of mediation, and this can be understood from the vision of the Son of man which follows immediately. We will see this in our analysis of the text, so here I will limit myself to observe, concerning the relationship between the angels and Jesus Christ, that in the vision Christ holds the "seven stars" in his hand (1:16). He explains to John that the stars are "angels." The meaning of the scene is clear: the angels (*all* the angels, as is indicated by means of the number seven) are in the hands of Christ. This means that he has dominion over them, having imposed his superiority upon them, as is explicitly stated shortly after (see 2:1) and repeatedly affirmed throughout the book.

The Pauline letters to the Colossians and the Ephesians

and the Apocalypse, far from being in contrast, both attempt to deepen and further illuminate the early Church's growing Christology. This had to happen as both traditions grew in an atmosphere full of cultural, philosophical and religious ferment. Both John and Paul allow us to understand that, behind it all, there is a lively Jewish community which, perhaps even before the beginnings of Christian preaching, had initiated a dialogue with the surrounding Hellenistic philosophical and religious culture. The primary importance which the question of angels has in the Pauline letters and in the Apocalypse could be an indication that, in this encounter, angelology played a central role. In fact, belief in mediating beings between the divinity and the world was one of the few points which Judiasm and Hellenism had in common.

Jesus' "Apocalyptic" Discourse in the Synoptic Gospels

Strange as it may seem, commentators generally do not devote a great deal of attention to the relationship between the Apocalypse and the three similar, but different in detail, synoptic "apocalyptic" discourses of Jesus (see Matt 24:1-44; Mk 13:1-37; Lk 21:5-36). Those who have compared these texts with the Apocalypse show the presence of a certain literary scheme in both. For example, there is a succession of punishments announced by Jesus (wars, civil wars, hunger, disease, persecution, cosmic catastrophe) which would correspond to those described by John in the succession of the seven seals. The messianic figure of the Son of man is also present in both. The list could go on. These and other common details have been explained by a mutual dependence upon a common source, or by the fact that both belong to the same "apocalyptic" literary genre. Nothing more is said, because the discussions of Jesus' eschatological discourse are always polarised around Jesus' announcement of the destruction of the Temple. All the synoptic discourses begin with that announcement.

As that announcement has been always linked with the

historical event of the destruction of Jerusalem in 70 A.D., the major concern of the exegetes has been to distinguish which parts of the discourse go back to the historical Jesus speaking of the return of the Son of man, the end of time, judgment, etc., and which parts refer to the destruction of Jerusalem. This is never really successful, as there appear to be so many contrasts and contradictions in the discourse as reported by the three Evangelists.

The contradictions find their roots in the very substance of the discourse itself, in the difficulty of reconciling the three elements which form its heart: the destruction of the Temple (and of Jerusalem), the coming of the Son of man, the end of the world. These events are presented as intimately connected, impossible to unravel. One thing is clear in all three synoptics: the end of the world, understood as the end of history, is not imminent. It cannot take place before the Gospel is preached to all the nations of the world (see Matt 24:13; Mk 13:10; Lk 21:24).

Contrasting with this, however, one finds in all three accounts the description of the coming of the Son of man amid a series of phenomena (cosmic catastrophes, judgment, the gathering of the chosen ones) portrayed in such a way that it appears obvious that there is a description of the end of the world. Also in all three accounts this is followed by a solemn affirmation from Jesus that all this must take place during the life span of the generation living at that time (see Matt 24:34; Mk 13:30; Lk 21:32).

How can all this be explained? For those who argue that Christianity had its origins in "apocalyptic," these discourses are an indication of the attempts of the early Church to modify the message of Jesus centred on his proximate return for judgment and the establishment of his kingdom. For others, it is a question of the intertwining of diverse traditions which had not been perfectly sorted out as the Gospels grew through their various stages.

We cannot hope to solve this massive problem. One observation, however, must be made. There are too many presuppositions which are taken for granted and have not been proved. One of these is that the prediction about the

Temple (as well as that on Jerusalem) is concerned with the destruction of 70 A.D. But this link, accepted explicitly or implicitly by everyone, is not as obvious as it may seem. It is worth the effort, therefore, to examine this question briefly. It is also important for us, because the theme of the destruction of the Temple, along with the end of the Jewish cult, is something which we will see recurring in the Apocalypse.

The "Destruction" of Jerusalem and of the Temple

It is claimed that, in all the Synoptic Gospels, the discourse of Jesus begins with a prediction about the destruction of the Temple. Faced with the splendour of that building, Jesus becomes sad and speaks of its destruction in the near future through a series of images which indicates that it will be a material destruction caused by a foreign enemy (see, for example, Matt 24:2: "There will not be left here one stone upon another"). It is natural to think of the Roman invasion, and this is strengthened by the fact that in Luke's Gospel the same sadness and the same sort of prediction are addressed to a deaf and hostile Jerusalem (see Lk 19:41ff).

Nevertheless, concerning the destiny both of the Temple and of Jerusalem, one can notice a marked difference between Luke's report and the other two Gospels. In Mark there is no reference to the destruction of Jerusalem, while in Matthew it comes as a conclusion to the violent discourse of Jesus against the teaching and the teachers of Judaism whom he accuses, not only of hypocrisy and hardness of heart, but above all of violence against the just, the prophets and the ones sent by God, whom they have persecuted and slain (see Matt 23:1-36). In the city of Jerusalem, Jesus sees the symbol of all the negative aspects which he is denouncing, and for this reason, he announces the imminent punishment through the words of the prophet Jeremiah: "Your house is forsaken and *desolate* (*erēmos:* Matt 23:38. See Jer 22:5).

In Luke there are two passages where Jesus laments over

Jerusalem and foretells its destruction. The first is found during Jesus' journey with his disciples towards Jerusalem, and is close to Matthew's version (see Lk 13:34-35). The second, however, takes place as he is about to enter the city. As he sees it, he is moved to tears by the thought of the calamity and destruction which is about to occur (see Lk 19:41-44). The description of detail here is so accurate that there can be no doubt that the prediction refers to the events of 70 A.D.

An analogous situation can be found in Jesus' prediction about the destruction of the Temple. In Matthew and Mark not only is there no clearly identifiable link with the events of 70 A.D., but on close examination it may not even refer to a material destruction. It is true that in both of these Gospels (as in Luke) the starting point for the discourse appears to be a reference to a material destruction: "There will not be left one stone upon another." Nevertheless, both in Matthew and in Mark the discourse itself seems to speak of a ruination which will be caused by an act of profanation. In each case, the profanation precedes an eventual destruction in so far as one has to suppose that the Temple has to be standing for its profanation to take place. Only in Luke does the ruin and destruction of the Temple predicted by Jesus have clear links with the events of 70 A.D.

The difference between Luke and the other two synoptics on this point is important. He does not refer to the profanation which the Temple is about to endure. Perhaps it is better to say that, for Luke, the profanation takes place in the events of 70 A.D., with the invasion of the city and the Temple by the Romans. In fact, both Matthew and Mark speak of the profanation of the Temple by means of an expression from Daniel, the famous "abomination of desolation" taken from the prophecy of the seventy weeks (see Dan 9:27). In Luke this citation from Daniel is missing, but it is still echoed in the term "desolation" which Jesus uses to speak of the material destruction of Jerusalem (see Lk 21:20). This is another indication that for Luke the two predictions on the Temple and Jerusalem are understood as intimately linked with the tragic events of 70 A.D.

The Profanation of the Temple and the Coming of the Son of Man

It is a pity that these differences have not been given their full importance by the commentators. Taking them into account, the first deduction which one can draw is that, while for Luke there is a clear link with the events of 70 A.D., this is not quite so obvious for Matthew and Mark. Another conclusion is that, in Matthew and Mark, it is not the Temple's destruction, but its profanation which constitutes the "sign" of the coming of the end time, given to the disciples at their request (see Matt 24:3; Mk 13:4; Lk 21:7). This becomes even more significant when we notice that the "sign" is given by Jesus through an explicit citation of one of the most famous messianic prophecies, that of Daniel on the seventy weeks (see Dan 9:27). In addition to this, we find that the second part of the eschatological discourse, fixed upon a description of the parousia, calls upon a further equally famous messianic prophecy from Daniel, that of the Son of man coming upon the clouds of heaven (see Dan 7:13-14).

Reduced to its essentials, the eschatological discourse placed on the lips of Jesus has as its object the way and the circumstances in which he will reveal his messianic nature, in conformity with the promises of Scripture and in accord with contemporary expectations. The biblical passages which are most important are those from Daniel. In the prophecy of the seventy weeks it was not so much the chronological calculation which struck the imagination of the time, but more the precision with which certain facts which were to usher in the messianic era were indicated. In the second part of the seventy weeks, Daniel claimed that certain extremely serious events would take place: the slaying of a consecrated person, the profanation of the Temple and the prohibition of Jewish cult. All this would happen because of a cruel and wicked persecutor.

It does not matter that the prophet is referring to historical facts, already past; to the persecution of Antiochus IV.

These things are clear to modern scholarship, but for the people of old, both before and after Christ, Daniel was used as he presented himself: a prophet who lived in the time of the Babylonian exile. As this was the case, the facts which he described were considered as what would happen on the occasion of the coming of the Messiah. This is the way these prophecies were understood, especially at a popular level. In fact, they were often enlarged upon or broadened to refer to events which would involve a crisis of the whole of created reality, as signs of the end of the world. The profanation which would put an end to Jewish cult soon took on the proportions of a general destruction which would carry with it, not only the Temple and the city of Jerusalem, but the whole of the existing order.

This is the mentality which was behind the question which the disciples posed for Jesus. It was not only a question of the Temple. This event, for them, meant at the same time the end of the world and the glorious triumphant coming of the Messiah, the establishment of the kingdom of God. All of this had been described in the other prophecy from Daniel: the coming of the Son of man upon the clouds to the throne of the divinity to receive unending authority, glory and a universal kingdom (Dan 7:13-14).

In the reply of Jesus one can trace a first concern to separate all that touched upon the messianic coming from the end of the world. The latter is not connected with the way in which he would be and act as the Messiah. Jesus characterises his messiahship as a fulfilment, closely linked with the two prophecies of the destruction of the Temple and the coming of the Son of man (the Messiah) on the clouds. In connection with the latter prophecy, he also hints at the fulfilment of other messianic prophecies (Isaiah, Ezekiel, etc.) concerning a cosmic catastrophe, the darkening of the sun and the moon, the falling of the stars.

The Death of Jesus as the End of Jewish Cult (Profanation of the Temple) and the Fulfilment of the Judgment of God (The Coming upon the Clouds)

The eschatological discourse of Jesus is, therefore, not concerned with the end of the world, but rather the fulfilment of the prophecies about the coming of the Messiah. It is precisely the coming of the Messiah with its outstanding features (profanation of the Temple, the coming of the Son of man on the clouds, cosmic catastrophe, the judgment and the gathering of the chosen ones) whose proximate fulfilment Jesus announces, a fulfilment which would take place under the very eyes of the ones who are listening to him. Clearly he is referring to something in which he will be the protagonist, an event in which his being the Messiah will be revealed.

What is this event? It has been thought, and scholars continue to insist, that he is alluding to his return, to his second coming in power and majesty to exercise judgment and to set up the kingdom. Such an interpretation, however, poses the same problems as the eschatological interpretation of the Apocalypse. Is it really thinkable that the effects and the significance of the messianic work of Jesus Christ (judgment, gathering of the chosen ones, the establishment of his kingdom) are linked only with the glorious return of Christ in his second coming? Moreover, given the distance between the final writing of the gospels and the death of Jesus, why did the Evangelists have him speak the words about the fulfilment of the eschatological events to people who were his contemporaries?

These are not the most serious obstacles for the above interpretation. It leaves without any explanation the whole section which deals with the Temple. This is an important theme. It is from the Temple that the discourse has its starting point, and the only eschatological "sign" which he gives to his disciples refers to it. On the other hand, the eschatological discourse takes place in Jerusalem, and from the moment of his entry into the city, the Temple is the scene of his preaching, and also his activity: the purification of the Temple.

It is thus worth the effort to ask what Jesus means when he alludes to the profanation of the Temple.

Jesus had already seen a type of profanation in the presence of the merchants, and this fact is stressed by his hard words, taken from Jeremiah: "You make it a den of robbers" (Matt 21:13; Jer 7:11). Yet there is something even more serious to be traced in Jesus' powerful invective against the religious leaders of Judaism and against Judaism, guilty of having poured out the blood of the saints and the prophets, even within the Temple (see Matt 23:35). It is precisely in reference to the slaying of the saints and the prophets that, as we mentioned above, Jesus recalls the prophecy of Jeremiah, according to which their "house" had become a "desert" (see Matt 23:38). The prophecy of Jeremiah, used by Jesus in Matthew's Gospel, takes us back to the expression from Daniel "the abomination of desolation" which is quoted shortly after in the eschatological discourse (see Matt 24:15; Mk 13:14). In Greek, the noun which we translate as "desolation" (*eremosis*) is derived from the adjective which we translate as "deserted" (*eremos*). The idea under both expressions is that of solitude and abandonment.

Therefore, when Jesus speaks of the Temple in terms of an "abomination of desolation," the meaning of his words is more or less as follows: an act of profanation which produces solitude in the Temple, its being abandoned by the faithful. In other words, it is the end of the cult which takes place there. This can be ascertained not only from the meaning of the word "desolation" but also from what Jesus commands must be done as soon as "the sign," the profanation of the Temple takes place: to flee from Judea, from their own houses, from their own tasks (see Matt 24:16ff; Mk 13:14ff). The flight renders the Temple desolate and deserted.

In Luke, as we have seen, Jesus' request that they flee is linked with the events of 70 A.D. This reverses the presentation of Matthew and Mark. For them, the appearance of the "sign" of the profanation not only precedes the flight, but determines it. It happens while the Temple is still standing, even though it now contains the "abomination of desolation," the profanation which forces the faithful to abandon it.

What then, is the profanation of the Temple? It is the slaying of Jesus, planned, ordered and led by the religious leaders (the High Priests) who have the Temple as their dwelling place. It is their presence which profanes and contaminates it. What Jesus commands and advises is not a flight from a besieged Jerusalem, but the abandoning of Judaism and its cult. The break with Judaism, so long avoided despite his many difficult encounters with it, now becomes inevitable for Jesus, as he looks forward to the final breach caused by his being slain by them.

He thus indicates to his disciples that his death finally fulfils the prophecy of Daniel on the slaying of a consecrated person, the profanation of the cult. But he also indicates the fulfilment of other messianic prophecies, especially those concerning the coming of the Son of man on the clouds. In Daniel it alluded to the revelation of the Messiah at the moment of his greatest authority, as he exercises the judgment of God upon the world. Jesus quotes it in reference to his proximate death to indicate that there the judgment will take place as redemption will be realised, as the chosen ones from the four winds, the whole of humanity, will be gathered.

The cosmic catastrophes involved in certain prophecies which Jesus recalls also point in the same direction. The images of the darkening of the sun and the moon, the falling of the stars, the tearing open of the heavens, etc., are simply symbolic descriptions of the great judgment of God which should take place at the final coming of the Messiah. They are used by Jesus to speak of his coming again.

The function of the eschatological discourse placed upon the lips of Jesus by the Synoptic Evangelists is to provide, on a solid Old Testament basis, a key to understand the events which were to take place from that point onwards in his story: the arrest, the condemnation, the passion, the death and resurrection. They are to be understood as the most important and glorious moment, as the revelation of Jesus as the Messiah. It is not by accident that in all the Synoptic Gospels his death is accompanied by references to some sort of cosmic catastrophe (see Matt 27:45; Mk 15:33; Lk 23:44) and to the end of the Jewish cult, symbolised by the tearing apart of the veil of the Temple (see Matt 27:51; Mk 15:38; Lk 23:45). The message of the eschatological discourse is fulfilled.

If the eschatological discourse has this meaning, then it has a great deal more in common with the Apocalypse than its literary genre, sources, or certain formal elements. It has its whole argument in common: to show that the concluding events of the whole life of Jesus Christ were a vital part of that mission. It is not by chance that the two prophecies of Daniel, the seventy weeks and the coming of the Son of man on the clouds, are the essential background to a correct understanding of both the eschatological discourses in the Synoptic Gospels and the Apocalypse.

The Johannine Writings

The discussion of the relationship between the Apocalypse and the other New Testament documents attributed to "John" by tradition deserves a lengthy treatment of its own. It is intimately related to the questions of authorship and time and place of composition. Our limitations will not permit such a treatment. We are more concerned to spend our efforts on a study of the structure and theology of the Apocalypse. Nevertheless, what we have already seen in the contacts with the Pauline literature and the eschatological discourses from the Gospels, it can be claimed that the Apocalypse has some sort of relationship with the literature which preceded this document. As far as the Johannine literature is concerned, the contacts can be seen through individual points of contact or divergence, similarity or dissimilarity, at the level of overall content and structure.

Traditional research in this area has stressed the differences between the documents, and then has adopted various positions to explain them. In the past there was a considerable study of the formal differences, but of recent times this seems to have been replaced by an insistence that we are dealing with two different literary genres. As far as content is concerned, one's conclusions about the relationship between the Apocalypse and the rest of the Johannine literature depends heavily upon one's ideas about the respective genres. If the Apocalypse is a piece of "apocalyptic" literature in the generally accepted sense of that term: a looking forward to the second coming of Christ for the realisation of the messianic promises, then it is quite clear that there can be little relationship between the Apocalypse and the Johannine literature.

The Johannine Gospel and Letters are shot through with a joyous certainty that the messianic promises are already present: the communication of the divine life (eternal life), the gift of the Spirit, the knowledge of truth, the victory of Jesus Christ over death, etc. The attitude of these documents is, therefore, clearly anti-apocalyptic. The First Letter says explicitly that the whole of the Christian life is already being lived in the eschatological times. It goes so far as to say that the coming of the Antichrist has already taken place, along with its accompanying apostasy and signs of his arrival (see I John 2:18ff).

However, if the Apocalypse is to be read in the perspective which is being proposed by this study, then the relationship between these writings has no need of lengthy demonstrations. More than this, those aspects which have always been noticed as common between them: the definition of Jesus Christ as the Logos, the insistence upon the theme of "witness," the presentation of a spiritual Judaism which is continued into the new reality of Christianity, can now take on their full relevance.

The Composition and Structure of the Apocalypse

The text of the Apocalypse which we find in our New Testament today is made up of twenty-two relatively brief chapters. This subdivision had its origins in the late Middle Ages, and it is sometimes difficult to see just what criteria were being used for such a division. For example, the seventh and final seal, even though it is the last of a long series, and forms one verse only, has been placed as the first verse of ch. 7, whereas it clearly belongs to ch. 6, where the other six seals are found. Naturally, most modern commentators suggest their own divisions and structure of the book, but not all are equally successful.

The reason for these difficulties is obvious, as we do not have the slightest indication of how the original author wished to subdivide his work. If one observes the oracular style of the book, and the way in which the author seems to go ahead by a continual statement and restatement of themes, it is legitimate to ask if we should even try to divide the book into chapters, as that gives the idea of a series of units, each one with its own particular theme and argument. Naturally, we must continue to refer to chapter and verse, as this facilitates reference, but we must not be slaves of that system.

There have, of course, been many attempts to trace the basic structure and message of the work. Most claim that there are three basic divisions:

    1—3   Introduction
    4:1—22:5   Prophetic part of the book
    22:6-21   Epilogue

This division presupposes that 4:1—22:5 are a prophecy about a future coming, and that the first three chapters introduce that prophecy. It overlooks that chs. 2-3 contain the "seven" of the letters, the first of a series of four "sevens" found throughout the work: letters, seals, trumpets and bowls. How is it that the first of these "sevens" is only introductory, while the other three are "prophetic"? This question is usually answered through a consideration of the words of Jesus Christ in the vision of ch. 1, where John is commanded: "Now write what you see, what is and what is to take place hereafter" (1:19). "What you see" refers to the vision of the Son of man in ch. 1; "what is" to the present state of the Church (contained in the letters to the Churches of chs. 2-3); "what is to take place hereafter" refers to the second coming of Christ, announced in the prophetic section of the book, from ch. 4 onwards. But why is "what you see" restricted only to the vision of the Son of man in ch. 1? Is not the whole of the book, and especially the so-called "prophetic" sections made up of visions? Surely these visions must also be described as "what you see"? We would like to suggest a different structure.

The most important feature of the book is the *four groups* of *seven events:*

2—3	The Seven Letters
6—8:1	The Seven Seals
8:6—11:19	The Seven Trumpets
16	The Seven Bowls

These four "sevens" determine the whole structure and message of the book, which can be seen as unfolding in the following fashion:

1:1-8	*Proemium.* Introduction and theological theme
1:9-20	Introduction to the Seven Letters
2—3	*The Seven Letters*
4—5	Introduction to the Seven Seals
6—8:1	*The Seven Seals*
8:2—8:5	Introduction to the Seven Trumpets
8:6—11	*The Seven Trumpets*
12—14	A recalling and deepening of the message of the Letters, Seals and Trumpets, especially the last two, a deepening of that message, as an introduction to the Seven Bowls, in the following fashion: 12: The creation and fall of man.

	13: The corruption of political and religious authority.
	14: The old economy as the first salvific intervention.
15	The Bowls are given
16	*The Seven Bowls* are poured out
17:1—19:10	The death of Christ as judgment upon history
19:11—20:15	The death of Christ as the final destruction of evil forces
21:1—22:5	The death of Christ and the heavenly Jerusalem
22:6-21	*Epilogue*

From this structure we can see that the Seven Bowls, introduced, given and poured out, and the description of the subsequent effects, dominate the second half of the book, running from ch. 12 till 22:5. The full significance of such a lengthy treatment will be appreciated in the light of the study which follows.

One final point. Although the account is often read as a continual progression, this is not the case. Like the Gospel of John, the same theology is repeated over and over again, each time going a little deeper, and carrying the message further, like waves on a seashore. It is a story of sin and redemption, of suffering and hope, told four times – the number four (four corners of the earth) representing the whole of the earth and its history. This story is dominated by the first coming of Jesus, the "Revelation of Jesus Christ" (1:1) central yet culminating in its role in salvation history both before and after the actual presence of Jesus of Nazareth among us.

THE PROLOGUE (1:1-8)

THEME: The "Revelation of Jesus Christ" (1:1) as the putting into reality and action of the divine plan to save all men, fruit of the love of God for his creatures, and necessitated by the sin of man. It has, as its high point the sacrifice of the Cross, which is the messianic revelation of Jesus Christ.

1The revelation of Jesus Christ, which God gave him to show to his servants what must soon take place; and he made it known by sending his angel to his servant John, 2who bore witness to the word of God and to the testimony of Jesus Christ, even to all that he saw.
3Blessed is he who reads aloud the words of the prophecy, and blessed are those who hear, and who keep what is written therein; for the time is near.
4John to the seven churches that are in Asia: Grace to you and peace from him who is and who was and who is to come, and from the seven spirits who are before his throne,
5and from Jesus Christ the faithful witness, the first-born of the dead, and the ruler of kings on earth. To him who loves us and has freed us from our sins by his blood
6and made us a kingdom, priests to his God and Father, to him be glory and dominion for ever and ever. Amen.
7Behold, he is coming with the clouds, and every eye will see him, every one who pierced him; and all tribes of the

earth will wail on account of him. Even so. Amen.
⁸"I am the Alpha and the Omega," says the Lord God, who is and who was and who is to come, the Almighty.

Structure of the Prologue

Most commentaries see the whole of ch. 1 as a general introduction to the whole book. It appears to me, however, that there is a clear break at v. 8. In v. 9 we are brought into contact with the personal experience of the author:

> "I John, your brother... was on the island called Patmos on account of the word of God and the testimony of Jesus."

From here on we have a gradual growth into a series of visions, without a break, up to the epilogue in 22:5. The section starting in 1:9 is an introduction to the Seven Letters, which fill all of chs. 2-3. Only vv. 1-8 have the character of an introduction, preceding the description of the experience of Patmos.

Some scholars argue that this introduction shows that the document was originally a letter, as it is similar to some of the greetings of the Pauline letters:

> "John to the seven Churches that are in Asia: Grace to you and peace" (1:4).

This idea is strengthened by the fact that in the epilogue he again returns to the first person to speak to those for whom the document was written:

> "I warn every one of you who hears the words of prophecy of this book" (22:18).

The matter is not quite so simple, especially in the epilogue, as we will see, but the general idea of a letter is quite possible, as long as we leave the "form" of the Apocalypse, something quite unique, not to be forced into the literary form of a letter.

In fact, there is no "introduction" in the true sense of that word. These few verses draw us immediately into the whole theme of the work, containing, in fact, a synthesis already containing hints of what will later become major issues. Despite this, the passage is not simply a summary of what will follow. Rather, here we have a model of John's method, his way of gradually unfolding and developing his theme. As he does this he develops his argument more amply or more profoundly, without ever changing or going beyond his original statement in these opening verses.

In other words, John's method is a continual going back upon what has already been seen and said, yet without repeating himself. He simply goes further, wider and deeper as he works with and meditates upon his fundamental message. There is a continual movement from the universal to the particular, from the simple to the complex, as the reader is led further into a reflection upon the relationship between God and creation (especially mankind), between eternity and time, between being and becoming. This sounds like a description of the history of mankind, but for John, it is something more. For him, history is essentially a history of salvation, of the gradual working out of a divine plan which is aimed at saving man from the miserable condition into which he has fallen, to bring him back to his original blessedness. Because of this, the end will correspond to the beginning, but at the same time, it will be even further reinforced, more powerful in its simplicity and its universality.

The Problem of Mediation

The first words "The revelation of Jesus Christ" show immediately the theme and the exclusive message of the book: it will explain the continual self-revelation of Jesus in history. This revelation is described in the first verse with two balancing expressions, of which the second takes up and develops the first.

In the first expression, the revelation of Jesus is described as something which has its origin in God; a gift of God, passing through and concentrated in Jesus Christ to reach mankind.

> "The revelation of Jesus Christ which God gave him to show to his servants" (1:1a).

All is said: nature of the revelation = a gift; the origin of the revelation = God; through whom the revelation passes = Jesus Christ; for whom it happens = humanity, his servants. There are two poles: God on one hand, mankind on the other, and between the two, the mediator: Jesus Christ.

In the second part of the verse, however, we meet a further mediation:

> "And he made it known by sending his angel to his servant John" (1:1b).

We are now at the level of a moment in history, where two more mediators are in action: the angel and John. The revelation which John performs is to make concrete and historical "the revelation of Jesus Christ" in a given place and time. Just when, we will see later. This brings with it a problem. The simplicity of the affirmations of the communication of God to mankind through Jesus in 1:1a has now been complicated and made more distant by the insertion of further mediators: angel and John. There is, therefore, a contrast between the directness of the mediation of Jesus in v. 1a, and the distancing from Jesus through further mediation in v. 1b.

This contrast between the initial statement of v. 1: "the revelation of Jesus Christ" and the successive "made... known by sending his angel to his servant" is quite marked and deliberate. The contrast has not been noticed by the commentators, as they are convinced that what follows the initial statement is simply an illustration of the normal way in which, according to John, the "revelation of Jesus Christ" would take place within the Christian community, through the mediation of angelic and human agents. Such an interpretation, however, not only misunderstands v. 1, but it fails to appreciate the line of argument of the whole of the Apocalypse. In chs. 21-22, dedicated to the description of the heavenly Jerusalem, the relationship between the divinity and humanity spoken about in 1a becomes a reality: the divinity, because of the decisive intervention of the mediator Jesus Christ (his death and resurrection) dwells directly in the midst of mankind:

> "Behold the dwelling of God is with men. He will dwell with them, and they shall be his people, and God himself will wipe away every tear from their eyes" (21:3-4).

The two extremes between which the "revelation of Jesus Christ" must work itself out now appear to join and they are bound tightly together by the constant presence of the Lamb, a symbol of the death of Christ, the culminating moment of his "revelation."

Beginning and End

This means that the end of the Apocalypse recalls the beginning of the book, reflecting a basic idea of John that the history of salvation reaches its high point when man returns to his original state of perfection, in perfect communication with the divinity. This is made possible, as the book will show, through the direct intervention of Jesus Christ – indirectly in the Old Testament, but reaching its culminating point in his messianic presence in history as Jesus of Nazareth.

The historical coming of Jesus Christ, and especially his death followed by his resurrection, represented the culminating moment of his revelation and, thus, of his mediating task. It is therefore impossible to think that after such an event his revelation, to reach his own Christian communities, would still have to pass through human or angelic mediators. It is clear that such a situation of lesser mediation reflects the period previous to the event of Jesus Christ. Both the opening verse and the concluding chapters indicate this, and the rest of the prologue speaks of the event of revelation as in the future.

That this is the case is made immediately clear by John, in the vision of the Son of man in the midst of the lampstands (see 1:9ff) which immediately after the prologue begins the section on the seven letters. There the "revelation of Jesus Christ" will be presented in its definitive stage, where Jesus Christ, victorious over death and hell and living forever (see 1:17-18) communicates directly. We find no angel, and even John is merely one of the community (see 1:9: "I John, your brother, who share with you"). He has the spirit of prophecy (1:10) but this is merely a manifestation of the gift of the Spirit which belongs to the whole community. The witness "to the word of God and to the testimony of Jesus Christ" (v. 2) was an exceptional thing in the Old Testament period (see 6:9-11; 20:4-6) but is a normal part of the task of a Christian after the coming of Christ (see 1:9).

It appears that this question of the mediation between God and man is a central problem for the Book of Revelation, and John wants to show that there is only to be one mediator, Jesus Christ.

It will be central to the section on the Seven Letters (especially the introduction to them: the vision of the Son of man) and the section on the new Jerusalem where the problem of mediation has been resolved, by the person and the sacrifice of Christ, the Lamb.

Nevertheless, in perfect accord with his method, the final solution is already anticipated by John in the second part of the prologue (see 1:4-6). After having presented a "revelation of Jesus Christ" which passes laboriously through a series of mediators, John allows us to see that there can be a community, the ecclesial community to which he belongs, where there is no shadow of that complicated series of mediators. It is a community of kings and priests (v. 6, see also 5:10) to whom grace and peace are possible because of God, the Spirit and Jesus himself (vv. 4-5). There is a mediation (v. 5: "from Jesus Christ"), but it is exclusively Jesus, a mediation which has happened because of an act of love:

> "To him who loves us and has freed us from our sins by his blood" (1:5b).

He is the source of authentic testimony to which all others, both before and after him, refer; he is the source of the victory over death which has given back to man a life in the Spirit and has returned to him, within the created world, his dignity of priest and king. John will tell his readers later (see 5:3) that this was a task that could be performed by no other created being. Only Jesus could perform it because of his divine nature, boldly mentioned here in close association with "his God and Father" (v. 6), and picked up again in the vision of the Son of man which follows immediately (see 1:13ff) where the attributes which the Old Testament scriptures gave to Yahweh are applied to the figure standing amidst the lampstands.

Thus, this book, generally understood as concentrating entirely on the end time, begins with a praise of the love of Jesus which gives life as a fruit of that love. The visions which follow will certainly be full of pain and suffering, but, as we will see, this is not the action of God, but the sinful will of angels and men whose pride attempts to take over and destroy all other beings. They are attempting completely to overthrow the situation described in vv. 4-6. The battles of this book must not be seen as physical battles, but they are a symbolic description of the spiritual warfare carried on between God and these evil powers: angelic and human. Above all, God uses the spiritual weapon beyond all weapons to defeat this evil: the death of Jesus. All the descriptions of cataclysms, battles, slaughter and the destruction of human pride throughout the book are, as we shall see, symbolic descriptions of that event. This event is again taken up in v. 7, through a citation of Zechariah (12:10-14) applied by John to the crucifixion. He also links it to the famous vision of the Son of man coming on the clouds from Dan 7:13. Most see this as a reference to a future coming, but, as we will see, it is all a reference to the death of Jesus. The use of "the Son of man," throughout the work, is unfailingly a reference to the death of Jesus. It is important to notice that here in v. 7, at the very first hint of John's use of Dan 7, he associates it with Zech 12. The identification of the one "who is coming with the clouds" with the crucified one, the pierced one, is something which must be kept in mind throughout this book, where Dan 7:13-14 will appear and reappear as a sort of unifying thread.

The Revelation of Jesus Christ

We must be careful not to simply take this expression as the title of the book. It is the *theme* of the book. It can mean two things:
(a) The revelation *about* Jesus Christ
(objective genitive)
(b) The revelation which comes from Jesus Christ
(subjective genitive)

My interpretation is based on an acceptance of the first of these possibilities. While some scholars choose one or the other, most claim that there is probably a little of each in the mind of the author. From what I have already argued, it is clear that the words "the revelation of Jesus Christ" indicates a revelation, that is a manifestation of Jesus Christ himself, of his person and his task, in which John sees the manifestation and the gradual putting into effect of the divine plan for the salvation of mankind. This meaning appears to me to be not only the best interpretation from a purely linguistic point of view, but it also corresponds to the structure of the book and the developing argument which gradually emerges from that structure. It allows the Apocalypse to be what it claims to be: "prophecy" in the authentically biblical sense, as John understands it, a meditation upon human history, finding its sense and purpose in the light of the revealed word of the Sacred Scriptures.

It appears to me that John finds the meaning of history as a continual working out of the judgment of God upon mankind and upon the world. This judgment is seen, on the one hand, as a punishment from God for the sin of man, but on the other as the possibility of salvation and life. For John, the one who executes this divine judgment which has been going on from creation itself, is Jesus Christ. In this way, the whole of history, and not only its conclusion, is "apocalypse": "revelation of Jesus Christ."

"What must soon take place" (v. 1)

These words, which close the very first affirmation of the Apocalypse, refer to the content, the object of the "revelation" which Jesus Christ has received from God so that he might communicate it, "show to his servants" (see 1:1). In contemporary interpretation there is not the slightest doubt that these words refer to some sort of final moment, and it is also clear that this moment is referred to as the "revelation of Jesus Christ." At this point, however, the choice which I have just made between the secrets which Jesus Christ might reveal and the revelation which is Jesus Christ himself begins to appear as very important. In fact, if it is a question of certain secrets which Christ reveals to John, then some sort of "prophetic" foretelling of a future event is a perfectly logical interpretation. However, if the "revelation of Jesus Christ" means, as I believe, his gradual revelation of himself through history understood as a history of salvation, its fulfilment has to be placed on another level. It must mean that the divine salvific plan has been realised.

The rest of the book will show that this is what John means. In the four "sevens" which form the work (letters, seals, trumpets and bowls) there is the description of disorder, physical and moral evil, in various forms, all of which is moving towards some sort of final moment. That event is explicitly described by the "seven" of the trumpets as the "mystery of God" (see 10:7), and which is gradually identified with the death of Christ. This is the fulfilment which John has in mind: the death of Christ which puts into effect, in a total and definitive fashion, the mystery of God, that is, his plan to save humanity. In so far as this is a fulfilment of the will of God, it is "necessary" (see 1:1; 4:4; 22:6). It does not refer to the destruction of the world which must happen "soon," but to the perfection of the mystery of God: the coming and the death of Christ.

If this perfect fulfilment of the mystery of God is the death of Christ, the word "what must soon take place" should be read in connection with the situation which preceded that event, the period of waiting, the period of promise, the old economy. This situation is recalled immediately afterwards by the presence of the angel as mediator. If this is the case, then the expression used by John for "soon" (Greek: *en tachei*) carried with it the hint of a time which is near at hand, and it bears also the nuance of a word of consolation and comfort. This hint becomes clearer in the words of the angel of the sixth trumpet who announces that very shortly the "mystery of God" will be fulfilled (see 10:7). It is also clear from the "Seven" of the letters, especially in the final section (see 2:16; 3:3, 11, 20).

But precisely in the letters (which, we shall see, are to be read as an allegory on the time of waiting) there appears to be yet another hint of just how this fulfilment will take place. The expression used by John indicates that the events will happen in a short time; there will be a rapidity, an immediateness in the divine action which no obstacle can hope to block or delay. That is obvious as with any action of God, but there is also the idea that what will happen will come unexpectedly. Twice in the Apocalypse (see 3:3; 16:15), as also in the Synoptics (see Matt 24:43), Christ compared his coming to that of a thief in a household.

The Angel and John

I have now mentioned several times that the reference to the mediation of the angel and John refers to the situation *before* the event of Christ. We have seen that v.1a speaks simply of a mediation of God →Jesus Christ→the faithful community, but in v. 1b new intermediaries are needed – the angel and John. This insertion of the angel and John does not only happen here, but is fundamental for the further development of the Apocalypse. In fact nearly always in the visions which depend upon a direct contact between John and angelic figures the latter have a function of making him see. They explain the visions. Most of the book seems to have angels performing the function ("show to his servants") which 1:1a gives to Jesus Christ.

This has seemed to commentators as normal practice for apocalyptic literature, but there is more to it here. John seems to be very concerned about the mediation between God and man, and has his own ideas of how things were and are mediated: in the old economy it happened through angels, who, even then, were acting as agents of Jesus Christ, the real author even of that economy. Even there one could find salvation (see those killed for their witness in 6:9ff). Nevertheless, after the coming of Christ, the mediating function of the angels is over – only Jesus mediates:

> 1:16: "In his hand he held seven stars, and from his mouth issued a sharp two-edged sword, and his face was like the sun shining in full strength." (See also 4:9-10; 5:8, etc.)

The angels are reduced to simple "fellow servants" (see 19:10; 22:9).

The same must be said for John. He is always the human who receives the revelation, and he is the one who has to "write" what he sees or hears (see 1:11, 19; 14:13; 19:9). For this reason he considers himself a prophet, or a brother of the prophets (see 19:1; 22:9).

In this function, however, he seems to have two different moments or levels in his activity:
1. He is subservient to the angels, and even tempted to adore them. Everything is done at their command.
2. He sometimes appears to be on the same level as the angels. One could almost say that he is at times superior.

This situation is described in the introduction to the Seven Letters (1:9-20) where in the vision of the Son of man, the vision is communicated directly from Jesus Christ to John. This is clearly a superior revelation.

These two stages, I believe, are to be seen as the two stages in the history of salvation:
1. The "signs" which need the mediation of angels to John refer to the old order.
2. The direct mediation of Jesus refers to his coming and its fruits, the major one being his presence among men.

The personality and figure of "John," then, is used to present the situation of man in the two situations, a pre-Christ stage where the mediation of angels is needed, and a situation during and after Christ, when Jesus communicates directly.

This clarifies the two-fold reference to John in ch. 1. Recalling what we said earlier about witnessing to the word of God and to the testimony of Jesus Christ, as an exceptional way to come to divine life in the old economy, we find John referred to in such a capacity in 1:2. He represents the ancient witness to the word of God. In 1:9 he is still a witness to the word of God and to the testimony of Jesus, but here he expresses himself differently: he is "your brother, who shares with you the tribulation and the kingdom and the patient endurance, a fellow member of a Christian community."

> *"From Him who is and who was and who is coming, and from the seven Spirits who are before his throne and from Jesus Christ"* (1:4-5).

Verses 4-7 contain a great deal of material which could be the opening of a letter, similar to the letters of Paul: the name of the author (John), the type of greetings generally found in Christian greetings (grace and peace), these gifts are asked from the divinity. In vv. 4-5, the formulae used by John to describe the divinity, and especially Jesus Christ, have the atmosphere of a confession of faith.

What is impressive is the rhythmic three-fold formula which appears to be too contrived to be accidental:

> "From him who is and who was and
>   who is coming
> And from the seven spirits who are
>   before his throne
> And from Jesus Christ, the faithful
>   witness, the first born of the dead"

John asks that these divine realities pour out grace and peace upon the people who are receiving the document.

The first of these realities – clearly the divinity, God himself, is given a threefold qualification: "he who is, and who was and who is coming." Jesus Christ is the recipient of a sort of hymn which seems to be in two sections, each one made up of three elements:
1. The quality of his life:
   — the faithful witness (v. 4) — he who loves us (v. 5)
2. His death and resurrection:
   — firstborn of the dead (v. 4) — has freed us from our sins by his blood (v. 5)
3. The glorious effects which follow:
   — the ruler of kings on the earth (v. 4) — made us a kingdom of priests (v. 5)

Keeping this in mind, we can perhaps identify the third section of a hymn to Christ which is made up of the combination of Daniel and Zechariah (Dan 7:13; Zech 12:10ff).
1. A basic attribute of Jesus: he is Messiah:
   "He is coming with the clouds"
2. Reference to the death and resurrection:
   "Every eye will see him, everyone who pierced him"
3. The judgment upon humanity which is the effect of this:
   "And all the tribes of the earth will wail on account of him."

The insistence on the number "three" also makes it clear that already here there is a consciousness of the "threeness" of the divinity: God, the seven spirits, i.e., the totality of the

Spirit and Jesus Christ (see vv. 4-5). The location of Jesus Christ in the third place probably is used to stress his mediating function between the divine and the human, but it could also be due to the fact that John, basing himself upon a combination of Isaiah and Zechariah (see Is 11:1ff and Zech 4:10) appears to regard the Spirit as a possession of Jesus Christ in so far as he is the Messiah (see 5:6 and 4:5).

We should notice the correspondence which exists between the threefold formula used to define God: "he who is and who was and who is coming," and the above continual use of a threefold pattern to refer to Jesus. The name given to God is the name which is addressed to God as the Father of Jesus (see 1:6; 3:5, 21, etc.). Thus we can speak of God the Father, who is defined in a way which comes directly from the Jewish usage, avoiding the name of God. It has its origins in the name Yahweh, which is a form of the verb "to be" (see Exod 3:14: "I am who am") which had been filled out by later Judaism into, "who is and who was and who will be."

As can be seen, John changes the last expression "who will be" away from the verb "to be," into the verb "to come": "who is coming." We have already mentioned that this is typical of John's use of Scripture; he returns to the biblical tradition, but he varies some small detail. This arises from his plan to furnish a further fulfilment and explanation of the original Scriptures. In the use of the verb "to be," the *transcendence* of God was made clear. By changing the verb, and making it a present participle, John wished to stress the link between the divinity and the world, his presence in history, a presence not limited to a point in time or a circumstance (as is indicated by John's use of the present participle, often badly translated into a future: "he who will come," thus missing the point). The presence is from always, for always, and constant.

All this is reflected in what is said in the formulae applied to Jesus, but in Jesus the threefold formulae speaks of his relationship with humanity, with history understood as a history of salvation. When Christ presents himself to John in 1:17-18 there is the same past, present and future being all caught up in the one salvific plan of God, whose putting into action is the perennial "revelation of Jesus Christ."

> "I am the first and the last, and the living one; I died, and behold I am alive for evermore, and I have the keys of Death and Hades."

"Behold he is coming with the clouds" (v. 7)

These words, along with the rest of v. 7 are those which are more influential than any other factor in Apoc 1:1-8 for leading the interpreter to claim that the book is about the second coming of Christ at the end of the world. What seems to be missed is that this passage comes to John from Dan 7:13 and that it is used here in connection with another messianic text, Zech 12:10ff. We have already mentioned that John does not use the Sacred Scriptures to fill out his images or to add colour. He uses it to provide himself with a sure footing and basis for the truth which he is trying to communicate.

The truth which stands so close to his heart, and which he will be attempting to prove throughout the whole work is that the historical coming of Jesus Christ, in his incarnation, death and resurrection are the final fulfilment of the promises, the prophecies, the prefigurations and the hopes expressed in the Old Testament. We can already see this in these verses of the prologue to the work. The greeting which John had for the Churches of Asia gave him a chance to stress the divine nature of Jesus Christ, by placing him firmly in a trinitarian context (1:4-5). After this, in two blocks of material, he speaks of his work of redemption and salvation in favour of humanity (1:5-6). The two scriptural quotations from Daniel and Zechariah which follow are the scriptural proof of all that John has just said about Jesus Christ: the redemption and the salvation brought to humanity by Jesus is no less than the bringing to fruition of what had been forecast and promised concerning the Messiah in Daniel and Zechariah: The Messiah comes, and he sets up a situation of judgment in his coming.

In this way, v. 7 anticipates several of the most important themes which will be taken up and further developed by John:
— Jesus Christ is the Messiah announced by Scripture.
— His messianic revelation is fulfilled in his death and resurrection.
— In his death the judgment of God comes into effect.

It is for this reason that this prophecy of Daniel will be regularly taken up through the book, and always in association with the death and resurrection of Jesus:
— The vision of the Son of man (1:12ff).
— The vision of the throne of the Lamb (chs. 4-5).
— The vision of the Son of man on the white cloud (14:14).
— The word of God who comes down from heaven mounted on a white horse (19:11ff).

THE SEVEN LETTERS TO THE CHURCHES (1:9—3:22)

THEME: The 'mystery' of the seven stars and the seven lampstands. The whole of the revelation has Jesus Christ as author, and it is summed up in his person and his messianic work of death and resurrection. This coming has shed light on the meaning of the old revelation and has begun to realise the promises within the ecclesial community.

Structure and General Theme

According to the division which I have proposed, immediately after the Prologue, the Seven Letters to the Churches begins. It becomes fully developed in chs. 2-3. Like all the other "sevens" (seals, trumpets and bowls) the letters are preceded by an introduction which is associated with the prophetic visionary experience which he has on the Island of Patmos, occupying the second half of ch. 1 (vv. 9-20). The indications that 1:9-20 is connected with the letters is best seen in the fact that at the beginning of each letter there is a return to some attribute of the description of the Son of man who appears before John.

The clearest link, however, is found in the fact that the

so-called Seven Letters are the uninterrupted continuation of the words which Jesus directs to John, after he turns around "to see the voice" (1:12) and finds himself before the Son of man. The effect of this vision is that John falls to the ground "as though dead" (1:17), but Christ raises him, insisting on the fact that he has conquered death and is now in possession of an endless life (1:18). He then commands that John write what he had already heard from the "loud voice" behind him that told him to write (vv. 10-11), explaining it more fully by giving further explanation (v. 19) and speaking of the symbols which surround him, the seven stars and the seven lampstands (v. 20). Then follows, without any break (the division into chapters comes from the Middle Ages) the messages of the angels of the Seven Churches.

It is important to see this connection between the vision of the Son of man and the seven letters, as without it the most immediate point of referral to what is written in the letters is lost. The vision is then seen as some sort of inaugural vision, standing on its own, and the letters also remain somewhat of an enigma, whose presence in the overall structure and message of the book becomes almost impossible to decipher. Tying them together, I believe, helps one to explain the other. We must also pay attention to detail which is often missed, thus leading to quite anachronistic interpretations of the letters, e.g., the explanation of the angels of the Churches as the bishops of the various communities. This does not tie in with the message, and I hope that what I offer will be seen as matching the theology of the whole book.

Considered as belonging to the experience of Patmos, the letters move around the great basic theme of the book: the transmission of revelation. This is already indicated by a consideration of the verbs used: "to hear," "to see," "to write" – i.e., register the things seen and heard, to communicate them to others. The "writing" which appears several times in the book (see 10:4; 14:13, etc.) is always in terms of communicating a received revelation. The being "in the spirit" (1:10) is a clear "prophetic" sign, intimately linked, as we have seen, with revelation.

We must insist on certain particulars which do not appear to mean a great deal to contemporary interpreters, but would have certainly been noticed by John's contemporaries. They would have known that there is a difference between hearing behind oneself "a great voice like a trumpet" (1:10-11) and seeing Jesus Christ face to face and hearing a revelation directly from him (see 1:17ff). Already in the New Testament there is a distinction drawn between "a voice" (John the Baptist), and the presence of Jesus (see Matt 3:1-6; Mk 1:2-3; Lk 3:1-6).

We will hope to demonstrate that it is precisely these two *different* "prophetic" situations which John wishes to illustrate through his use of Seven Letters. The two situations are certainly connected. It is always John who receives the revelation; the message has to go always to the communities in Asia (see 1:11 and then the geography of the Churches in chs. 2-3). There is, of course, only one "book" which has to be written.

The position of the human instrument who receives the revelation varies: first he hears a voice from behind him, and then he has a face to face encounter. The voice is described in different terms. The voice from behind is "a loud voice, like a trumpet" (1:10). When, however, John hears the voice of Jesus Christ, it is described as follows: "his voice was like the sound of many waters' (1:15). There is another *very important* detail. After the revelation passes between Jesus and John, he is commanded to communicate it to the angels. This changes what we read in the second part of 1:1: Christ ⟶ angel ⟶ John. Finally, even though the "book" is the same, in the second case, the contents are fuller and much more precise (compare 1:11 and 19).

These similarities, yet differences, this continuity, yet diversity, in an author as controlled as John, must signify something. The mediators (Jesus – John – angels) are those of 1:1b, and the figure of the Son of man in 1:12-20 takes up again the use of Dan 7:13 in 1:7. These carry on, but are taken further and deeper.

The Introduction to the Seven Letters 1:9-20

1⁹I John, your brother, who share with you in Jesus the tribulation and the kingdom and the patient endurance, was on the island called Patmos on account of the word of God and the testimony of Jesus.
¹⁰I was in the Spirit on the Lord's day, and I heard behind me a loud voice like a trumpet
¹¹saying, "Write what you see in a book and send it to the seven churches, to Ephesus and to Smyrna and to Pergamum and to Thyatira and to Sardis and to Philadelphia and to Laodicea."
¹²Then I turned to see the voice that was speaking to me, and on turning I saw seven golden lampstands,
¹³and in the midst of the lampstands one like a son of man, clothed with a long robe and with a golden girdle round his breast;
¹⁴his head and his hair were white as white wool, white as snow; his eyes were like a flame of fire,
¹⁵his feet were like burnished bronze, refined as in a furnace, and his voice was like the sound of many waters;
¹⁶in his right hand he held seven stars, from his mouth issued a sharp two-edged sword, and his face was like the sun shining in full strength.
¹⁷When I saw him, I fell at his feet as though dead. But he laid his right hand upon me, saying, "Fear not, I am the first and the last,
¹⁸and the living one; I died, and behold I am alive for evermore, and I have the keys of Death and Hades.
¹⁹Now write what you see, what is and what is to take place hereafter.
²⁰As for the mystery of the seven stars which you saw in my right hand, and the seven golden lampstands, the seven stars are the angels of the seven churches and the seven lampstands are the seven churches.

In vv. 9-10 there is a description of a concrete place: "on the island called Patmos," in an interior condition which was somewhat extraordinary: "I was in the Spirit," and a day is given, "on the Lord's day." There is no reason why any of this should be doubted, or spiritualised. He was on the island, "on account of the word of God and the testimony of Jesus," which could be as a prisoner, engaged in forced labour, or on some missionary activity, and the reference to the day could well be a reference to a liturgical celebration, on a Sunday. The Greek expression, (*en tē kuriakē hēmera*), may even indicate Easter Day.

We must, however, be concrete in our interpretation of the expression "I was in the Spirit." This does not mean that he fell into some sort of trance, but it is closely associated with the many occasional experiences of the early Church: tongues, prophecy, healing, etc., which were manifestations of the Spirit who was *always* there. For John, as for Paul, it is a question of the illumination of the Spirit, producing a prophetic activity: a deepening, under the guidance of the Spirit of certain mysteries, so that they can be communicated to others (see also I Cor 14:1ff).

These personal details go even further; they tie John closely to the prophetic experience of the Old Testament. Patmos indicates isolation and separation; Ezekiel and Daniel both are portrayed as prophesying during the Babylonian exile. John, even as these Old Testament witnesses, was persecuted and exiled because of his faithfulness to the Law and for maintaining the messianic hope (6:9ff; 11:3ff). Like them, too, he possessed the Spirit (see 19:10; 22:6).

"I HEARD BEHIND ME A LOUD VOICE LIKE A TRUMPET" (V. 10).

The prophetic experience of Patmos has two moments:
(a) First John hears a voice behind him which orders him to write what he sees in a book and send it to a list of Churches in Asia, a list which is then repeated in the letters themselves (see 1:10-11 and chs. 2-3).
(b) He turns around and he sees Jesus Christ (Son of man) in the midst of seven golden lampstands. He repeats the

order, and then dictates the letters, one by one. (see 1:12-20 and chs. 2-3).

Although this has not been noticed by commentators who tend to move quickly to the vision of the Son of man, it is important, and has serious consequences for the interpretation of the rest of the book, not only for the link between the Patmos experience and the Seven Letters. In ch. 4, the *first* phase of the Patmos experience is taken up again at the opening of the section on the Seven Seals. 4:1: "The first voice, which I had heard speaking to me like a trumpet, said...." In the section which follows (see 8:2: "seven trumpets were given to them") the trumpet theme comes back. In chs. 4-5 the vision of the Son of man returns (vision of the throne and the Lamb) and is repeated in ch. 14, where the Son of man is seated between two groups of angels (Son of man between the lampstands) and it returns again in ch. 19: the Logos of God on a white horse.

It could be said that we are here in touch with a key to the reading of the Apocalypse. I have already mentioned that John takes up and deepens the same arguments as the book unfolds, but the vision in 1:12-20 of the Son of man is more majestic than the repeated references in the rest of the book (Lamb, Son of man on a white cloud, Logos on the horse). Here it is clearly a "Revelation of Jesus Christ" in a supreme and final way. It will not be repeated until the final scenes which speak of his permanent presence among the believers in ch. 21:22-27; 22:1-5 and his direct communication with them (22:16-17).

I have already suggested that the two phases of revelation in 1:9-20 represent an indirect (from behind) and a direct (face to face) revelation. This could refer to the two moments in the revelation of Jesus – the indirect revelation of the Old Testament, and the direct revelation of the person preaching and works of Jesus Christ. There is a continuity; one leads to the other, but there is still a distinction. This objective plan could also have a subjective reference. The "turning towards" Jesus could be a reference to the need for faith in him, possible only through "conversion," a turning around towards him.

In Jesus, scripture, the Old Testament, finds its final explanation. This, in my opinion, is why the Letters are really a reading of the ancient scriptures done by Jesus himself, an explanation of their significance in the light of his coming – his *first* coming. The "loud voice" from behind calls for all the intermediaries of the Old Economy: a superhuman intervention (loud voice), a human instrument (John), the prophetic mission (write a book), those for whom it is intended (the Seven Churches). He has to write what he sees (v. 11). In the vision of the Son of man the communication is direct, the command is the same, the Churches are the same and he has to write what he sees (v. 19). Only the *mode* of communication is different. There is only one "revelation of Jesus Christ," but there are two phases in its communication. The second is perfect and direct, a result of the messianic coming of Jesus Christ, but it was already contained, in an imperfect, embryonic way in the Old Economy. The agent (John) is always the same, but in the first moment he is specially called out from the people; in the second he is their brother, one of them, receiving the trumpets of Jesus Christ.

The "loud voice" which comes from behind John is the voice of an angel. This is always found in the Apocalypse when mention is made of a "loud voice" (see 5:2, 11; 7:2; 8:13; 10:3, etc.). This is a further indication that we are in the period of the Old Economy, the period of the Old Testament, which takes place, in John's vision of things, through the mediation of an angel. The same thing is indicated by the reference to a "trumpet." This is not just an interesting description, especially as he picks up the image again in 4:1: "And the first voice, which I had heard speaking to me like a trumpet, said, etc.," and we find that what follows is an allegory on the Genesis story of Creation. The trumpets also return in the seven trumpets which is, as we shall see, an exposition of the Old Economy. The reference to trumpet probably also contains an allusion to the revelation at Sinai, the basic and central event in the Old Economy. See Ezek 19:16-19:

"On the morning of the third day there were thunders and lightnings, and a thick cloud upon the mountain and a very loud trumpet blast... And as the sound of the trumpet grew louder and louder, Moses spoke, and God answered him in thunder."

The voice of Jesus Christ is "like the sound of many waters" (1:15). The image is still one of power, but it has to be understood as a spiritual, and not a material power. Again we are dealing with a biblical citation. Ezek 43:2:

"And behold the glory of the God of Israel came from the east: and the sound of his coming was like the sound of many waters" (see also Ezek 1:2).

Fortunately, in this case the author himself gives us an explanation of the symbol. In ch. 17 John describes the prostitute as "seated upon many waters" (17:1), which further on he explains as: "The waters... are peoples and multitudes and nations and tongues" (17:15). This is a regular formula in the Apocalypse to indicate the totality of humanity (see 5:9; 7:9; etc.).

Thus the voice of Jesus alludes to the universal character of his "revelation," in contrast to the "particularism" of the revelation of the Old Testament, reserved for the Hebrew people. John will do this throughout the work, but we must not forget the fact that these two moments, even here, are closely linked, and the "loud voice" is also directed to the Seven Churches. What the loud voice brusquely asks be done is further clarified by the voice of Jesus Christ with the explanation of the "mystery" of the seven stars and the seven candelabra (symbol of Judaism in its totality) which become the "Seven Churches," i.e., the totality of the Church, to which now even the angels have become a part "fellow servant with you," as the angel will explain in 19:10 and 22:9. This is fully confirmed at the end of the book:

"I Jesus have sent my angel to you with this testimony for the Churches" (22:16).

THE VISION OF THE SON OF MAN — THE MODELS

The second part of the prophetic experience of Patmos, the appearance of the Son of man among the lampstands has two sections:
(a) vv. 12-15: The description of the figure
(b) v. 6 —: The words of the Son of man which, however, in my argument, do not finish till the end of ch. 3: the message to the Churches.

This section is full of Old Testament background, and especially the description of the Son of man. I will attempt to draw them out. There are two Old Testament models behind the figure which John, in his usual method, takes over but alters:

(a) Always noticed is the general background of the great opening vision of the Book of Ezekiel (1:4—3:37). In its essentials, the vision in Ezekiel is made up of:
   1. A vision of the throne of Yahweh carried by the four Cherubim with the multiple arrival and human appearance (1:4-26).
   2. The apparition of a person who appears to be like Yahweh, so much so that the prophet prostrates himself before him, but is picked up and given a mission to Israel. This mission is strengthened by the vision of the scroll which is devoured (1:26-36).
   3. The prophet is taken by the Spirit on high and he hears behind him the great noise of Yahweh departing (3:12-14).
   4. After a period of doubt, affliction and suffering, the prophet finally comes to a place where he sees Yahweh in his glory and is confirmed in his mission which is explained to him (3:22-27).

   This vision is taken up here and later in the book (ch. 4: the four Cherubim around the throne of the divinity; ch. 10: the scroll which is devoured, etc.). The difference here is that the vision of the person like Yahweh is placed in a second moment, after hearing the "loud voice." We have already seen the significance of this, the Old and the coming of Jesus, a theme which will return, especially in chs. 4 and 10.

(b) This transposing of the Ezekiel scene into a first and second part leads to John's second Old Testament model: The visions of the prophet in the section chs. 7-12 of his prophecy: symbolic beasts, the ancient of days on his throne, the Son of man coming on the clouds. In Daniel there is a first explanation given by a person who seems like an angel (Dan 7:16ff: explanation of the four beasts, the ancient of days, the Son of man; 8:15ff: the explanation of the two beasts). The definitive explanation is, however, given to Daniel by a person, also probably an angel who has a description that makes him very like the Ancient of Days (Dan 10:5-15; see 7:9-10). It is this two-fold "revelation" that John picks up, the second being superior to the first, and John pushes it to its limits, making the second personality, the Son of man himself, the definitive revelation.

THE SON OF MAN

In Dan 7:9-10 and 13-14 the Son of man appears after the vision of the ancient of days, and the character is a promise that, in the end, a suffering Israel will be released in a messianic intervention of God, and all power and authority will be given to the Son of man (Israel). John, as usual, adapts this. The Son of man who appears among the lampstands (1:13) takes on the characteristics which Daniel gave to the Ancient of Days (Yahweh), and also Daniel's "second revealer" from Dan 10:5-14. For John, however, following the Gospel tradition, the Son of man is Jesus Christ.

Jesus Christ is the Son of man. That means that he is the Messiah announced by Daniel in his vision. The quotation from Dan 7:13 in Apoc 1:7: "Behold he is coming with the clouds" was already an anticipation that Jesus was the

Messiah announced by the prophets in the Old Testament. The vision of the Son of man at Patmos takes this up and explains it further, picking up a theme simply stated in the Prologue. This will happen repeatedly throughout the book (chs. 4-5; 14; 19), always to show that the coming of Jesus was a messianic coming, the definitive fulfilment of revelation, completely and finally illuminating all of the promises of the Old Testament.

The Son of man is described by John as having the characteristics which Ezekiel and Daniel had attributed to the supreme divinity, Yahweh: "hair as white as white wool" (1:14 and Dan 7:9); "eyes like a flame of fire," a symbol of the power of universal judgment (1:14 and Dan 10:6); "Feet like burnished bronze, refined as in a furnace," a sign of absolute transcendence (1:15 and Dan 10:6); his voice "like the sound of many waters," the symbol of the universality of his revelation (1:15 and Ezek 43:2). There can be no mistaking John's idea: Jesus Christ, the Son of man, is of divine status, a God equal to Yahweh. Again this has been prefigured in the Prologue (vv. 4-5) and will appear again in the vision of the Lamb in ch. 5, another re-use of the vision of Daniel, as we shall see. There it will be carried further, as John wishes to make it clear that the messianic activity of Jesus is not political or "this worldly," but a redemption through the sacrifice of self.

This idea of the salvific action of the Son of man is also hinted at here. In the description of the Son of man, the eternal, the godly and the transcendent are stressed. The very use of "one like a son of man" indicates a presence among men, in history. He is, as we have repeatedly said, the continuation and the perfection of the Old Economy, and thus also in history, as was that Economy. Above all, however, he has passed through death and this gives him power over death (v. 18). We have already read in the Prologue that he has "freed us from our sins by his blood." The salvific action of the Son of man is repeated here in another way. In v. 17, at the sight of the Son of man, John "fell at his feet as though dead." Jesus places his hand upon him and raises him (see 1:17). This is certainly taken from Dan 10:9-12, but for Daniel the restoration is after fear. Here it is after "as though dead," the situation of man before the presence of the divine life made possible by Jesus:

> "Fear not, I am the first and the last, and the living one; I died, and behold I am alive for evermore, and I have the keys of Death and Hades" (1:17-18).

He restores man to a life lost because of sin. This theme, perhaps hinted at here, will become more fully developed in the allegory of Death riding the fourth horse, followed by Hades (6:7).

THE SON OF MAN, KING, PRIEST AND UNIVERSAL JUDGE

The Son of man is presented as a divine being who has lived, died and risen, and thus given life (1:12-18). He has overcome death and hell, and this is another key theme of the book. During the rest of the book what has been announced here as achieved will be repeated in the battle with these powers. The final victory will not be heard again until 20:13-14:

> "Death and Hades gave up the dead in them, and all were judged by what they had done. Then Death and Hades were thrown into the lake of fire."

We read in the Prologue that he "made us a kingdom, priests to his God" (1:6) and the Son of man also seems to have the attributes of King and Priest. He is described as "clothed with a long robe and with a golden girdle round his breast" (v. 13). This is the clothing of the Hebrew High Priest (see Exod 28:4; 29:5; Lev 8:7). It is also the prerogative of kings, and their dignitaries (see I Macc 10:89; 11:58). Most commentators see the reference here to the Kingship of Jesus. The same garment is worn by the angels in 15:6. This need not worry us, as John will show in chs. 4 and 5, the angels also have a royal and priestly function (see 4:4; 5:8; 8:2). The function common to angels and Jesus is, of course, that of "revelation." Thus, Jesus is Priest and King, like the angels, but he is the perfection of all that they (the necessary mediators in the old order) had done.

There is, however, something more. We must recall that what we have here is a use of Daniel. What he is wearing is, in fact, the same as the garments worn by the person who, in Dan 10:5ff, gives Daniel the definitive explanation of his vision. In the Apocalypse, however, as we have seen, this personality is not another angelic figure, but Jesus, Son of man in so far as he is Messiah. It is not absurd, therefore, to see here in the Apocalypse the use of "gold" (in Apoc a symbol of contact with the divinity) an allegory of the incarnation, Son of man, Messiah, Jesus of Nazareth, yes – but clothed with gold, in contact with, possessing the divinity.

This explanation will help us understand better the reason why the angels of ch. 15, who receive cups to be poured out, have a similar garb (see 15:6). I said above that it was an allusion to the angels, priestly and kingly mediators in the old order. The cups poured out are, however, a representation of the death of Jesus. This event is a decisive event for *God's* salvation of *mankind*. It would not be possible without *incarnation*. The angels, clothed like kings and priests with a golden sash, receive the cups, and this signifies that they too are closely associated with the link between incarnation and the death of Jesus Christ.

The Son of man, however, (and this is important) unlike the angels in ch. 15:6 is not dressed in "bright linen." He is "clothed with a long robe," a technical term referring to the priestly garment. The symbol seems to be that not only is he a priest, but by the different garment we are told that he has already performed his sacrifice. That this is the case is indicated in v. 18. No matter how close the mediation between the angels and Jesus may be in their both having performed the priestly task of bringing the heavenly to earth, he is King and Priest forever (v. 18). He has performed his once-and-for-all sacrifice and is now King and Priest over a kingly and priestly people (1:6).

It is in that function that Jesus is also judge. The attributes of the flaming eyes and the "sharp two-edged sword" (vv. 14 and 16) indicate his role as judge. Again this is a function which he exercises in his coming and in his death and resurrection. For the Jewish tradition, the great division between the good and the bad was to happen when the Messiah came. We have already seen that John presents Jesus as Son of man, Messiah, but a messiahship exercised in victory over death through death (v. 18). This makes him judge, as will be repeated in ch. 19 where the Logos of God will come down from heaven to meet and divide men who are lined up against him (19:11). There he also has the flaming eyes and the double edged sword (19:12-15), but the judgment is about to happen. Here he is already judge, and dressed in his priestly robe; there he wears a "robe dipped in blood," symbol of the sacrifice which still has to be undergone; and his royal name as yet is known only to himself (see 19:12-16).

THE "MYSTERY" OF THE SEVEN STARS AND THE SEVEN LAMPSTANDS

The order of the Son of man (v. 19) repeats that of the "loud voice" (v. 16), but further and finally explained, as happened in the book of Daniel. This second instruction has also the revelation of a "mystery" – that of the seven stars and the seven lampstands (see 1:20) and then the dictation of the letters (chs. 2-3). Both are part of what John is commanded to write. The symbolism of the seven stars and seven lampstands is always difficult for interpreters, and many suggestions help little in tracing an unfolding logic here.

It is clear that the "mystery" forms part of what John has to write:

1:19: "What you see, what is, and what is to take place hereafter."

Of these many "things," the "mystery" of the stars and the lampstands are a continuation, or better, the result, the meaning and explanation.

We are not dealing here with a simple identification. We are warned that it is a "mystery." We must start from the word "angel" which has a specific sense in Apoc. The angels, we have already seen (1:1), are the intermediaries for the transmission of the revelation of Jesus Christ in the stage before the coming of Jesus. Therefore, when Jesus says that they are "the angels of the seven churches" he simply means that they had the mission in the Old Order of preparing for the advent, the foundation of the seven Churches, i.e., the totality of the Church, the new people of God from all humanity and redeemed by Jesus. This is clear from the epilogue:

"I Jesus have sent my angel to you with his testimony for the Churches" (22:16).

This, therefore, means that after his coming, their role as mediators fades, and they become members of the community, without any special superiority or function. They are "fellow servants with you" (19:10; 22:9). For this reason they are totally subject to Jesus: "The seven stars which you saw *in my right hand.*" He is their lord and master. They are under his control.

The lampstands are well-known as a symbol of the cult and the spiritual heart of Judaism. It is already found in Zech 4:1-14, and will be further used by John to speak of the two witnesses – representing Judaism (prophets and Law), and they will be called "the two lampstands which stand before the lord of the earth" (11:4).

If this is the case, when John writes: "and the seven lampstands are the seven Churches" he wishes to say that with the coming of Jesus Christ, Judaism with its cult and spiritual heritage has become the Church (7 of each = perfection of each). This is the high point of the "revelation of Jesus Christ," the fulfilment of the "mystery" and the meaning of the whole book of the Apocalypse.

The "Letters" to the Churches of Asia Minor (chs. 2-3)

THE PROMISE OF REDEMPTION
2—3

2 ¹"To the angel of the church in Ephesus write: 'The words of him who holds the seven stars in his right hand, who walks among the seven golden lampstands.
²"'I know your works, your toil and your patient endurance, and how you cannot bear evil men but have tested those who call themselves apostles but are not, and found them to be false;
³I know you are enduring patiently and bearing up for my name's sake, and you have not grown weary.
⁴But I have this against you, that you have abandoned the love you had at first.
⁵Remember then from what you have fallen, repent and do the works you did at first. If not, I will come to you and remove your lampstand from its place, unless you repent.
⁶Yet this you have, you hate the works of the Nicolaitans, which I also hate.
⁷He who has an ear let him hear what the Spirit says to the churches. To him who conquers I will grant to eat of the tree of life, which is in the paradise of God.'
⁸"And to the angel of the church in Smyrna write: 'The words of the first and the last, who died and came to life.
⁹"'I know your tribulation and your poverty (but you are rich) and the slander of those who say that they are Jews and are not, but are a synagogue of Satan.
¹⁰Do not fear what you are about to suffer. Behold, the devil is about to throw some of you into prison, that you may be tested, and for ten days you will have tribulation. Be faithful unto death, and I will give you the crown of life.

¹¹He who has an ear, let him hear what the Spirit says to the churches. He who conquers shall not be hurt by the second death.'

¹²"And to the angel of the church in Pergamum write: 'The words of him who has the sharp two-edged sword.

¹³"'I know where you dwell where Satan's throne is; you hold fast my name and you did not deny my faith even in the days of Antipas my witness, my faithful one, who was killed among you, where Satan dwells.

¹⁴But I have a few things against you: you have some there who hold the teaching of Balaam, who taught Balak to put a stumbling block before the sons of Israel, that they might eat food sacrificed to idols and practice immorality.

¹⁵So you also have some who hold the teaching of the Nicolaitans.

¹⁶Repent then. If not, I will come to you soon and war against them with the sword of my mouth.

¹⁷He who has an ear, let him hear what the Spirit says to the churches. To him who conquers I will give some of the hidden manna, and I will give him a white stone, with a new name written on the stone which no one knows except him who receives it.'

¹⁸"And to the angel of the church in Thyatira write: 'The words of the Son of God, who has eyes like a flame of fire, and whose feet are like burnished bronze.

¹⁹"'I know your works, your love and faith and service and patient endurance, and that your latter works exceed the first.

²⁰But I have this against you, that you tolerate the woman Jezebel, who calls herself a prophetess and is teaching and beguiling my servants to practice immorality and to eat food sacrificed to idols.

²¹I gave her time to repent, but she refuses to repent of her immorality.

²²Behold, I will throw her on a sickbed, and those who commit adultery with her I will throw into great tribulation, unless they repent of her doings;

²³and I will strike her children dead. And all the churches

shall know that I am he who searches mind and heart, and I will give to each of you as your works deserve.

²⁴But to the rest of you in Thyatira, who do not hold this teaching, who have not learned what some call the deep things of Satan, to you I say, I do not lay upon you any other burden;

²⁵only hold fast what you have, until I come.

²⁶He who conquers and who keeps my works until the end, I will give him power over the nations,

²⁷and he shall rule them with a rod of iron, as when earthen pots are broken in pieces, even as I myself have received power from my Father;

²⁸and I will give him the morning star.

²⁹He who has an ear, let him hear what the Spirit says to the churches.'

3"And to the angel of the church in Sardis write: 'The words of him who has the seven spirits of God and the seven stars.

"'I know your works; you have the name of being alive, and you are dead.

²Awake, and strengthen what remains and is on the point of death, for I have not found your works perfect in the sight of my God.

³Remember then what you received and heard; keep that, and repent. If you will not awake, I will come like a thief, and you will not know at what hour I will come upon you.

⁴Yet you have still a few names in Sardis, people who have not soiled their garments; and they shall walk with me in white, for they are worthy.

⁵He who conquers shall be clad thus in white garments, and I will not blot his name out of the book of life; I will confess his name before my Father and before his angels.

⁶He who has an ear, let him hear what the Spirit says to the churches.'

⁷"And to the angel of the church in Philadelphia write: 'The words of the holy one, and true one, who has the key of David, who opens and no one shall shut, who shuts and no one opens.

⁸"'I know your works. Behold, I have set before you an

open door, which no one is able to shut; I know that you have but little power, and yet you have kept my word and have not denied my name.

⁹Behold, I will make those of the synagogue of Satan who say that they are Jews and are not, but lie – behold, I will make them come and bow down before your feet, and learn that I have loved you.

¹⁰Because you have kept my word of patient endurance, I will keep you from the hour of trial which is coming on the whole world, to try those who dwell upon the earth. ¹¹I am coming soon; hold fast what you have, so that no one may seize your crown.

¹²He who conquers, I will make him a pillar in the temple of my God; never shall he go out of it, and I will write on him the name of my God, and the name of the city of my God, the new Jerusalem which comes down from my God out of heaven, and my own new name.

¹³He who has an ear, let him hear what the Spirit says to the churches.'

¹⁴"And to the angel of the church in Laodicea write: 'The words of the Amen, the faithful and true witness, the beginning of God's creation.

¹⁵"'I know your works: you are neither cold nor hot. Would that you were cold or hot!

¹⁶So, because you are lukewarm, and neither cold nor hot, I will spew you out of my mouth.

¹⁷For you say, I am rich, I have prospered, and I need nothing; not knowing that you are wretched, pitiable, poor, blind, and naked.

¹⁸Therefore I counsel you to buy from me gold refined by fire, that you may be rich, and white garments to clothe you and to keep the shame of your nakedness from being seen, and salve to anoint your eyes, that you may see.

¹⁹Those whom I love, I reprove and chasten; so be zealous and repent.

²⁰Behold, I stand at the door and knock; if any one hears my voice and opens the door, I will come in to him and eat with him, and he with me.

²¹He who conquers, I will grant him to sit with me on my

throne, as I myself conquered and sat down with my Father on his throne.
²²He who has an ear, let him hear what the Spirit says to the churches.'"

This is the first of the four 'sevens.' The content of the messages can be structured:
(a) Introduction:
   (i) Address
   (ii) Presentation of the Sender, i.e., Christ
(b) Body of the Letter:
   Praise, correction, warning, advice to the Churches. Honouring the coming of Christ.
(c) Conclusion:
   (i) An invitation to listen to the voice of the Spirit.
   (ii) Promises to the victor.

It is not always exactly this form, and at times the order is reversed in the conclusion (the last four letters). The link with the vision of the Son of man is made by his presentation as "Sender" in terms taken from 1:12-16. There are other links in the body of the letters.

All of the cities are known places, north of Ephesus. The most important were Ephesus and Smyrna. Sardis and Pergamum had been great in the past while the rest were still flourishing commercial centres. From the rest of the New Testament only Ephesus is known to have a Christian presence, and Paul was there between 54-57 (Acts 20:31). Thyatira is mentioned as the birth place of a Pauline convert at Philippi in Acts 16:14.

Content of the Letters

EPHESUS

Titles of Christ: "He who holds the seven stars in his right hand, who walks among the seven golden lampstands." (see 2:1).

Body of the Letter: The community is praised for its endur-

ance in difficulty, for its non-tolerance of evil men and for having unmasked false apostles and for detesting the Nicolaitans. It is reproved because the members "have abandoned the love you had at first" (2:4). Christ threatens to come and remove the lampstand from its place.
Promises: To the conqueror is promised "to eat of the tree of life which is in the paradise of God" (2:7).

SMYRNA

Titles of Christ: "The first and the last, who died and came to life" (2:8).
Body of the Letter: The community is in a situation of persecution, poverty and hostility coming from the Jews. It is about to suffer a persecution of 10 days (2:10). No reproof. Exhortation to fidelity unto death.
Promises: Preservation from the "second death" (2:11) and the gifts of "the crown of life" (2:10).

PERGAMUM

Titles of Christ: "He who has the sharp two-edged sword" (2:12).
Body of the Letter: The community has its seat where Satan has established his throne. However, it did not deny Christ, not even in the days when Antipas, the faithful witness, was killed. There are, however, followers of Balaam and Balak and the Nicolaitans among them. Christ will come to fight them with his two-edged sword.
Promises: The victor will have the manna hidden in the Ark of the Covenant, and a white stone upon which will be written a new name "which no one knows except him who receives it" (2:17).

THYATIRA

Titles of Christ: "The Son of God, who has eyes like a flame of fire, and whose feet are like burnished bronze" (2:18).
Body of the Letter: The community has many good works

(love, faith, service and constancy) always growing. However, it allows space for the false prophetess Jezebel. Christ warns her, her lovers and her children of a terrible punishment when he comes. Up till then the community is to conserve what it has, and no further burdens are to be added.
Promises: To the victor is promised power over the nations and "the morning star" (2:26-28).

SARDIS

Titles of Christ: "He who has the seven spirits of God and the seven stars" (3:1).
Body of the Letter: Community living only by name, as in reality it is dead. There remains a small group also on the point of death (3:2). Christ exhorts them to wake up, to strengthen this group, to keep what they have received and heard, to convert, to watch: he will come like a thief. There are, however, in this community a few names (perhaps the small group of 3:2) who "have not soiled their garments" (3:4).
Promises: The victor will receive "white garments" and his name will not be blotted out before his Father and the angels (3:5).

PHILADELPHIA

Titles of Christ: "The holy one, the true one, who has the key of David, who opens and no one shall shut, who shuts and no one opens" (3:7).
Body of the Letter: A solemn reference to an open door before the community, a door which no one can close. The community is small and weak, but it has kept the word and not denied Christ. For this it will see the conversion of a part of Judaism and will be preserved "from the hour of trial which is coming on the whole world" (3:10). Christ announces: "I am coming soon" (3:11) and invites the community to keep what it has.
Promises: The victor will be placed like a column in the

temple of God and will have written on it the names of Christ, the Father and the heavenly Jerusalem.

LAODICEA

Titles of Christ: "The Amen, the faithful and true witness, the beginning of God's creation" (3:14).
Body of the Letter: Christ finds nothing good in the community. Luke-warm, vain, but unhappy, poor, blind and naked. Christ will repudiate it. An exhortation to get gold (i.e., to become richer), white garments (to cover nakedness), ointments (to cure blindness). The coming of Christ is near: "Behold, I stand at the door and knock" (3:20). Whoever opens will dine with Christ.
Promises: The victor will sit upon a throne, beside Christ and the Father.

PROBLEMS

The mixture of clear Old Testament reminiscences and the real facts of these cities has always made this section difficult to interpret. How does it fit into the argument of the Apocalypse? Why these cities, and not some of the famous early Christian cities? Some would suggest that emperor worship was there, while some see that there was an imperial road that linked them all. While there may be truth here, it does not provide an answer to the interpretation of the section within the whole document. Nearly all scholars accept that these are real letters, a pastoral attempt on the part of John. There is the major difficulty in integrating them within the whole of Apocalypse. I will take another line, suggesting that the letters are not real letters, but John's use of a letter form to make his own particular point clear.

REAL OR FICTITIOUS LETTERS?

Recent commentators have questioned whether behind these letters stand a series of authentic letters or not. Are we dealing with a pastoral letter directed to authentic problems, or has John merely used this form to develop his own ideas? For many scholars there can be no doubt that we are dealing with real letters, directed into the Churches actually nominated in the texts. Some would even suggest that the letters are earlier than the Apocalypse itself, and that they have been taken up and used by the author.

This realistic interpretation of the letters has become widespread in recent times under the influence of the historical-critical approach to the New Testament. This method attempts to find every possible link with the actual historical situation which has produced a document, and in dealing with the Apocalypse, the concrete indications of the letters has been one of the major points of interest. Very few interpreters argue that the letters are merely a literary invention to serve the purpose of the author. Among those who do there are some who concentrate on the actual message of the letters, reading the message as "prophetic," while others are more interested in their literary and formal aspects. The latter method, which I will be following, is really quite novel, and it will be for the reader to judge whether or not it is fruitful.

In so far as the "prophetic" content of the letters is concerned, it appears to me that there is already a certain contradiction in the arguments of those who see them as real letters. Some see in them a prophetic prefiguring of this history of the Church, while others tend to stress the presence of Old Testament images and detail in them. Our interpretation will attempt to take all of this into account.

THE "PROPHETIC" INTERPRETATION OF THE LETTERS

Reduced to its essentials, this method of interpreting the letters sees in them a prefiguring of various epochs in the history of the Church. It still has adherents, but it was particularly popular among the Fathers, and was continued to Bede the Venerable in England (7th-8th Century) and then among various medieval and more recent commentators. Perhaps the most famous of these interpretations,

which applied not only to the letters but to the whole of the Apocalypse, came from Joachim da Fiore (died in 1202). He divided the work into seven "periods":
1) The Apostles (chs. 2-3).
2) The Martyrs (chs. 4-7).
3) The Doctors of the Church (chs. 8-11).
4) The Virgins (chs. 12-14).
5) The struggle against the sinful and worldly Empire (chs. 15-18).
6) The coming of the Antichrist, destroyed by the return of Christ (ch. 19).
7) The thousand year reign of Christ, followed by the resurrection and the final judgment (chs. 20-22).

Joachim believed that he was living in the sixth of these periods, and that the seventh would begin in 1260.

Obviously, this form of interpretation will lead to many varieties of "prophetic" readings. Most of them come from authors or apocalyptic figures who see themselves as living in the last era. Such was the case with Joachim, and such is also the case with many of our contemporary readings of the document. This form of interpretation has little support from scholarship, but is widespread among popular groups.

THE LETTERS AND THE OLD TESTAMENT

It is clear that there are many Old Testament references in these letters. How should we interpret them? If we are to follow a strictly historical plan, and see them as real, pastoral letters, all the references to Balaam and Balak or Jezebel have to be seen as referring to a heresy or a personality in the community at that time. This often leads to great speculation and a variety of possibilities. We have already seen, however, that John does not use the Old Testament that way. His method is to take a passage in its original meaning, and then deepen it, altering it as he uses it. It is never used as a tool for symbolic reference.

Further, it has sometimes been noticed that there is a sort of historical progression in the biblical allusions, a history of salvation beginning with Adam and finishing with Christ.

Each episode refers to some progressing moment in the history of salvation. This approach seems to point in the right direction because it seems to fit in with John's continual and central concern to show that the coming of Christ is the perfection and replacement of the Old Testament economy. If this is the case in the reference to salvation in the letters, they carry further the programme announced in 1:1: "the revelation of Jesus Christ." He has clearly stated this with his vision of the Son of man, but now, in the three parts of each letter we can now see what corresponds to "what you see (titles), what is (salvation of each Church), and what is to take place here after (promises)," the "mystery" of the stars and the candelabra, i.e., a Judaism which has been done away with and substituted by Christianity.

THE HISTORY OF SALVATION

Let us see if we can pick up the traces of a history of salvation through a reading of the letters:
1. *Ephesus*
   There is reference to the fall, "You have abandoned the love you had at first"; (v. 4), also in "your works, your toil and your patient endurance" (v. 2). Further clear indications to this moment are found in the command: "Remember then from what you have fallen" (v. 5) and especially in the promise made to the victorious one: "I will grant to eat of the tree of life which is in the paradise of God" (v. 7).
2. *Smyrna*
   The situation described is that of persecution, poverty and hostility from the Jews, who have become "a synagogue of Satan" (2:9). This, of course, would be the situation of a Christian community, but it is not impossible that it harks back to another period of persecution and poverty: the slavery of the Hebrews in Egypt. This seems to be indicated by the "ten days" through which they will be tested (v. 10), probably a reference to the ten plagues which preceded the liberation (see Exod 7:14ff). The "Synagogue of Satan" could also be an allusion to

Egypt, as it would indicate the ultimate perversity of Israel which began so well, but finally led to the slaying of Christ. As a consequence, in 11:8, we will find Israel described as "Sodom and Egypt." The situation of suffering in Egypt prefigures the situation of the present, in which a new people of God is persecuted by a new Eypgt. Certainly, this may be the situation of the community at Smyrna, but John has in mind the old situation, as is made clear again by the promise of "the crown of life." This promise is made later in the book, as here, only to those who are "faithful unto death," i.e., those who are killed. It will be offered in the fifth seal (6:9ff) and in the reign of a thousand years (20:4ff) and also to those who are killed, during the period of the Old Economy.

3. *Pergamum*

There are clear references here to Israel's presence in the desert after the liberation from Egypt; the episode of Balaam and Balak (2:14, see Num 25:1-2; 31:16), the "hidden manna" (v. 17, see Exod 16:32ff; Heb 9:4) and also, perhaps, the "white stone" with a name written on it, which may allude to the two stones with the names of the tribes of Israel which the High Priest carried on the shoulders of the Ephod (see Exod 28:9ff). There is probably also a reference to the desert in the fact that the community dwells "where Satan's throne is" (v. 13), because Satan exercises his power in the desert, as well as his temptations and persecutions (see 12:13ff; 17:3ff).

4. *Thyatira*

Several commentators have already seen the description of the wealth and well-being of the community (v. 19) as a reference to the time of the Hebrew Kingdom. The spiritual prosperity came with David (see 2:19; I Kgs 1:47), but with Solomon, material and spiritual corruption (I Kgs 11:1ff). This is the theme indicated by the reference to Jezebel (v. 2) the cruel wife of Achab, foreign idolatress in the nation (see I Kgs 16:31ff). The terrible punishment warned against Jezebel recalls the prophecy of Elijah against Achab and his wife after the slaying of Naboth (I Kgs 21:21ff). The prophecy of

Elijah, however, also pointed forward to the end of the Kingdom of Israel when ten tribes broke away from the others in the time of Jeroboam, a man who came to power because of his closeness to Solomon (935 B.C.). The letter to Thyatira describes Israel at its period of greatest power and splendour (Solomon) which already contained the seeds of religious corruption and the loss of the major part of the people in the division of the nation.

5. *Sardis*

The description of this Church reflects the state of desolation and death which followed the destruction of the Kingdoms, Israel and Judah. The kingdom is as if dead, reduced to a small group (see 3:2), and one thinks immediately of the "remnant of Israel" spoken of by Isaiah (see Is 1:9; 6:13; 65:8ff) or of the vision of the bones in Ezek 37, the period of the exile.

6. *Philadelphia*

Here we find a small community, weak but praised for faithfulness in perseverance in faith. A coming in the near future is announced (3:8-11). In the promise of this letter, there are references to a building, construction, keys, door, column of the temple, city of God, the New Jerusalem. This could well be an allusion to the period of the return from the exile and the reconstruction of Jerusalem and of the temple.

THE SEVENTH LETTER

This letter to Laodicea has always caused problems because it is so difficult, and because we know nothing of the situation of a first century Christian community of Laodicea. I would like to offer a solution, following the line traced so far. This letter expresses a judgment and a condemnation of Judaism which, in its blindness and hard-headedness, has not recognised Jesus of Nazareth as the Messiah preannounced by the Scriptures.

The community is reproached for being neither cold nor

hot, but lukewarm (3:15-16), and this does not refer to spiritual fervour (our use!), but to a criticism of Jewish legalism, of a praise offered to God with the lips and not with the heart, with external signs, but not in spirit and in truth. This could, of course, be the situation of Laodicea, but we do not know this.

The references to the "counsel" of what the community must do has to be interpreted along the same lines (v. 18). What is the "gold refined by fire" which they must procure from Jesus? As we have already seen, in the Apocalypse, gold is a symbol tightly linked to the divinity: everything around him is "gold" (throne, altar, etc.), everything which comes from him is "gold." To purchase gold from Christ, therefore, means to recognise him as divine, and from the divine, and this is further specified by the description of the gold as being absolutely pure, without sully: "refined by fire" (see Ps 18:31; Prov 30:5). All this is an invitation to accept Jesus of Nazareth, purified gold from the Father, through his incarnation and especially through his death. The "white garments" in the Apocalypse are always a reference to the new life which comes as a consequence of the acceptance of Jesus. The same can be said of the "salve to anoint your eyes, that you may see": the gold, the white garments and the sight are the content and the result of the acceptance of the contents of the "good news" of Jesus Christ.

This may well apply to Laodicea, but we do not know. It would certainly apply to Judaism. In the words of this letter, the long and patient word of Christ in his patient pedagogy throughout the whole of salvation history, Law and Prophets, comes to a conclusion. His advent is now close: "Behold, I stand at the door and knock; if anyone hears my voice and opens the door, I will come in to him and eat with him, and he with me" (3:20). These words have been used as an interior and personal invitation, but in the context they are an invitation to Israel to come and take their place at the messianic banquet, at the wedding feast of the Lamb, which will be described in ch. 21. To Judaism, however, a condition is made: "If any one hears my voice and opens the door...." This is the stumbling block: the person of Jesus of Nazareth is to be accepted as the Messiah.

This, to John's eyes, is an offer refused. He is thus so damning in his condemnation: "I will spew you out of my mouth" (v. 16). They thought that they had everything: "You say, I am rich, I am prosperous and I need nothing" (3:17) and this is exactly the accusation which John will level against Babylon before her ruin in 18:7. It appears to me that the destruction of Babylon will not be about the material destruction of Rome, but about the spiritual destruction and end of Judaism: the earthly Jerusalem will disappear to leave place for the heavenly Jerusalem. This argument will run through the whole book, and has been initiated in this first section of the "sevens," which concludes by repudiating those who go on calling themselves "Jews," but who, in fact, no longer have a right to do so:

2:9 : "The slander of those who say that they are Jews and are not, but are a synagogue of Satan."

3:9 : "Those of the synagogue of Satan who say that they are Jews, and are not but lie."

As we will see, for John, they lost that right at the slaying of the Lamb.

OLD AND NEW

Thus, it appears to me, the letters present a summary of the history of salvation through seven successive portraits. The probability of this interpretation depends, not so much on the certainty of the internal hints from the letters themselves, but upon the way in which it corresponds to the structure and message of the other "sevens" in the Apocalypse. As we will see, they are also, in their own way, illustrations of various aspects within the history of salvation. They all conclude in the same way, with a reference to an end which is not the end of the world, but an end to the old ways and, in particular, an end to Judaism.

The "seven" of the letters appears, however, to be more comprehensive and complete than the other "sevens." It deals not only with the negative conclusion and condemnation of Judaism, but also with the positive aspects of the new reality which is coming to take its place. In the promises to the victors which conclude the letters, this reality is outlined in a way that will be taken up again and further developed in the magnificent portrait of the heavenly Jerusalem at the end of the book (chs. 21-22). The parallels between these two parts of the book have been noticed by all the commentators. It is obvious that the promises made to the victors is the reality described as the heavenly Jerusalem.

In the letters, as we have seen, the reality promised is certainly the Church. In this way certain disputed peculiarities of the letters can be explained. Are they real or fictitious? Probably a little of each. They certainly play an important literary role within the context of the whole work, as can be seen from the close links which exist between them and various other parts of the book. On the other hand, it also appears clear from the actual list of names that are given, with precise geographical identification, that John has something to say to those particular communities.

What is it that he wishes to say to them? In the first place, he wishes to communicate to them the promises made to the victors. Given that the Apocalypse sets out to throw light on the mystery of Christ, the building up of the Church and the deepening of faith, then it was of primary importance to both John and to his faithful ones (those who were the real victors) that they listen to these promises, and understand their significance in full. Maybe this is the reason why the invitation to listen to the voice of the Spirit is always made in the plural: "He who has an ear, let him listen to what the Spirit says to the *Churches*" (see 2:7-11-17, etc.). The promises are not made to a specific Church, but to all seven Churches, which means (given the significance of the number "seven") the totality of the Church as such.

Usually, however, it is taken for granted that the really significant part of the message is the section directed to the community in the body of the letter: praise or correction, advice and warnings, and the announcement that Christ is coming. But we have suggested that all this represents, at a literary level, a dramatic dialogue between Christ, who is the real source of revelation, and the Hebrew people. Is there any relationship between all this and the real life situations of the communities nominated by the letters? In other words, are these personalities and events which John takes from the Old Testament in some way being used in reference to circumstances, events and people from those communities? We asked this question when discussing the letter to the sinful community of Laodicea, and here we must conclude as we concluded there – we simply do not have sufficient information to decide one way or another.

Nevertheless, we can be certain of one fact. John's exposition of the history of salvation in the letters, no matter what contact it had or did not have with the concrete situation of the Churches, was a most efficacious means of teaching and encouraging a Christian community. We know that from its earliest days the Church has looked to the Old Testament as its basis for formation, exhortation and support, and as a major element in her liturgical life. It is probably along these lines that one must search in order to find the final reason for John's heavy dependence upon the Old Testament in these letters.

"TO THE ANGELS OF THE CHURCH...WRITE"

There is another detail about these letters which may find a satisfactory interpretation in the light of the explanation which we have just suggested. The letters are not directed to the Churches themselves, but to the angels of the Churches. In the past there have been various attempts to explain these angels: they are the Bishops of the various communities; they are the angelic representatives of the communities (according to a Jewish way of seeing things) or they are the personification of the community.

The use of angels in the Apocalypse, however, has a

character all its own which does not permit the use of any of the above suggestions, and they are so important to this document that it is a seriously defective interpretation which goes ahead as if they were not mentioned. There is probably a different way to explain the fact that John, under orders from Christ, must write to the angel of the Church. The letters are presented as dictated by Christ and written by John. This means that they are an authentic act of revelation which passes directly from Christ to John, while the angels come in third place, as the recipients of the revelation. The series established here: Christ – John – angel is in contrast with that of the prologue (see 1:1) and then again in the epilogue (see 22:6-16) and probably in the scene where John hears the "loud voice" behind him (see 1:10).

How is this inversion of the usual order of revelation to be explained? We are, evidently, in the second section of the experience of Patmos, when John, turning "to see the voice," finds himself before Christ and listens directly to his voice (1:12ff). In that moment, it will be recalled, the angels are in the right hand of Christ, which means that they are now subjected and subordinate to him. The fact that John, under order from Christ, turns to them in such an authoritative manner (remember that "to write" means to reveal throughout the Apocalypse) indicates that this situation of subjection is still in force. But it is not only that. We know that for John the angels are the representatives and the intermediaries of the Old Economy and in the revelation of that Economy. It is precisely in this sense that they become the receivers of the letters. The fact that Jesus dictates the letters and that the contents of the letters is concerned with the Old Testament now takes on a precise meaning. Here we find, on the authority of Jesus, an authentic explanation of the Old Economy and of the Old Testament revelation, which the angels represent. They were the ones who foretold Christ and they prefigured the Church. This has already been synthetically explained in the words of Christ in 1:20:

> "The seven stars are the angels of the Churches and the seven lampstands are the seven Churches."

The letters are the concrete spelling out of that explanation.

"THE WORDS OF HIM WHO..."

In the introduction to each letter Christ presents himself through a series of attributes which come, for the main part, for the introduction to the seven letters, from the vision of the Son of man. This is, as we have already said, the clearest indication of the literary link that exists between the introduction and the letters themselves. In all probability, the matter does not cease there. Some have noticed that there is a link between the attributes and the content of the letters, both body and conclusion (the promises to the victor). This is a further proof of the organic nature of the whole collection of letters and also of their insertion into the book as a whole. Other scholars have even noticed that there is a sort of *crescendo* in the attributes given at the head of each letter. This could also be explained as an indication of a gradual progression towards the coming of Christ, and especially towards the definitive revelation of his messiahship in his death and resurrection.

It is clear that, after a more universal reference to the "revelation of Jesus Christ" contained in the letter to Ephesus (see 2:1: stars and lampstands), his death and resurrection are immediately found at the heart of the titles given in the letter to Smyrna (see 2:8). The attributes of the letters which follow: two-edged sword (Pergamum: see 2:12); Son of God, eyes like a flame of fire, feet like bronze (Thyatira: see 2:18); seven Spirits and seven stars (Sardis: see 3:1); the Holy one, the True one, he who has the keys of David, who opens and no one shuts, who shuts and no one opens (Philadelphia: see 3:7); the Amen, the faithful and true witness, the beginning of God's creation (Laodicea: see 3:14), can all be identified with messianic privileges (judgment, divinity, possession of the Spirit and of his testimony, destruction of death and hell, the foundation of a new reality, of the new creation). All of this belongs to Christ because of his death and resurrection.

It may also be significant that the attributes of Christ which are used throughout the letters come originally from the figure of the Son of man in the introduction to the letters. If the series of letters really does represent the events of the Old Testament revelation, the taking of these attributes and using them at various stages of that representation may indicate the gradual movement towards the fullness of the revelation of Jesus Christ, already taking place within the old revelation, as yet incomplete. There is also a certain amount of obscurity. We are, in fact, dealing with symbols (stars, lampstands, sword, keys, abstract terms) whose significance will become clear only when they are gathered round the figure of the Son of man; only after the coming of Jesus Christ.

The titles, as we have seen, are largely taken from the description of the Son of man. They form, therefore, "what you have seen" (see 1:19), the first part of what Jesus commands John to write. And these things are certainly the equivalent of "what you see" which the "loud voice" orders him to write in the first part of the vision (see 1:11). They are the messianic prophecies, made up of symbols and visions, spread throughout the Old Testament. The "seeing" of the first section relates to the "have seen" of the second, just as the "loud voice" of the first section, relates to the Son of man: the ancient revelation of what will be new, the former to the latter.

"I KNOW YOUR WORKS"

In five of the seven letters the body of the letter is introduced by the expression: "I know your works." In the other two (Smyrna and Pergamum) there is a reference to the situation of persecution in that community. In all seven cases, therefore, there seems to be a reference to something very practical and concrete. This naturally leads interpreters to conclude logically that the letters are indeed directed into John's contemporary circumstances, to personalities and to events. But we have just seen that the matter is not quite so clear, as the body of each letter makes reference to some past event, as a first point of reference.

We have found an indirect confirmation of this interpretation in the fact that the letters are not directed to the communities as such but to the angels of the communities. Therefore, when Christ says "I know your works" we should also remember that the words are not directed to the commuunity, but to the angel which represents it. And we must not forget that this representation through the angels was possible only in the Old Economy and not in the new, where the only representative is Christ, the "King of Kings" (of the faithful: see 1:5-6), "the beginning of God's creation" (3:14).

The expression "I know your works" indicates, therefore, the divine judgment upon the Hebrew people. It is a judgment upon men, circumstances and concrete facts. We have here the equivalent of the "what is," which John must write (see 1:19). It is generally thought that this expression indicates the present, in contrast to the future ("what is to take place hereafter": 1:19). We can only accept this understanding of the expression if it is seen, not as some future end of the world, but as the establishment of the new reality which Christ came to complete, abolishing, yet in some way continuing, overcoming, yet in some way perfecting, the old order. "What is" thus represents the present, not so much in its temporal aspect, but as an existent order of things which is moving towards it end, to be replaced by "what is to take place hereafter," the new order, the New Economy.

"I AM COMING SOON"

In all the letters, except the second, Christ explicitly refers to his coming. Here also there seems to be a mounting intensity and precision in his announcements. The expression found in the last letter, to Laodicea: "Behold, I stand at the door and knock" (3:20) speaks clearly of an imminent coming, or even of his having already arrived. This feature has led many interpreters to see the Apocalypse as directed towards the end time. Our understanding of the document, however, permits us to interpret these expressions in a simpler and quite plausible fashion: an announcement of the coming of Christ which is referred to from start to finish in the letters. The letters, we have seen, are a sort of guided reading through the Old Testament scriptures, seen and understood as "revelation of Jesus Christ." This revelation, for John, has its fulfilment in the historical coming of Christ which has been constantly foretold in the ancient scriptures, inspired by Christ, who is the author of the whole of revelation.

The announcement of a rapid or proximate coming, therefore, is to be firstly understood as the witness to this coming already contained in the scriptures of old, acting as a "voice," like John the Baptist, to prepare the way of the coming Lord.

The announcement of the coming of Jesus Christ and the promises to the victors are the sections of the letters which correspond to "what is to take place hereafter," which John must also describe (1:19). This is especially true for the promises to the victors. They already contain, germinally, the whole of the reality which will be described, with great richness of detail, in the final chapters of the Apocalypse. Thus, even with this expression of rapid coming, we are still engaged in a reading of the Old Testament and the promises made there of the coming of the Christ, and of the new reality which his coming will bring.

In conclusion, the "seven" of the letters to the Churches represents a more global repetition of the initial theme of the "revelation of Jesus Christ" which has to be seen in two moments: in the Old Testament revelation and in his actual historical coming. In the vision of the Son of man, which we have understood as an introduction to the letters, these two moments were already represented by the two parts of the vision: the "loud voice" (see 1:10-11) and then the apparition of the Son of man (see 1:12-20). John, the human instrument of revelation, receives two commands to write.

The first ("write what you see in a book": 1:11) represents the Old Testament revelation, whose scope was to announce the coming of Christ and to prefigure the reality which he would bring: the reconciliation of humanity with God and the gift of divine and eternal life. The second ("write what you see, what is and what is to take place hereafter": 1:19) corresponds to the new revelation brought by Christ, contained in his person which illuminates and gives meaning to the whole of Scripture. In this way, while there may be two commands to write, the written book is one, just as the revelation is one and its author is one: Jesus Christ. Yet, there remain two ways, two intensities in "seeing" it: one through symbols and the other through the person of Jesus Christ.

John will take up this same concept in ch. 10, with his allegorical scene of the swallowing of the book, sweet upon the lips but bitter in the stomach, followed by an order to prophesy yet again: "about many peoples and nations and tongues and kings" (10:11). The letters are an example of this new "prophecy": they are an interpretation of the Old Testament in the light of Jesus Christ, finding there the promise and the foretelling of the new reality which he has brought: the Church, the new people of God, a people of kings and priests (see 1:6; 5:10).

THE SEVEN SEALS (4:1—8:1)

THEME: The History of Mankind: Sin and Redemption.

Structure and General Theme

The "seven" of the seals is much more developed than that of the letters. There is a prologue of two chapters (chs. 4-5) and the link will be made through the sealed book given by the one "seated on the throne" to the Lamb in 5:1.

The preface is made up of two visions, the vision of the divinity in ch. 4 and the Lamb in ch. 5. Both visions happen in heaven, and each one is preceded by a sort of introduction, a voice which is explained by John as the earlier voice "like a trumpet" (1:10), heard before the vision of the Son of man in ch. 1. This voice invites John to go up to heaven to receive the revelation of "what must take place after this" (4:1). The opening of the seals takes place in 6:1—8:1. Again we will see that the seals repeat the history of salvation, without any clear scheme, and the seals seem to be divided into two quite distinct groups, the first *four* and the second *three*. We will see that this scheme of 4 = 3 is repeated by the following "sevens," the trumpets and the bowls.

The group of four is marked by a greater unity than the

group of three. The very use of the number "four" connects it with earthly and historical realities; the four seals are, each in turn, linked with "a horse," again with historical significance, and the four colours may be a reference to the distribution over the face of the earth of the realities represented by the horses.

Less united and more complex is the second group of three, from the fifth to the seventh. In the series of the seals and the trumpets (less so in the bowls) the second group presents us with a movement *towards* man and the earth of an action which is outside both man and earth. In the seals the action begins in heaven and clearly has the divinity itself as its source. In the trumpets the point of departure will be outside man in so far as it comes from the abyss, the place of a spiritual power which is, however, corrupt: Satan and his angels. In the "seven" of the bowls, the movement will *always* be from outside man and history, "from heaven." The "seven" of the bowls, we shall see, represents a definitive intervention of God to judge man and the world. The distinction between the two groups in the bowls will depend upon the two realities which are judged, first man and creation (the first four bowls) and then the evil powers which have oppressed and corrupted both men and creation (last three bowls).

In both the seals and the trumpets there is a second feature to be noticed. In both, the sixth element is more fully developed. It is clear in the seals that this represents the inbreak of the divine into history. This intervention appears to be motivated by the divine anger which, after a long and patient wait, comes finally to destroy its enemies. This structure comes from the 1st Century Jewish idea of a "cosmic seven." In these speculations, the history and development of the world is based on seven series of a thousand years, corresponding to the seven days of creation. In the *sixth* millennium, corresponding to the day of the creation of man, the Messiah comes, bringing with him consternation, but creating the peace and tranquility of the final thousand years. We will see that the influence of this theory is strong in the book. Obviously, none of this refers to actual *chronol-*

ogy. It is all a backdrop for his central theme of the gradual "revelation of Jesus Christ." In this way, in the sixth seal it is not only a certain point of time when God intervenes, but a summary of all his interventions; in this case, the choice of the Hebrew people and the redemption of all people through the death of Jesus. (7:1-8: the 144 thousand marked on the forehead and 7:9-17: the innumerable peoples who come marked with the sign of victory).

The preface to the seven seals is complex. The vision of the door open in heaven, of the throne, the sealed book which passes from the one on the throne to the Lamb, all seem to represent a phase of the "revelation of Jesus Christ" which is previous to the situation reflected in the preface to the letters. These two chapters are allegories of creation and redemption which, however, John sees "in heaven," i.e., he sees their significance, not their actualisation in history.

This can be seen from a comparison of the visions. Both are based on the vision of the Son of man from Daniel. There are clearly two moments in Daniel, the vision of the Ancient of Days on the throne (see Dan 7:9-10) and then the Son of man coming on the clouds (7:13-14). The vision of Daniel has been used in ch. 1 in which, however, there was a superimposition of the divinity upon the Son of man. In the end, the two are one: the Son of man is the divinity. In chs. 4-5 they are clearly separate, and one follows the other.

The history of humanity is *not* in the visions, but it begins with the seven signs. It begins with the disasters of the first four horsemen which close with the domination over the dead. Only a few escape, and they are the ones who die for the word of God and their testimony to Jesus. They are found "under the altar," and they are rewarded by "rest" and they are given "white garments." Then, and only then, the divinity intervenes in the redemption of the 144 thousand and the whole of humanity. After this, there is the silence of the seventh seal.

We will read this as the story of the fall of mankind (the first four seals) and the salvific intervention of God (the remaining three seals). This is anticipated in the prologue;

the throne (ch. 4) and the Lamb (ch. 5) are allegories of creation and redemption.

The name of Jesus never appears. It is the Lamb, however, who opens the seven seals. For John, this means that the whole of history is a salvation history which can be seen and properly understood only in the light of its culmination in the sacrifice of Christ.

The Introduction to the Seven Seals (4:1—5:14)

> **4** ¹After this I looked, and lo, in heaven an open door! And the first voice, which I had heard speaking to me like a trumpet, said, "Come up hither, and I will show you what must take place after this."
> ²At once I was in the Spirit, and lo, a throne stood in heaven, with one seated on the throne!
> ³And he who sat there appeared like jasper and carnelian, and round the throne was a rainbow that looked like an emerald.
> ⁴Round the throne were twenty-four thrones, and seated on the thrones were twenty-four elders, clad in white garments, with golden crowns upon their heads.
> ⁵From the throne issue flashes of lightning, and voices and peals of thunder, and before the throne burn seven torches of fire, which are the seven spirits of God;
> ⁶and before the throne there is as it were a sea of glass, like crystal. And round the throne, on each side of the throne, are four living creatures, full of eyes in front and behind:
> ⁷the first living creature like a lion, the second living creature like an ox, the third living creature with the face of a man, and the fourth living creature like a flying eagle.
> ⁸And the four living creatures, each of them with six wings, are full of eyes all round and within, and day and night they never cease to sing,
>
> > "Holy, holy, holy, is the Lord God Almighty,
> > who was and is and is to come!"
>
> ⁹And when the living creatures will give glory and honor

and thanks to him who is seated on the throne, who lives for ever and ever,

[10]the twenty-four elders will fall down before him who is seated on the throne and worship him who lives for ever and ever, and they will cast their crowns before the throne, singing,

[11]"Worthy art thou, our Lord and God,
to receive glory and honor and power,
for thou didst create all things,
and by thy will they existed and were created."

5 [1]And I saw in the right hand of him who was seated on the throne a scroll written within and on the back, sealed with seven seals;

[2]and I saw a strong angel proclaiming with a loud voice, "Who is worthy to open the scroll and break its seals?:

[3]And no one in heaven or on earth or under the earth was able to open the scroll or to look into it,

[4]and I wept much that no one was found worthy to open the scroll or to look into it.

[5]Then one of the elders said to me, "Weep not; lo, the Lion of the tribe of Judah, the Root of David, has conquered, so that he can open the scroll and its seven seals."

[6]And between the throne and the four living creatures and among the elders, I saw a Lamb standing, as though it had been slain, with seven horns and with seven eyes, which are the seven spirits of God sent out into all the earth;

[7]and he went and he received from the right hand of the one seated upon the throne.

[8]And when he had taken the scroll, the four living creatures and the twenty-four elders fell down before the Lamb, each holding a harp, and with golden bowls full of incense, which are the prayers of the saints;

[9]and they sang a new song, saying,

"Worthy art thou to take the scroll
   and to open its seals,
for thou wast slain and by thy blood
   didst ransom men for God

from every tribe and tongue and
people and nation,
[10] and hast made them a kingdom and
priests to our God,
and they shall reign on earth."

[11] Then I looked, and I heard around the throne and the living creatures and the elders the voice of many angels, numbering myriads of myriads and thousands of thousands,

[12] saying with a loud voice, "Worthy is the Lamb who was slain, to receive power and wealth and wisdom and might and honor and glory and blessing!"

[13] And I heard every creature in heaven and on earth and under the earth and in the sea, and all therein, saying, "To him who sits upon the throne and to the Lamb be blessing and honor and glory and might for ever and ever!"

[14] And the four living creatures said, "Amen!" and the elders fell down and worshipped.

"IN HEAVEN AN OPEN DOOR" (4:1)

Like all the other "sevens" that of the seals is preceded by an introduction which provides the key for our understanding of the section. We have a series of three visions, closely linked together, in rapid succession: a vision of the door open in heaven, of the divinity seated upon a throne, of the Lamb who received the sealed book.

The first vision forms an introduction to the introduction. Its function is to introduce the visions which follow, clearly breaking the thread of the argument which has been developed so far. There is, despite this, a taking up and even a further stressing of something which we have already seen. In fact, after having seen the open door in heaven, John hears a voice "like a trumpet," which he further clarifies as the one which he had heard earlier (4:1). This is clearly the voice which he heard from behind, in the vision of the Son of man (see 1:10). We find here a significant example of John's method of carrying his argument further through a progressive repetition yet deepening of his themes.

From this literary point we can now move to an important point in the interpretation of the text. John, through the element of the voice, calls us back to the situation described earlier which was, as we have seen, a typically "prophetic" situation. This means, a situation where the divine revelation is transmitted through a human agent. The parallel nature of the situation can also be found in the repetition of the words "I was in the Spirit" (4:2), an expression which indicates the human experience of the divine illumination and inspiration.

The similarity between the two situations is such that it has led some scholars in the past to see it as a hint of an imperfect linking of the two parts of the book which were originally independent, but it appears to me that this taking up of the same situation is intentional, as John goes back to a previous theme, but develops it further. In other words, the prophetic situation described in ch. 4 is not only similar to the one described in ch. 1. It is the same. This means that the visions which John describes from now on form his obedience to the command which was given to him in 1:11: to write a book, describing what he was seeing, and to send it to the Churches.

Ch. 4, therefore, does not begin the prophetic part of the Apocalypse, as this is generally understood: predictions about the end time. On the contrary, here John takes up his presentation of the "revelation of Jesus Christ." He makes a link with the first of the two situations of the transmission of revelation described in ch. 1, that in which he only hears a voice (1:10). Certainly, here he does not mention that the voice comes from behind him. In ch. 1 it was an important observation, as he then turned to face the Risen Christ. Here, at a second moment, this turning towards the Risen Christ is not found. The vision of John here is indirect, reflected, veiled. The divinity has neither face nor name; the victorious Christ is presented under the symbol of a slain lamb, "standing" (see 5:6).

We are, therefore, in the first moment of the revelation,

when the loud voice, the voice of an angel, speaks of the old economy, the law and the cult in visions of her prophets. All these things are, however, announcing "what must take place after this" (4:1). The same truth is indicated by "the open door." In itself it would mean nothing, except that at the end of the book (ch. 19) the situation has changed. No longer is it a door, but heaven itself opening (19:11). Here the visionary goes to heaven, "in the spirit" (4:2), while there the Logos of God descends to the earth (19:13) to complete the redemptive action.

The door opened in heaven signifies the beginning of a revelation, the beginning of the divine salvific intervention. The visions of the throne and the Lamb will now show us that this revelation will have two moments, the creation, where it has its beginning (throne), and the redemption worked by his sacrifice (Lamb).

THE VISION OF THE THRONE: CREATION

After the vision of the open door and the summons to "come up hither" (v. 1), John sees the divinity seated upon a throne, surrounded by beings which make up the heavenly court. It is never directly said that it is God, but it is clear from various elements:
— the throne upon which God sits is clearly distinct from those 24 beings called "elders" (*presbuteroi*, 4:4).
— he is surrounded by a rainbow (4:3).
— before him are "seven torches of fire which are the seven spirits of God" (4:5).
— and also "as it were a sea of glass, like crystal" (4:6).

Throughout the whole vision, the throne and the person on it are the centre of all the attention and the action. Above all there are the "four living creatures" (4:6), externally like the famous cherubim from the vision of Ezekiel (see Ez 1:10) and, like them, in constant movement around the throne. Then there is also the incessant hymn of praise, taken from Isaiah (Is 6:3), and a further external sign from Isaiah, the six wings instead of the four which appear in Ezekiel. There is also the act of worship on the part of the "Elders," who throw down their crowns. This is mentioned twice in the introduction (4:9-10 and 5:8). There is, as well, the presence of an unnumbered group of angels: "the voice of many angels, numbering myriads of myriads and thousands of thousands" (5:11). Their voice is also in praise of the one seated on the throne, who, after he disappears and the sealed book is consigned, is associated with the Lamb. All of this adds up to the figure on the throne as God, the Father, possessing all power, dignity and authority, separated from everything else which, in turn, offers him homage in a way which is a true cultic act of worship.

This latter aspect gives to the vision of the one seated on the throne and of the Lamb a quasi-liturgical flavour. Though the setting is not mentioned at this point, these things are happening in a heavenly temple. John speaks later (11:19; 15:5) of "the temple of God which is in heaven" and makes reference elsewhere to altars in heaven (6:9; 8:3ff; 9:13; etc.).

Scholars have discussed this, but the problem is that "in heaven" is taken to refer to some geographical location not on earth. This is not John's meaning. John is "in the Spirit" when he goes into this situation (4:2), and the meaning of "in heaven" is that what happens is of the spiritual order. It is not the description of some "place." To contemplate a reality "in heaven" means, for John, to see its profound significance which goes beyond all appearances, i.e., to see it with the eyes of God, who is the real author of all things. It is "in the Spirit" that John receives illumination. In chs. 4 and 5, John does not see some distant picture-show, but he sees through all appearances to the ultimate significance of two basic mysteries, creation and redemption. The temple where this takes place is not in a geographical heaven, but in the whole of the created universe, in its totality.

THE COSMIC ORDER

Many commentators have noticed that this vision is an allegory of the creation. This is most clearly shown by the hymn which comes at the end of the vision in 4:11. The whole scene can be seen as a cosmology read with theological eyes. At the centre, universal creation and Lord, is God seated on his throne. The throne is upon "a sea of glass, like crystal" (v. 6) (which we can read as the land-sea-earth) upon which, in the biblical vision or myth, is the footstool of the throne of God (see Is 66:1). This idea becomes clear in ch. 15 when John describes the sea as no longer clear "like crystal," but "a sea of glass mingled with fire" (15:2), into which Satan and his angels (paralleled with "fire" in 8:7-11) have fallen.

This image takes us back to the act of God in the first verses of Genesis, when God creates "the heaven and the earth" from an indistinct reality which the author parallels to a sea over which the Spirit hovered. Here, also, before the throne, there are the seven Spirits of God (4:5), i.e., the totality of the Spirit of God.

The earth is at the centre of this universe. This is the function of the enigmatic groups which are around the divinity: the twenty-four Elders and the four "living beings." Commentators nowadays look to the twenty-four Elders as taken from astronomic speculations: a double zodiac, the twenty-four stars of Babylonian speculations, the twenty-four heavens of the Pythagorean system. The four living beings refer more specifically to the earth: four elements, four winds, four zones of the earth. This appears correct, although we will not delve into such obscurities. The general idea is of God as lord of the heavens (the 24) and the earth (the 4).

As far as the twenty-four Elders are concerned, they are seated on thrones, like the divinity. They, too, wear crowns on their heads (4:4). Clearly they can be seen as angelic figures who have been charged by the divinity to govern a part of the universe, an idea common in antiquity, which John seems to share (see 7:1; 16:5).

A prerogative to govern seems to be given in other places also to the four "living creatures." They appear to be linked to the earth. They are more closely attached to the throne itself which is based on the earth. Their cosmic significance comes to John from his source for these creatures (Ez 1:5ff). There John had already found the idea of many eyes (4:6-8; see Ezek 1:18), a symbol of an ability to see everything and, therefore, to look to, to provide for, everything.

As is usual in Apocalypse, John accentuates this cosmic significance through the variations which he introduces to his original source. Instead of the *four* wings which the Cherubim have in Ezekiel, they have *six* (4:8) like the Seraphim in Isaiah (Is 6:2). The number "six" in Jewish tradition has to do with the earth, in particular with God's creation and organisation of the earth, which he did, according to Gen 1, in *six* days. The other change is that, while in Ezekiel *each* being has four faces (lion, ox, man and eagle), in the Apocalypse each has one of these faces. This is an attempt to distinguish between them at the level of their individuality, and therefore in their function. This will become clearer and important when, at the opening of the first four seals, each one of these "living creatures" will be individually put into a relationship with each of the four horses as they are called forth (see 6:1ff).

THE SUBMISSION OF THE ANGELS

The four "living creatures," like the twenty-four Elders, have a function of governing the created world. Perhaps it would be better to speak of a function of mediation between God and the world, and the world and God, for all of these angelic beings. In one direction it is a function of governing – God to the created, but in the other direction it is a liturgical, cultic function – creation to God.

If mediation is the task of all the angelic beings, what explanation are we to give to the two groups of angelic beings which we find in ch. 4 (24 Elders; 4 "living creatures"; innumerable angels)? The distinction between the Elders and the "living creatures" is quite clear at the level of function. We must not move from this to a type of speculation, widely used, on various hierarchies of angels at the level of their "nature." John is interested in function. Of the two classes which we find here, one is clearly of biblical origin (the four creatures comes from Ezekiel). The other, the Elders, is probably a creation of John, although even here there may be a biblical contact. Not a few exegetes have put the number 24 in parallel with the members of Hebrew priestly classes (see I Chron 24:4ff). This is probable if we adopt the line mentioned earlier of the created universe as moving toward God in a sort of cult of praise.

The two "classes" of ch. 4 is clearly a question of *function*, and not of *nature*. The parallel with the classes of Hebrew priesthood comes from John's conviction, taken from Jewish thought, according to which the human temple (the Ark of Moses and then the construction in Jerusalem) is merely a copy of the heavenly temple. This applies to the decoration, the cult and the people who perform, and must be kept in mind in interpreting the Apocalypse. In the "sevens" which follow, in the trumpets and the bowls, a part of the action takes place "in heaven," that is "in the temple of God which is in heaven" (see 8:22ff; 11:19; 14:17ff; 15:5ff; etc.). This must not be understood in a mechanical, spatial way, but the "heavenly" indicates the spiritual dimension, belonging to God and to his action. In this way, "heaven" indicates the whole universe, created by God, governed by him through angels, redeemed by him through the sacrifice of Christ, the Lamb. Little wonder then, if in this universal reality, John sees an immense temple, in which there is a perfect and immense liturgy, of which the Jewish cult is simply a miniature reproduction. Thus, for John, the heavenly and perfect liturgy has its continuation and pale copy in the historical and earthly cult of Judaism.

On various occasions John will allude to an event "in heaven" which appears to be an interruption of the liturgy there. The silence of half an hour which follows the opening of the seventh seal (8:1); the tearing open of the veil which covers the Ark of the Covenant in the heavenly temple in 11:19, etc. All this, as we will see, is the sign, in the "heavenly" sphere, i.e., in the spiritual and divine, of something which happens on earth; the death of Christ which puts an end to the Jewish cult.

Something like this is already foreshadowed in the visions of chs. 4 and 5 in two parallel and partially corresponding scenes. At the end of ch. 4, after having described the twenty-four Elders and the four living creatures and their functions, John adds:

> "And when the living creatures will give glory and honor and thanks to him who is seated on the throne, who lives for ever and ever, the twenty four elders will fall down before him who is seated on the throne and worship him who lives for ever and ever, and they will cast their Crowns before the throne..." (4:9-10).

This has always been understood in a repetitive sense. The twenty-four Elders *repeat* their gestures *every time* the creatures give glory and honour.

This does not do justice to the Greek, which has a temporal conjunction – "when" (Greek = *hotan*), used with a verb in the future tense "they will give." This *must* be a reference, not to a continued motion, but to a specific moment in the future when this gesture will take place. At that moment the twenty-four Elders perform all the gestures of a complete renunciation of authority, etc., total submission. In the light of this, I suggest that the end of ch. 4 projects into the future. John wants to contrast a situation described in the chapter as a whole with a future moment where something happens which is caused by some specific circumstance.

What that circumstance was is presented as realised in ch. 5, "And when he (the Lamb) had taken the scroll the four living creatures and the twenty-four Elders fall down before the Lamb" (5:8) and again: "And the four living creatures said 'amen!' and the Elders fell down and worshipped" (5:15). It appears that this act of submission takes place when the Lamb takes the book, an act which only he can perform (see 5:2-5). This gesture is a symbol of the redemption of mankind by Christ, a redemption which has its culminating point in his death on the cross.

It is, therefore, the death of Jesus which causes the prostration of the heavenly court. This signifies the definitive recognition of a supremacy, and a renunciation of certain privileges, synthesised by the crowns of gold (see 4:10). Recognition is not made to the divinity on the throne, but to the Lamb when he takes the scroll (see 5:8). What is announced at the end of chs. 4 is fulfilled in ch. 5 when the whole of the angelic court, all their mediation and authority in government, revelation and cult is over, and assumed by the Lamb. This was already indicated in the prologue when we were told that the Son of man held the seven stars (the totality of the angelic world) in his right hand (1:16 and 2:1). Now this is spelt out in more detail: the circumstance and the modality of this subjection, the divine Christ (ch. 5), has passed through death, thus conquering it. Only the Lamb could do this.

Therefore, both visions of chs. 4 and 5 conclude with the subjection of the angels to Christ. For John, this indicates that the mediating function of the angels ceases, and thus, the Old Economy is over. These ideas will return again and again in the Apocalypse. The scene of the prostration of the angels will be repeated at the end of the "seven" trumpets (11:16) and after the destruction of Babylon at the pouring out of the seventh bowl (19:4). The same thing is signified by the great silence which follows the opening of the seventh seal (8:1). Always, this is caused by the event of the death of Christ.

THE REDEMPTION

The vision of ch. 5 is clearly the continuation of the vision in ch. 4. New elements are immediately obvious: the sealed scroll and the Lamb. These two elements dominate the chapter. The scroll appears suddenly at the beginning of the chapter:

> "And I saw in the right hand of him who was seated on the throne a scroll written within and on the back, sealed with seven seals" (see also Ez 2:9-10).

The important factor, in the light of what follows, is the seven seals, which no one "in heaven or earth" was able to open (v. 2), except the Lamb (vv. 6-9). Uniting both visions is the one seated on the throne, who hands the sealed scroll to the Lamb who then will break the seals. There are two separate visions, and two separate events, one following the other but intimately linked.

The symbol of the scroll seems important, and we must notice that it appears again in Apocalypse. It was a "scroll" which John had to write to the communities of Asia (1:11); it will be a "scroll" which the angel holds in his hand in the vision of ch. 10. In both of these cases it is something given from above and which brings, in a more or less full way, happiness and sweetness to whoever receives it (see 1:3; 10:9ff). It is obviously the word of God, revelation which can give life to man.

The basic idea of the "scroll" in Apocalypse, a communication of God's word to man, is the idea of a gift of life which passes from God to man. This becomes clearer when we see that John, following a biblical expression (see Ps 69:28ff; Eccl 24:32) speaks repeatedly of a "book of life" (see 3:5; 13:8; etc.). To have one's name written in that "book" signifies to share in the divine life. Over this book, which clearly belongs to God, Jesus Christ has special power: it is, in fact, within his power to leave or erase from it the names of every man (see 3:5). Several times it is said clearly that this power over "the book of life" comes to Jesus in so far as he is the Lamb, i.e., he has died and risen (see 13:8; 21:27). It also appears, from these passages, that this is an authority which he has possessed "from the creation of the world" (see 13:8 and 17:8), and that it has as its basis the eternal and universal value of the sacrifice of Christ. The "book of life" is often referred to as "the book of the life of the Lamb" (13:8; 21:27), and the sacrifice of the Lamb has been in action "since the creation of the world" (13:8).

The book with the seven seals, therefore, has its origins in God, and comes from him. The first to receive the communication of this book is Christ. Most translations read: "He went and took (the scroll) from the right hand of him who was seated on the throne" (5:7), but two important details must be noticed here. There is, in v. 7, of the Greek text, no use of the word "scroll" (Greek = *biblion*). Then in v. 8, the word is used: "And when he had taken the scroll." The other detail is that in v. 7 the perfect tense is used, in v. 8 the aorist tense is used. I would like to tease out these details.

It appears possible that v. 7 speaks about the Lamb, who receives all that he is and has from the one seated on the throne, God. This is expressed in the use of a perfect tense of the verb *lambano* indicating an action which took place in the past, but whose significance and fruit continues into the present. It should be translated: "And he went and he received from the right hand of the one seated upon the throne." This means that all that he is and has comes from all time and unto all time, from God, his Father. John, however, is never interested in the origins and nature of the Lamb for their own sake. This must flow over into salvific action, and this leads us to v. 8. Here he actually receives the scroll, the gift of life between God and man which *only* the Lamb is able to reveal through his sacrificial death, and this is the significance of the use of the aorist, a reference to an "event."

If the "book" is a symbol of the divine life which the Lamb gives to mankind, as he breaks through the seals, what then, are the seals? They are clearly the reality of sin, starting with the original sin and then all that follows, through which man has been excluded from the divine life. Only the Lamb is able to break through that reality. This means that only the sacrificial death of Jesus Christ can restore mankind to a free access to divine life.

THE LAMB

The significance of this symbol is quite clear. It recalls bloody sacrifice. Evidently it is connected with the slaying of a lamb by the Hebrews the night before their liberation from Egypt (see Exod 12:21ff), a rite which had become fixed in the paschal ritual. This symbol is at the basis of John's use of the Lamb in reference to Jesus Christ. By virtue of the identification between the Lamb and Christ which is constant through all of the book, the sacrifice of the Cross must stand at the centre of the Christology of the Apocalypse. This assumes a particular importance here, where, beginning with the vision of a door open in heaven (4:1) John attempts to synthesize, through the visions of the throne and the Lamb, the profound significance of the Old Testament revelation. The Old Testament is regarded as the Law and the Prophets. The Law is summarised by taking its central affirmation, that there is only one God, creator and lord of heaven and earth to whom, without any exception, is due all homage and adoration. The Prophets, as far as the early Christians were concerned, were directed towards the pre-announcing of the Messiah.

This twofold message of the Law and the Prophets is behind John's use of the two visions in chs. 4 and 5. The first is a vision of God seated on a throne, surrounded by the heavenly court, rendering homage as the heavenly representatives of created beings, especially the whole of mankind. The second, the Lamb who receives the book from the Father, is an allegory on the redemption wrought by Jesus through his sacrifice.

In the vision of the Lamb and the sealed scroll are summarised all the messianic expectations of the Prophets of the Old Testament. The Lamb, therefore, is a symbol of the Messiah. He possesses the fullness of power – the seven horns and the fullness of the spirit: "seven eyes, which are the seven spirits of God" (5:6). It is important to notice that in 4:5 the seven spirits of God stand immobile before the divinity and over the sea like crystal, but possessed by the Lamb, they are clearly there for a mission: "the seven spirits of God sent out into all the earth" (5:6). This confirms further the messianic status of the Lamb.

This is further indicated by the context within which the Lamb is presented. I have mentioned that the visions of chs. 4 and 5 recall the two visions of Dan 7: the Ancient of Days (Yahweh) on the throne and the Son of man coming on the clouds to receive from the Ancient of Days the seal of his messianic function and authority (see Dan 7:9ff). We have already seen a use of this vision from Daniel in ch. 1, but there the Son of man takes over the description and characteristics of the Ancient of Days.

Here, however, the original distinction seems to be kept. First there is the vision of the one seated upon the throne, and then the vision of the Lamb coming to the throne to receive his messianic authority. There are, as usual, variations on the Danielic scheme which need attention. In Dan 7:9-10 the vision of the one seated on the throne is described in great detail, while his surrounding court is left shadowy. In the Apocalypse, the opposite happens. The divinity is without a name (4:2: seated on a throne) without a face ("he appeared like jasper and carnelian" – 4:3), immobile and silent. Even the flame, which in Daniel is pouring out from the scene to show the power and incessant activity of the divinity, is reduced by John to a slow burning presence (4:5: "before the throne burn seven torches of fire"), and he goes further to explain that they are the fullness of the Spirit (seven spirits of God). Only after it is taken over by the Lamb does the Spirit move out over the earth. In Daniel the angels are reduced to a presence (Dan 7:10) while in John they are carefully grouped and described, both in their appearance and their movements.

We claimed that the vision of ch. 4 was an allegory of the creation, but now can go further and claim that it is an allegory of the Old Economy. Through this scene John wishes to express the character and content of that revelation. The heroes were angels; they governed the world, they were mediators in cult, they were the mediators also of revelation. All this happened in the presence of the all-creating God who, therefore, had to be adored and worshipped. In this, John has summarised the Old Testament, a period described also by Paul:

> "Ever since the creation of the world his invisible nature, namely, his eternal power and deity, has been clearly perceived in the things that have been made" (Rom 1:20).

Equally notable are the changes which John introduces to his use of Dan 7 in ch. 5. Above all, there is the scroll. He must have picked this up from the fact that in Dan 7:10, before the court of the Ancient of Days, "books" are opened. Common to Dan 7 and to Apoc 5 is a judgment of God on mankind. John, however, transforms the symbol to the extent that the whole act of judgment, of condemnation or salvation, is the exclusive prerogative of the Lamb.

The most outstanding variation which John has introduced is the substitution of the Lamb for the Son of man. In Daniel, the figure is clearly messianic and he comes to the Godhead. To him is given all power to free Israel, and eventually to have all authority. John certainly has the scenes from Daniel before him, but the Lamb figure alone retains all the messianic significance. For Dan 7 the Son of man is the Messiah. In Apoc 5, the Lamb is also the Messiah, but his messiahship is exercised in a different way. He does not "come to" Yahweh, but from the beginning he is with God:

> 5:6: "Between the throne and the four living creatures, I saw a lamb standing."

We have already seen that 5:7 speaks of the origin of his authority. He has it because he takes it from God. He too shares in all that is the divinity. We have also seen that he has the totality of power (5:6: the seven horns) and possesses the totality of the Spirit (5:6: the seven spirits of God).

The Lamb, therefore, is the Messiah; this he has from his taking over the role of the Danielic Son of man. He is different from that messianic figure, however, because he is also divine. The way he exercises his messianic function is also different, and John explains this by writing of:

> "A Lamb *standing* as though *it had been slain*" (5:6).

He has exercised his messianic function through his death ("it had been slain") and his resurrection ("standing"). This comes to John, not through apocalyptic speculation, but from the events of the life, death and resurrection of Jesus of Nazareth. John believes that these "events" have freed all mankind, not from a political slavery, but from the slavery of sin. All that I have been saying is well summed up in the words of John himself, in the hymn of the four living creatures in vv. 9-10:

> "Worthy art thou to take the scroll and to
> open its seals,
> for thou wast slain and by thy blood
> didst ransom men for God
> from every tribe and tongue and people and nation,
> and hast made them a kingdom and
> priests to our God,
> and they shall reign on earth."

The ultimate reason for the substitution of the Lamb for the Son of man is because the latter offered the political restoration of the people in a temporal sense. Not so the Lamb. He will offer the whole of mankind freedom from sin, but only by being "slain" and by rising again – "standing."

The First Four Seals: The Creation and Fall of Man 6:1-8

> 6 ¹Now I saw when the Lamb opened one of the seven seals, and I heard one of the four living creatures say, as with a voice of thunder, "Come!"
> ²And I saw, and behold, a white horse, and its rider had a bow; and a crown was given to him, and he went out conquering and to conquer.
> ³When he opened the second seal, I heard the second living creature say, "Come!"
> ⁴And out came another horse, bright red; its rider was

permitted to take peace from the earth, so that men should slay one another; and he was given a great sword.
⁵When he opened the third seal, I heard the third living creature say, "Come!" And I saw, and behold, a black horse, and its rider had a balance in his hand;
⁶and I heard what seemed to be a voice in the midst of the four living creatures saying, "A quart of wheat for a denarius, and three quarts of barley for a denarius, but do not harm oil and wine!"
⁷When he opened the fourth seal, I heard the voice of the fourth living creature say, "Come!"
⁸And I saw, and behold, a greenish horse, and its rider's name was Death, and Hades followed him; and they were given power over a fourth of the earth, to kill with sword and with famine and with pestilence and by wild beasts of the earth.

The opening of the first four seals happens in a series of short scenes which are parallel. The Lamb opens, one by one, the four seals; the four living creatures, also in succession, issue an order: "Come!"; one after another four horses appear differentiated by colours – white, bright red, black, greenish. On every horse, there is a rider, each different in aspect from the other. Thus we can see that certain things remain the same (voice of the living creatures; horse, rider) while others change (colours, face and decoration of the riders). There is a unity in the four scenes, and there is also an allegory upon one and the same reality, described under different aspects.

We must make this unity the prime criterion in our interpretation. Many scholars draw a parallel between the first horseman and the vision of the Logos on a white horse in 19:11. As we will see, there is a link, but the first horseman and the Logos belong to their own context, and must be first interpreted there. The unity of the series of horsemen is further indicated by the fact that all four are under the jurisdiction of the four living things. We must not separate the first of the horsemen from them, even though there is an important parallel in 19:11.

What, then, is the significance of this allegory? What we have said already indicates that here we find four moments in one event. There are four phases in which there is one protagonist, symbolised by four horsemen and horses. The symbol of the horse is regular in the Apocalypse, and its reference is always connected with warfare. The horse must be further specified by the horseman upon it. This also relates to the idea of warfare, which is involved in the symbol. The idea here is clearly a negative one, like the frightful horsemen in the sixth trumpet (see 9:15ff). Only destruction and death are given to mankind. The Logos in 19:11ff also brings division and destruction, but only to the enemies of humanity (the dragon and the beast). To humanity itself it brings salvation and life.

The horsemen and the horse must be understood together. In the case of the scene of the Logos descending from heaven on a white horse we will see that it is an allegory of an incarnation of Christ, which has its culmination in the death of Christ on the Cross (his cloak soaked in blood, the battle of Armageddon). Therefore it is not absurd to see in the white horse a symbol of human nature which, in ch. 19, Jesus takes back to its original condition of innocence indicated by the colour white. An analogous message is found in the horses and the horsemen of the sixth trumpet (see 9:15ff). The horsemen are also marked by colours (9:17), red of fire, the blue of sapphire and the greenish colour of sulfur, and these are reproduced by the substances which come from the mouths of the horses – fire, smoke and sulphur. These are a symbol of the corruption of humanity by the demons. We can also see the horses as human nature, and the horsemen as some sort of incarnation within human nature which comes from another outside power, in this case, an evil power.

This leads us deeper into the truth which is hidden behind the veil of the allegory of these first four seals. It is aided by the fact that the scene of ch. 19 and also the sixth trumpet in ch. 9 allows us to reconstruct the indications of the four colours, and to see how they match the colours which follow one another in the four seals: white, bright red, black (a deep blue), greenish. It is not an accident that the colour white is matched with the only positive scene here, while the following three colours are close to the colours of the sixth trumpet, and they are all negative, as are the colours in ch. 9.

Gathering all this together, I suggest that the one common theme, the horse, is a symbol of human nature, and the colours which modify each horse and the different horsemen are shadows of various moments of humanity's history. It is possible, therefore, to see in the series an allegory of the spiritual history of man before the coming of Christ, a story which John has from the Genesis account of the fall of man (Gen 1:26ff).

Man, according to the biblical story, was created perfect and in a privileged situation, lord of the universe and a friend of God. But man sinned. The consequences were the loss of the blessedness of the original situation and exile into a strange, arid and hostile land, where man must suffer and work to survive, and eventually die. It was a severe condemnation, but not without hope. Man was promised a liberator who would redeem him from guilt and punish the tempter. The tempter, however, does not stop in his attempts to lead mankind astray, as John will show in later visions. He will use man's pride, his desire to make his own way to lead mankind into rebellion against God. This is the war which John, both here and elsewhere, presents to us as the consequence of original sin.

This is what he is describing in the scene of the first four horses. In the first, through the colour of the horse (white) and the appearance of the horseman (crowned and victorious), John presents humanity in its ideal perfection, as it was at the beginning, and as it will be when the Logos (Jesus Christ) will have assumed it in the incarnation, and redeemed through his sacrifice. He carries a bow in his hand, the weapon which shoots forward to a distant target, a symbol of the inherent possibilities of human nature. He has a crown on his head, a symbol of victory and, at the same time, of the supremacy of man over the whole of creation.

With the second horseman the scene changes brusquely.

The colour of the horse, bright red, is already a symbol of violence and destruction. The horsemen of the sixth trumpet will carry it on their breastplates and it will be the distinctive colour of the dragon. The appearance of the horseman is not described, but he is given "a great sword" (v. 4). There can be no doubt about his intentions and attitude. The task he is given is "take peace from the earth so that men should slay one another" (v. 4). This is the pain of warfare. John places it first among the consequences of original sin, not only because it is the most evident, but also because it is the one most in contrast with God's original plan for mankind, peace and order, according to the Old Testament. As we will see later, warfare is the bloody basis upon which a certain wicked, oppressive political power will rise up. A central biblical fact is that the first consequence of original sin was that brother killed brother in the Cain and Abel story (see Gen 4:1-16).

The opening of the third seal presents a series of details which are not altogether clear, but the significance can be quickly grasped. At the opening of the seal, called forth by the voice of the third living creature, a black horse enters bearing a rider who carries a balance (v. 5). A voice, which comes from the living beings, speaks a message which refers to the lack of what were then the staple foods: bread, wine and oil (v. 6).

Even though many commentators have seen in this a reference to some contemporary problem, the message that comes from its context refers to the suffering situation of man at all times, his struggle for food being the result of his initial disobedience.

The fourth seal is most frightful and also the most enigmatic. The colour is already quite a puzzle. John describes it with a Greek word *chloros*, which literally means "green." We have already seen that these colours are symbolic, and the previous colours lend themselves to an interpretation. This is not the case here; there is no such thing as a "green" horse. Many have associated the colour with death, and this led to the later translation "pallidus" – pale. Various other translations have gone in this direction, associating it with death, and the colour of dead bodies. The translation "greenish" is applicable to a dead body. The message is, without doubt, a reference to the most difficult and painful of all consequences or original sin: death, a result of humanity's disobedience (see Gen 3:19).

This is a terrible and a universal punishment, but there is more than physical death. Repeatedly in the Apocalypse John shows his concern over another consequence of sin: the breach set up between man and God, which has caused man to lose forever the possibility of communicating with the divinity, of receiving the divine life – i.e., he is placed in a continual situation of spiritual death. Physical death is merely the external symbol of this deeper reality. According to Jewish tradition, after death man went to "Sheol" which John translates into Greek as "Hades." John places "death and Hades" one after the other, as one leads to the other, the latter being the "place" where the dead go. But for John it is not only this. Death and Hades are mentioned elsewhere in Apocalypse (see 1:19; 20:13-14), both referring to the same reality. Here and in 20:14, the two terms are treated almost as personifications, and they clearly are the manifestations of Satan. This is why, in ch. 20, John can speak of Death and Hades being thrown down into the lake of fire (20:14), which is then paralleled by 20:10: "The devil who had deceived them was thrown into the lake of fire."

The scene of the fourth seal, therefore, in as allegory of the triumph of Satan over humanity, a triumph which resulted in the fall of man, resulting in a double death, the physical death and the spiritual death: Death and Hades. This could go further to explain the colour. It is not just "pale" as for a physically dead body, but the Greek word has clear links with "green." The translation "greenish" could cover both the reality of physical death and also the nature of external death, spoken of through the symbol of "sulphur" (see 19:20; 20:10, 14-15). The same image and elements will be taken up by the breastplates and horses of the sixth trumpet (9:17-18). This is the ultimate destiny of mankind, without the salvific intervention of Christ's victory over death and Hades (1:18).

THE FOUR HORSEMEN AND THE FOUR EMPIRES

The four coloured horses and their horsemen, therefore, symbolise the story of the creation of man and his fall. This will be taken up again and deepened in the following "sevens," the trumpets and the bowls. In the first four trumpets we will see the story of what preceded the fall of man, the fall of the rebellious angels (see 8:6-12). In the first four bowls (see 16:2-9) the theme of the fall of man will be taken up again, with a heavier stress on the spiritual fall, the loss of grace and of eternal life.

The first four seals stressed the physical consequences of sin, although the fourth, with the linking of Death and Hades, also opened up the theme of the spiritual loss. The most important issue, however, seems to be the outbreak of murderous violence and war, introduced in the second horse and horseman. The idea of war and violence is already inherent in the symbol chosen, a horse. This is already also evident in the biblical background for his use of a horse, Zechariah 1:8; 6:2-8. There the horses are symbols of the four empires, the fruit of violence and war. We have seen that John uses the symbol in a wider sense, to refer to the experience of humanity in the light of the history of salvation. Does this mean that John abandons any reference to history and politics, and lifts it all to the level of the spiritual? There were certainly political implications in Zechariah. We have already seen that John takes his references from the Old Testament, that he remodels them, but that he always leaves intact something of the original meaning. It is also clear that John knows the theory of the four empires, and uses it in the Apocalypse. This tangle of interpretations of the symbol of the four horses cannot fail to be confusing and so needs patient unravelling.

This theory of the four empires was a concept widely used in antiquity both in the Bible and outside of it. The key idea is that the human population of the world and political power over it is divided into four regions or zones of the earth. Sometimes these four empires are seen as existing at the same time, sometimes in succession. The latter is more common and generally used either to prove the worth of the present regime, the fourth, or, on the contrary, to show that it must be destroyed. This idea is very common in the struggles between the Persians and the Macedonians (400 B.C. and following) and then the Macedonians and the Romans (200 B.C. and following).

In the biblical tradition it is probably already present in Ezekiel (the four Cherubim who carry the throne of Yahweh, Ezek 1:5ff); it is clear in Zechariah (horses and horsemen in 1:8ff and the vision of the four carriages drawn by multi-coloured horsemen in 6:1ff) and further developed in Daniel (Dan 2:31-38: the dream of Nebuchadnezzar of the statue made of four metals; 7:2ff: the four beasts which rise from the sea). In Zechariah and Daniel we see a differing use of the same theory. In Zechariah, the four empires appear simultaneously, but they are not completely negative. They collaborate with God for the maintaining of earthly order. In Daniel, this is radically changed. They follow one another, and destroy and devour one another. They are totally negative, with a gradually increasing intensity in their wickedness. The last empire, the worst of all, will be destroyed and replaced by a fifth, the messianic reign of the Son of man.

Here the Apocalypse seems to be closer to Daniel. In fact, there will be an explicit use of Daniel's idea in 13:1ff to speak of corrupt political authority. John is also negative about the action of these historical powers, and he seems to see them as arising in a succession. There are other uses of the idea in Apocalypse, however, which hint that John was subject to other influences as well. In ch. 7, during the sixth seal, he has a vision of "four angels standing at the corners of the earth, holding back the four winds of the earth, that no wind might blow on earth or sea or against any tree" (7:1). The action of these angels is explained immediately as the putting into action of the order of a further angel, coming from the East, to sign the foreheads of 144 thousand "servants of God" (7:2-3). In ch. 9, during the sixth trumpet, an analogous scene takes place, but in an opposite direction. A voice comes from the four corners of the heavenly altar (the living creatures?) ordering the angel who has the sixth trumpet "Release the four angels which are bound at the great river Euphrates" (9:13-14).

The two scenes correspond as an antithesis to one another. Following an order, something is either held or liberated. Is it the same reality which is held and then liberated? Apparently not, because, in the first case, it is "four winds," while in the second, it is "four angels." Nevertheless, it is clear that in both cases we are dealing with forces which are hostile to humanity on the level of salvation. While they are bound, a small portion of humanity (144 thousand) are saved and receive the divine life ("the seal of the living God: 7:2) whereas, when they are freed, there is ruination (spiritual death) for a large part (a third: 9:15, 18) of humanity.

It is not too difficult to see in these hostile forces the rebellious angels, the demons and, in the last analysis, Satan. It is also clear that these forces do not act directly, but by using an instrument of another nature which, in the first case is given the name of "the four winds of the earth" (7:1) and in the second, an army of horsemen (9:16). In the first case, the instrument of the diabolical action is held in check by an angelic intervention. In the second case, the instrument seems to be the angels themselves who were at first bound, but who are then freed. It cannot be quite like that, because in both cases the action is a demonic action; even the first is to be seen as such, from the description of the horses and the horsemen (see 9:17). It is not, therefore, the angels who are liberated, but a reality which they encounter and hold, and with which, precisely because of this relationship, they are somehow identified. An identification can also be found in the first case, in so far as it is not to "the four winds" but to the "four angels" who hold them who have the power to harm the sea and earth (7:2). In the sixth seal and in the sixth trumpet the same situation is clearly described: "the four winds of the earth" and the army of cavalry are the same thing.

How are we to explain, in both cases, the different names given to the hostile forces which are somehow under the control of the angels? As we will see in its own place, the invasion of the cavalry in the sixth trumpet is foreshadowed by the rising of the four conquering empires whose first origin, according to a widespread belief in antiquity, took place in the land of the Euphrates (see 9:14 and then 16:12). Moreover, "the four winds of the earth" in biblical language, stand for the four empires. This is said explicitly in Zech 6:5: "They are the four winds of heaven which go forth after presenting themselves before the Lord of all the earth." From here Jewish thought identified "the four winds" as a symbol of the four empires. There is an indirect indication of this in Dan 7:2: "I saw in my vision by night, and behold the four winds of heaven were stirring up the great sea."

After this lengthy background, we are in a position to explain a few details of the vision of the four seals which do not receive a great deal of attention from commentators.

First of all, it becomes clearer why the symbol of horses is used to represent the human situation. That symbol in Zechariah had a political-historical significance. To take it over and place it in a scheme where the Lamb breaks the seals one by one means to place all the story of humanity (which is, for John, essentially political) into the light of Christ. John was not interested in political history in itself, in contrast to Zechariah and Daniel, who saw the hand of Yahweh in human, political events (e.g., the interpretation of Zech 1:12 and 6:8 as the occupation of Babylon by Cyrus, King of the Persians, and Dan 10-11 as a reference to Macedon and the Persians, and then the various Macedonian kingdoms).

John does not have this approach. He knows that the political history of mankind is essentially a history of wars, of kings and empires which come and go. He knows, too, that man can never recover his freedom, lost in sin, through these political means. His liberation can never be achieved by any human or spirit. Because of this, he takes from Zechariah and Daniel their political symbols, but transposes them to a more universal level, where even political and historical values can receive their real explanation. He does not deny or ignore political and historical values. Thus, it is quite possible that the four horsemen which follow one another in the first four seals are also symbols of the four empires which, according to the biblical tradition, come before the messianic moment.

In fact, only in this way can certain facts be explained, e.g., the colour of the horses. Certainly, there is a relationship between the four colours of the horses and the characteristics of the horsemen, as we have already explained, but alongside this meaning, the original biblical idea which referred to the distribution of the reality symbolised by the four zones of the earth remains present in the Apocalypse.

This distinction, in a political sense, is clearly referred to in the words of 6:8: "And they were given power over a fourth of the earth, to kill with sword and with famine and with pestilence and by wild beasts of the earth." Although many link this only with the fourth horse, to Death and Hades, this cannot be the case, as two of the elements referred to, sword and hunger, refer explicitly to the second and third horsemen. To Death and Hades belong "death" (physical and spiritual) and the "wild beasts" (in the sense which John will explain later, as the instruments of corrupt political and spiritual authority used by Satan to oppress humanity). Even less can the expression "power over a fourth of the earth" refer *only* to Death and Hades. This expression makes sense only if it is applied to each one of the four horsemen, understood as a political reality.

Only by grasping this connection of the horses and the horsemen with history and politics which the horses and horsemen have can one also understand that the four living creatures call them forth. Despite the negative aspect of these realities called forth, the fact that their origins are determined by these living creatures can be seen as somehow tied in with God's action. They are a part of the contingent world of history and politics looked after by the angels. They are not an essential part of the history of salvation, which is the exclusive prerogative of the Godhead. The same thing will happen in the sixth trumpet, where the four corners of the altar (probably also a reference to the four living creatures) order the angels to free the four angels tied at the Euphrates (9:13) and one of the living creatures will give the seven bowls to the seven angels in 15:7.

If, therefore, the four horseriders in the Apocalypse keep the symbol of the four empires, the relationship which John establishes between them and the four living creatures indicates that this symbol has been transferred to a more universal plane. What John has at heart is not to identify in these symbols any particular historical-political empire, or any particular battle as the sign of a coming empire, as did the old symbol. He wishes to show first of all that *all the empires*, are the result of original sin, a consequence which, like everything connected with the divine punishment, is not evil *in itself*, but forms a part of the period of trial and suffering before the final liberation. In this way we can also see the connection between these scenes with the four living things and, even more profoundly, with the Lamb who breaks the seals.

Nevertheless, the link with the Lamb, that is, with the slaying of Christ, tells us that the consequences of sin, in so far as they were punishment and trial allowed by God, were not accepted as such by mankind, and they became, eventually, an occasion to continue the rebellion against God. Because of the seduction of Satan, as John will explain as we go further, political authority became corrupt and an instrument for the oppression of the weak. The slaying of Jesus is the symbol of this, but it has been true from the very beginning of history. In the fifth seal, John will give us a dramatic presentation of this situation.

The Fifth Seal: The Salvation of the Just Ones in the Old Economy (6:9-11).

> 6⁹When he opened the fifth seal, I saw under the altar the souls of those who had been slain for the word of God and for the witness they had borne:
> ¹⁰they cried out with a loud voice, "O Sovereign Lord, holy and true, how long before thou wilt judge and avenge our blood on those who dwell upon the earth?"

¹¹Then they were each given a white robe and told to rest a little longer, until the number of their fellow servants and their brethren should be complete, who were to be killed as they themselves had been.

This is the famous scene, dramatic and complex. At the opening of the fifth seal John sees "under the altar the souls of those who had been slain (the same term as the one used for the Lamb) for the word of God and for the witness they had borne" (6:9).

From this group comes an invocation, or better, "a cry" to vindicate their slaying and do justice on the inhabitants of the earth who are responsible (6:10). A voice (probably of God) invites them to "rest" for a vague period of time: "until the number of their fellow servants and their brethren should be complete, who were to be killed as they themselves had been" (6:11).

CHRISTIAN MARTYRS (WITNESSES)?

The general meaning of the scene is clear. John wishes to say that those who die because of the word of God and of their witness, those we call "martyrs," will receive reward after death. When one descends to particulars, however, many difficulties arise.

At the root of all the discussions stands the universal agreement that John is talking about Christian martyrs here. This gives rise to many problems: who are they? why under the altar? why do they have to wait? who are the rest of the martyrs who are yet to come?

It is essential, therefore, to be clear on who these slain ones are. They were slain, says John, "because of the word of God and the witness they bore" (6:9). This formula, with slight variations, appears many times in the Apocalypse. John uses the expression, witness to the word of God (i.e., his law, his will expressed in the commandments) and to Jesus, to convey an idea of a religious attitude. He speaks of himself in this way (1:2, 9). Yet, in the other cases in the

Apocalypse it always appears to be associated with, on the one hand, a sacrifice of life on the part of the witness, and on the other, the reward for the slain ones on the other side of death. The closest situation to the one described in the fifth seal is found in ch. 20, connected with the reign of a thousand years. There John also speaks of "souls" of those who have been "slain because of the witness to Jesus and because of the word of God" (20:4).

The situation in chs. 6 and 20 is clearly the same. In both there is a connection with the reign of a thousand years, and both speak of "those who have been slain because of their witness to Jesus and because of the word of God" (6:9-11; 20:4). Moreover, many particulars which are missing or vague in ch. 5 are present or made more precise in ch. 20. The reward is given to the "martyrs" during the thousand year reign of Christ. They gave witness in favour of Jesus. The reward is given to the martyrs, and "all the other dead" are explicitly excluded (20:5). The content and meaning of the "rest" and the "white robe" which the martyrs of the fifth seal receive is explained as "to have life," "to reign with Christ," "to be priests of God and of Christ" (20:4-6). The period of waiting is a thousand years, after which Satan will be released from his prison (20:7) for his final assault on the divinity and his final defeat (see 20:8-10). After this there is the second coming. What is said in ch. 20 on the thousand years is a further spelling out of the scene of the fifth seal.

How is it that those who are "killed" for religious motives are the only ones saved? Is it possible that this situation describes the followers of Christ after his coming? Scholars divide on the explanation of this, but their answer is generally found in 14:13. "Blessed are the dead who die in the Lord henceforth." They are those slain by the beast. Also in ch. 20 only those who die for the double witness, to God and to Jesus, are admitted to happiness on the other side of death. Are they the same as those who "die in the Lord henceforth" in 14:13?

THE "REST" AND THE WHITE ROBE

Do they have to be Christian martyrs? The terms "rest" and the "white garment" are certainly used to speak of the divine life given to the just. While "rest" indicates this in a rather negative way, (it is the end of human problems), the white garment indicates the content of eternal life. White is a colour used in the Apocalypse to speak of justice and sanctity (not victory, as many commentators claim). The first horse and horsemen are white (6:1: man's original condition at creation); white is the cloud upon which the Son of man comes (14:14); the horse of the Word of God is white (19:11); the throne from which the judgment of God upon the world is pronounced is also white (20:11). The white garments, therefore, are in the first place a symbol of the justice and sanctity of those who wear them. White garments are given to the martyrs, and therefore they are symbols of their justice and sanctity.

Notice, however, that the witnesses are *"given* a white robe." How is this so, as they are just, and they were the ones to perform their just deeds? In other places, Jesus is presented as the one who *gives* the white robe. To Laodicea he says: "I counsel you to buy from me...white garments to clothe you" (3:18). In the letter to Sardis, Christ promises to give white garments to the conqueror (3:5). It appears that there is a distinction between the white garments merited by human virtue and justice on the one hand, and those given by Jesus to another, where there is no indication of any virtue or justice on the part of the receivers.

The garments given by Jesus are white since they have been washed "in the blood of the Lamb"; so those to whom the white garment is given have been freed from sin and written in "the book of life." The white garments are a symbol of the redemption which Jesus has obtained, and the gift which he has given to humanity (freedom from sin and communication of divine life). Because of this, they also mark the great crowd of the sixth seal (7:9ff) a symbol of humanity redeemed by Christ, a humanity receptive in its human suffering, valor, virtue and justice.

The white garments which are given to the "souls of those who had been slain" in the fifth seal, however, indicates their reception of the effects of redemption as a result of death because of their testimony. The same idea will be expressed in ch. 20 in more explicit terms (see 20:4-6). The "slain ones" of the fifth seal (as also in the reign of a thousand years) receive something after death which humanity, redeemed by Christ, the new people of God, the members of the Christian community, possess already in this life (see 1:5-6; 5:9-10; etc).

THE SALVATION OF THE ANCIENT WITNESSES (MARTYRS)

Thus it appears that one group: those "slain" in the fifth seal, and the same group in the reign of a thousand years, receive the white garments *after* their death, while all the faithful have it already in this life. It appears to me that the former groups refers to those who were slain for this witness, their justice and sanctity, in the period of the Old Economy. We have already argued that the witness given: to the "word of God" (observation of his commandments – see 12:17; 14:12) and to Jesus (faith in Jesus: 14:12) can be seen as a summary of the whole of the Old Testament, the Law of God (his commandments) and the Prophets (the announcing of the coming of the Messiah).

Such witness must continue *after* the period of Jesus. The whole Christian community is called to it. John sees himself as giving this kind of witness, and to him, as to all others in the community who do likewise, the white garment, the kingship and the priesthood have already been given. But what is done in the fifth seal and in ch. 20 seems to have something exceptional about it, and cannot be after Christ, as then it is the possession of all believers. The reason for the privilege which has been granted to them is not so much the heroism with which they went to death because of their witness, but lies rather in the fact that their death was not only an announcing of Christ, but in some way a prefiguration and an anticipation of the death of Christ. The immolation of the Lamb, according to John, has been going on "before the foundation of the world" (13:8).

The salvation of those who died in the Old Economy comes not from their own death, but from the death of Christ which is unique and life-giving. John expresses this idea in many ways. There are the 144 thousand (those we meet in the next seal) who stand with the Lamb on Zion, and follow him wherever he goes (14:14). This signifies that they are already inserted into the sacrifice of Christ and reaping the benefits of its effects. So also with the "slain" of the reign of a thousand years who already have life and reign "with Christ" (20:4).

In the fifth seal John expresses this idea with a very suitable image. The "souls of those who had been slain" are "under the altar" (6:9). For John, the altar was the centre of the old cult (see 8:3-4). Both the altar and the cult, however, were only symbols of the supreme act of cult which would take place in the death of Christ (16:7). Thus, to say that these souls were "under the altar" means that they were in Christ and already participating in the effects of his sacrifice.

Perhaps the use of the preposition *"under"* the altar is a hint that they are enjoying the effects of the sacrifice which has not yet taken place *upon* the altar. If this is so, then we have a further indication that the passage refers to those who have died as witnesses in the Old Economy. Whatever the case might be, it is clear that their situation is only provisional. They are not in a position of lesser importance, but they are to wait "until the number of their fellow servants and their brethren should be complete (6:11). What is this "completeness" that they are awaiting?

We have already indicated that John will take up this theme of the salvation already gained by those fallen in the Old Economy because of their testimony, especially in the reign of a thousand years in ch. 20. Before that, we will find that the testimony offered by the ancients to the Law of God and the messianic coming of Christ is acted out dramatically in the experience of the two "witnesses" in ch. 11 (see 11:3). These are symbols of the Law (Moses) and the Prophets

(Elijah), witnessing the Law of God and the coming of Jesus in the period of the Old Testament. John tells us there that they are killed by "the beast that ascends from the bottomless pit" (11:7) which he will later explain as being Satan in so far as he incarnates the two authorities among men: political and religious authority, corrupted by him and put into his service in a wicked alliance (chs. 13 and 17). The two witnesses also receive reward after their death, analogous to that of the "slain" of the fifth seal and the reign of a thousand years: they receive "a breath of life coming from God" and they are taken up into heaven (see 11:11-12).

Nevertheless, even the situation of the "witnesses" appears to be provisional, as something still has to come. Their story, in fact, closes the sixth trumpet story. This trumpet is dedicated to the ancient phase of the history of salvation (the perversion of humanity as a result of the diabolic attack and the first salvific intervention of God in the period of the Old Testament). The seventh trumpet announces the fulfilment of "the mystery of God" (10:7). This fulfilment, as John will make clear to us, is the death of Christ.

Something similar happens with the fifth seal, where the "slain" are to wait for "their fellow servants and their brethren" who are also to be killed, as they were killed (6:11). In the sixth seal, John will present, first a definite number, obviously symbolic, of 144 thousand saved (marked with the seal of the living God, see 7:2, 4), and after them an immense crowd which cannot be counted (7:9ff). There is a clear distinction between two groups, and the origin of the second group is determined by the death of Christ (see 7:14). Thus this group is the "fulfilment" of the former group. This means that the group of 144 thousand marked by the seal refers to the same reality as the "slain" of the fifth seal. This idea will be further deepened and explained by John especially in ch. 14.

The Sixth Seal: The Two Moments of the Divine Salvific Intervention (6:12—7:17)

6 ¹²When he opened the sixth seal, I looked, and behold, there was a great earthquake; and the sun became black as sackcloth, the full moon became like blood,
¹³and the stars of the sky fell to the earth as the fig tree sheds its winter fruit when shaken by a gale;
¹⁴the sky vanished like a scroll that is rolled up, and every mountain and island was removed from its place.
¹⁵Then the kings of the earth and the great men and the generals and the rich and the strong, and every one, slave and free, hid in the caves and among the rocks of the mountains,
¹⁶calling to the mountains and rocks, "Fall on us and hide us from the face of him who is seated on the throne, and from the wrath of the Lamb;
¹⁷for the great day of their wrath has come, and who can stand before it?"

7 ¹After this I saw four angels standing at the four corners of the earth, holding back the four winds of the earth, that no wind might blow on earth or sea or against any tree.
²Then I saw another angel ascend from the rising of the sun, with the seal of the living God, and he called with a loud voice to the four angels who had been given power to harm earth and sea,
³saying, "Do not harm the earth or the sea or the trees, till we have sealed the servants of our God upon their foreheads."
⁴And I heard the number of the sealed, a hundred and forty-four thousand sealed, out of every tribe of the sons of Israel,
⁵twelve thousand sealed out of the tribe of Judah, twelve thousand of the tribe of Reuben, twelve thousand of the tribe of Gad,
⁶twelve thousand of the tribe of Asher, twelve thousand of the tribe of Naphtali; twelve thousand of the tribe of Manasseh,

⁷twelve thousand of the tribe of Simeon, twelve thousand of the tribe of Levi, twelve thousand sealed out of the tribe of Benjamin.

⁹After this I looked, and behold, a great multitude which no man could number, from every nation, from all tribes and peoples and tongues, standing before the throne and before the Lamb, clothed in white robes, with palm branches in their hands,

¹⁰and crying out with a loud voice, "Salvation belongs to our God who sits upon the throne, and to the Lamb!"

¹¹And all the angels stood round the throne and round the elders and the four living creatures, and they fell on their faces before the throne and worshipped God,

¹²saying, "Amen! Blessing and glory and wisdom and thanksgiving and honor and power and might be to our God for ever and ever! Amen."

¹³Then one of the elders addressed me, saying, "Who are these, clothed in white robes, and whence have they come?"

¹⁴I said to him, "Sir, you know." And he said to me, "These are they who have come out of the great tribulation; they have washed their robes and made them white in the blood of the Lamb.

¹⁵Therefore are they before the throne
   of God,
and serve him day and night
   within his temple;
and he who sits upon the throne
   will shelter them with his
   presence.
¹⁶They shall hunger no more, neither
   thirst any more;
the sun shall not strike them, nor
   any scorching heat.
¹⁷For the Lamb in the midst of the
   throne will be their shepherd,
and he will guide them to springs
   of living water;

and God will wipe away every tear
from their eyes."

The sixth seal is more developed than the others, and this is due to the fact that John wished to represent through it the totality of the salvific interventions which God has made in favour of mankind. Here he concentrates his attention on the two most important interventions:
(a) What he did for the Hebrew people (liberation from Egypt, the Covenant and the Law at Sinai, and the messianic promise).
(b) What was done in Jesus Christ (redemption of the whole of humanity, freedom from sin and diabolic domination, the establishment of the new Covenant).

Here, too, as in the rest of the book, the two interventions, although distinct and qualitatively different, are seen in continuity, like two moments or stages in the one intervention in which the first appears to be a prefigure of the second. The second is the perfect and final salvific intervention already on the way in the former.

This explains why the first moment of the events of the sixth seal which look to the intervention of the Old Economy of Salvation (the 144 thousand "signed" ones of the tribes of Israel, see 7:1ff) is placed within the general context of a great earthquake and cosmic disaster (darkening of the sun and moon and the falling of the stars (see 6:12ff), which are "signs" of the death of Christ. In John's vision of things, all the salvific interventions refer ultimately to the culminating point, and here they find their value, even though, as yet, partial and provisional.

The death of Christ, as John will later explain (especially in the seven bowls) is the acting out of God's final Judgment on the world and upon history. Even the earlier interventions form part of that judgment, as yet only partial, upon Satan, the rebellious angels, man submerged in the flood, on Sodom and the Pharaohs of Egypt and the rest of fallen humanity. All this is dealt with in the first part of the opening of the seal (6:12-17) through a diverse use of biblical citations, especially of the Prophets.

All the events which follow, through the whole of ch. 7 represent the salvific effects which the judgment of God has had for men. There are, therefore, two distinct, but linked scenes:
(a) The marking on the forehead of the 144 thousand "servants of God" (7:1-8).
(b) the appearance of the immense crowd of people dressed in white garments (7:9-17).

To show the break between the two, John uses an expression "after this" (7:9) which he commonly uses to mark a break in his events which marks a step forward.

THE 144 THOUSAND

It is not difficult then, to see the two scenes as representing the two stages in the divine intervention. We can now notice that, in the first scene, all the activity linked with the theme of salvation is entirely handed over to the angels, which is an indication of the mediation used by God in the Old Economy. Angels hold back the demonic forces (7:1: "the four winds") to make possible the marking of the foreheads of the 144 thousand "servants of God" with the "seal of the living God" (7:2).

What is represented by this sealing on the forehead? The link with "the living God" clearly allows us to see it as a communication of the divine life. This means that the 144 thousand are granted salvation, just as the "slain" of the fifth seal were granted salvation. Are they the same group? What John tells us about the 144 thousand in ch. 14:1ff allows us to say from this point that they are. There he will see them gathered around the Lamb "on Mt. Sion," bearing his name (i.e., the name of the Lamb) and the name of his Father on their foreheads (14:1) for even the 144 thousand have rendered testimony to the Law and to the messianic prophecies.

That the scene refers to the Old Economy is proved by further elements: the number of those "sealed" and their origin. The number, though symbolic, is clearly defined, indicating a severe selection. Their origin is limited to "the tribes of Israel" (7:4). These rather negative points will be picked up by John later, and especially in chs. 10-11, where he will show that, in the Old Economy, there is a severely limited number of the saved, who all come from the Hebrew people. It is not mere chance then that these two limitations are immediately contradicted in the vision which follows of the white clothed crowd: immense numbers coming from the whole of humanity (7:9).

The exact same pattern is found in ch. 20:1ff. There we will find also an angelic intervention which immobilises the action of Satan, making possible the reign of a thousand years, restricted to a closed number of just ones receiving life, while the rest of humanity is excluded (20:4-5). We can, therefore, consider the first part of ch. 20 (tying Satan and the thousand years) as a taking up of the first part of the vision of the sixth seal. The only thing that is missing in ch. 20 is the reference to their coming from the Hebrew people. This may be implicit, in so far as they have given witness to the Law and the messianic prophecies, but it may have even more significance. The fact that the origin in Israel is *not* mentioned in ch. 20 may indicate that this is not absolutely essential, not even in the Old Economy. If, in fact, those saved according to the old law did all come from the Hebrew race, this does not eliminate the possibility that even in the Old Economy all that was asked was an adhesion to God's word and a trust in his promise. This would, in theory, even then be possible for everyone, and could be called a "spiritual Judaism." It is this spiritual reality which is transformed, but not done away with, through the coming of Christ. Such a concept of a "spiritual Judaism" could not be limited to any ethnic group not even before the coming of Christ.

THE GREAT MULTITUDE WHICH NO MAN COULD NUMBER

Again the symbol is clear. The immense number, their origin from the whole of humanity, the white garments and the palms which they hold in their hand all indicate that they are the whole of humanity redeemed by Christ, given the divine life by him (white garments) and given a victory over sin and demonic forces (the palms, primarily a symbol of victory *not* martyrdom).

Many commentators have seen this. What has created difficulty are the words of the four Elders who explain the nature of this group to John: "These are they who have come out of the great tribulation; they have washed their robes and made them white in the blood of the Lamb" (7:14). This has always been seen by commentators as a reference to persecution (under Nero or Domitian) or the final moment of the Antichrist, but I believe that this is a mistaken view, as the words of the Elder do not refer to a tribulation suffered by the "crowd." This is shown by the second part of the phrase: "They have washed their robes and made them white in the blood of the Lamb." The "tribulation" out of which they have come, of which they are the product, the fruit, is the tribulation of the Lamb. For this reason it is called "the *great* tribulation," in which the persecuted is no less than the incarnation of the divinity – Jesus Christ. The immense crowd of the redeemed is the product of that sacrificial death, a new people of God.

The description of this new people of God which follows in vv. 15-17 has many words and concepts which are repeated, very often word for word, and which are further developed in the final part of the book, dedicated to the description of the new Jerusalem. The central idea is that this new people of God offer to God and to the Lamb an everlasting cult, as the divinity has now come to dwell among them (see 7:15 in parallel with 21:3 and 22). For this reason, all their spiritual needs (life, truth and justice) will be abundantly satisfied (see 7:16-17 in parallel with 21:3, 23-27).

The Seventh Seal: The End of the Old Economy (8:1)

8:1 When the Lamb opened the seventh seal, there was silence in heaven for about half an hour.

This is the shortest of all the seals. We are simply told that when it is opened it produces in heaven "silence for about half an hour" (8:1). This seal has caused great difficulty for commentators of all ages. Many have argued that this "silence" signifies the end of history and the beginning of eternity. The difficulty lies in the expression: "for about a half an hour." This has led many contemporary exegetes to see it as a sort of interlude, and it is created by John to set up a tension, a moment of suspense, before introducing the visions which follow, especially the "seven" of the trumpets.

I find this unsatisfactory, basically because it calls for an interpretation of the various "sevens" as a progression from one to another, along an ever-developing line. I have been arguing that this is not the case, but that there is a continual statement and re-statement of the same basic themes. I will attempt to explain this seventh seal along these lines.

In his statement and re-statement process, John does not simply say the same things over and over. Each time a theme is taken up a further time, it recalls and repeats something that has already been said, but it is never identical with it. It must be noticed therefore that all four "seventh" episodes of the "sevens," even though different in many ways, represent the end, the interruption, the destruction of something: the relationship between Christ and the community (seventh letter: 3:15-17), the cult led by the angels in the heavenly temple (seventh trumpet: 11:19), the reality represented by Babylon (the seventh bowl: 16:19). The seventh seal is no exception: the silence ends all sound: word, indistinct voice or noise, whatever it may be.

To understand fully the significance of the silence we must notice that it occurs "in heaven." The earlier part of the vision was full of sound as the angelic voices sang a perpetual liturgy, raising hymns of praise to the divinity. To this immense chorus we must add the weaker voices of the "prayers of the holy ones" which, passing through the mediation of the angels, also arrive to the divinity (see 5:8; 8:3-4). To this one must add the cry of the "souls of the slain ones" beseeching God to render justice, to vindicate their death (6:10). All of this comes to a halt in the "silence" of the seventh seal.

What can this signify? The supplications of the slain and the angelic choirs all cease because of the same event – the death of Christ. This has already been indicated at the beginning of the sixth seal (6:2), where earthquake, cosmic disasters and the flight of the inhabitants of the land are put into action. We will see in our study of the "seven" of the bowls (chs. 17-20) that the judgment set in action by the death of Christ has an immediate effect of the destruction of evil forces and the vindication of the innocent's blood (18:24).

Even this interruption of the heavenly liturgy is closely linked with the death of Christ. The synoptic Gospels all speak of the end of Jewish cult at the death of Christ, through the image of the veil of the temple (Matt 27:51; Mk 15:38; Lk 23:45). John's use of the cessation of the heavenly choir refers to the same thing. Because the heavenly temple was the model of the Jewish earthly temple (see Exod 25:9, 40), as the cult is performed – or not performed – in heaven, so will it also be on earth. Yet John probably wants to convey yet another profounder truth through this cessation of the heavenly liturgy. It is presided over by the angels, and the earthly cult passed to the divinity by means of the angels (see 5:8; 8:3-4). The end of the heavenly liturgy means the end of the angelic mediation. In this silence we can trace a hint of the angels' falling to the ground in adoration in 4:9-10 and the repetition of that act when the Lamb took the scroll in 5:8.

If this is the meaning of the silence, then we can offer a better solution for the reference to "for about half an hour." It is clearly an indication of a short period of time, but it must not be seen as indicating some chronological and historically controllable "half hour." It is a line of demarcation between something which finishes (the old cult), and something which beings (the new cult, in spirit and in truth, which the sacrifice of Christ founds and makes possible).

It is possible that we have here a veiled biblical reference. This unit of time, an "hour," which is divided into two makes one think of the subdivision which Daniel makes of the last of the seventy weeks into two "half weeks" (Dan 9:27). It is not only the analogy of the division of a unit into two which makes one look there, but it is in the second "half week" that Daniel placed the profanation of the temple and the forbidding of Jewish cult by Antiochus IV. These things, for John, were to be seen as a prefiguring of what would happen in a much more serious way at the death of Christ. Here at the instigation of the Priests themselves, who acted as judges, there is the definitive profanation of the temple, and the final cessation of true Jewish cult.

Therefore, the "half hour" corresponds to the period between the death and the resurrection of Jesus, a period of time which John (as we will see from the episode of the two "witnesses" who prefigure the experience of Jesus in 11:11) calculates as "three and a half days," i.e., "half a week." There are traces of this duration of time also in the Synoptic Gospels (see Matt 12:40 – Jonah in the belly of the whale). During this period there is "silence." The ancient cult administered by the angels has come to an end; all creation waits for the new cult that will begin with the resurrection of Christ, the new Passover.

THE SEVEN TRUMPETS (8:2—11:19)

THEME: The Old Economy: the first stage of the divine salvific intervention which can be seen in the struggle between the good and the bad angels.

Structure and General Theme

The "seven" of the the trumpets is more developed than either of the two previous "sevens" (letters and seals), but the basic structure of 4 and 3 appears again. There is a further development in the final three trumpets which receive a fuller description. As well as being three trumpets, they are also the three "woes" announced by the angel flying in midheaven (8:13).

Differences and similarities can also be seen in the movement involved. In the first four seals we had a complex movement which began in heaven (the voice of the four living creatures) yet at the same time from hell (the fourth horseman). The point of reference was the earth (the four horsemen). In the second group of three we had a movement which went as follows:

heaven (fifth seal)

heaven ⟶ earth (sixth seal, the falling of the stars)
heaven (seventh seal)

In the first group of four trumpets, we find immediately the movement heaven ⟶ earth (first four trumpets: the falling of burning heavenly bodies). In the second group the movement starts from hell (fifth trumpet: the shaft of the bottomless pit) and widens out over the earth (sixth trumpet: the descent of the angel with the book open in his hand) and finally, like the seventh seal, the movement closes in heaven (seventh trumpet: the opening of the temple of God in heaven).

Comparing the two, we can see a reversal of movement. The first four trumpets take up and develop the sixth seal, while the fifth and sixth trumpet, at least structurally, seem to do the same with the first four seals. The same themes are certainly repeated, but their presentation is different. How is this to be explained?

We have seen that the argument of the seals is a sort of mediation on the history of man seen from one side as a consequence of the original fall (the first four seals) and from the other as the salvific intervention of God which works itself out in the form of judgment, bringing both salvation and condemnation. The argument of the trumpets is a meditation on history, but now not as a succession of events which grow from an original fall. Here history is seen in its totality, and therefore right from the beginning it is presented as a judgment of God on the world.

If the whole of history is a judgment of God, then he intervenes constantly, although in various forms and with a varying activity. This is what John wishes to communicate by his inversion of the scheme. In fact, the whole of the trumpets is a development of the sixth seal which is dedicated to the description of the divine salvific intervention. In claiming this, John presents a more unified picture of the history of mankind, in contrast to the seals where it was presented in two stages: the negative sign of the domination of Death and Hades (first four seals), and then the positive sign of the progressive salvation from God (last three seals). Both, as John will teach us in the trumpets, are the effect of the one judgment of God. In fact, the trumpets teach us that the judgment of God is not only found in history, but also precedes it. Even before the world of mankind, the angelic world (or, better, a part of it) was cast down from heaven from a condition of perfection and nobility, cf. the first four trumpets. The human story begins with the fifth and sixth trumpets. It is the story of the evil which the fallen angels let loose from the abyss into which they have been cast. It rises to darken the light, to torment man, to cover creation with blood, to suffocate justice and truth. The three "woes" which coincide with the last three trumpets underline in a dramatic way the apparently irresistible growth and spread of this ruinous activity.

Human history, however, is not only the story of evil unchecked. As violence and pride rise from below we find in the sixth trumpet itself another sign which moves in the opposite direction, from heaven down to the earth. This sign is also in the persons of angelic beings, and is a force for good which brings help to mankind (ch. 10). It is, moreover, apparently victorious over the rising evil. Nevertheless, the development of this "seven" still leaves a most disconcerting impression. At the end of it all it appears as if the victory of the good forces is limited to the heavenly world. The two witnesses saved from the death inflicted upon them by the beast which rises from the abyss are taken to heaven, and there also praise is sung for the establishment of the kingdom of God. But the earth, where the "strong angel" of 10:1 has descended from heaven to dominate, still seems to perish as a victim of the "Angel from the abyss" who is called *Apollyon*, i.e., "exterminator" (see 9:10-11). The book handed over by the angel is sweet at first, but then turns bitter in John's stomach (10:10). The holy city is invaded and stamped under foot by the pagans, and the profanation is not only at the material level, because it is transformed from a "Holy City" into "Sodom and Egypt" (11:8). The temple itself appears to be profaned, as the veil which covered the Ark of the Covenant is pulled back in the heavenly temple, the model of the earthly temple (11:19).

For an answer to these problems we must keep in mind the chief protagonists in the story: the good and bad angelic creatures. They are present in the other "sevens," but here they are in the forefront of all the action, as if they were the cause of the good and evil which are described in this "seven." This does not surprise us greatly in the case of the bad angels, as it is the result of their rebellion against God and their hatred for humanity. But how are we to explain that the authors of the good are the good angels who should be always subordinate to God and especially to Jesus Christ? Here God is only alluded to, and Jesus Christ is passingly mentioned in the seventh trumpet by the heavenly choir singing praise to the establishment of the messianic kingdom (11:15).

The explanation can be found by recalling again the function which the angels have as mediators of the Old Covenant. Their presence and function in the seven trumpets is to be explained, by this "seven," which as we shall see from a more detailed analysis, is an allegorical representation of the covenant, and the economy of the Old Testament. This is presented by John as the first stage of the divine salvific intervention which is described through the terrible battle between the angels who have remained faithful and the rebels. In a first moment, the faithful ones win. Satan and his companions are driven from heaven, thrown down to the ground and (as John will later clarify) closed within the abyss, but they are not definitively defeated. In fact, from the abyss Satan sets free his wicked influence on humanity, where he finds certain allies who favour his resurrection and rising up from the prison of the abyss. The final victory will only be won when he and his allies, both angelic and human, are overcome by the victory of the death and resurrection of Christ. That final victory is reported in the final "seven," that of the bowls, from ch. 12 till the end of the book.

THE "SEVEN" OF THE TRUMPETS AND THE OLD TESTAMENT

It is generally taken for granted that the symbol of the trumpet belongs to the eschatological symbols. Thus, the whole of the "seven" is about the end time. This makes the "seven" extremely difficult to understand, because it is clearly not "the end." There is so much that is incomplete. It is quite clear that the final victory has not been won. Therefore, we suggest that the trumpet signal is *not* eschatological here, but it is linked with the imperfect situation of the Old Economy, revealed in the Old Testament.

In fact, this "seven" has many echoes and memories of the Old Testament. We have already mentioned the intermediary of the angels. As well as that, there are contacts between the punishments produced by the trumpets with the plagues in Egypt. Linked to this are allusions to the presence of the Hebrew people in the desert, and the foundation of the old covenant at Sinai. This dominates the message of ch. 10, and is carried further by the "two witnesses" of ch. 11, an allegory on the Law and the messianic expectation of the Prophets.

It appears possible to see a reference to the Old Testament, and especially to the Exodus, in the structure of this "seven." Between the first and the second group of trumpets there is a sort of intermezzo: the vision of an eagle which flies in midheaven and announces to the inhabitants of the earth a threefold "woe" (8:13). The image of the eagle is regular in the Old Testament and refers to the care, at the same time both powerful but loving, which God shows for his people Israel. It is an important symbol when the Old Testament speaks of the liberation from Egypt (see Exod 19:4; Deut 32:11). This reference to the Exodus will be taken up by John again in ch. 12 when he will write of the second flight of the woman into the desert (12:14), another allegory on the Hebrew Exodus.

It is not surprising, therefore, that the group of trumpets dedicated to the exposition of the first salvific intervention, the Old Economy, is under the sign of the eagle, a symbol of the help which Yahweh gave his people. We can also understand how this coincides with a series of "woes." This first intervention, as John will explain in ch. 12, consists essentially in the punishment of the rebellion of Satan and his being driven out from heaven by the angels. It is a judgment, as are all the interventions of God, but this judgment, through the angels, is provisional: Satan is driven out of heaven but he is not definitively overcome. From the prison of the abyss into which he was closed by the faithful angels (20:1ff) he gradually frees himself, and at first works upon earth through his two agents (the two beasts) and then comes up again himself to perform the greatest of all his acts against God, the slaying of Jesus Christ.

The final three trumpets, while they describe on the one hand the first salvific intervention of God which happens through the angels (symbolised by the eagle), on the other hand show a gradual rebirth of Satan who, coming from the abyss, carries his attack upon humanity and the divinity through a series of growingly serious "woes." These move through the temptation and the fall of man (fifth trumpet – first "woe"); the corruption of human history and its most important manifestations, political and religious authority (invasion of the cavalry, wars, profanation of the temple and the holy city, the killing of the two witnesses (the second "woe") to the death of Christ (seventh trumpet – the third "woe"). These are the three "woes" announced by the eagle and recalled, in ch. 12 by the chorus of angelic voices, praising the driving out of Satan from heaven (12:12).

As can be seen from these rapid indications, the presence of the Old Testament in the "seven" of the trumpets is not something of marginal importance. It is symbolic, and makes all of this section appear as an allegory on the Old Testament revelation. This being the case, we must understand the eschatological (end time) significance of the trumpets in a way different from the usual interpretations. The "end" referred to by the strong angel descended from heaven (10:7: "In the days of the trumpet call to be sounded by the seventh angel, the mystery of God...should be fulfilled"). That mystery coincides with the death and resurrection of Jesus; an end of time, certainly, but in the sense of a history of salvation where all historical events converge upon the promise made by God in the very moment that punishment was inflicted as a result of the original fall. Seen from the point of view of the history of mankind, this does not mean an "end" in the normal sense of that expression, but a complete change in the spiritual order, where the old is cancelled and substituted by a new order, a "new heaven" and a "new earth," a "new Jerusalem," as John will illustrate in the final chapters (see 21:1ff).

Here in the seven trumpets, however, we are in a preceding stage. It precedes, but it is not foreign or radically opposed to the new. It is a preparation, an announcing and even an anticipation. In this way, only some aspects will be completely done away with, while others will move on to their perfection. John thinks that this perfection comes about with the coming of Jesus Christ, an event which has been announced and prefigured in the preceding events, especially within the revelation of the Old Testament, which had its high point in the covenant made on Sinai between God and his people. In this covenant John sees the essence and the value of the Old Testament economy. All the signs and events which preceded it, especially all the signs of the liberation from Egypt, have value only in so far as they lead into the establishment of the Covenant.

The establishment of the Covenant on Sinai, as it is told in the book of Exodus (see Exod 19:16ff) took place amidst lightning, thunder and a growing intensity of trumpet blasts. For this reason the Old Economy is placed within the sign of the trumpets. Thus, John takes a current apocalyptic symbol and uses it for his own particular purpose: a sign of the divine salvific intervention of Sinai, the Old Economy in its highest moment.

Nevertheless, the covenant of Sinai is, in turn, only a preparation for the covenant which Jesus Christ would set up between God and man. Thus the trumpets not only recall the pact of Sinai, but look forward to the final, definitive perfection of that covenant in Jesus Christ. This covenant will be amply described by John in the "seven" of the bowls, from ch. 12 to the end of the book.

The succession of the two "sevens," the trumpets and the bowls is, therefore, a taking up again and a development of the situation synthetically described in the vision of the Son of man in ch. 1. It is not chance that there the two phases were symbolised by John's hearing "a loud voice like a trumpet" which sounded from behind him (1:10). And it is the same "voice...like a trumpet" which introduced the episode of the throne in 4:1, during which we see another allegory of the Old Testament revelation.

The Introduction to the Seven Trumpets (8:2-6)

THE ANGELIC LITURGY

> **8** ²Then I saw the seven angels who stand before God, and seven trumpets were given to them.
> ³And another angel came and stood at the altar with a golden censer; and he was given much incense to mingle with the prayers of all the saints upon the golden altar before the throne;
> ⁴and the smoke of the incense rose with the prayers of the saints from the hand of the angel before God.
> ⁵Then the angel took the censer and filled with fire from the altar and threw it on the earth; and there were peals of thunder, voices, flashes of lightning, and an earthquake.
> ⁶Now the seven angels who had the seven trumpets made ready to blow them.

Like the other "sevens," the trumpets were preceded by an inaugural vision. It begins with the handing over of the trumpets to the "seven angels who stand before God" (v. 2). John speaks of these angels as if the reader already knew about them. This has troubled commentators, and reference is usually made to the so-called "angels of the presence" which are found in the Old Testament (see Tob 12:15; Is 63:9). The solution is probably much simpler, if we remember that in the Apocalypse the number "seven" has a symbolic value, indicating "totality": Seven Churches = the totality of the Church; Seven spirits = the totality of the Spirit; Seven candelabra = the totality of Judaism and its cult, etc. So the angels here have been mentioned, as the reference is to all the angels, and we will remember that they were described in 1:20 as seven stars, under the authority, in the right hand of the Son of man. Their standing before God indicates their fidelity to him, and their readiness to put his commands into action.

The scene which follows (vv. 3-5) still has an angel as the protagonist. He is officiating at a sacrifice to God offered on an altar which is clearly the altar of incense from Jewish cult. In fact, the smoke of incense and the prayers of the saints rise from it to God. The scene makes explicit what was implicit in 5:8 where the twenty-four Elders and the four living creatures fell down before the Lamb "with golden bowls full of incense which are the prayers of the saints." What John wants to make clear in both cases is the idea of a human cult (the prayers of the saints) which, to reach the divinity, must pass through the mediation of an angel. This is one of the differences the early Christians pointed to between their cult which had Jesus Christ as mediator, and the Jewish cult which was mediated by angels. The Letter to Hebrews argues such a case strongly.

John's scene however does not appear to be polemical. It is used to characterise the Old Economy, and the seven trumpets will be described after this introduction. The polemics do emerge later from the brusque way in which the scene closes. The angel takes the fire from the altar, fills the censer and throws it on the earth. Then follows: "peals of thunder, loud noises, flashes of lightning, and an earthquake" (v. 5). Commentators argue that this announces a fresh series of plagues which are about to strike humanity, brought by the seven trumpets. While this is true, it is still too superficial.

Can we give a more precise significance to this brusque action of the angel which, above all, puts a sudden end to a liturgical action? We saw something similar in the "silence for about half an hour" which was produced in heaven by the opening of the seventh seal (8:1). The silence, we said, was an allusion to the end of the angelic liturgy which was going on in heaven (see ch. 4), and this in turn was the sign "in heaven" of what was happening on earth, i.e., the end of the Jewish cult, which the first Christians associated with the death of Christ. The conclusion of this liturgical scene probably has the same meaning. It is an indirect reference to the death of Christ and its effects, the end of the angelic mediation and the end of the cult which depended upon it. The conclusion of the seven trumpets continues the same theme, as the veil which covered the Ark of the Covenant in the heavenly temple will be torn away, and there also we will find "flashes of lightning, loud noises, peals of thunder, an earthquake" (11:19).

If this is the meaning of the interruption to the angelic liturgy described here, it will be possible to give a less fantastic interpretation to the fire taken from the altar and poured out on the ground. The first meaning is a symbol of the judgment of God which strikes the world. The consequence of the judgment is firstly the condemnation of Satan and his being driven, along with his followers, from heaven. The first four trumpets will illustrate this first effect of the divine judgment which has struck the most noble of his creatures, and it is shown through the allegory of flaming bodies which fall from heaven to earth.

This is its first significance, but it also indicates the end of the Jewish cult. Both of these meanings are clearly negative. Is there anything positive in it? There could be, as the symbol of fire which comes from heaven is used in the New Testament to speak of the purifying effect of the message of the Gospel (see Lk 12:49) or even of the Holy Spirit communicated to the believers (Acts 2:3ff). This is often overlooked as commentators are so taken up with the idea of a final sad destruction. We know that such is not to be the case. The scene of the pouring out of fire upon the earth is a sign of the judgment of God on the world, a judgment which has been going on since the beginning of time, or at least since the events of the sinfulness of God's creatures, both angelic and human. The judgment of God however is not only punishment. It is always accompanied by the divine will to draw from it salvation and life for mankind. This applies especially to that final and decisive judgment, which took place in the death of Jesus, a final judgment which produced a new reality, the new people of God, a regal and priestly people. Could this pouring out of fire, symbolising the judgment of God upon earth and the end of the Jewish cult, also signify the spreading over the earth of a new cult, the adoration of the Father in spirit and in truth?

The First Four Trumpets: The Fall of the Angels (8:7-13)

> 8⁷The first angel blew his trumpet, and there followed hail and fire, mixed with blood, which fell on the earth; and a third of the earth was burnt up, and a third of the trees were burnt up, and all green grass was burnt up.
> ⁸The second angel blew his trumpet and something like a great mountain, burning with fire, was thrown into the sea;
> ⁹and a third of the sea became blood, a third of the living creatures in the sea died, and a third of the ships were destroyed.
> ¹⁰The third angel blew his trumpet, and a great star fell from heaven, blazing like a torch, and it fell on a third of the rivers and on the fountains of water.
> ¹¹The name of the star is Wormwood. A third of the waters became wormwood, and many men died of the water, because it was made bitter.
> ¹²The fourth angel blew his trumpet, and a third of the sun was struck, and a third of the moon, and a third of the stars, so that a third of their light was darkened; a third of the day was kept from shining, and likewise a third of the night.
> ¹³Then I looked, and I heard an eagle crying with a loud voice, as it flew in midheaven, "Woe, woe, woe to those who dwell on the earth, at the blasts of the other trumpets which the three angels are about to blow!"

The first four trumpets, like the first four seals, are clearly a unit and very homogeneous, with both fixed and changing elements. The fixed element is always the proportion which is damaged by the punishments – a third. The variable appears to be the object of the punishments: earth, sea, rivers and fountains, stars. There is however a unity behind all of these: the punishment strikes creation in its spatial dimension, heaven and earth, and the life which is found there, from plant life to man himself. Man is mentioned only in the third trumpet (the bitter waters); in the others he is only indirectly present. Clearly John wishes to speak of the damage meted out to the physical and subhuman life.

The other variable is the way in which the punishments strike: in the first three trumpets, there is a falling (specified in the first two as being "thrown") of fiery bodies from on high (heaven) to below (earth: seas, rivers and fountains). In the fourth trumpet there is no fall; something "strikes" the stars and reduces their splendour by a third.

These variables are not really so different. In the first three, John is really describing in different ways the same thing, the falling of heavenly bodies. He begins with a rather vague description: "hail and fire mixed with blood" (8:7). In the second it is clearer: "a great mountain burning with fire" (8:8). In the third it is quite direct: "a great star." What is then described in the fourth trumpet, i.e., the darkening of a third of the stars, is the effect, or better, the explanation of what has been described in the first three: something has struck a part of the stars to the extent that they lose a third of their splendour. Something in their nature has been changed. This has to be connected with what has happened to the "great star" which, in the first three trumpets, has been described as falling.

What is the significance of this cosmic catastrophe? The star – angel parallel which we found in ch. 1 (1:20) is enough to tell us that these four scenes are about the fall of Satan (first three trumpets) and his followers (fourth trumpet), but what follows will confirm this interpretation. That Satan is hinted at by the "great star" becomes clear in the fifth trumpet: "I saw a star fallen from heaven to earth, and he was given the key of the shaft of the bottomless pit" (9:1). In ch. 12 John will have a short summary of the history of salvation. The fall of Satan and his angels is described: "Behold a great red dragon...his tail swept down a third of the stars from heaven, and cast them to the earth" (12:3-4).

The connection with the first four trumpets is clear.

It is difficult to know exactly where John learned this story of the fall of the angels, but there is much speculation in Jewish literature which may have served him. Whatever his source, there is one important particular that needs attention: the effect of the fall of the angels is that a third of creation is corrupted. How is this to be understood? The first reply which comes to mind is that John anticipates here the disastrous effects which the fall of man will have on creation, a fall which is also a consequence of the fall of the angels. There may also be a further aspect. John, together with biblical and extra-biblical thought, sees the creation as being governed by the intermediary of angels. We have already seen this dramatically portrayed in ch. 4. Thus, the rebellion of the angels, and the disaster which results, happen also to that part of creation which they govern.

In any case, all the evils described touch physical and cosmic realities. The fall of the angels produces the corruption of creation as a direct consequence, and the fall of man as an indirect consequence. In other words, it produces an enormous upsetting of the existing order of things in creation. We have noticed that all of this seems to happen as a result of a divine punishment, which is the result of a divine anger.

I have suggested that this is not the whole story. These elements which fall from the heavens also have intelligence and a will of their own. Certainly their fall (described in the first trumpet as their being "thrown") is the result of an act of God which strikes them. The fall also brings disastrous effects of the elements into which they fall. These are consequences for the physical world (the first four trumpets) and for the human world (the "woes" announced by the eagle, the three following trumpets).

These effects, however, are not the direct consequence of the divine judgment. This is evident in the case of man. The "woes" which strike him certainly have their source in the diabolic jealousy, but his yielding to the temptation is also involved, and thus he is ultimately responsible himself. As far as creation is concerned, the biblical tradition has already made it clear that its pains are the result of the sinfulness of angels and men: pride, violence, a desire to dominate and to destroy. For this reason later in the book we will find that the liberation of man from the domination of those who destroy (11:18) and the renewal of cosmic order (21:1: the new heaven and the new earth) is one of the effects of the establishment of the messianic kingdom.

Of all of this the first trumpet and its products are a sign: hail and fire mixed with blood. This is the vaguest of the symbols, leading to the clear indication of the falling of the stars. In reality, the description of the punishment of the first trumpet gives us a key to an understanding of the whole "seven" of the trumpets. Not only does it contain something of all the rest, but, as many commentators have noticed, there is a clear reality of the so called ten plagues of Egypt (see Exod 9:23ff). They are also recalled in the following trumpets: second trumpet: water changed into blood; fifth trumpet: darkness and locusts; seventh trumpet: once again, hail. There are further references to the Exodus experience of Israel: third trumpet: bitter waters (see Exod 15:22ff); sixth trumpet: the setting up of the Covenant at Sinai.

We have already glanced at the trumpets and the Old Testament. Some further reflections should be added because of these contacts with the Exodus. We have seen that they serve to characterise the whole of the seven trumpets as a representation of the Old Testament economy, whose high point John presents as the liberation from Egypt and the establishment of the Covenant at Sinai. This is a prefiguring of the new Exodus and the new Covenant which the death of Jesus has realised in favour of the whole of humanity.

But there is even more. In the first four trumpets we have seen the presentation of the fall of the angels as the source of the corruption which is produced in the creation. The fifth, sixth and seventh trumpets (the three "woes") will show its spreading among men. The fact that John chooses elements from the Exodus story to tell of the tragic beginning of a history of salvation means that he sees a contact between the two moments. The liberation of the Hebrew people from

Egypt was the result of a divine intervention which manifested itself through a series of punishments. Israel also felt the pain of this, as each plague was met with even greater persecution from the Pharaoh. This, according to John, is a symbol of how things had been in the affairs of men since the beginning of time. All humanity has fallen under an oppressor, upon whom the wrath of God fell, and this also led to exasperating oppression for mankind. Such a situation went on until there was a final liberation in the human event of Christ. Through the trumpets, God's anger is reflected, but there is also a hint of the future liberation through the use of the Exodus story. In the sixth trumpet John will, in fact, show the limited value of this stage, the Old Testament economy, in the salvific plan, especially in the visions of ch. 10, (descent of the angel with a small scroll in his hand) and ch. 11, (the event of the two "witnesses").

The Fifth Trumpet (The First "Woe"): The Fall of Man (9:1-12)

> 9 ¹And the fifth angel blew his trumpet, and I saw a star fallen from heaven to earth, and he was given the key of the shaft of the bottomless pit;
> ²he opened the shaft of the bottomless pit, and from the shaft rose smoke like the smoke of a great furnace, and the sun and the air were darkened with the smoke from the shaft.
> ³Then from the smoke came locusts on the earth, and they were given power like the power of scorpions of the earth;
> ⁴they were told not to harm the grass of the earth or any green growth or any tree, but only those of mankind who have not the seal of God upon their foreheads;
> ⁵they were allowed to torture them for five months, but not to kill them, and their torture was like the torture of a scorpion, when it stings a man.
> ⁶And in those days men will seek death and will not find it; they will long to die, and death will fly from them.
> ⁷In appearance the locusts were like horses arrayed for

battle; on their heads were what looked like crowns of gold; their faces were like human faces,
⁸their hair like women's hair, and their teeth like lions' teeth;
⁹they had scales like iron breastplates, and the noise of their wings was like the noise of many chariots with horses rushing into battle.
¹⁰They have tails like scorpions, and stings and their power of hurting men for five months lies in their tails.
¹¹They have as king over them the angel of the bottomless pit; his name in Hebrew is Abaddon, and in Greek he is called Apollyon.
¹²The first woe has passed; behold, two woes are still to come.

The fifth trumpet is linked to the four preceding ones through the initial vision: "a star fallen from heaven to earth" (9:1), clearly Satan driven away from his place of origin. He is given the key to the shaft of the bottomless pit. The shaft is opened and dense smoke comes out darkening the sun and the air. From the smoke locusts spread over the earth (vv. 2-3). The use of the locusts forms only a link with the analogous plague in Egypt, because the appearance and the activity of these beings have nothing to do with locusts. They do not harm the vegetation, but only mankind, and their description in vv. 7-10 has little to do with locusts. At their head is the "angel of the bottomless pit" whose name in Hebrew is *Abaddon* (ruin, perdition) or in Greek *Apollyon*, the Exterminator (see vv. 4-11).

Scholars usually link this diabolic attack to some future moment, but it is better seen as the spiritual attack against mankind which has been going on from all time from the world of the fallen angels, with Satan at their head. This is the explanation of the limitation of the invasion to men. The diabolic temptation is directed to man, and not to the rest of creation. It has been with man from all time in his desire to be his own master, a proud challenge to heaven and the divinity. The smoke which ascends to darken the sun and the air is a good symbol for it. This challenge is punished, however, and the instruments of the punishment are the very ones who created the pride, the demons. John tells us this symbolically through his use of the locusts which come forth from the smoke to torment mankind.

These torments are unbearable, but they do not produce death. John carefully stresses that point: "They were allowed to torture them for five months, but not to kill them" (9:5). How is this to be understood? In the symbolic sense of the fifth trumpet, we have a description of the original fall of man as a consequence of diabolic temptation, and the consequences of that fall.

These first happen on a physical and material plane, but John is thinking beyond that. He wants to present the torment which flows from the loss of divine life, from the separation from God. This is the suffering which creates the desire of v. 6: "And in those days men will seek death and will not find it; they will long to die, and death will fly from them."

The death which men seek is the loss of their very selves, but the demons do not have the authority to allow that sort of death. They can only mete out torment, take man away from the fullness of life which he has from his contact with God. They have done this by drawing man to pride and guilt.

The spiritual ruin brought by the powers of evil is further indicated by the two names given to the head of the attack: *Abaddon*, which is synonymous with "hell" and *Apollyon,* which means "the one who destroys, who sends things to ruination." There is a clear link between these two names, and the two names, "Death and Hades," which came at the end of the four horsemen of the seals. The action of Satan against man begins in hell (the bottomless pit) and finishes there.

What is the significance of the "five months" which John gives to the action of the locusts? The only satisfactory explanation comes from John's use of the "cosmic week," in which the establishment of the messianic presence of the sixth millennium is always preceded by five millennia of suffering and domination by the powers of evil. We have already seen in the seals, and especially in the special place of the "sixth" seal and trumpet, that John uses this scheme. It must never be forgotten that John is making no suggestion of chronology at all. It is the use of an apocalyptic background to convey a spiritual message. We will find further traces of this in ch. 17, in the explanation of the seven heads of the beast (17:9-11).

The Sixth Trumpet (The Second "Woe") The Value and Limitations of the Old Economy (9:13—11:14)

9 [13] Then the sixth angel blew his trumpet, and I heard a voice from the four horns of the golden altar before God, [14] saying to the sixth angel who had the trumpet, "Release the four angels who are bound at the great river Euphrates.

[15] So the four angels were released, who had been held ready for the hour, the day, the month, and the year, to kill a third of mankind.

[16] The number of the troops of cavalry was twice ten thousand times ten thousand; I heard their number.

[17] And this was how I saw the horses in my vision: the riders wore breastplates the colour of fire and of sapphire and of sulphur, and the heads of the horses were like lions' heads, and fire and smoke and sulphur issued from their mouths.

[18] By these three plagues a third of mankind was killed, by the fire and smoke and sulphur issuing from their mouths.

[19] For the power of the horses is in their mouths and in their tails; their tails are like serpents, with heads, and by means of them they wound.

[20] The rest of mankind, who were not killed by these plagues, did not repent of the works of their hands nor give up worshipping demons and idols of gold and silver and bronze and stone and wood, which cannot either see or hear or walk;

²¹nor did they repent of their murders or their sorceries or their immorality or their thefts.

10 ¹Then I saw another mighty angel coming down from heaven, wrapped in a cloud, with a rainbow over his head, and his face was like the sun, and his legs like pillars of fire.
²He had a little scroll open in his hand. And he set his right foot on the sea, and his left foot on the land,
³and called out with a loud voice, like a lion roaring; when he called out, the seven thunders sounded.
⁴And when the seven thunders had sounded, I was about to write, but I heard a voice from heaven saying, "Seal up what the seven thunders have said, and do not write it down."
⁵And the angel whom I saw standing on sea and land lifted up his right hand to heaven
⁶and swore by him who lives for ever and ever, who created heaven and what is in it, the earth and what is in it, and the sea and what is in it, that there should be no more delay,
⁷but that in the days of the trumpet call to be sounded by the seventh angel, the mystery of God, as he announced to his servants the prophets, should be fulfilled.
⁸Then the voice which I had heard from heaven spoke to me again, saying, "Go, take the scroll which is open in the hand of the angel, who is standing on the sea and on the land."
⁹So I went to the angel and told him to give me the little scroll; and he said to me, "Take it and eat; it will be bitter to your stomach, but sweet as honey in your mouth."
¹⁰And I took the little scroll from the hand of the angel and ate it; it was sweet as honey in my mouth, but when I had eaten it my stomach was made bitter.
¹¹And I was told, "You must again prophesy about many peoples and nations and tongues and kings."

11 ¹Then I was given a measuring rod like a staff, and I was told: "Rise and measure the temple of God and the altar and those who worship there,
²but do not measure the court outside the temple; leave

that out, for it is given over to the nations, and they will trample over the holy city for forty-two months.

³And I will grant my two witnesses power to prophesy for one thousand two hundred and sixty days, clothed in sackcloth."

⁴These are the two olive trees and the two lampstands which stand before the Lord of the earth.

⁵And if any one would harm them, fire pours from their mouth and consumes their foes; if any one would harm them, thus he is doomed to be killed.

⁶They have power to shut the sky, that no rain may fall during the days of their prophesying, and they have power over the waters to turn them into blood, and to smite the earth with every plague, as often as they desire.

⁷And when they have finished their testimony, the beast that ascends from the bottomless pit will make war upon them and conquer them and kill them,

⁸and their dead bodies will lie in the street of the great city which is allegorically called Sodom and Egypt, where their Lord was crucified.

⁹For three days and a half men from the peoples and tribes and tongues and nations gaze at their dead bodies and refuse to let them be placed in a tomb,

¹⁰and those who dwell on the earth will rejoice over them and make merry and exchange presents, because these two prophets had been a torment to those who dwell on the earth.

¹¹But after the three and a half days a breath of life from God entered them, and they stood up on their feet, and great fear fell on those who saw them.

¹²Then they heard a loud voice from heaven saying to them, "Come up hither!" And in the sight of their foes they went up to heaven in a cloud.

¹³And at that hour there was a great earthquake, and a tenth of the city fell; seven thousand people were killed in the earthquake, and the rest were terrified and gave glory to the God of heaven.

¹⁴The second woe has passed; behold, the third woe is soon to come.

As is usual, the sixth trumpet is more fully developed. We can distinguish two groups of visions. The first, a negative sign, takes in the loosing of the four angels tied at the river Euphrates, followed by a dreadful vision of cavalry which kills a third of humanity (9:14-21). The second vision is of the descent of the strong angel from heaven with the small scroll open in his hand (ch. 10), the measuring of the temple (11:1-2) and finally the episode of the two "witnesses" (11:3-14).

The visions in the second group are positive, as interventions in favour of the chosen ones are described. We should notice however that all these visions conclude in a fashion which is not completely negative but still unsatisfactory: the small scroll, when eaten produces bitterness in the stomach; the holy city, the place of the temple, is invaded and trampled down by "the nations" (pagans); the two witnesses are killed and left unburied in the square of Jerusalem, the holy city changes its name into the opposite, Sodom and Egypt.

These unsatisfactory endings are not however, final and definitive. They all point forward to the future positive stage of the seventh trumpet, where the mystery of God will be accomplished. The bitterness of the book is overcome by a new prophecy which is universal (10:11); the bodies of the witnesses are raised and assumed into heaven (11:11-12). Even the invasion of the holy city is presented as a consequence of the exclusion of the pagans from the Temple, and thus the destruction may point to a mysterious plan of God which brings them into contact with revelation and salvation.

WAR AS A CONSEQUENCE OF ORIGINAL SIN

The vision opens with the freeing of the four angels tied at the Euphrates. This scene has contacts with two earlier ones: the chaining of the four winds by the four angels in the sixth seal (see 7:1ff) and the calling forth of the four horsemen of the four living creatures in the first four seals (6:1ff). Common to these scenes, above all, is the scheme: a command comes from on high and imposes the tying or the loosing of four beings which have a nature or an activity which brings evil and destruction.

The correspondence with the earlier times is intentional, even though contrasting, especially in the case of the scene of the sixth seal (chaining of the four winds) and that of the sixth trumpet (loosing of the four angels). That here it is angels, while in ch. 7 it was winds, is not a great difficulty, in so far as John sees created realities (winds) as subject to angels: "After this I saw four angels standing at the four corners of the earth, holding back the four winds of the earth" (7:1). A close relationship remains, even when the elements are used symbolically. In the sixth seal, the four winds represent the diabolical attempt to take possession of the whole earth through violence. It may be possible to see also in the four winds a symbol of the four empires through which, in historical fact, the diabolical power concretely spread its domination. This would also help to explain the difference between the seals and the seventh trumpet. In the sixth seal, the winds and their lords were placed in the four zones of the earth, while in the sixth trumpet they appear to be concentrated upon the Euphrates. On the banks of this river, in fact, the ancient historians normally placed the rising of the first of the great conquering empires.

It is not essential to insist on these historical aspects. John working with this idea which he has from apocalyptic traditions, and especially Daniel, certainly has it in mind, but he is far more interested in conveying to his readers the spiritual meaning of history than history itself. What he describes in this first scene of the sixth trumpet is certainly the scourge of war, and he may be referring to the empires, from which historical wars have their source. It is clear, however, that the scourge is presented in a theological key, as the first and gravest consequence of original sin, the fall of man under the diabolic instigation described in the fifth trumpet.

In fact, the army of horsemen described is more realistic than the locusts in the fifth trumpet. And here, in marked difference from the locusts, men are killed. This has to be understood in a physical way, but the horsemen and their horses are not a historical phenomenon pure and simple. The horses emit strange substances from their nostrils: fire, smoke and sulfur, which are duplicated in the colours imprinted upon the breastplates of the horsemen: bright red, a deep blue; sulphur. The colours of the second, third and fourth horsemen of the seals come to mind: bright red, black and greenish. There are other links between the two scenes. In the sixth trumpet the voice which orders the loosing of the four angels is four-fold: "from the four horns of the golden altar" (9:13), while in the four seals it is the four living creatures who called them forth. In the sixth trumpet, there are three colours, leaving out one from the seals. The colour "white" does not appear here.

It is precisely the absence of "white" which strengthens the impression that the scenes are linked. The scene of the white horse described humanity in its original perfect state. This will also be its final state (see 6:2: "he went out conquering and to conquer"), while the other colours were signs of his decadence, both physical and spiritual, which resulted from original sin. This is why the sixth trumpet recalls only these three colours, and not the first. Here John is describing the condition of humanity after the original sin, already foreshadowed in the fifth trumpet.

It should also be noticed that, in the sixth trumpet, the evils which follow the fall are all concentrated in the scourge of war, while, in the seals, there was a list of different consequences. For John, war is the most serious of the evils, and even in the seals it was the bright red horse and the horseman with the sword which began the list. There is more to it than this, however. The central place of war in the "seven" of the trumpets is due to the fact that John is gradually bringing his message from a symbolic level to a historical level, because God's salvific interventions happen in history. In the "seven" bowls, where the decisive intervention of Jesus Christ is dealt with, this aspect will become even more explicit. This will be especially true of ch. 13 where the great instrument of Satan will appear: the beast from the sea, a sign of corrupt political authority. Nevertheless, this reality has already been clearly foreshadowed here, in the substances which come out of the horses and which are reflected on the shields: red (violence), smoke (pride) and sulphur (spiritual death). Sin, as the biblical tradition had taught John, is made up of these elements: pride which leads to injustice and violence and has death as a result. In this sense sin, before it penetrates the structures (the state, for example), takes over the hearts of men.

THE OLD AND THE NEW REVELATION

The vision of ch. 10, with the mighty angel descending from heaven and offering a small open book, breaks suddenly into the spectacle of desolation created by the cavalry. Again, this break is intentional. The scenes that follow are to be seen as a positive, and in the end victorious, reply to the sea of evil which has come up from the abyss. In fact the angel is not only "mighty," but he is described with characteristics of such majesty and power as to resemble the divinity, and his voice "like a lion roaring" is used in the Old Testament to refer also to the manifestation of Yahweh. John wishes to present this angel as a representative of Yahweh. It is in the name of Yahweh that he offers the book, takes possession of the sea and the land, and solemnly proclaims the coming of "the mystery of God" (10:7).

It is not difficult to see in this detailed scene an allegory on the Old Testament revelation or, to be more precise, to the Covenant set up between God and man in the "former times." The Covenant, according to the traditions which John is following, had the angels as its mediator. It also had various stages:
— the promise made to the couple as they were driven out of Eden
— the pact set up between God and Noah after the flood (see Gen 9:8ff)
— the vocation of Abraham (Gen 12:1ff)
— the actual Covenant set up during the Exodus experience

A great deal of this is summed up in the mighty angel: the rainbow (as at the end of the flood), the legs which are like "pillars of fire" (as those pillars which led Israel in the desert), especially the promise that the "good news" is about to be given "to his servants, the prophets" (10:7).

The clearest indication of the old Covenant, however, is given in the symbol of the small, open book. It is quite evident that John wishes to contrast it with the other book which, in the vision of ch. 5, passed from the hands of the one seated on the throne to the Lamb (5:1ff). That book was a symbol of the work of salvation, the redemption of mankind, which only Jesus Christ was able to perform. The basic symbol of the book handed over by the angel here is the same. It also refers to a salvific intervention of God for mankind, but this is of lesser importance. In fact, the book is described as "small." Three times John uses this diminutive "small" to refer to the book. As well as that, in contrast to the scroll of ch. 5 which was sealed with seven seals which no one except the Lamb could open, the book is described here as already "open" (10:2). Who opened it? John does not say, but in so far as it is not the same as the earlier book, it may well have been the angel. Certainly, it is the angel who brings it to earth. We are now quite aware of the significance and role of the angel: that of the mediator of the Old Covenant.

The small book offered by the angel is, therefore, a symbol of the salvific intervention which took place in the Old Testament. It took place as God revealed himself to man through his word, communicated to man. It appears that two points are important to John: the proclamation of the existence of a unique God, creator of the universe, and the confirmation of the fact that God promised the liberation of mankind from the very beginning of time. From the first truth flows the Law, which John summarises in the commandment to adore the unique God, and to refuse all form of idolatry. From the second we find the heart and substance of prophecy. John always comes back to the Law and the Prophets to characterise the salvific economy of the Old Testament period. We will find that they return again in the two "witnesses." It is also hinted at in the oath of the angel in v. 6:

> "And swore by him who lives forever and ever, who created heaven and what is in it, the earth and what is in it, and the sea and what is in it,"

and the indication that he is about to reveal the "mystery of God," announced to his servants the prophets (10:6-7).

What value does John give the ancient economy? The symbol itself, the same as that used for the action of Christ, the placing of this scene as breaking in upon the infernal invasion, the majesty of the angel – all of this indicates that John sees the small book as a real and efficacious intervention of God for salvation. Nevertheless, as he has already done in the sixth seal, John is always anxious to stress that the Old Economy has its limitations. In the sixth seal this was indicated by the limited number of elect as against the great crowd of humanity. Such clear indications, though not to be found in this instance, are repeated throughout the account. The character of the Old Testament economy as "revelation" is clearly shown. The fact that the book is "open" points in that direction. But all the scene is full of allusions to the transmission of revelation. It is found in the oath of the angel. When he begins to speak he "calls out" (10:3) and also the "seven thunders" (the divinity) speak. John sets out to write what they are saying, but he is prevented (10:4). At the end of the scene, after he has swallowed the small book given by the angel, another voice says to him: "You must again prophesy about many peoples and nations and tongues and kings" (10:11).

This form of revelation is clearly the old one. It is certainly true and valid, but it is incomplete. In fact, the message of the angel is reduced to the announcing of something ("the mystery of God") which will happen in the future. That old revelation is not only incomplete, but in a certain way, John indicates that it is not altogether comprehensible. There is a series of images: the voice, a cry like a roaring lion and claps of thunder. These are traditional images of the Old Testament to indicate the presence of the divinity. They also stress his terrible, inaccessible, impenetrable and incomprehensible majesty. The revelation of the Old Testament is an indirect revelation or, to use John's words, it is "sealed up" (10:4). Only Jesus Christ can open those seals (5:9), i.e., bring to man the word of God in a direct fashion and reveal its true nature. Therefore, after his coming, revelation can take a new direction (10:11) and there will no longer be any seals (22:10: "Do not seal up the words of the prophecy of this book").

But the word of God in the Old Testament is not only incomplete (a pre-announcing) and indirect (under seal). The salvation offered by it is still imperfect. This is the meaning of the swallowing of the book. He is commanded to come and take the book and to swallow it. He is also told that it will be sweet to taste but will turn bitter in the stomach. It happens just like that, and then he is given another command: "You must again prophesy" (10:8-11). John takes this scene from Ezekiel (Ezek 2:1-3, 3) but he adds some very important details. The first is the effect of the eating. In Ezekiel it is only sweetness, but here it is followed by bitterness. The other is the order to prophesy. Ezekiel is told to prophesy to "the house of Israel" with all others excluded. John is told to prophesy "about many peoples and nations and tongues and kings" (10:11).

Again we see the limitations of the old order. As word and Law of God, it certainly does good for the man who meditates and observes it. John takes up here a theme not only from Ezekiel, but from the whole of the Old Testament (see Ps 19:11; 119:103; Jer 15:16), but he adds that in the end it produces bitterness, which in John's language refers to spiritual death (see 8:11). Here we can see the polemics of the early Church, claiming that the Old Testament can be fully understood only in the light of Jesus Christ (see, for example, Rom 3:19ff; 7:5ff).

John sees the bitterness in perhaps a more complete way. It is not a question only of "understanding" the Old Testament, but of seeing the Old Testament as essentially an incomplete divine salvific action. The coming of Jesus completes that action, makes the whole mystery of the Old Testament economy comprehensible, and broadens the salvific intervention of God to the whole of mankind (10:11).

THE MEASURING OF THE TEMPLE

After the descent of the mighty and with the open book (ch. 10), there follows another positive scene, in contrast with the invasion of the infernal cavalry which opened the sixth trumpet. This is the measuring of the temple (11:1-2). Again Old Testament models form the background (Ezek 40:3ff and Zech 2:5ff) and again, however, we find John interpreting them, as he introduces variations. While in the Old Testament the measuring is done in great detail, here we find simply the order that it be measured. We are not told that it happens. John is also warned not to measure the "court outside the temple" (11:2). This is not only found in the Old Testament models, but it appears superfluous, as everyone knew that that court was available to the pagans. Finally, John links the presence of the pagans in that court directly to invasions suffered by the "holy city," Jerusalem, and evidently of the Temple itself.

The general sense of the passage is clear enough. The order to measure the Temple indicates, as in the Old Testament models, that the place is the object of a particular divine affection, chosen by the divinity as his own dwelling, where he receives the cult of his adorers. This is, of course, the Jewish Temple. Coming after the account of the open book, it moves to another important aspect of the old economy: cult. This has already been somewhat anticipated in the liturgical scene which served as an introduction to the "seven" of the trumpets (8:2-5), but here the reference is more precise, clearly speaking of the earthly Temple, and relating it to "the holy city" and to certain historical events (the invasion of pagan peoples). The fact that it is to be measured shows its validity.

As with the revelation transmitted by the angels, the

divine cult prescribed by that revelation was also valid and efficacious. As John showed in the introduction to the "seven," here, too, there is a mediation between God and humanity entrusted to the angels (8:2-5). This does not take away the fact that the Temple was a real Temple, and it was filled with authentic worshippers of the divinity. Nevertheless, John wishes to also show its limitations. This appears in the order not to measure the outside court, "for it is given over to the nations" (11:2). Again John shows that the Jewish cult was restricted only to a portion of humanity, whereas the salvation of Christ was for all. There are other limitations, e.g., the invasion of foreign peoples, a continual experience of the history of Jerusalem and her inhabitants. These invasions produced destruction and desolation, and the original prophecies of Ezekiel and Zechariah were written in the context of the worst of these, the destruction of the Temple of Jerusalem, described and measured in all the beauty of its restoration on the return from the Exile.

That Temple, according to John, was a material temple, tied to a city (Jerusalem) and made of stones. The cult, therefore, had this limitation. Both Temple and cult suffered from the ups and downs of historical experience, of political and military events. Not even the restored Temple was free from that, as the reasonably recent desecration at the hands of Antiochus IV showed clearly.

The authentic cult of the one true God could not be restricted to a material place, restricted to one people only (the chosen people), nor limited by material artifacts, nor subject to the conditioning of time and human history with all its vicissitudes. The cult of the new religion which John followed was an adoration of the Father in Spirit and in truth (see Jn 4:23). John will describe it symbolically in his closing section of the new Jerusalem, where its description will not be interrupted by disastrous events, as here (see 21:9ff). It will be a new reality inaugurated by Christ.

THE "WITNESS" OF THE LAW AND THE PROPHETS TO JESUS CHRIST

The scene of the measuring of the Temple which we find at the beginning of ch. 11 is an allegory of the ancient Jewish cult, truly a valid cult, but provisionary, destined to pass away and to be absorbed into a higher and truer form which is spiritual and universal. John repeats of the ancient cult what he has said of the old revelation. With the revelation, however, there was an idea of continuation, while with the cult there is the idea of an "end," as the pagans trample over it (11:2). They will trample it for "forty-two months" which is a reference to the three and a half years which Daniel described as the worst times of the persecutions of Antiochus IV (see Dan 7:25; 12:7). This means that there is a definite material end, tied to the idea of ruin and physical destruction: the cult ceases because the Temple in which it was performed is, from time to time, systematically destroyed.

It is this reference to the "forty-two months" which suggests the idea of an "end" of Jewish cult, tied to a destruction of the Temple which suggests that the end is spiritual as well as physical. The persecution of Antiochus IV is the background for the whole of the Book of Daniel. Daniel sets up its duration of a "week of years," which he then subdivides into two "half-weeks." The second of these is the worst precisely because the destruction is also spiritual: the profanation of the temple and the prohibition of cult (see Dan 9:26-27).

In ch. 12, John sees symbolised in the week of years of the persecution of Antiochus IV the whole period of the messianic waiting, the period from Adam to Christ. The persecution in the Apocalypse is that waged by Satan against humanity, and he too has his second "half-week" of violence, both physical and spiritual, to be seen in the affairs of the religious history of the Jewish people. At the centre of this argument John places the Temple which, like the Judaism which it represents, has been subject to violence of all sorts: material (destruction by Nabuchadnezzar) and spiritual (profanation and prohibition of Cult: Antiochus IV). In the prophecy of Daniel, also, the phase of spiritual violence against the Temple and cult characterise the second "half-week" of the persecution of Antiochus IV. John then applies the idea of this second "half-week" to designate all of the religious and historical experiences of the Hebrew people. What happens to the Hebrew people, violence and spiritual suffering, is the assault against the first salvific intervention of God (Law, messianic prophecies, Jewish cult).

The episode of the two "witnesses" which now follows, is therefore closely linked to what we have just seen, the Temple, the cult and the "holy city." As these latter were trampled upon and destroyed by foreign powers, agents of Satan, so too are the two "witnesses" slain by "the beast that ascends from the bottomless pit," and their bodies are left in "the street of the great city" clearly Jerusalem (11:7-8). Another link is made through the terms "two olive trees" and "the two lampstands" (11:4). These images are taken from the vision of Zechariah (see Zech 4:3 and 14) and they refer to the construction of the Temple.

Who are these "witnesses"? Most commentators see some reference to Moses and Elijah. This comes from their authority to make fire come down from heaven, to close the sky, preventing rainfall (Elijah: I Kgs 17:1ff; II Kgs 1:10ff), and change water into blood (Moses: Exod 7:14) attributed to them in vv. 5-6. As the apocalyptic literature associates these figures with the coming of the Messiah, commentators see it as an announcing of the end time. Our study of the book leads us in another direction.

It is important, firstly, to remember that we are still in the middle of the sixth trumpet, and that the episode of the two "witnesses" is the third in a series of which the former two (small open book and the measuring of the Temple) referred to the Old Testament economy. The episode of the two "witnesses" is no exception. It is quite clear that under Moses and Elijah we can see a figure of the expression used to speak of the whole of the Old Testament: the Law (Moses) and the Prophets (Elijah).

The meaning of the episode depends upon the concept of "witness" used to name these two characters. How is it to be understood? We are used to seeing this word (Greek: Marturia) used almost exclusively in reference to people who witness to Christ after his coming. In the New Testament itself, however, we can find a use of the word which implies the witnessing to Christ before he came, and this usually happens in a context of polemics with Judaism, over the significance of the Old Testament and its heroes. The concept is very important in the Fourth Gospel: the Old Testament writings and heroes gave witness to Christ (see Jn 5:31ff; 8:54ff; 12:40-41). John the Baptist is often seen as the end of the Old Testament (see Matt 11:13 and esp. Lk 16:16).

It is in this light that we are to explain the episode of the two "witnesses." They symbolise the witnesses to Jesus given by the Law (Moses) and the Prophets (Elijah), before his coming. This very issue stands at the heart of the Gospel accounts of the Transfiguration (see Mk 9:2-12; Matt 17:1-3; Lk 9:28-36). In this way, the duration of their witnessing is also explained: "one thousand two hundred and sixty days" (v. 3), which is the same as the "forty-two months" during which the "holy city" is under pagan attack (11:2). In other words, through all the physical and spiritual suffering of the Hebrew people, this witness was active, i.e., throughout the whole story of the Old Testament economy.

How was this double testimony, Law and messianic prophecy, expressed? Only in word? John's use of the episode of the two "witnesses" shows that if the two figures symbolise what they represent, then what they represent is something absolutely real and concrete. It is a question of people who are slain precisely because they stand for these two basic aspects of the Old Economy: the Law and the prophetic mission. They are killed because of these two, and as John explains later (19:10) this means that they are killed because of their witness to Christ.

We discover, in this way, a profound unity between various groups in the Apocalypse:
- those in the fifth seal who are slain "because of the word of God and the testimony which they bore" (6:9).
- those who descend from the Women, "those who keep the commandments of God and bear testimony to Jesus" (12:17), and are pursued and slain by the dragon
- those "saints, who keep the commandments of God and the faith of Jesus" who fall victim to the violence of the beast (14:12).

The theme runs even further, as in ch. 20, speaking of the reign of a thousand years, John says that the only ones who are admitted, to the exclusion of all others are "the souls of those who had been beheaded for their testimony to Jesus and for the word of God" (20:4). Their blessedness lies in their reigning with Christ and being priests of God (20:6). They participate, *after death*, in a fullness of life which is exactly the same as that offered to the followers of Christ, *already in* this life (1:6: "He has made us a kingdom, priests to his God and Father"). The situation of those participating in the reign of a thousand years is exactly the same as that of those killed from the fifth seal. *After death* they are "under the altar," they receive "white garments" and they are asked to "rest" for a certain time (6:9, 11). Here also the slain receive, *after death*, "white garments" (i.e., the communication of the divine life) which the followers of Christ possess *already in this life* (3:4; 3:18; 7:14). In both cases it is temporary, as they are both waiting for something further: in ch. 6 it is the number of the elect, while in ch. 20 it is the "thousand years."

John is describing something similar in his episode of the two "witnesses." They are also slain for the witness given to the Law and to the prophetic mission. After death they are called to a new life and invited to go up to heaven (11:11-12). This is a resurrection, but it has to be understood in a particular fashion. Notice that they are not simply restored to the life which they had formerly. What enters them and makes them "stand up on their feet," a symbol in the Apocalypse of resurrection, is "a breath of life from God" (v. 11). They receive a communication of life from God himself. This is exactly the same gift as is symbolised by the "white garments," given to the martyrs of the fifth seal and to those participating in the reign of a thousand years. Similar also is the provisional nature of what is given to the "witnesses." They too have to wait for the fulfilment of the "mystery of God" which has been announced by the mighty angel (10:7). Here, as in the fifth seal and the reign of a thousand years, we are in the moment which comes *before* the decisive salvific intervention of God, the decisive judgment of God on the world which is, for John, the death and resurrection of Jesus.

All these, the slain of the fifth seal, the two witnesses and the final participants in the reign of a thousand years reap the benefits of the final and decisive intervention of God in Jesus *before* it actually takes place. This, however, is given *only* after a death of a certain type and quality: those who are slain because of witness given to the word of God (the Law) and its promise of messianic redemption (Prophets).

The Apocalypse clearly looks to those who in the Old Economy gave their lives in this witness, because, in John's vision, their deaths have in some way anticipated the death of Christ. John makes it clear that the privileges are not the result of their own deaths – they are "under the altar" (6:9), i.e., already inserted into the death of Christ:

— they are signed with the sign of the living God (7:2).

The same point will be made in later chapters:

— 144 thousand will stand *with the Lamb* on Mt. Sion (14:1)
— those who conquer against the beast sing the hymn of Moses *and of the Lamb* upon a sea of glass (15:2-3)
— those who participated in the reign of a thousand years live and reign with Christ (20:4-6).

As far as the "witnesses" are concerned, this relationship with the sacrifice of Christ is shown by the similarity between their deaths and resurrection to the death and

resurrection of Jesus, whose crucifixion is explicitly recalled (11:8). There is one important difference: because of their enemies, their bodies are not buried, but left in the street of Jerusalem, while Jesus' burial is in all the Gospels (and Paul). This is significant. In the New Testament the burial of Jesus is important for:
— resurrection from the dead as a salvific act, a new creation
— Jesus' descent to the dead, to save the holy ones of old (Acts 2:31; Rom 10:7; Eph 4:8ff; I Peter 3:19).

The fact that there is *no* burial would indicate that this death is not salvific, neither for themselves or for others. Their resurrection is also different. They do not take up life again, but are given life and called up to heaven, all normal "post death" experiences for the follower of Jesus in the period of the Church.

The rest of the details are close to the experience of Jesus, even the three and a half days (see Matt 12:38ff), and this is to be linked here also with Daniel's theory of a "half-week" of suffering.

THE END OF JERUSALEM AND OF JUDAISM

Among the points which link the experience of the "witnesses" and Jesus is the earthquake which accompanies their resurrection. In the Apocalypse, the resurrection of the witnesses produces an earthquake which destroys a tenth of the city (evidently Jerusalem) and causes the death of seven thousand men (see 11:13). Earthquake is a sign which accompanies the *judging* intervention of God. John uses it often. We found it at the opening of the sixth seal (6:12); we find it at the end of the sixth trumpet (destruction of Jerusalem); we find it again at the end of the seventh bowl (the destruction of Babylon in 16:18ff).

It appears clear that John uses the symbol to indicate the beginning and the end, i.e., the totality of the intervention of God in history. The conclusion of the account of the two "witnesses" probably gives us the explanation of this fact.

An earthquake accompanies the resurrection of the "witnesses" and also of Jesus (see Matt 28:2). It also accompanies the death of Jesus (see Matt 27:51ff). There is a clear link. What is going on through the whole of the witness of the Old Testament, from its beginnings will come to its culmination in the death and resurrection of Jesus. It is always *judging* activity. Here in Apoc 11 the witnesses receive life and are taken to heaven, while the city which has refused their witness and slain them is destroyed and its own inhabitants slain.

At the stage of the "witnesses" God's intervention is still only partial. It will not be fulfilled until the sounding of the seventh trumpet and the "mystery of God" (10:7) is fulfilled. As well as that, we have seen that only to the witnesses is given a reward, and only to a part of the city and its inhabitants is the punishment meted out. The city which was earlier called "the holy city" now no longer has a name indicating its spiritual value. Its name is changed to "Sodom and Egypt" (v. 8). All of this indicates that there is worse to come, i.e., the final repudiation of the city, i.e., Judaism itself. Again we are in a biblical and New Testament tradition, as Jesus quoted Jeremiah 12:7 (see also 22:5): "Your house is forsaken and desolate" (Matt 23:38), and refers immediately to the total destruction of the Temple:

> "Truly, I say to you, there will not be left here one stone upon another, that will not be thrown down" (Matt 24:1).

In this way the account of the two "witnesses" concludes the exposition of the Old Economy which began in ch. 10 with the descent of the mighty angel. John has shown the value of the announcing and the testimony of that economy, as it looked forward to the future fulfilment of the "mystery of God." He has also indicated it limitations. The same must be said of the witnesses. Despite all their positive aspects, on the level of history, the final victor is "the beast that ascends from the bottomless pit" (11:7), Satan. This victory lies not so much in the slaying of the "witnesses" as in the profanation and corruption of the "holy city," which becomes

"Sodom and Egypt." It is this aspect which gives to the sixth trumpet its character as a "woe" (the second "woe"). Even though the Old Economy was an intervention of God, Satan still appears to be victorious. After having tempted man and caused him to fall from his position of privilege and friendship with God (fifth trumpet, first "woe"), he continues to persecute him during the whole of his history on earth, corrupting political authority and making it his instrument for the oppression and death of mankind (the invasion of the cavalry) and finally destroyed the "holy city," a symbol of God's first intervention in Judaism (the slaying of the two "witnesses").

The responsibility for the slaying seems to belong to Jerusalem. Did Jerusalem do it or allow it to happen? There is not a great difference. In fact, John says that it is the beast which ascends from the bottomless pit which kills them (11:7), an expression which clearly refers to Satan here. We must notice however that in ch. 13 the term "beast" will be used to indicate the two historical instruments which Satan uses to slay the just ones: corrupt religious and political authority. There is a close collaboration between the two, and it is, in fact, this collusion between corrupt political and religious authority which sets up, in practice, the ascent of Satan from the bottomless pit.

But that is yet to come. Here it is still implicit. It will be fulfilled when the two authorities combine, not to slay the two "witnesses," who are precursors and models, but to slay Jesus Christ. Then Satan will really appear to have come up from the pit and to have had a total victory. Then Jerusalem will no longer be "Sodom and Egypt," but Babylon (ch. 17) and her destruction will be celebrated in ch. 18.

Certainly the Babylon of chs. 17-18 is not only Jerusalem, but all the wicked presence of Satan in corrupt political and religious authority wherever it is found; but the documented history of Jerusalem, the slaying of the prophets and then of Jesus Christ himself, represents the most wicked success story of Satan. For this reason, after the resurrection of the "witnesses" she is struck down by an earthquake, a symbol of the divine judgment which condemns her and destines her to destruction.

The earthquake is only a pre-announcing of that which will cover Babylon after the pouring out of the seventh bowl which is a symbol of the death of Jesus. The city struck is clearly the same, given the same title: "the great city" (11:8 and 16:19), but the second destruction is total. This total destruction will be a symbol of the end of Jerusalem in all its manifestations (Law, revelation, cult), the definitive repudiation of Israel with its dreams of a political Messiah.

It is not only the end of Judaism. Not only in the slaying of Christ is the perversion of Jerusalem wiped out, but the consummate collusion of corrupt political and religious authority within her has come to pass and Satan has risen from the bottomless pit.

Babylon is a symbol of all this. The earthquake which destroys her at the pouring out of the seventh bowl, i.e., at the death of Christ, will mark the final end of Satanic domination over mankind.

The Seventh Trumpet (The Third "Woe"): The Fulfilment of the "Mystery of God" (11:15-19)

> 11:15 Then the seventh angel blew his trumpet, and there were loud voices in heaven, saying, "The kingdom of the world has become the kingdom of our Lord and of his Christ, and he shall reign for ever and ever."
> 16 And the twenty-four elders who sit on their thrones before God fell on their faces and worshipped God,
> 17 saying, "We give thanks to thee, Lord God
>   Almighty, who art and who
>   wast,
> that thou hast taken thy great
> power and begun to reign.
> 18 The nations raged, but thy wrath
>   came,

and the time for the dead to be
judged,
for rewarding thy servants, the
prophets and saints,
and those who fear thy name,
both small and great,
and for destroying the destroyers of
the earth."

¹⁹Then God's temple in heaven was opened, and the ark of his covenant was seen within his temple; and there were flashes of lightning, voices, peals of thunder, an earthquake, and heavy hail.

We already know the contents of the seventh trumpet: "the mystery of God" announced by the mighty angel in 10:7. We have already had clear hints of what the mystery might be. After the sounding of the seventh trumpet, a heavenly choir is heard, praising the establishment of the Reign of God and his messiah on earth (11:15). We shall see in 11:17 that it is a messianic reign whose beginning is presented as a putting into action the ultimate and definitive judgment of God: judgment upon the dead, retribution for the just, condemnation and destruction for the evil ones "the destroyers of the earth" (11:18).

The "mystery of God" is fulfilled in the coming of the messianic kingship and the universal judgment which established that kingship. These, for John, are positive, but the seventh trumpet is still the third "woe," clearly announced in v. 14:

"The second woe has passed; behold the third woe is soon to come."

While it is explicitly announced at the end of the first and second "woe" that they are over, this is not said of the third (see 9:12 and 11:14), which is explained by the fact that the "seven" which follows, the bowls, is a further taking up of the last three trumpets, and especially the final trumpet. It is sufficient to notice that John places the handing over and the pouring out of the bowls between the opening of the Temple of God in heaven (15:5) and the appearance of lightning, voices, thunder, earthquakes, etc. (16:18), both of which (heavenly Temple and commotion) are reported *together* in 11:19 at the end of the seventh trumpet.

Most of the problems which have arisen for the interpretation of the seventh trumpet come from its having been traditionally understood as referring to the end of the world, the "mystery of God" which is the establishment of his reign and judgment outside of history. This is not the case. The "mystery of God" is the coming of the liberation and the redemption which have come about in and through the death of Christ. This is what John means by the fulfilment of the "mystery of God," the judgment of the world and the beginning of the messianic kingdom (see 1:5-6).

Therefore, as in the seventh seal, so also in the seventh trumpet, the theme is the death of Christ. Here also, as there, the event itself is not described, but only its effects. In the seventh seal there was a brief interruption in the angelic liturgy. In both places there is something new in the functions and prerogatives of the angelic world. We have two allegorical scenes:

— the prostration of the angelic court (11:16)
— the opening of the heavenly Temple which allows the ark of the Covenant to be seen (11:19)

We have seen in chs. 4-5 that the prostration of the angels signifies a subjection of all their powers (governing the world and mediation in cult) to the universal lordship of Christ. Here the prostration seems to accentuate their loss of position in the domination of the world. In fact, only the twenty-four Elders who were described in ch. 4 with regal characteristics (thrones and golden crowns: 4:4) are mentioned. This is quite understandable in a context which celebrates the advent of the messianic kingdom:

> "The kingdom of the world has become the kingdom of our Lord and his Christ, and he shall reign for ever and ever" (11:15).

The second scene, the opening of the Temple, is only indirectly connected with the angels. The opening must mean the tearing down of the veil which separates the body of the Temple from the "holy of holies," where the Ark was kept. The Ark was always hidden, but now it is available to all who would wish to look, so John's message is clearly that there is a change in the structure of the temple, a change and an end of a certain type of cult – i.e., the ancient cult presided over by the angels.

This opening of the heavenly Temple which ends the seventh trumpet is parallel to the "silence for about a half an hour" which took place at the end of the seventh seal, and it indicates the same thing: the interruption of the angelic liturgy. But the real significance of the scene takes us even further. The interruption is further clarified by the scene of the angel taking the fire from the altar and casting it upon the ground, which appeared in the prologue to this "seven" (see 8:5). There the gesture of the angel was followed by thunder, voices, lightning and earthquake, as here in the opening of the Temple.

But the opening of the Temple, in comparison with the silence of the seventh seal, is clearer in another sense. In both cases the events happen "in heaven," but the heavenly Temple, for John and his readers, was a model of the Jewish Temple on earth (see Exod 25:9, 40). What happens in the heavenly Temple happens also in the earthly model. Thus the opening of the Temple is an explicit reference to the death of Christ, as we know from all the synoptic Gospels, where the death of Jesus is marked by the tearing asunder of the veil before the Holy of Holies (see Mk 15:38; Lk 23:45). Thus the death of Christ, symbolised by the opening of the Temple in the seventh trumpet, is the fulfilment of the "mystery of God" announced earlier as for "in the days of the trumpet call to be sounded by the seventh angel" (10:7).

In this way it is also a "woe." The death of Christ has boundless positive effects, but it is also the moment of the judgment of God upon the world. In this sense, the death of Christ is a "woe" which strikes the earth, both because it brings to a pitch the wicked activity of Satan and because, in this apparent victory of the forces of evil, they are definitively destroyed.

Certainly, the positive effects of the event are also clear here. They are found, above all, in the hymn raised by the heavenly voices. What happens at the level of action, prostration of the Elders, opening of the Temple, lightning, voices, thunder, earthquake and hail, all looks in another direction, that of judgment and condemnation: the end of the angelic mediation and of the Jewish cult. This opening of the Temple also points to a vaster revelation, a freer access to the divinity, a theme found elsewhere in the New Testament (see, for example, Heb 6:19-20; 9:3, 6-12).

THE SEVEN BOWLS (12:1—22:5)

THEME: The second stage of the redemption. The death of Christ as the judgment of God: the destruction of the evil forces and the gathering of the chosen ones.

Structure and General Theme

The so-called second part of the Apocalypse, which runs from ch. 12 almost to the end of the book, develops one theme only: the death of Christ as the judgment of God on the world and on history and the two consequences of this, the destruction of the forces of evil and the gathering of those chosen to become part of the new people of God, founded by Christ.

The theme is gathered around the "seven" of the bowls which, in itself, happens rapidly (chs. 15-16). In this case, all the elements of the seven have the same content: the historical death of Jesus. The theme has a very full preparation, running from ch. 12 to ch. 14. Both in the preparation and in the seven bowls themselves there is a continual recalling, deepening and historicising of the content of the preceding "sevens," especially the seals (in chs. 13-14) and the trumpets (in ch. 12 and then in chs. 15 and 16). Then comes even further explanation, again very full, in chs. 17-22, where we find that there is a repeated recalling of the seven letters, in relation to the two effects of the death of Christ.

Thus, both the preparation and the further explanation of the theme is really made up of the preceding "sevens" (letters, seals and trumpets). What is significant, however, is that the discussion is carried on at a much more clearly *historical* level. In the "seven" of the bowls, man is at the centre of the stage.

In fact, even if the struggle is always between the forces of evil and of good, the episodes of the struggle are now seen as events which form a part of concrete human history. The action of Satan is seen as the wicked collusion between two human agents: political and religious authority (the two beasts of ch. 13), joined to damage mankind, and now instruments for the domination of Death and Hades. Even the divine intervention is no longer indirect, through the intermediary angels. It takes place in the Incarnation of Christ (ch. 19).

For this reason, the "seven" of the bowls has the visions as "signs." The "sign" is a concrete, extraordinary intervention of God in history to defend and to free his people. The Old Testament spoke of it in the liberation of the Hebrew people from Egypt. This was the supreme divine intervention. John, while accepting the reality and the value of that intervention, is convinced that the only true and definitive intervention took place in Jesus Christ, because it touched no longer just one people, but the whole of humanity. The activity of Satan is no longer just *contained* (ch. 12: Satan thrown down to the earth; ch. 20: Satan bound) but eliminated forever (ch. 20: Satan thrown into the lake of fire and sulphur).

Despite the efforts of scholars to find seven signs in the "seven" of the bowls, there are only three: the "sign" of the woman, the "sign" of the dragon (see 12:1 and 3) and the angels who have the bowls (see 15:1). In these three "signs" are contained the whole of human history, understood as a history of salvation: the creation of Man (1st sign), the fall of man through diabolic temptation, yet the promise of redemption (2nd sign), the putting into action of the redemption of man through the work of Jesus Christ (3rd sign). In the three "signs" are shown the power of God, a power which gives life to man, just as the three "woes" of the last three trumpets (see 8:13ff) showed the activity of Satan. This activity brought death to man, a corruption of his human nature and the loss of his original privileges (1st woe); the corruption of political authority in wars and destruction, together with the corruption of religious authority in the slaying of the two witnesses (2nd woe); and the slaying of Christ (3rd woe). The very arrangement of the material gives to the event of the death of Christ (foreshadowed through the image of a bowl) a central position in the development of the theme. The theme has, of course, been with us from the very first lines of the book, and has been carried on in the vision of the Son of man in ch. 1, that of the Lamb in ch. 5, always, as we have seen, based on Daniel's vision of the Son of man coming on the clouds (Dan 7:13-14).

The vision of the Lamb and the use of Daniel return to play a central role in this section of the Apocalypse (see ch. 14). They have the function of linking the internal logic of the section itself and also looking back to the earlier sections. This confirms what we have already said about the central function of this messianic vision of Daniel in the composition of John's book. As always, this basic text will be entwined with other biblical citations which are used according to a definitive plan and criterion. A first group of citations will refer to that original situation – no longer of the Hebrew people at the Exodus (heavily present in the earlier sections, and still used here) – but of the origins of the whole of humanity described in the Book of *Genesis*. This is particularly the case of ch. 12. Another group of texts seems to come from history books, Psalms and Prophets, all linked with the end of the Kingdom of Judah, with the Exile and the hopes of a future return and restoration. This will appear especially in the second part of the section, where John describes the effects of the death of Christ: judgment and redemption. Especially prominent are passages from

Ezekiel, Zechariah (reconstruction of Jerusalem and the Temple) along with the later Isaiah and Daniel on the times and the form of the establishment of the messianic kingdom.

At the end of the section, in the description of the defeat of Satan (ch. 20) and the new Jerusalem, the two motifs (Genesis and prophecy on restoration) are blended, to stress skilfully that the restoration brought about by the death of Jesus does not touch only the Hebrew people, but the whole of humanity. The destruction remedied by Christ is not only that caused by Nabuchadnezzar on a material level, but also that caused from the very beginnings of humanity, on a spiritual level by Satan. In fact, the material destruction symbolised by Nabuchadnezzar, and all violence on a material level along with him, is a consequence of that original spiritual destruction.

The great length of this final "seven," when compared with the others, is explained by the importance and centrality of the argument which John sees as fundamental. Here the "revelation of Jesus Christ" reaches its highest moment, the death of Christ. From the point of view of the internal links between the "sevens," that of the bowls is seen as a development of the seventh trumpet. That moment concluded with the opening of the Temple of God in heaven, followed by lightning, voices, thunder and earthquake which follows the final bowl (16:18). But, as we saw earlier, the "seven" of the trumpets can be seen as a development of the sixth and seventh seal. There will also be a deliberate recalling of the seals, especially the sixth and the seventh, in the "seven" of the bowls.

Exegetes have always seen these links, and there have been many attempts to explain them. Perhaps it is not possible to discover rules for John. From what we have seen, we can already say that he has only one theme: "the revelation of Jesus Christ," and this varies, according to the perspective from which he is looking at it. Thus the series of "sevens" are best seen not as a chain of events but as a series in succession, progressively carrying the same argument further and deeper. It remains true, of course, that we are dealing with "events" in history, of which the Cross of Jesus is the culmination. This series of events has been taken up in *all* the sevens, all of which have concluded in the same moment, the Cross of Jesus Christ. This is why there are always close links between the last two elements of each "seven," because here the central and culminating issue is being discussed in all the "sevens."

THE PREFACE TO THE "SEVEN" OF THE BOWLS: THE FIRST TWO "SIGNS" (12—14)

The Creation and Fall of Man (ch. 12)

12 ¹And a great prophet appeared in heaven, a woman clothed with the sun, with the moon under her feet, and on her head a crown of twelve stars;
²she was with child and she cried out in her pangs of birth, in anguish for delivery.
³And another portent appeared in heaven; behold, a great red dragon, with seven heads and ten horns, and seven diadems upon his heads.
⁴His tail swept down a third of the stars of heaven, and cast them to the earth. And the dragon stood before the woman who was about to bear a child, that he might devour her child when she brought it forth;
⁵she brought forth a male child, one who is to rule all the nations with a rod of iron, but her child was caught up to God and to his throne,
⁶and the woman fled into the wilderness, where she has a place prepared by God, in which to be nourished for one thousand two hundred and sixty days.

⁷Now war arose in heaven, Michael and his angels fighting against the dragon; and the dragon and his angels fought,
⁸but they were defeated and there was no longer any place for them in heaven.
⁹And the great dragon was thrown down, that ancient serpent, who is called the Devil and Satan, the deceiver of the whole world – he was thrown down to the earth, and his angels were thrown down with him.
¹⁰And I heard a loud voice in heaven, saying, "Now the salvation and the power and the Kingdom of our God and the authority of his Christ have come, for the accuser of our brethren has been thrown down, who accuses them day and night before our God.
¹¹And they have conquered him by the blood of the Lamb and by the word of their testimony, for they loved not their lives even unto death.
¹²Rejoice then, O heaven and you that dwell therein! But woe to you, O earth and sea, for the devil has come down to you in great wrath, because he knows that his time is short!"
¹³And when the dragon saw that he had been thrown down to the earth, he pursued the woman who had borne the male child.
¹⁴But the woman was given the two wings of the great eagle that she might fly from the serpent into the wilderness, to the place where she is to be nourished for a time, and times, and half a time.
¹⁵The serpent poured water like a river out of his mouth after the woman, to sweep her away with the flood.
¹⁶But the earth came to the help of the woman, and the earth opened its mouth and swallowed the river which the dragon had poured from his mouth.
¹⁷Then the dragon was angry with the woman, and went off to make war on the rest of her offspring, on those who keep the commandments of God and bear testimony to Jesus.
¹⁸And he stood on the sand of the sea.

THE "SIGN" OF THE DRAGON

With ch. 12 the presentation of the first two "signs" begins, approaching human history as under the wicked influences of Satan who, after having led humanity into disobedience and causing it to lose its original privileges wishes to bring it completely under his dominion, a dominion of Death and Hades. This presentation goes on till the end of ch. 14 and takes up themes and motives which have been developed earlier. Here, however, they come back in less obscure form and more clearly situated within historical reality.

The narrative of ch. 12 is made up of an implacable hostility between a woman and a dragon. These are, of course, two symbols. We must not see the symbol of the woman, which we will later consider in detail, as an analogy of a person signified, even though it is closely associated with a human reality. The same thing must be said for the dragon. We must not look at "dragons" as such, because the ultimate source of the image is found in its biblical allusions. It comes from Genesis and is a recalling of the story of the temptation. This is made quite explicit in 12:9, where John identifies the dragon with "that ancient serpent, who is called the Devil and Satan, the deceiver of the whole world."

The symbol, nevertheless, keeps the external signs of a dragon: red colour, seven heads, ten horns, seven diadems, one for each head (12:3). John has added this dragon aspect, changing the serpent model from Genesis. Why? He will take up this symbol, with slight variations, in chs. 13 and 17, and will give a fuller explanation in ch. 17, which we will examine there. For the moment we will suggest some possible origins for this curious presentation. It probably comes from Daniel's use of the seventy weeks of waiting for the Messiah (7 × 10. See Dan 9:24ff). If this is the case, then we can see John bringing his symbols closer to history, a feature of this section. We must ask how this dragon can be a "sign in heaven." If, as I claimed above, "sign" is a manifestation of the creative and life-giving power of God, the dragon is such. This is so because, according to the Jewish tradition which John is following (an echo of it is also found in Gen 3:1) he was the most noble, intelligent and perfect of all creatures. Therefore, in the dragon John wishes to summarise the creation of the angelic world, presented as one "sign in heaven," face to face with another "sign," the woman, that is, the world of human beings.

It is precisely the most perfect among the creatures then who harbours ideas of jealousy towards God, and has plans of rebellion. Because of this, his perfection is changed to misery, and he thus presents himself before the woman as a monstrous and murderous dragon. Then follows the presentation of the woman and her descendents. For John this persecution is the continual temptation from the dragon to cause man who had been promised a glorious future (Wis 2:23-24), to break from God. It happens for the first time, with terrible results, in the garden of Eden.

THE "SIGN" OF THE WOMAN AND THE SON

The symbol of the woman is much more complex. Most commentators see her as representing some historical reality, and the various suggestions can be summed up in three major ones: Israel, the Virgin Mary and the Church. It appears to me that the reality symbolised is much vaster than any of these interpretations. In fact, as the symbol of the dragon can only be fully understood by seeing how it is used throughout the whole of the section, so it must be with the symbol of the woman. The author takes up the theme of a woman, certainly with variations, in the prostitute of ch. 17 and the spouse of the Lamb in ch. 21 (see 17:1ff and 21:9ff). Through all the differences, the basic symbol of "woman" mentioned in ch. 12 for the first time, remains.

We will come back to the connections between these three "woman" figures, but already in ch. 12 it is clear that any identification of "the woman" with the suggestions made above is too narrow. All three (Israel, Mary, Church) could fill the description of v. 1: "A woman clothed with the sun, with the moon under her feet, and on her head a crown of twelve stars"; but the next verse already causes difficulty for any of them: "She was with child, and she cried out in her pangs of birth, in anguish for delivery" (v. 2). All agree that the child to be born is Jesus Christ, but this is precisely what causes the difficulty for further interpretation of the figure, and really needs further consideration. In fact, there is only one characteristic of the child which suggests that it might be Christ: "one who is to rule all the nations with a rod of iron" (v. 5). This is a messianic attribute (see Ps 2:9) and will be applied to Jesus in 19:15, but it is not *only* that. It also expresses one of the two characteristics which the "kings and priests" (1:6) of the new humanity redeemed by Christ will have, and it forms part of the "promise to the conqueror" in the letter to Thyatira (see 2:21ff).

Nothing tells us that the ruling over the nations which will be the destiny of this Son must be restricted to Jesus and not to the one who has been promised the same prerogative if he has faith in Jesus and gives witness to him. It could be the case that the child carried by the woman is a symbol of the promises made by God to mankind right from the first moments of creation. In fact, it is impossible that the child be Jesus. John writes: "She brought forth a male child, one who is to rule all the nations with a rod of iron, but her child was caught up to God and to his throne" (v. 5). To see this as a reference to the ascension is not impossible, but what of the punishment, violence and persecution which happens to the woman as a result of this action? One also needs to explain the use of a strong expression which says that the child was "caught up," or better "torn away." How is all this to be explained if the child is Jesus Christ and the woman one of the three realities suggested by scholarship? Only as "Israel" can it be explained: Christ, even though born from Israel, has been taken from her because of her lack of faith. How then are we to explain the care and attention which God gives to the woman after the child has been taken away?

THE DESERT

The relationship which John sets up between the symbol of the woman and that of the desert is the other element which must be accounted for, if we hope properly to understand the significance of this female figure. Some scholars see the desert as a reference to some historical fact, e.g., the flight of the Christians from Jerusalem in 70 A.D. Others go in the opposite direction and explain it away as a metaphor to speak of a brief period of difficulty, physical or moral persecution, temptation.

The desert has a profound and clear biblical background, even if ambivalent: it is a place of refuge, but also of difficult trials, of encounter with God, but also of diabolic temptation. This ambivalent character of the symbol of the desert, found in the lives of many biblical personalities (Abraham, David, Elijah, Jesus himself) has it basic source in the situation of the Hebrew people after their liberation from Egypt and the crossing of the Red Sea. The desert was for them a place of refuge against aggression, a place of privileged encounter with God (Sinai), but also a place of difficult physical and moral trials, of temptation and sin.

It is in this sense that "the desert" is used here. For the woman it is a place of refuge, as God extends his protecting wing and gives his providential care (v. 6). It does not however have only positive characteristics. The woman flees there after she has lost the fruit of her womb. The protection offered has to be seen as totally spiritual, because it is clear that physical violence reaches her there, as "war arose" (v. 7), and the dragon departed "to make war on the rest of her offspring" (v. 17). Moreover, her presence in the desert is for a strictly limited period: "one thousand, two hundred and sixty days" (v. 6) or, for a period which is the same: "for a time, two times and half a time" (v. 14). As we have seen, this period of three and a half was the time of persecution, the preaching of the two witnesses (11:3), the pagan domination over the holy city (11:2) and we will see, the authority granted to the activity of the beast from the sea (13:5).

THE TWO FLIGHTS INTO THE DESERT

John's insistence upon the period of time makes us ask if there is, beyond this symbolic meaning, reference to a historical situation. We know that the reference is not to three and a half chronological years, but to a period of persecution, but can this be further specified? From v. 13 onwards it looks as if a definite situation is described. The devil, thrown down from heaven to the earth, rages against the woman, but she escapes from his assault, lifting off into flight, and escaping into the desert with the wings of an eagle which she is given. The dragon tries again, vomiting against the woman a flood of water to drown her, but the earth saves the woman, opening up and swallowing the water (12:13-16).

It is not difficult to trace in this allegorical account the basic lines of the Exodus event under the protection of God: the crossing of the Red Sea and the gift of revelation (the Law and the Prophets; "the two wings of the great eagle" – see Exod 19:4; Deut 32:11). There is a further allusion to the Law and the Prophets when the "seed" of the woman pursued by the dragon is further described as "those who keep the commandments of God and bear testimony to Jesus (v. 17).

Is Israel, then, the woman who waits and then gives birth to a son, loses him and then flees to the desert? Many have suggested such an interpretation, and there is a great deal of Old Testament background for Israel as a woman (see Is 37:22; 54:1; 62:4; Ezek 16:1ff; Hos 2:2ff; Cant *passim*). Behind the cosmic images used to describe the woman could be Joseph's dream in Gen 37:9. All of this seems to solve the problem.

Before the flight into the desert which we have just described John mentions another, immediately after the woman has given birth and has had the child taken from her (12:6): "And the woman fled into the wilderness." Is it the same flight? All take it for granted, but it may not be so. The repetition of the same incident so quickly would seem pointless; the only thing that coincides is the duration of the period; the circumstance of the two flights seem to be profoundly different, as between them there is the account of the fall of the angels. This must have some particular significance.

THE FALL OF THE ANGELS

The first flight of the woman into the desert is mentioned immediately after John tells us that the woman gave birth to a son, who was taken from her. If one is not a consequence of the other, they are, at least, linked. The woman goes into the desert *after* the son is taken from her. In any case, the "desert" represents for the woman a change of "place." She is no longer "in heaven" (v. 1), but "in the desert" (v. 6), even though she is under the care and providence of God. The situation of the woman who appeared as "a great sign in heaven" is clearly changed.

At this point John, after having finished dealing with one "sign in heaven," returns to the other "sign in heaven," represented by the dragon. What he now describes (vv. 7-12) is still something that takes place "in heaven," an epic battle between the rebellious angels and the faithful angels, led respectively by Satan and Michael (12:7ff). It is a clash between two different attitudes towards God: one is "the deceiver of the whole world," as we know from Genesis, a creature who asserted that one could be like God (Gen 3:5). The other attitude proclaims: "Who is like unto God." This is what the name Michael means in Hebrew. The result of the battle is unfavourable for the rebels, and they are driven out of heaven forever (v. 8). Satan is cast down upon earth, and the voices which celebrate the victory of the faithful ones announce already to the earth the "woes" which his presence will bring. They begin immediately:

> "And when the dragon saw that he had been thrown down to the earth, he pursued the woman who had born the male child" (v. 13).

The woman flees a second time into the desert on the wings of the great eagle, but even there her adversary follows and attacks her ferociously, turning then to persecute her offspring, i.e., the just ones who observe the Law of God and give witness to Christ who must come (12:17).

This second flight is, evidently, the continuation of the first, but it is not the same. What John has described between the two flights has changed the "place" and the circumstances of the diabolic aggression against the woman. What was one, for both of them "in heaven," is not on earth. A clear indication that John is referring to earthly events and experience, the progress of human history.

The devil has been thrown down as a result of his failed rebellion. We will know from what follows that this is not a final defeat. He has received a mortal wound (13:3) which has reduced his power, and this will be also shown in his chaining in 20:1ff. For the moment he is described as standing still "on the sand of the sea" (v. 17), meditating his return to the history of mankind, to carry on his rebellion against God and his project of world domination through the agencies of corrupt political and religious authority (ch. 13).

This story of the experience of the devil, told in ch. 12 and made even more explicit in what follows, has already been told in more veiled terms in the earlier parts of the book, especially in the "seven" of the trumpets:
— falling of the stars and other heavenly bodies on the earth and the sea (1st four trumpets)
— the influence of the devils who come up from the bottomless pit to torment mankind (5th trumpet)
— the corruption of political and religious authority: wars, destruction, the slaying of the witnesses (6th trumpet)

CREATION AND FALL OF MAN

And the woman? We have seen that her flight into the desert is mentioned by John twice, and she is in two different circumstances. We have also seen that it is especially the first flight where the condition of the woman is radically changed, in so far as she passes from "heaven" to "the desert." In this change of situation, something analogous to the experience of Satan happens to the woman. He was cast from heaven to earth, and the woman, in some way, also passes from heaven to the earth, to seek refuge in the desert.

Obviously, these changes of place are to be interpreted symbolically. It is a question of a movement from one condition to another, a change, however, which has as its basis the symbolic opposition between "heaven" and "earth"; it is a movement towards a worse situation. This is clear for both Satan and the woman. The fact that in both of her flights the woman finds something positive in the desert must not distract us. This has to be understood in relation to the aggression which the woman suffers, but it does not totally eliminate the negative character of the desert. It is indicated by the fact that the woman is to remain there only for a brief, clearly defined period of persecution and temptation. If she were to stay there forever it would mean a complete submission to her persecutor, and a betrayal of God who has destined her to flee there for a limited period only. The great prostitute, whose place of permanent abode is "in the desert" points to such a betrayal. Her relationship with the desert and the beast must be understood as a development of the "flights" into the desert in ch. 12.

The ambivalent character of the "desert," positive and negative at the same time, is particularly stressed by John in the second flight, in which we have traced a recall to the historical situation of the Hebrew people who have come out from Egypt. The same thing has to be said for the first flight. Is there, perhaps, a reference here to some precise historical event? It appears that we now have sufficient elements to claim that the first flight is an allegory on the original fall of mankind, which brought with it the loss of the prerogative of divine promises (the Son is taken away), the loss of a condition of friendship with God (heaven), the abandoning of the garden of Eden to live in a land, cursed because of the fault of man, now arid and resistant to the work of man (desert. See Gen 3:17-19).

John does not describe the sin itself, but alludes to its consequences. Even this allusion is veiled because in the midst of the condemnation consequent to the sin, John also intends to put into evidence the positive aspect, that which was linked to the promise of redemption made by God to the woman (Eve) in the very act of imposing upon her the punishments which were the consequences of her sin (see Gen 3:15-16). This promise was sufficient, in the eyes of John, to change what was a punishment into an act of mercy, of loving providence. The "desert" of punishment therefore becomes the "desert" of refuge, where God feeds the woman for one thousand, two hundred and sixty days (see 12:6). This means that he does not abandon mankind to the demonic attack, but continually renews his promise of liberation, as he did for Noah and all the Patriarchs.

The first flight of the woman into the desert signifies the first intervention of God in favour of mankind after its sin. This intervention is remarkable, not only because the promises far exceed the guilt, but also because it is the first moment in a divine intervention which will conclude with the sending of his Son. This is the background to the ancient Christian idea of this first sin, in some way being "a happy fault," sung in the Easter *Exultet*. In this way, it is the beginning of a series of divine interventions, among which, for John, the most important were the freeing of his people from the Pharaoh (a symbol of Satan), his leading them into the desert, and his sealing a Covenant with them. The Hebrew people, after that intervention, were now in a position where they had a new relationship with God, the Law and revelation (the two wings of the great eagle in 12:14). In this situation there could now be born from "the woman" further "offspring...who keep the commandments of God and bear testimony to Jesus" (v. 17). In other words, it was possible to return to the original condition of innocence, of justice and of trust in the promises of God symbolised by that "Son" carried in the womb of the woman.

THE TWO FLIGHTS INTO THE DESERT AS A TIME OF MESSIANIC EXPECTATION

A comparison of the two flights, therefore, shows that the second is a reality which the first one merely promised. It is here that John sees the error of Judaism. The Jews thought that God's action in the liberation from Egypt was the definitive one. They saw it as definitive in two ways:
(a) That only Israel would be subject to God's salvific intervention.
(b) That every further salvific intervention would take place in the same material, physical and temporal fashion.

This latter idea grew to the conviction that the Messiah would be a political figure, as against the spiritual dimensions foretold by the prophets. John has already denounced this attitude in the episode of the two "witnesses" (ch. 11), and the symbol of the destruction of the other woman, the prostitute of ch. 17, will take up the theme again.

John shows the faulty nature of this form of messianic expectation by inserting the two flights. In the second, we have the story of the divine intervention absolutised into a political messianism. Both periods in the desert, however, are the same: the three and a half years of the bitter persecution of Antiochus IV against the Hebrews (168-165) from which Daniel (see Dan 7:25; 12:7) onwards became a symbolic number for persecution. Thus not only the first period in the desert (the original fall and its promise) but also the second (Exodus and its Covenant) is also a period of waiting for a solution yet to come.

For John the definitive liberation came only in Jesus Christ who took the woman to live on "a great high mountain" (21:10), the Mt. Sion of the new Jerusalem. The woman "in the desert" of ch. 12 represents a period *before* the great event of the death and resurrection of Jesus. It is a symbol of humanity after the fall, but it is also a symbol of the Hebrew people, whose being chosen was not the conclusion of the divine salvific intervention, but only the proximate preparation and the prefiguring of the final act, which takes place in Jesus Christ.

The general background of Daniel could be further indication why there are two periods of three and a half years. We have already seen that Daniel sees the persecution as lasting a week of years, divided into two half-weeks. It is the second three and a half years which are the most difficult. Here again we find the dragon ceaselessly persecuting the offspring of the woman in the second of the two periods "in the desert." The use of the dragon with the seven heads and the ten horns also goes back to Daniel. In ch. 17, the seven heads will be explained as "seven kings," or as "seven hills on which the woman is seated" (17:9). In all probability, this refers to seven demons ready to rule for the seven millenia of history. The ten horns are also explained as "ten kings" who, however, receive authority only for a brief period, in service of the beast (that is, Satan) (see 17:12). One can see in this case, a symbol of wicked earthly rulers.

The figure of the dragon carries in itself the figure which sums up human history (seventy weeks), understood as the effect of the combined forces of demonic lords of the world and their perverse human and historical representatives. Seen from the point of the messianic hopes and expectation, this history is made up of a continual period of persecution. It is the final "week" of waiting, which Daniel speaks of, divided into two, marked by a twofold divine intervention, but also a twofold diabolic intervention. This latter first took away from man his original state (first flight into the desert), and secondly continued his attack on the Jewish people, drawing them away from a proper understanding of divine intervention of the Old Economy (second flight into the desert).

THE WOMAN OF CH. 12 AS A SYMBOL OF HUMANITY AND ISRAEL

We can now see that ch. 12 is a meditation of the significance of human history from creation to redemption. It is a story, on the one hand, of a continual falling away of man, and on the other, progressive intervention of God to save him. Man is created in a perfect condition, centre of all creation and having dominion over it (12:1: the woman clothed with the sun, stars around her head and the moon at her feet). But this is all physical and material. An even greater, spiritual perfection is promised to man (12:2: the son which the woman carries). This, however, is not simply given. It has to be won by man's working through trials and sacrifices. This is why the woman is described as crying out in her pangs of birth, in anguish for delivery (12:2). This is a frequent Old Testament image for the difficulty which accompanies spiritual rebirth (see Is 66:6ff; Jer 13:21; Rom 8:22ff).

The allusion to the cost of spiritual birth is an allusion to the limitations placed upon man in Eden, his separation from the tree of life and the tree of knowledge (see Gen 2:9 and 17). Only in the New Jerusalem will the trees be reunited (22:2). Man, however, does not remain faithful. As soon as the child is born, it is taken away from the woman. The violent character of this "taking away" refers to the aggression of Satan and the punishment of God upon man when he disobeys.

What follows then is the change of the condition of the woman. She passes from the privileged position (heaven) into another where, although still enjoying the protection and assistance of God she is now in difficulty (desert). In this desert stage John distinguishes two moments, or rather two corresponding periods during which, on the one hand, there is the gradual unfolding of the promises of God, but on the other there is a sort of resurrection of Satan who, although defeated in a first battle and also driven from "heaven," takes up again on earth his project to rule, and develops a growing crescendo of corruption and physical and moral destruction.

The woman of ch. 12 is, therefore, a symbol of humanity, in its complex and troubled relationship with God. As such, the symbol came to John from the Old Testament where the relationship between Israel and Yahweh is often shown through the image of a woman. John does not discard this. As we have seen, the second flight into the desert is a representation of the religious history of Israel, but John is convinced that the history of Israel is not an end in itself; it only plays a part in a vaster plan of God which embraces the whole of humanity. By linking the same symbol with Eden and then the Exodus, John shows that the history of Israel must not be understood in a particularist way. It is a part of the whole of the history of mankind, and can only be properly understood when read in that context.

In this way, John has stated the premises for the description of the universal effects of the action of Christ through the seven bowls. At the end of that, in the description of the new Jerusalem, the symbol of the woman will come back again: "spouse, woman (wife) of the Lamb" who comes down from heaven (21:9). This is a symbol of the new humanity, raised up by Christ through the incarnation, death and resurrection. She is no longer "in the desert," but upon a high mountain which is the spiritual Mt. Sion. A woman does remain "in the desert" however, and she is the one who has made a temporary resting place a permanent habitation, and has found only spiritual death: the great prostitute of chs. 17-18.

The Corruption of Political and Religious Authority (ch. 13)

13 ¹And I saw a beast rising out of the sea, with ten horns and seven heads, with ten diadems upon its horns and a blasphemous name upon its heads.
²And the beast that I saw was like a leopard, its feet were like a bear's, and its mouth was like a lion's mouth. And to it the dragon gave his power and his throne and great authority.
³One of its heads seemed to have a mortal wound, but its mortal wound was healed, and the whole earth followed the beast with wonder.

⁴Men worshiped the dragon, for he had given his authority to the beast, and they worshiped the beast, saying, "Who is like the beast, and who can fight against it?"
⁵And the beast was given a mouth uttering haughty and blasphemous words, and it was allowed to exercise authority for forty-two months;
⁶it opened its mouth to utter blasphemies against God, blaspheming his name and his dwelling, that is, those who dwell in heaven.
⁷Also it was allowed to make war on the saints and to conquer them. And authority was given it over every tribe and people and tongue and nation,
⁸and all who dwell on earth will worship it, everyone whose name has not been written in the book of life of the Lamb that was slain from the foundation of the world.
⁹If anyone has an ear, let him hear:
¹⁰If any one is to be taken captive,
   to captivity he goes;
 if any one slays with the sword,
   with the sword must he be slain.
Here is a call for the endurance and faith of the saints.
¹¹Then I saw another beast which rose out of the earth; it had two horns like a lamb and it spoke like a dragon.
¹²It exercises all the authority of the first beast in its presence, and makes the earth and its inhabitants worship the first beast, whose mortal wound was healed.
¹³It works great signs, even making fire come down from heaven to earth in the sight of men;
¹⁴and by the signs which it is allowed to work in the presence of the beast, it deceives those who dwell on earth, bidding them make an image for the beast which was wounded by the sword and yet lived,
¹⁵and it was allowed to give breath to the image of the beast so that the image of the beast should speak, and to cause those who would not worship the image of the beast to be slain.
¹⁶Also it causes all, both small and great, both rich and poor, both free and slave, to be marked on the right hand or the forehead,

¹⁷so that no one can buy or sell unless he has the mark, that is, the name of the beast or the number of its name. ¹⁸This calls for wisdom: let him who has understanding reckon the number of the beast, for it is a human number, its number is six hundred and sixty-six.

"ON THE SAND OF THE SEA"

Ch. 13 contains the description of the two famous beasts who represent, in the section on the bowls, the two instruments of satanic action in history. John sees them emerge, one from the sea and one from the earth. "Earth" and "sea" are obviously terms with a symbolic meaning. "The sea" represents the cosmic yet historical reality of the bottomless pit, while "the earth" is the place of man's dwelling after the fall, the cosmic yet historical reality which is equivalent to Eden. The "sea" according to the Jewish tradition already present in Daniel (see Dan 7:2ff) is the symbolic place or origin of political authority. So it is also for John. The "beast from the sea" in ch. 13 represents political authority. In fact, this beast sums up in itself the four beasts of Daniel 7 (the four empires).

To the power which comes from the sea to bring evil, i.e., political authority, adding the beast from the land, John adds another evil authority, equally important, and perhaps even more significant. We will see this later. For the moment I must simply indicate that the very fact that the beast comes from the earth shows that we are dealing with a reality which was, in itself, originally a good thing. The "earth," in fact, comes to the rescue of the woman when she fled for the second time into the desert (12:14-16). Therefore, if "the earth" produces such a terrible monster, it means that the earth is no longer what it was before, and that its originally good nature has been changed and corrupted.

The corruption of the "sea" and the "earth," represented by the two beasts, is the work of Satan, the dragon, thrown from heaven to earth. The beast from the sea, in fact, reproduces its exterior (seven heads, ten horns: 13:1; 17:3), the beast from the land, under the form of lies, reproduces the dragon's mentality and behaviour (it is similar to the Lamb, but "speaks" like the dragon: 13:11). The wicked influence of the dragon goes in two directions, upon the sea and the earth, and is symbolised by the position which he took up at the end of ch. 12: "And he stood on the sand of the sea" (12:18), i.e., the line of demarcation between the two elements.

This must not be ignored. It is important even at the level of John's composition: it links ch. 12 which is a summary of the history of salvation, and ch. 13, which takes up, in its own turn, certain points from the preceding chapter to carry them deeper. His standing on the sand of the sea is, on the one hand, the result of his being defeated by Michael and his angels (12:7ff), and on the other, a link with the emergence of the two beasts which follows. In this scene, the "woes" forecast for the sea and the land by the heavenly voices which celebrated the expulsion of Satan from heaven (12:12).

By placing Satan between the earth and the sea, John stresses further the universal character of the wicked influence which Satan now prepares himself to exercise, a lordship over both the elements. From both he calls up his agents, giving to them his authority and his dignity. In them and through them he regains what he lost in his initial defeat, and he prepares his counter-attack against the one who drove him out of his original dwelling place. The appearance of these two beasts, and particularly the first, sets up that gradual curing of the apparently mortal wound inflicted upon Satan, a fact which so astounds men that they are led to think that he is the supreme divinity (see 13:3-4).

In the rising of the first beast, Satan obtains, even though only on earth and thus passing, the recognition of his absolute dignity which he sought vainly to establish in heaven. At the cry "who is like God"? (the name Michael) he was driven from heaven. Now on earth we hear another cry in v. 4: "Who is like the beast?" The second beast, John tells us, comes to consecrate and make legitimate this pretension. The description of the beast as "standing" on the sand of the sea picks up the same expression used for the slain lamb, who "stands," also a reference to the resurrection of Jesus (see 5:6; 14:1).

His standing within the limitation of the sand on the seashore ultimately indicates, however, that his real home cannot be found in either sea or earth. Even though he calls forth beasts from the sea and from the earth and gives them his power as agents, they are clearly quite separate from him. They represent not Satan, but historical and human realities which he takes over. The dwelling place of Satan is the bottomless pit, where he was thrown, locked in and chained from the beginning. John will make this clear in only ch. 20 when he wishes to stress the ultimate impotence of Satan against Christ's reign of a thousand years, i.e., the salvation already possible in the Old Economy. If he now appears to be out of the bottomless pit, that has to be understood in relation to human history, where his presence is constant and growing through the agency of the two beasts. This very need to delegate ultimately shows his difficulty in acting. He is present only to carry on the assault against the divinity in the final stage of the "revelation of Jesus Christ," which is, for John, historically speaking, in the incarnation and the death of Jesus: the battle of Armageddon (16:12ff; 19:19) and of Gog and Magog (20:7ff).

We have already found an analogous situation in the "seven" of the trumpets. The first five trumpets represent the fall of the angels and its consequences, but even there the "star fallen from heaven to the earth" (evidently Satan), seems to work indirectly, opening the bottomless pit from which come the physical and moral evils which torment man during the messianic expectation (9:1ff). There also the succession of evils which are produced by the influence of Satan follow the same order as we find with the two beasts. After the fall of man, indicated in the fifth trumpet, follows the sixth trumpet and the breaking forth of the plague of warfare (the corruption of political authority, the first beast) and then the persecution and the slaying of the two witnesses (the corruption of religious authority, the second beast). For John, this last episode is the worst aspect of Satan's persecution of humanity. The two witnesses are slain in Jerusalem, and the responsibility for the slaying lies with Jerusalem herself. Therefore, even Judaism suffers a corruption caused by Satan. It is this last fact which marks the effective return of Satan from the bottomless pit. The slaying of the two witnesses is, in fact, attributed to "the beast that ascends from the bottomless pit" (11:7), an ambiguous expression which refers to both the agent of Satan (the beast) and the place of origin of Satan himself (the bottomless pit). The slaying of the two witnesses is the immediate prelude for the slaying of Jesus Christ, which John presents in the "seven" of the bowls as the common deed of the dragon (Satan), the beast from the sea (political authority) and the beast from the earth (religious authority).

THE BEAST FROM THE SEA: THE CORRUPTION OF POLITICAL AUTHORITY

The first beast which John sees is the one coming from the sea (13:1ff). Nearly all the commentators see here a symbol of Rome and her empire. This interpretation is basically true, but there is much more to it than a simple identification. The external description of this monstrous being shows two distinct parts. On the one hand, the beast from the sea reproduces the externals of the dragon of ch. 12 (seven heads and ten horns). On this is superimposed another description, a person of three animal forms (leopard, bear and lion). The diadems here are no longer on the heads, but on the ten horns, and the heads are covered by "a blasphemous name" (13:1).

John, following his usual pattern, is taking a symbol which was already known (here, the dragon), modifying it and adding further elements for more precision and depth. We know that the dragon symbolises Satan, and the basic similarity with this beast tells us that it is a wicked, demoniacal being. It represents a continuation and a manifestation of the dragon. There are two parts: that which comes from the dragon (seven heads and ten horns) which must be distinguished from the other: the animal aspects, the changing of the diadems to the horns and the blasphemous names.

For this reason we cannot see the head which has been wounded and then healed as an allegory on a human man, like the legend of *Nero redivivus*. The seven heads belong to the dragon, i.e., Satan, to his nature and to his story, from the first moment of his rebellion against God and of his corruption, as we learnt from ch. 12. Even if one admits that John knew of the legend of *Nero redivivus*, all he would be saying here is that what happened to Nero was but a reflection of what happened to Satan. In the history of salvation the fall of Satan and his angels stood at the beginning, according to John, of a whole series of negative historical events, of which Nero and other wicked rulers are the continuation. In this way, the episode of Nero or of any other *single* episode is not symbolised by the mortally wounded and healed head. What is represented is the whole complex of wicked political authority, which brings the resurrection of Satan into history.

We must now see the ways in which the beast *differs* from Satan. In the description of the dragon in ch. 12 the diadems, a symbol of royal authority and dignity, are on the seven heads (12:3). Here, instead, they decorate the horns. In the explanation of these symbols which John offers in 17:9ff, we learn that both the heads and the horns are kingly beings. The horns are lesser than the heads, lesser not only in dignity (they receive power *like* kings) but in their rule for a briefer period (17:12). They are human kings whose reign is very weak in comparison with that of the seven demons (the seven heads) put forward by Satan as governors of the seven millennia of human history.

The *equality* in the dignity between human beings and demonic rulers is here expressed by the passing of the diadems from the heads to the horns. This stresses even more the function which the beast from the sea (political power) has in relation to the dragon (Satan). John then says it explicitly: "And to it the dragon gave his power and his throne and great authority" (13:2). The animal forms (leopard, bear and lion) make the red colour of the dragon even more explicitly ferocious but they signify far more. The mention of the three animals is an obvious citation of the vision of Daniel, who sees four beasts rise from the sea (Dan 7:2ff). The first three beasts have the same appearance as those in Apocalypse. In Daniel, the fourth beast is not described, but from his subsequent actions, he is all the former three put together. This is what John takes over. It could have two explanations: it could be a description of the Roman Empire, the sum total of all the evil beasts, or it could be that John wishes to speak of a universal symbol of political authority, historically incarnated in the four world empires common to ancient history, apocalyptic, and already present in Daniel.

These two explanations are, in fact, complementary. Certainly Rome is involved in the symbol, but it does not exhaust all its meaning. The ultimate reference is not to some historical power, but to the one who is using these historical powers for his wicked designs. It is an important distinction. We have seen that the beast from the sea takes over, changes and adds to the symbol of the dragon. There is a transference of properties of the dragon to the new manifestation, but not vice-versa. While Satan (the dragon) can influence political authority, the contrary influence is not possible. This has two important consequences:

(a) It is not the action of certain historical forces which produces Satan in the world, and therefore, the Apocalypse does *not* have a pessimistic view of history.
(b) Political authority and, speaking more generally, historical forces, can certainly suffer from the influence of Satan and become his wicked instruments, but they are not realities which are in *themselves* necessarily wicked.

Certainly, John is no great friend of the Roman Empire, but he is a long way from having that blind fanatical fury which many see in him. This is above all, because his message is basically spiritual, centred upon the history of salvation which certainly embraces also secular history. He is judging and evaluating it from quite a different perspective from that which many commentators have suggested. In the vision of John, what is central is creation, fall and redemption. This will not allow of any reality, cosmic or human which is intrinsically negative. It is all the word of God, and even if corrupted, it is still marked with the sign of his presence. As we saw in ch. 12, the earth has become "desert" because of the sin of man, but it maintains its good aspects, a sign of the providential care of God for humanity.

The same thing has to be said for political authority which John is presenting here in its monstrous degradation, and for religious authority, the beast which will follow. Clearly, they are presented as the agents and almost the incarnation of Satan, but they were not that way from the beginning, and they are not that way of their very nature. Throughout the Apocalypse there is also the presence of good angelic beings in the context of political and religious authority.

There were the four living beings who called forth the four horsemen who, we saw, catch up the idea of the four successive empires common to the apocalyptic tradition (6:1ff). The angels faithful to God hold back the four winds of the earth to allow the sealing of the foreheads of the faithful ones in the sixth seal (7:1-3), and these four winds also are a symbol of the four empires.

What is this corruption of political authority by Satan? The indication is given in the blasphemous names carried by the heads. The greatest blasphemy for the Apocalypse is that of those who, like Satan, try to place themselves on a level with God, or even to take his place. The "blasphemous names," therefore, represent the temptation to divinisation, which accompanies political authority when it sees itself in absolute authority. This temptation was already present in the fall of the angels and in the fall of man. Even after his fall, Satan perseveres in this line, and when rendered impotent, passes it on to political authority, along with "his power and his throne and his great authority" (13:2).

The "blasphemous names" which cover the heads of the beast from the sea represent the pretensions of the state to take absolute and supreme authority. This leads to the denial of God (blasphemy) an extension of Satan's dominion over all the earth, imposing terrible conditions on all who live there, claiming that only to the state is adoration due. The second beast will attempt to give this pretension a divine seal, profoundly abusing the use of the Word of God.

All of this could be identified in the Roman Empire, but John simply does not wish to stop there. The Roman Empire was the confirmation and the aggravation of something which has always been present in history. John, a careful reader of Daniel, could see the same things in the pretensions of Nabuchadnezzar and of Antiochus IV. In fact, it is probably Nabuchadnezzar and his golden statue before which all his subjects had to prostrate themselves in adoration (see Dan 3:1ff) which is behind John's allusion when he is speaking of the activity of the second beast in favour of the first (see 13:14ff).

THE "FORTY-TWO MONTHS"

The authority of the beast from the sea, says John, lasts for forty-two months (13:5). This is the same duration as the domination of pagan peoples over the "holy city" (11:2), the mission of the two witnesses (11:3) and the first and second flight of the woman (12:6 and 14), and clearly symbolic. It is to be linked with the three and a half years from Daniel, used to refer to the fierce persecution of Antiochus IV (see Dan 7:25; 12:7). Even in Daniel, this period is the second half of a duration of a "week of years" of Jerusalem against the Hebrews by this arch-enemy (see Dan 9:24ff). It is the half a week in which the persecutor, after having put to death a consecrated person (the "anointed one," possibly the High Priest Onias III), profanes the Temple in Jerusalem with the erection of a statue to Zeus, and prohibits the celebration of Jewish cult. In Jewish apocalyptic, this second "half week" had come to symbolise the period of persecution which would precede the coming of the messianic kingdom. Even in Daniel, what happened in this period was the worst of all iniquities: profanation and destruction of sacred things.

John is using this background for his presentation of the

beast from the sea in ch. 13. The very figure of the dragon with the seven heads and the seven horns is a probable reference to Danielic background. A more precise reference is made by the "forty-two months" of authority, granted to the beast from the sea (13:5). This figure is a synthesis of the four beasts from Daniel, and takes over their symbolic significance. The beasts in Daniel are figures of the four world powers which followed one another in the passage of human history. This is also true for the beast from the sea, although here there is a distinction, as the succession of world powers has less importance. John is chiefly concerned to stress and denounce the demonic character of political domination, in so far as it is the consequence of sin and violence, expressed in the self-glorification of man.

With all this, however, there is still in John a series of world empires which come before the messianic advent, and it is fixed at the number "four." We gather this not only from the beast, but also from other elements in Apocalypse: the four horsemen, the four winds held back by the angels of the sixth seal (see 7:1ff), the four angels at first bound, and then let loose in the sixth trumpet (9:14f). This was already fixed in the apocalyptic vision of history which Daniel certainly confirms (Dan 2:31ff; 7:2ff). John uses it in this way. The beast from the sea, who takes up the elements of the four empires, is a representation of the period of messianic expectation now moving towards its culmination: the death of Christ described in the seven bowls.

If this is the case, then the actual period of time of the authority of the beast from the sea (the worldly empires) extends over the whole of human history, seen as a history of salvation, from the beginnings until Christ. This would mean that it should cover the whole of the "week" which John takes from Daniel. Why, then, does he use "forty-two months," i.e., three and a half years? He does this because in the whole "week" of messianic expectation which runs from Adam to Christ, he fastens particular attention on that second "half week" which coincides with the flight of the woman into the desert, i.e., the phase which is devoted to the religious and political history of the Hebrew people. There

John sees the partial and provisional first phase of the divine salvific intervention. He has already clarified this in the seven letters (chs. 2-3), in the sixth seal (7:1ff, the 144 thousand "signed ones"), in the sixth trumpet (chs. 10-11: the angel with the book, the two "witnesses") and which he now prepares to describe further in the visions of chs. 14 and 15.

This explains why the duration of the authority of the beast from the sea is the same as that of the holy city, trampled on by the pagan peoples, and the mission of the two "witnesses." In the historical experiences of the Hebrew people, from the slavery in Egypt up to the death of Josiah in the battle of Meggido, he sees an uninterrupted period of violent aggression against Israel from neighbouring powers: Egypt, Assyria, Babylon. To help John in his reading and understanding of this period, he has looked especially to the prophets of the Babylonian exile and of the post-exile period, and to the apocalyptic literature which had developed in the period just before Christ, Nevertheless, John sees, above all, a reflection of the diabolic persecution against man which had its origins in the fall. He then sees the particular concentration of the diabolic fury against the Hebrew people, because they were the chosen place for the promises of the final liberation of man which had been made from the time of the original fall. For this reason, God had freed them from the slavery of Egypt and had guided them through the desert to the promised land, giving them *the Law*, and continually renewing his promises through the *messianic prophecies* of a final liberation. For this very reason too, Satan attacked through the agency of political authority (and also through corrupt religious authority – the two "witnesses"), in his fiercest possible fashion. We have already read this at the close of ch. 12: "Then the dragon was angry with the woman and went off to make war on the rest of her offspring, on those who keep the commandments of God (the Law) and bear testimony to Jesus (the Prophets)" (12:17).

THE NUMBER SIX HUNDRED AND SIXTY-FOUR

If the beast described by John illustrates the theory of the four empires, then we may be able to see just which empire is referred to, though here we run into serious difficulty. Even though John using a model which, in Daniel, is of a historical character, he is stressing the spiritual and demonic, and thus discarding much of Daniel's obvious historical references. John clearly refers to the universality of political power, and also to a universality of its extension through his use of the number "four" which refers to all the regions of the earth.

Given this tendency in the Apocalypse, it is risky to try to be precise about the exact empires, but, if it is universal, it certainly embraces the Roman Empire. We have already insisted that it is not correct to take characteristics which belong to the dragon (seven heads and ten horns) and apply them unequivocally to the Roman Empire. In particular, we must not pick out certain events and personalities (e.g.: Nero) as the complete explanation of John's imagery (e.g.: the healed wound). We said that John's major idea was an allusion to the apparent resurrection of Christ. This will appear even more clearly in 17:8: "The beast that you saw was, and is not, and is to ascend from the bottomless pit and go to the bottomless pit." These words refer to Satan, to his original perfection, his fall and then his gradual return throughout the Old order up to his final liberation in the slaying of the Messiah (Jesus Christ).

We have already said that this gradual rise is made possible through the agency of corrupt political and religious authority. Even though it is impossible to identify all the Empires, it is evident that the Roman Empire is being considered. This will become clearer in the seven bowls, when the joining of the two beasts, from the sea and from the land, takes place at the death of Christ in the collusion of the Roman Empire and the Jewish Synagogue. Nevertheless, John never makes a direct reference to the Roman Empire. There will be a clear hint, however, in ch. 17 when the prostitute is destroyed by the beast, a reference to Rome's destruction of Jerusalem, her former ally, in 70 A.D.

Is there a reference to Rome in the passage which concludes ch. 13: "This calls for wisdom: let him who has understanding reckon the number of the beast, for it is a human number, its number is six hundred and sixty-six" (13:18)? It is a famous passage and the suggested solutions are innumerable. All the solutions, from St. Irenaeus onward (2nd century) have looked to an allusion to Rome. Irenaeus rightly saw the main idea as that of an anti-religious theme (based on the name of Titan: Adversus Haereses V. 30:1-3), but modern scholars have many complicated systems to find the name of almost all the first century Roman Emperors: Caligula, Titus, Domitian, and especially Nero.

What forces the exegetes to see it as an individual figure rather than an abstract concept like the Empire are the words: "it is a human number." What must be understood in ch. 13 however is that John is simply stressing that it is a human reality, and not a diabolic one. We have already insisted that we must not *identify* the beast with Satan whose agent it is while maintaining its own nature (political authority). This "human number" is the political authority which has a grave responsibility for what is described in the seven bowls, and thus there is a historical link here with the Roman Empire, as we know of her link with the death of Jesus.

If we grant that the solution lies in equalling the letters of the alphabet with numbers, then the suggestion of Irenaeus remains the best. He read there the Greek word *Teitan*, i.e., Titan. In Greek mythology, the Titans were the giants who had dared to challenge the divinity and those who dwelt in heaven. They were defeated and buried alive under Mt. Olympus. There is, in the book of Genesis also, a human challenge to the heavens, the story of Babel. Most contemporary exegetes read the story as reflecting the pride of political authority, already shown in Genesis, and the identification of Babel with Babylon and its Empire has confirmed this interpretation.

With this background, Irenaeus goes beyond any identification of a single person, and reading 666 as equal to Teitan interprets the beast as an expression of historical and human power (the Roman Empire) which, driven by inordinate pride and under the influence of an even greater pride (the dragon), moved to attack the divinity. This seems to be the best line of approach, but we can add some further contemporary suggestions. Many begin from the number "six" as the number of man (based on the creation of man on the sixth day: Gen 1:26-31) and see in 666 a threefold repetition of man's fruitless attempt to reach the fulness of perfection (represented by the number "seven") by his own power.

Taking into account more biblical ideas, and also the argument of Apocalypse itself there is a further possibility. We have seen that the beast from the sea represents the four empires which endured through all the period of the messianic expectation. We have also seen that, for John, it is not the four successive Empires which interest him, but the extension of the "four" into the four divisions of the geographical structure of the earth. For this reason one can think of a fourfold division, not only of the geography, but also of "the week" of the messianic expectation which runs from Adam to Christ. Subdividing into four parts this time of expectation, worked out in days (the thousand two hundred and sixty days plus thousand two hundred and sixty days, i.e., the equivalent of the two "half weeks" of the flights of the woman in the desert), we come to 630 days for each Empire. To this number one must add 36, which is the square of the number of man, i.e., 6.

The number 666, therefore, would result from the sum of 630 (the symbolic time assigned to each Empire) and 36 (the symbolic number of man, multiplied by itself). In other words, 666 is the number of human empires, and contains within it the two characteristics which result from John's meditation on this reality: the duration of authority allowed to each Empire (630) and the self-exaltation of man typical of a political institution, especially in the case of human kings and emperors (36). In this sense, it is a "human number." It represents the political institution, which is the highest and most complete synthesis and realisation of the great variety of human attempts to control.

We have seen that the political institution also has a positive aspect. If 666 sounds so sinister, it is because it comes at the end of an argument which develops a picture of corruption of political authority. Thus, even though "a human number" is used to express its distinction from the diabolic, at this stage, the human institution has become perverse, and is using the authority given to Satan in a battle against God. With this remark we are back to the suggestion of Irenaeus, and his use of Teitan to speak of a monstrous and proud revolt against God. For Irenaeus this certainly meant the persecuting power of the Roman Empire, but this was not such a fierce and widespread reality at the time of John. He is not fixing his attention on the persecution of the Roman Empire against Christians, but the diabolic use of political power (certainly the Roman Empire included) which led to its collusion with religious authority including the Jewish Synagogue) which eventually led to the death of Christ, an event which John will describe in the chapters which follow.

"THE LAMB WHICH WAS SLAIN FROM THE CREATION OF THE WORLD" (13:8)

Pride, therefore, is the principal characteristic of political authority, in so far as it seeks the *absolute* affirmation of man against the divinity. In this way, it is the continuation in history of what happened at the original fall. John sees behind it all the design of Satan to oppose God and to take over from him. The first consequence of pride and the desire for self-affirmation is the will to impose oneself on others, to desire to dominate them. This desire is evil because it is man's claim to be more than he really is, whence come jealousy and violence. This stands behind John's use of the biblical story of the fall in ch. 12. Satan (the dragon), moved by pride and a desire to dominate, is infuriated by man created by God to be lord of the earth. He attempts to devour the son which the woman is bringing into the world. He attempts the ruination of man by communicating to him his own diabolic pride which leads him to seek to obtain with rebellion and violence what God has promised as a free gift of love (i.e., participation in the divine life).

This attempt only partly succeeds because God intervenes, punishing Satan, the author of it all, and reconstituting mankind in his promises, even though this will now only happen after a long and painful period of trial (flight into the desert). The trial is, essentially, a continuation of the situation of the original temptation. Satan, although now reduced, continues to suggest to man that he take with his own power and authority what was, in fact, a promise which had already been made by God to man, as a free gift of love.

Kingship and lordship over the earth also form part of the promises which God made to man. The son which the woman carried in her womb in ch. 12 is a symbol of that (12:5), but it is a lordship which must work itself out through love and respect for creation. Man is its king in so far as, through him, creation can become conscious of its own worth and dignity, and thank the creator for this. So, the kingship of man is most clearly expressed in cult, where he is capable of praising God in the name of the whole of creation. The kingship of man is also priesthood: all men are kings and priests because Christ, through the redemption, took man back to his original spiritual condition, establishing once again the correct relationship between man and the divinity (see 1:6).

It is exactly the corruption of these two fundamental prerogatives of man, kingship and priesthood, that John is describing through the allegory of the two beasts in ch. 13. The beast from the sea obtains "authority...over every tribe and people and tongue and nation" (13:7). The formula indicates the universality of the authority conceded and universality has, for the Apocalypse, a positive character. The same formula is applied to the universality of redemption wrought by Christ (5:9-10; 7:9; etc.). As well as that, it appears that the authority granted to the beast is of divine origin. We can gauge this from the expression "To him was given authority," using the passive, as very often in Apocalypse, to show the divine origin of all things. Even the authority "to make war on the saints and to conquer them" (13:7) is something which "was allowed" – a sort of divine permission to do evil, or rather, to put to evil use something which was really good.

What has just been said does not contradict John's affirmation that Satan gives the beast "his power and his throne and his great authority" (13:2). Everything which Satan possesses comes from God, therefore, the evil which Satan communicates to political authority is the use of authority for its own ends, its own exaltation and glorification. Such a lordship necessarily brings with it the smothering and violent subjugation of creation and of the rest of mankind, which is a monstrous caricature of the kingship promised to man in his first creation.

The upsetting of the regal function of man by political authority influenced by Satan has its confirmation and its culmination in the abuse of the other function of man, his priesthood. We will see this in the allegory of the beast from the earth. For the moment John shows the extreme point of man's ruination. The beast from the sea, i.e., political authority makes all the inhabitants of the earth adore him, as he has subjugated them with violence (see 13:8). In doing this, he not only takes over the place of God, whose authority he has usurped, but he makes himself the absolute norm of good and evil, justifying all his actions by his own authority to come to his evil ends. To do this he is helped by the beast from the earth, i.e., religious authority which has become worldly and corrupt.

The Apocalypse makes it clear that not all humanity gives in to the pretensions of the beast from the sea, not even when more subtle violence is exercised by the support of the spiritual authority of the beast from the land. We know the destiny reserved for those who oppose these pretensions: the beast from the sea (political authority) with the support and advice of the beast from the land (religious authority) kills them (13:5). This is finally summed up in the death of Jesus, put to death as a result of a conspiracy between the Jewish High Priests and the Roman Imperial authority. According to John, however, this situation belongs not only to Jesus and those who later followed him, but also to some who went before him. We have already seen this on several occasions, especially in the scene of the sixth seal (6:9ff) and the episode of the two "witnesses" (11:3ff).

John's lament over these "slain" is never sterile or desperate, as he is convinced that they are the ultimate victors. As he will say explicitly in 15:2:

> "And I saw what appeared to be a sea of glass mingled with fire, and those who had conquered the beast and its image and the number of its name, standing beside the sea of glass with the harps of God in their hands."

We already know what happens to "witnesses" slain before Christ. Because of their sacrifice, they are already admitted to participate in the divine life. John expresses this in many ways: the giving of white garments (6:9-11); the spirit which comes from God and makes the witnesses ascend to heaven (11:11ff); the song which no one can understand, sung by the 144 thousand who follow the Lamb wherever he goes (14:1-5). In the final survey of salvation history which John will make in ch. 20, the destiny of these witnesses will be spoken of as the putting into action of the first judgment, and the first resurrection of the thousand year reign of Christ.

The destiny, reserved for the victims of the two beasts, their tangible sign of victory, is not the effect of their sacrifices. The only sacrifice which has absolute value is that of Christ, and in virtue of that sacrifice, those of the witnesses also have value and merit reward. This appears clear for us for the period *after* Christ, but it was also the case, in John's vision of things, for the period which preceded Christ. He repeatedly argues this case, especially in the reign of a thousand years "with Christ" in ch. 20. Throughout, there is one criterion for this period before Christ, to have rendered testimony to the word of God (the Law) and to Jesus (the Prophets).

Because John has this way of seeing things, he must also have the idea that the death of Christ cannot be contained within the categories of time, nor can the application of its effects. It is an act of the divinity. The sacrifice of Christ has been perfected from all eternity. For this reason, in ch. 5, when Jesus is presented as standing in the heart of a threefold divinity, he is presented as "slain" and "standing," i.e., his death and resurrection, through which he has performed his redemptive mission, forms an integral part of his divine nature.

In virtue of the eternal value of Christ, in so far as he is God, the "book of life" which contains the names of the elect was written from all time, "from the foundation of the world." As we have seen from ch. 5, this book is to be identified with the redemptive action of Jesus for the world. It is a total redemption: valid for everyone and from all time. Even before the historical actualisation of Jesus' death, some participate in its effects, those just ones who fall to the violence of authority, but it is also valid for the others, even if John gives us to understand that some must wait for the historical event of the Cross, so that they can be judged "according to their works" (20:12-13).

The eternal and universal value of the sacrifice of Christ is stressed in ch. 13, just as the description of the beast from the sea is closing, with a formula which, from a theological point of view, is the most daring thing in the whole of the Apocalypse. Speaking of the pretensions of political authority to impose itself as an object of cult upon its subjects, John says:

> "And all who dwell on earth will worship it, every one whose name has not been written in the book of life, of the Lamb that was slain before the foundation of the world" (13:8).

Much the same thing is repeated in ch. 17, where again it is a question of the relationship between political authority and its subjects:

> "And the dwellers on earth whose names have not been written in the book of life from the foundation of the world, will marvel to behold the beast, because it was, and is not and is to come" (17:8).

The two affirmations are clearly close, so much so that commentators, baffled by 13:8 generally read it as a reference to the "book of life from the foundation of the world" (see RSV; TOB) or "written down from the foundation of the world" (JB). The Greek, however, is clearly to be best rendered: "slain since the foundation of the world." This is what John means. Not only is it a question of the timelessness of the action of God, but also the intimate link which John sees between Christ and the world. This relationship begins with creation itself, of which the redemption is the continuation, or better, the perfection. John has already made this clear in the link between the two visions of chs. 4 and 5: allegories on creation and redemption. He will pick it up in chs. 21-22 where the new Jerusalem will be described as a new creation (new heavens, new earth). Because he sees it this way, he can also speak of the Lamb "slain from the foundation of the world."

There may also be a further meaning, suggested by the context within which the expression is found. It comes at the end of the description of the beast from the sea, political authority which has used violence to spill the blood of the just ones who oppose it. John argues that they participate in the divine life even before the coming of Christ because of the eternal efficacy of the death of Christ. In the *divine plan*, the sacrifice of Christ precedes the death of his "witnesses," on the *level of history* their physical death precedes his and in some way "prefigures" it, as we have seen especially in the episode of the two "witnesses." In this way we can say that the death of Christ is already at work and being performed in the deaths of these innocent just. John can thus speak of the "Lamb slain from the foundation of the world."

John is certainly convinced that the death of Jesus is unique, never to be repeated, but it takes up into itself all the deaths and oppression suffered for the love of truth and justice, and is finally victorious over this death and oppression. This is why this statement comes at the end of the description of corrupt political authority whose chief weapon is violence. Against violence, the fruit of pride, John counterposes the Lamb, the symbol of non-violence, a meekness which, in divine obedience, brings him to death. It is precisely through this experience that violence is defeated through the resurrection. In this victory, Jesus triumphs for *all* who have suffered from pride and violence. In the city of evil "Babylon" which the death of Christ destroys for ever, one finds all forms of corruption and impurity. But in ch. 18 the visionary comes to see a tangible and bloody conclusion to all this and the blood which is justified is not only the "blood of the prophets and the saints," but also the blood "of all who have been slain on earth" (18:24).

"THE ENDURANCE AND THE FAITH OF THE SAINTS"

This now helps us to understand the obscure warning which is directed to the reader after the description of the beast from the sea, at least in its general meaning. It is introduced by a common expression: "If anyone has an ear, let him hear" (3:9. See also 2:7, 11, 17, etc.). What follows is somewhat obscure, not helped by the fact that the correct text is disputed. First there are two phrases, of which the first has no verb:

> "If anyone... for captivity, to captivity he goes" (13:10).

It is perhaps clearer in a second pair of phrases:

> "If anyone slays with the sword, with the sword he must be slain" (see also Matt 26:52).

If the two couplets are parallel, then the first one must read (supplying a verb):

"If anyone leads into captivity, to captivity he goes."

We have, in the reconstruction, in two pairs of phrases, the *lex talionis* which rules in the world and which is used by the beast from the sea, political authority.

Even more than the *lex talionis*, it appears that the logic of violence is described here: violence is matched by violence. The only way to overcome this logic is to reject it absolutely, but to do this the "endurance and faith of the saints" is needed. In fact, the beast persecutes and slays those who oppose him: endurance and faith are needed not to weaken, but to resist the temptation of meeting violence with violence and to remain staunch. This was a warning already issued by Jesus in the Gospels. The Apocalypse warns also but from a different point of view. The importance which John gives to the death of Christ as the central fact of his messianic revelation is already in itself a condemnation of violence and of the authorities who exercise it. But the fact that Jesus has defeated violence and its representatives precisely through his death causes the refusal of violence to be something more than a moral attitude. It provides a new key to the understanding of history and of its values, a key which reverses all previous understandings. This was of great importance in the spread of Christianity in the early centuries. It is only with the vision of the Apocalypse that one can explain the phenomenon of martyrdom, a vision which has nothing to do with disregard for the world, fanaticism, or an impatient eschatological expectation. It is based on the serene certitude of a victory already won by Jesus Christ, and of a judgment on violence already in progress.

THE BEAST FROM THE EARTH: THE CORRUPTION OF RELIGIOUS AUTHORITY

After the beast from the sea, John's vision describes a second beast coming from the earth. The author dedicates almost the whole of the second part of ch. 13 to it (vv. 11-17). The fact that it is described after the beast from the sea does not necessarily mean that the second beast arises *after* the former. It is nevertheless true that the rising of this beast in some way presupposes the existence of the former beast. In fact, we are told that "it exercises all the authority of the first beast in its presence" (v. 12), and places itself completely at the former's service. In this sense, one can say that it comes after the first beast and represents the effect of the corruption created by it.

In reality, both beasts are the effect of the wicked action of Satan in two different human areas: political and religious, which John symbolically describes as "sea" and "earth." In this sense their origins are contemporaneous and independent of one another, even if their development as presented is closely tied together, inter-dependent and complementary.

The explanation of the beast from the earth has not created great difficulties for the commentators, even though they have undervalued its importance. Most see it as a sort of "spiritual double" of the first beast. Most see the first beast as Rome, they see the second as pagan cult, or more specifically the cult of Emperor worship, the mystery religions or magic practices. These interpretations are not entirely wrong, but they are too limited and precise. It is clear that this beast has an activity in the area of the psychological and spiritual, in an attempt to lead man to accept the domination of the first beast, i.e., political authority. While the activity of the beast from the sea is described by John through images of brute force and violence, the beast from the land acts more subtly, through the temptation to error which arises from man's mind (13:13 – false signs and symbols) and from his natural attachment to his own ease (13:17). In the beast from the land we can see hints of what today we would call the techniques of authorities to widen their influence, propaganda, organisation and popular acceptance. There is no doubt that John could have seen here the superb example of the religious, cultural and administrative organisation of the Roman Empire of his time. We must repeat that this does not appear for the first time with the Roman Empire. The whole of the Bible is full of condemnations of Kings who wished to take upon themselves divine authority, and impose themselves upon their subjects as such. The book of Daniel, a great favorite of our author, portrays two of them: Nabuchadnezzar and Antiochus IV. These are placed at the beginning and at the end of the great crises which will precede the coming of the Messiah, at the beginning and at the end of the famous seventy weeks.

Thus John is not concerned only with the Roman Empire. In fact, the sign of the cult rendered to earthly sovereigns is the erection of a statue (see 13:14), and John uses this example often, and it clearly refers to the historical actions of Nabuchadnezzar and Antiochus IV. The former put up an immense golden statue and demanded that his subjects adore it (see Dan 3:1ff) while the second had a statue to Zeus placed in the Temple, thus profaning it (see Dan 9:27). Even if John saw the cult offered to the Roman Emperor, this would only confirm his conviction, which he had from the Word of God, that the desire to be adored was a constant fact in political authority which had been corrupted.

The identification of the second beast with the cult and priesthood of the pagans is therefore not quite as clear as many would think. What was in the Romans had already been present in the Canaanites, the Egyptians, the Phoenicians, the Babylonians, etc., and all of this had been condemned in the Old Testament. So the demands for adoration of a human political authority, and the persecution which met refusal cannot be simply limited to the Roman Empire.

"IT HAD TWO HORNS LIKE A LAMB AND IT SPOKE LIKE A DRAGON"

Even the wider identification just suggested of the beast from the earth does not explain all the details of John's description. The fundamental characteristics of this monster seem to be his double-nature and ambiguity. He looks like something yet behaves differently. He appears to be good, in the form of a lamb, but he "speaks," i.e., behaves, like the dragon (13:11). John then says immediately that this second beast "exercises all the authority of the first beast" (13:12). This shows ambiguity, because the second beast invades the area of the first, exercising authority which belongs to the first beast.

In the chapters which follow, John will no longer speak of the beast from the earth. In its place, with an identical function but a different symbol, appear "the false prophet" (16:13; 19:20; 20:10) or "the prostitute" (17:1ff). Again we have symbols with an ambiguous meaning. The double character of this being is shown particularly in its relationship with the beast from the sea, political authority. The work of the second beast appears as a total dedication to the cause of the first, a collaboration to achieve the same ends, but this is false. In reality, the second beast is working for its own ends; admittedly the same as the first, but in opposition, as the second beast also wants to dominate the world. John will make this clear through the figure of the prostitute, who is also "Babylon the great" (17:5). In ch. 17, too, we will read of the deadly conflict which breaks out between the two former allies (17:16).

The fact that the beast from the earth has his own projects appears already from the fact that he "exercises all the authority of the first beast" (13:12). This is generally understood as some sort of delegated authority. John tells us the second beast behaves like the first. Is it of the nature of the second beast to do this or does he decide to behave that way? There is not much information on this, but v. 12 says that the second beast "exercises all the authority of the first beast *in its presence*." This is a biblical expression meaning "to obtain the recognition or favor of someone." This is the first indication of a free choice on the part of the second beast to behave in a certain way, because he fears the former. He is afraid of its anger, and he seeks to please it; yet another sign of duplicity. In fact, everything John tells us of this second beast's relationships with the first has two characteristics: it comes from its own initiative, and it is insincere. The latter aspect is an attempt to hide behind a mightier figure, and to see that all responsibility rests on that figure. The second beast has the initiative of leading all the inhabitants of the earth to adore the first beast, to raise up a statue and prostrate themselves before it, to receive the sign of submission on their foreheads and their hands (13:12-17). To the second beast is given the power to "give living breath to the image of the beast, so that the image of the beast could even speak and to cause those who would not worship the image of the beast to be slain" (v. 15). This means that the brutal and blind violence of political authority is manoeuvred and directed by a power which hides in its shadow.

The beast from the earth appears to have a personality and an autonomy which are difficult to identify merely with the pagan priesthood and cult, as they were really the *tools* of the political authority. In Apoc 13 political power is being used. A religious and sacred cult which has such independence can be found only in Judaism. This is what John has in mind in his description of the second beast which arises from the earth. We must not forget that we are in the introductory section to the seven bowls, where the topic is the death of Christ. The description of the two beasts in ch. 13 represents the previous historical events which lead to that highest point in the history of salvation. These are the corruption of the two powers and their alliance to destroy humanity.

This situation does not happen only in the death of Jesus, but in all the other deaths where there has been violence against the innocent and the witnesses to justice and truth. In this way, as the beast from the sea represents the political authority of all times, which has exercised violence, the beast from the earth represents all that which, on a spiritual and moral level, has approved, supported and justified this violence. Naturally, also the religious and cultic side of paganism will enter here.

But most serious of all, for John, was the responsibility of Judaism. Judaism was chosen by God as the first stage, even though provisional and partial, for putting his plan of salvation into action. Her function was to witness to "the word of God" (Law of God, true cult) and above all the faith in the divine promise of liberation (witness to Jesus). But she fell short in this function, as she yielded to a material, political and worldly interpretation of these divine promises. It is Judaism that John says: "exercises all the authority of the first beast" (13:12). It is in seeking for conquest and dominion in the worldly political scene that Judaism becomes corrupt. To gain her ends, she leant upon profane political authority, partly because of sly skill, and partly because of fear. Again we see this in the behaviour of the second beast, who leads the political authority to condemn and put to death the "witnesses" to the word of God (which prohibits the practice of idolatry), but is careful to hide behind the massive statue of political authority.

What John has given here, through a different literary form, is a symbolic description of what the Gospels tell us about the trial, the condemnation and the execution of Jesus. In the allegory of the statue which speaks and issues sentences of death at the wicked suggestions of corrupt religious authority which stands at its shoulder (13:15), it is not difficult to see the complex intrigue which grew between the High Priest and the Roman authorities which led to the death of Jesus. John sees this as happening daily in his own situation, as also in the whole period previous to Jesus, (cf. the episode of the "witnesses" of ch. 11). In fact, as Jesus himself recalls (Matt 23:29ff), the prophets and those sent by God were stoned and slain always with the direct or indirect approval of Jewish religious authority.

If the beast from the earth represents the corruption of Judaism, and in this, the corruption of a fundamental aspect of human dignity, i.e., the priestly function, this explains why further reference through the Apocalypse can speak of it as a false prophet and a prostitute. It appears that the first characteristic is duplicity, in the sense of hypocrisy, the taking on of an externally good feature, but hiding a wicked nature. This is clear from the subtlety of action and appearance of the second beast, which behaves in reality in the same brutal way as the first beast. But John points to a reversal here, for the second beast is actually something which is good by nature but which behaves badly. As it becomes clear later, through the images of the false prophet and the prostitute, evil has finally taken over so completely that there is now no trace of the good. It is not so with the beast from the earth. This is made very clear from his description of the beast as like the lamb, but speaking like the dragon. This is not simply hypocrisy. The second beast described by John has in his nature something which is close to the essence of Jesus Christ as the one who realises God's salvific plan as the Lamb.

For John, Jesus Christ is the perfect product of the authentic spiritual Judaism. The other, the second beast, has refused what could be his true nature, to take on a search for glory, and worldly dominion, forgetting his true nature. He still believes that he is the true Judaism, now he is "the synagogue of Satan" (see 2:9; 3:9), "Sodom and Egypt" (11:8), "he speaks like the dragon" (13:11). In successive developments the perversion of Judaism will be taken further by the symbols of the false prophet and the prostitute. These two images also come from the Old Testament, where they are used to speak of the relationship between Israel and Yahweh. This is the source of John's symbols.

The figure of "prophet" is closely associated with the coming of the Messiah. Echoes of this are found in the New Testament, especially in the Gospels. There is the figure of John the Baptist and of Elijah (Matt 11:14; 17:10) and there is also the use of "the prophet" to speak of the Messiah himself (from Deut 18:18. See Jn 6:14; Acts 3:22). "False prophets," therefore, are false Messiahs: "For false Christs and false prophets will arise and show great signs and wonders, so as to lead astray, if possible, even the elect" (Matt 24:24). This is very close to the words of the Apocalypse. The beast:

> "works great signs... and by the signs which it is allowed to work in the presence of the beast, it deceives those who dwell on earth" (13:13-14).

The same will be said of the false prophet in 16:13-14, clearly another indication that the identity of the beast is to be found in Judaism, and not in pagan religion and cults.

The false Messiah indicated by the beast from the earth, and its equivalents (false prophet, prostitute) is not however a personality from history, but a whole attitude to messianism in Judaism, a search for a political, nationalistic Messiah. John is against this *material* interpretation of the Word of God and the promise of God to serve their worldly ends as a betrayal of the authentically spiritual tradition of Judaism, of which Jesus is the perfect product. By doing this, Judaism places itself on the same level as corrupt political authority. Moreover, as it has misappropriated the Word of God, Judaism's responsibility is more serious, in fact, that it is partly responsible for the corruption of political authority, which works because of the insidious suggestions of the second beast.

For this reason, even though they were slain by "the beast which rises from the bottomless pit," the bodies of the "two witnesses" lie unburied in the street of Jerusalem (see 11:7ff); in the same way in Babylon we will find not only "the blood of the prophets and the saints" but also "of all those who have been slain upon earth" (18:24). This is the accusation which Jesus lays against the Jews and Jerusalem in Matt 23:19ff: "murdering the prophets." The same will be said in Acts 7:51ff. John is merely translating the same message into his more symbolic language.

The First Divine Salvific Intervention: (The Old Economy) as an Announcing and Prefiguring of the Second (The Death of Christ) ch. 14

14 ¹Then I looked, and lo, on Mount Zion stood the Lamb, and with him a hundred and forty-four thousand who had his name and his Father's name written on their foreheads.

²And I heard a voice from heaven like the sound of many waters and like the sound of loud thunder; the voice I heard was like the sound of harpers playing on their harps,

³and they sing a new song before the throne and before the four living creatures and before the elders. No one could learn that song except the hundred and forty-four thousand who had been redeemed from the earth.

⁴It is these who have not defiled themselves with women, for they are chaste; it is these who follow the Lamb wherever he goes; these have been redeemed from mankind as first fruits for God and the Lamb,

⁵and in their mouth no lie was found, for they are spotless.

⁶Then I saw another angel flying in midheaven, with an eternal gospel to proclaim to those who dwell on earth, to every nation and tribe and tongue and people;

⁷and he said with a loud voice, "Fear God and give him glory, for the hour of his judgment has come; and worship him who made heaven and earth, the sea and the fountains of water."

⁸Another angel, a second, followed, saying, "Fallen, fallen is Babylon the great, she who made all nations drink the wine of her impure passion."

⁹And another angel, a third, followed them, saying with a loud voice, "If any one worships the beast and its image and receives a mark on his forehead or on his hand,

¹⁰he also shall drink the wine of God's wrath, poured unmixed into the cup of his anger, and he shall be tormented with fire and sulphur in the presence of the holy angels and in the presence of the Lamb.

¹¹And the smoke of their torment goes up for ever and ever; and they have no rest, day or night, these worshipers of the beast and its image, and whoever receives the mark of its name."
¹²Here is a call for the endurance of the saints, those who keep the commandments of God and the faith of Jesus.
¹³And I heard a voice from heaven saying, "Write this: Blessed are the dead who die in the Lord henceforth." "Blessed indeed," says the Spirit, "that they may rest from their labors, for their deeds follow them!"
¹⁴Then I looked, and lo, a white cloud, and seated on the cloud one like a son of man, with a golden crown on his head, and a sharp sickle in his hand.
¹⁵And another angel came out of the temple, calling with a loud voice to him who sat upon the cloud, "Put in your sickle, and reap, for the hour to reap has come, for the harvest of the earth is fully ripe."
¹⁶So he who sat upon the cloud swung his sickle on the earth, and the earth was reaped.
¹⁷And another angel came out of the temple in heaven, and he too had a sharp sickle.
¹⁸Then another angel came out from the altar, the angel who has power over fire, and he called with a loud voice to him who had the sharp sickle, "Put in your sickle, and gather the clusters of the vine of the earth, for its grapes are ripe."
¹⁹So the angel swung his sickle on the earth and gathered the vintage of the earth, and threw it into the great wine press of the wrath of God;
²⁰and the wine press was trodden outside the city, and blood flowed from the wine press, as high as a horse's bridle, for one thousand six hundred stadia.

STRUCTURE AND GENERAL THEME

From a literary point of view, ch. 14 is one of the most beautiful in the Apocalypse. It is made up of a series of visions which follow, at first sight without internal logic, but in fact in two sections, at the centre of which is placed the figure of Christ, presented under two symbolic forms: the Lamb and the Son of man upon a cloud.

The first series of visions is shorter and simpler. The symbol of the Lamb, opening the account: "stood the Lamb on Mount Sion" (14:1), dominates the whole scene, illuminating with his light everything that surrounds him, and especially the one hundred and forty-four thousand who came to the fore. In fact, all this first section is devoted to them (14:1-5).

The second series is longer and more complex, made up of a series of visions and the presentation of seven personalities. Six of these persons are clearly angelic, while one is presented as "like a Son of man." He is seated upon a white cloud with a sickle in his hand and a crown of gold upon his head (14:14), clearly a presentation of the person of Jesus Christ. His appearance is placed fourth in the series of seven, and thus there remain two groups of three angelic personalities, divided by the figure of the Son of man. Again we have a presentation of Jesus Christ at the centre of reality, this time of an angelic nature, which is illuminated by him and has its sense in him, but which at the same time in some way produces him as the fruit of its own womb (14:6-20).

The position of Christ at the centre makes the surrounding visions symmetrical, with a close correspondence between the themes discussed therein: the Lamb stands with the 144 thousand which surround him just as the Son of man is situated in the midst of the angelic figures. This consideration will help us to understand correctly the full significance of all the elements which make up this scene.

This does not exhaust the skill of the structure. The two sections are not only symmetrical, but are also united by profound links which make them complementary. This is shown by the dual symbolism used to present Christ: the Lamb and the Son of man on the cloud. The difference between the symbols is only apparent. The substitution of the Lamb for the Son of man has already happened in ch. 5, where John is interpreting Dan 7, but makes the Son of man of 7:13 into the Lamb. They both refer to the death of

Christ, understood as the salvific sacrifice which is the definitive working out of the divine plan for salvation.

The two sections of ch. 14, centred as they are on the symbol of the Lamb and the Son of man, are complementary in so far as both refer to the death of Christ, but there are differences in the way they approach that central issue. We can assert already, with certainty, that the one, central theme of ch. 14 is the death of Christ. The examination of the text will show that this event is not described, as yet, in terms of the historical detail of the event, but rather hinted at through the form of symbols which prefigure it. This gives ch. 14 the character of a short "pause," as if the author looks back over what he has said before, as he prepares to go further, taking up his usual method of an ever-deepening, cyclic argument. One can thus see the brusque taking up of the fact of the death of Jesus, in itself disturbing and painful, as both breaking away from the account of "the two beasts" of ch. 13 and yet continuing that argument. The dominant characteristic of the beasts is violence; the symbol of the Lamb as a denial and negation of violence, on a practical level, is the ultimate effect of the violence perpetuated by the beasts.

We noticed a similar sort of contrast at the opening of the seals, between the fierce series of horsemen, and the scene of the souls of the slain ones who were under the altar in the fifth seal (6:9ff). The analogy is not casual, because the horsemen also carried the idea of the corruption of political authority, and the souls of the slain ones of the fifth seal are the same as the 144 thousand who stand with the Lamb on Mt. Sion. There are even more powerful reminiscences of the earlier parts of Apocalypse, especially to the 144 thousand in ch. 7:4 and the symbols used to speak of the death of Jesus: the Lamb and the Son of man. The Lamb goes back not only to the grandiose vision of ch. 5, but also to various theological aspects which speak of the redemption, spread throughout the earlier part of the book (12:11; 13:8). In reference to the death of Jesus, it especially takes up the sacrificial aspect, in harmony with certain messianic prophecies, and with the valid cult and liturgy of the symbol of the Lamb itself in Judaism. Paradoxically, in ch. 5, John includes under this symbol the idea of victory. The Lamb is, in fact, "the Lion of the tribe of Judah," "the root of David" (5:5), gifted with the fulness of authority (seven horns) and stands at the centre of the throne, still bearing the signs of his immolation ("as one slain") but "standing," i.e., risen and victorious over death.

In ch. 14, the Lamb is presented as "standing," and placed "upon Mt. Sion" (14:1). This "mountain" (in 16:16, named Armageddon) is clearly the mountain where the immolation took place, and also the one mentioned at the end of the book descending from heaven, "the holy city, Jerusalem." There the marriage of the Lamb will be celebrated and the bride will be the New Jerusalem (see 21:10). In the opening scene of ch. 14 we have none of this, yet there is an anticipation, a prefiguring, a "first fruit" (see 14:4), which is, concretely, the one hundred and forty-four thousand.

The victory of Christ over death, which marks simultaneously the destruction of the forces of evil and the foundation of the New Jerusalem, at once judgment and redemption, is represented by the other symbol, the Son of man. From the beginning of the book till now, John has been using the book of Daniel, and especially Dan 7 and its background and theology, as a *leit-motif*. We have seen it in the prologue (1:7), indirectly in the vision of Jesus among the candelabra (1:13ff), in the visions of chs. 4-5, where there was a use of Dan 7:13, with the imposition of the symbol of the Lamb, instead of Daniel's Son of man.

In ch. 14 the two symbols are again separated, but what has gone before serves to modify and make clearer their meaning. The symbol of the Lamb is no longer only the sign of an immense task, impossible for any other creature "in heaven, on earth or under the earth" (5:3). The contact with the prophecy of Daniel has identified this Lamb with the concrete figure of the promised and expected Messiah, Jesus Christ. Now he is placed in a specifically precise and definite *place*, "on Mt. Sion." Certainly, this "place" is also symbolic, and all the scene happens in heaven "before the throne" (14:3) so that even this must not be understood in a strictly material way, but as an allusion to the spiritual dimension which comes from the presence of the divine, always involved in John's description of events "in heaven." Nevertheless, the proper name, Sion, is clearly a reference to Judaism, a reality which is concrete and precise. It is not by chance, therefore, that when the new Jerusalem descends upon the same mountain, the term "Sion" is omitted, and it is referred to as "a great high mountain" (21:10). It is no longer Israel, but the whole of humanity. The account of the one hundred and forty-four thousand is linked strictly with Judaism, and the very number is a further clear indication that we are dealing with a historically precise reality.

The symbol of the Son of man who comes on the clouds, used here again, is profoundly changed as a result of its contact with the symbol of the Lamb in ch. 5. The putting together of the two symbols there has removed any doubt about the revelation of the Son of man in Daniel. We now know that John intends to see in the signs of Dan 7 an announcement on the part of the ancient prophet of the absolute power of God. This is not shown, however, in line with certain Jewish thinking, through the distinction of one worldly, material and political power replaced by another of the same type, but as the announcement of something much greater and invincible: the victory over death by passing through it as a destruction of its roots. The modifications in the Danielic prophecy can be found in the way John cites it in earlier uses of the Old Testament. In ch. 14, the citation is direct (14:14), but with greater variation. The Son of man does not come "with the clouds of heaven" (Dan 7:13), but appears seated "upon a white cloud," crowned with a gold crown and carrying a sharp sickle (14:14). All these elements have been added to the basic vision of Dan 7, as also is the task of "reaping" performed by the Son of man.

We will analyse all of this later, but the changes and additions are surely meant to carry further the reinterpretation already begun in ch. 5 when "Son of man" was substituted by the Lamb. In general, we can say that these particulars are connected with the messianic revelation of Christ, understood in the specific sense of his actual historical coming, his incarnation and death on a cross.

That this is the case can be seen from a comparison between the Son of man on the white cloud in ch. 14 and the Logos descending from heaven, seated on a white horse, with many diadems on his head and a sharp two-edged sword coming from his mouth in 19:11ff. The latter takes up the former, carrying it further and making it even more specific, and is also a reinterpretation of the messianic prophecy in Dan 7. This has not been noticed, as it is so subtle: the vision of ch. 19 goes back to that of ch. 14 which, in turn reaches back to the vision of ch. 5. This is a further indication of the fact that ch. 14 forms a sort of bridge in the structure of the whole book. The links with the latter part of the book are not limited only to ch. 19. In fact, the link with ch. 19 is only an indication of a re-reading and further deepening of the message of ch. 14 which is carried on throughout the whole of ch. 17 till the end of the book. We will see as we go further how John seeks to reproduce the scheme of the second part of ch. 14: the two groups of angelic figures with Christ at the centre. In fact, there are three angelic apparitions which lead up to the vision of the Son of man in ch. 14, proclaiming the majesty, the power and law of God which determine the fall of Babylon (14:6-11). The three angelic appearances which follow help the Son of man in his "reaping," i.e., in the judgment which is at the same time the condemnation of the wicked and the salvation of the good (14:15-19). In perfect symmetry, the reference again to the three angels later in the book will be in close relation with the destruction of Babylon (17:1ff; 18:1ff; 18:21), while the three which follow the descent of the Logos are related to the double function of judgment (19:17; 20:1ff; 21:9ff).

Yet the function of "bridge" which I have described does not exhaust the message of Apocalypse 14. We must remember that it still forms a part of the introduction to the "seven" of the bowls, which speak of the death of Christ as the perfection of the divine salvific plan. Ch. 14 still serves as the presentation of a stage of waiting and preparation for the historical working out of that salvific action. It portrays the moment of the announcing of that event, not only in words, but also in action, as it prefigures the action being prepared for and announced. Clearly John draws his symbols and imagery from the Old Testament from the world of Judaism. This is important, as the visions of the Apocalypse are not an attempt to describe an undescribable future, but a meditation on the Word of God contained in the Sacred Scriptures, in the light of the person and work of Jesus Christ, whom John sees as at the origin and at the centre of that Word.

THE DEATH OF CHRIST IN THE WITNESS OF THE ANCIENT MARTYRS: THE LAMB AND THE ONE HUNDRED AND FORTY-FOUR THOUSAND UPON MT. SION

There have been various attempts to describe the significance of the first scene: 14:1-5. There is agreement on the Lamb, but who are the one hundred and forty-four thousand? They represent the elect, gifted with a special perfection and therefore having a position exceptionally superior to all others. It is generally explained that they are Christian martyrs, or (and sometimes combining both) they are Christians who exercise particular virtues: charity, continence, virginity. All of this sees the group as post-Christ, members of the Church, but if this group is identical with the group mentioned in the sixth seal, as is commonly accepted, then I argue that it refers to the Old Economy, as we saw there. Why does John call them back at this stage of the book? The answer is that here John wishes to establish something which was not mentioned in the sixth seal: a close link with the figure of the Lamb. This link leads to an exchange of features between the two symbols which relate very closely with one another.

The meaning under the symbol of the Lamb is clear: it evokes the idea of an innocent who is slain because of the violence and the guilt of others. In ch. 5 John, inserting this symbol into the Danielic messianic prophecy, adds the idea of an immolation which is a freely made sacrifice of expiation. Even more, given the divine nature of the one who is subjected to the immolation, this is not the end of the story. It is followed by a reversal: death becomes life, defeat becomes victory. The sacrifice, therefore, becomes redemption.

The Lamb "standing on Mt. Sion" (14:1) recalls all of this. The light of this symbol shines, above all, on one hundred and forty-four thousand, who are thus further clarified. In the sixth seal, several things were said of them: they come from the tribes of Israel (7:4ff), they were the object of a special choice, shown through the seal on their foreheads: the seal of the living God (7:2-3), this "sealing" took place in a moment of provisional freedom from violence, made possible by the angels' holding back the four winds (7:1ff). The full significance of all of this comes out now in ch. 14, which is not a repetition, but a further deepening of what was said earlier. It is clear that the one hundred and forty-four thousand are martyrs. The link with the Lamb is enough to indicate this fact. John says that they "follow the Lamb wherever he goes" (14:4), which must be given the full meaning of "follow," to witness to him to the extent of going to his same destiny, death.

The one hundred and forty-four thousand are, therefore, "martyrs" in the first sense of the word: "witnesses" of the Lamb, shown by the name they have on their foreheads: "his Father's name written on their foreheads" (14:1). To carry the name and the sign of someone means, in the language of the Apocalypse, to witness with external performance, the deep internal belonging to someone. They are also "witnesses" of God (the Father) and of Jesus Christ (the Lamb), and in the full sense of the word, because it has also cost them their lives.

The name of God and of Jesus Christ carried by the one hundred and forty-four thousand on their foreheads clarifies the meaning of their being "signed" in the sixth seal, and links them with other groups of people who are frequently mentioned in the Apocalypse, first of all, with the slain of the fifth seal. They too paid with their lives for their witnessing to the word of God and to Jesus Christ (see 6:9ff). Then, it links them with the descendants of the woman, "those who keep the commandments and bear testimony to Jesus" (12:17) who are persecuted and slain by the dragon. Further it links them with the "saints" whom the beast slays because of the "endurance" with which they "keep the commandments of God and their faith in Jesus" (14:12), and with those who are admitted to share with Christ in reign of a thousand years in ch. 20. John tells us that they too were "beheaded for their testimony to Jesus and for the word of God" (20:4).

In all of these cases John refers to the witness which took place in the Old Economy, before the coming of Christ: Witness to God (to the Word of God, i.e., the Law) and to Jesus Christ (i.e., to the messianic prophecies and waiting for his coming). This is what John illustrated in the symbolic account of the two witnesses in ch. 11. From that account, as also from the scene of the fifth seal, and even more explicitly in the reign of a thousand years in ch. 20, we learn of the destiny reserved for those who have lived this double "witness" unto death. Because of their sacrifice they are admitted, in contrast to all other men, to participate in the divine life even before the historical event of the redemption. The one hundred and forty-four thousand of the sixth seal, recalled in ch. 14 and probably also in 15:2 ("those who had conquered the beast and its image") are a further indication of the great value which John gives to the ancient witness. They have, in fact, in dying for witness to the Law and the messianic promise, prefigured and already put into action, the death of Jesus Christ himself. Their witness is described here as a correctness of behaviour: "in their mouth no lie was found for they are spotless" and a purity in their life of faith and cult, for this is what is meant by "these who have not defiled themselves with women," and their being "virgins," taking up the Old Testament expression of impurity of cult and idolatry in terms of prostitution and unchastity of the nation (see 14:4-5).

Like all the other ancient witnesses, the one hundred and forty-four thousand receive a reward which sets them apart from all other men: "These have been redeemed from mankind as first fruits for God and the Lamb" (14:4). This expression has not received sufficient attention, as in itself it is enough to show that the one hundred and forty-four thousand are not Christian believers. The text speaks of "redeemed," a term used to speak of the work of Christ, which cannot, however be limited to a small group, for its efficacy is universal. Here, however, the reference is to a special group, the "first fruits" of the pre-Christian era. They are not the complete harvest, but a small gathering made previous to the harvest. The image is not casual, as the second section of the chapter is devoted to Jesus, Son of man, at a harvest of judgment which coincides with his coming on the white cloud. That will be the universal harvest, the redemption and salvation for the whole of humanity in the sacrifice of Christ.

The one hundred and forty-four thousand, therefore, are those saved in the Old Economy. This emerges from other particulars. They sing before the throne, before the four living beings and the twenty-four Elders, that is, before the exponents of the Old Ecnomy, and they sing a new song which only they can learn (14:3). They alone are inserted into salvation and redemption, something which the Old Economy, in itself, could not achieve, because they are intimately linked with the Lamb, pariticipating already in the salvific effects of his sacrifice, as those of the fifth seal "under the altar" already receive the white garment before the number of their brethren is completed (6:9ff). This is the meaning of their standing upon Mt. Sion even before the New Jerusalem descends upon it, and the meaning of their being the "first fruits."

If this is the case, then the two sections which make up ch. 14 repeat exactly the situation of the sixth seal where we found the contraposition of the one hundred and forty-four thousand and the "great multitude which no man could number, from every nation, from all tribes and peoples and tongues" (7:9), fruit of the "great persecution" (7:14), the death of Christ. In the "great multitude" we see the new humanity redeemed by Christ, which in ch. 14 is described as the fruit of a general harvest, of a reaping and a vintage upon the earth.

In this account, however, the link between the two realities, the Old and the New Economy is more clearly a continuity than in the sixth seal. The function of the one hundred and forty-four thousand as regards to the immense crowd is not precise. We do not find out if the privileges are the same. Ch. 14 takes away all doubt. Each is on the same plane. Their recompense, their salvation, consists in being united to God and to Jesus Christ. This is the case for the great crowd of the sixth seal (7:10) and also for the inhabitants of the New Jerusalem (21:22; 22:3). Between the two, however, exists a difference. For the inhabitants of the New Jerusalem, who are the fruit of the redemption worked by Christ (the great persecution, the reaping and vintaging of the earth), the union with the divinity is already with them in this life, and is prolonged into the life after death. For the one hundred and forty-four thousand, however, who lived before the historical coming of Christ, the participating in the divine life is possible only after death, and this death is a sacrifice of their own lives.

If we follow the indications of ch. 11, the martyrs who are saved come exclusively from Judaism. Only there was it possible to give witness to the Law and the messianic prophecies. Elsewhere, in the fifth seal and the reign of a thousand years, such indications are not found. Moreover, the one hundred and forty-four thousand who are described in the sixth seal as from the tribes of Israel, are, in ch. 14, "redeemed from the earth" (14:3) and "redeemed from mankind" (14:4). Does this indicate that John sees a universal possibility even before Christ? This cannot be excluded *a priori*. There may be a hint that authentic Judaism, which means the realisation of all the *spiritual* dimensions of the old covenant was not to be limited to a race or a people. It is difficult to think that the cry to God from the slain of the fifth seal, that he render justice and vindicate their blood (6:10) is a hope which arose only in the Jewish world. In fact, when Babylon is condemned and destroyed, the blood which she is guilty of pouring out is not only "the blood of the prophets and the saints," but also "of all who have been slain on earth."

THE DEATH OF CHRIST IN THE WITNESS OF THE LAW AND THE PROPHETS: THE FALL OF BABYLON, REAPING AND VINTAGING OF THE EARTH

The second section of ch. 14:6-20 is longer and more complex, but repeats basically the scheme: the figure of Christ is placed at the centre of a series of personages and of visions which look to his figure for their meaning. In particular, the figure of Christ divides the series of angelic appearances into two groups of three. Christ appears as "one like a Son of man" seated upon a white cloud. He is graphically presented as one who stands alone, yet the angelic figures assimilate some of his features.

The symbol of the Son of man seated upon a white cloud contains an explicit reference to the vision of Daniel (Dan 7:13). We now know how John uses this vision, after ch. 5 where he substituted the Lamb for the Son of man: it is the revelation of the glory and the power of the Messiah, which the prophet, with great imagination, spoke of as coming with the clouds of heaven, now indicated as taking place in the death and resurrection of Jesus Christ, the effect of which is the redemption of humanity. The section of the chapter which deals with the Son of man is to read now in the light of the symbol of the Lamb. This is clear from the variations which John introduces to his citation from Daniel. Some touch the figure of the Son of man himself, where some descriptive particulars are added (as in ch. 1). The figure here wears a crown of gold. Unlike the figure in Daniel, the Son of man here is already in possession of the authority and dignity of a King, and the use of gold indicates that he derives it from the godly sphere. Even more explicitly, in the light of the visions of chs. 1 and 5, we can say that this royalty comes from the pre-existent divine nature of the

Christ, who comes on a cloud; an incarnation which brings to perfection the messianic task of redemption. In an analogous way, in 19:12, the Logos of God descends on a white horse, wearing many diadems on his head.

The Son of man, here, does not come "with the clouds," as Daniel says, and he is cited in 1:7 (see Dan 7:13); but seated "upon a cloud." In Daniel's version, the one seated is not the Son of man, but the Ancient of Days (Yahweh). This indicates the sitting of the supreme judge and the beginning of the judgment, now attributed to the Son of man, not only because he is equal to Yahweh, which we already learnt in ch. 1, but because he is seated upon "a white cloud." This is related to the incarnation and the death of Christ, (shown by the parallel with the "white horse" upon which the Logos is seated in ch. 19).

They are the symbol of the truth and the justice to which he gives witness. It is with his coming and especially with his death (see 19:11), that the Son of man is given authority to judge. In fact, in ch. 20 with the inauguration of the second, final and definitive judgment of Christ, there is first an installation of a "great white throne" (20:11), which is linked with the image of the white cloud and the white horse.

The symbol of the white cloud contains an allusion to the death of Christ, which was the main point of the symbol of the Lamb at the opening of the chapter. It is clear, therefore, that the central theme of ch. 14 is the death of Christ, and the two symbols, the Lamb and the Son of man on the white cloud, in many ways mean the same thing. Nevertheless, there are differences, and John has used them here in rapid succession to throw into relief two different aspects of the one theme. The symbol of the Lamb, together with the one hundred and forty-four thousand, is used to speak of the death of Christ in so far as it is a sacrifice of expiation and works the salvation of mankind. Then the Son of man on the white cloud begins to present to us that death as a judgment of God upon the world. It is this theme that will dominate the later chapters.

In the second part of ch. 14, the theme of judgment, identified with the death of Christ, is stressed by the presence of the two groups of angels which are on either side of the Son of man on the white cloud. They are, as I will explain, the representatives of the Law and the Prophets which give witness to the coming of Christ and to his death and, in doing this, also assist and collaborate in putting his judgment into effect. This is referred to by the other feature added to the Son of man. He carries a sharp sickle. No doubt this is also a symbol of death. Linking it with the scenes of the reaping and vintaging which follow, the scholars have seen in all this the pre-announcing of the terrible and indescribable slaughter which will fall upon the human race at the end of time. This is not the true interpretation. The death indicated is the death of Christ, and is, for John a positive thing. The reaping and vintaging image has in it the idea of a "gathering in" of the chosen ones, the redemption of humanity. The pain that is there indicates that the death of Christ involved thorough pain, and thus brings a painful aspect in the negative result of judgment: the condemnation and destruction of the wicked.

In this way, the sharp sickle in the hand of the Son of man is equivalent to the "double edged sword" which comes out from his mouth in 1:16 and from the mouth of the Logos in 19:15: a symbol of the judgment of God on the world which takes place with the coming and the death of Christ. The replacing of the sword with the sickle is connected with the further image of the reaping and vintaging. It is all taken from Joel 4:13, where these images are used to present the final judgment as a prelude to the messianic kingdom. This prophecy was popular in Jewish apocalyptic and there are echoes of it in the New Testament (see Matt 13:3ff and Jn 4:35ff). Thus John places two prophecies side by side. The prophecy from Daniel he has already explained in ch. 5 as a pre-announcing of the salvific death of Christ. Taking it up again in ch. 14 he entwines it, through the use of reaping and vintaging images, with the prophecy from Joel. In this way, the coming of the Son of man on the clouds (death of Christ) is seen as the fulfilment of the judgment of God upon the earth.

In the messianic prophecies and in apocalyptic, the judgment of God and the separation of the good and the evil precedes the coming of the messianic kingdom, which then sees the destruction and the blessedness of each group respectively. This idea of separation is clear in the image of the two-edged sword, but here is made even clearer through the harvest image. The positive aspect, however, the gathering of the fruit, predominates here. The other aspect, the selection and then the rejection of the bad part of the harvest, is only implicit. It is perhaps for this reason that John adds the vintaging image, the scene of the pressing of the grapes within the wine-press (14:19-20).

In this image the threatening tone which runs through the whole scene reaches its high point and makes quite clear the idea of judgment which has already been evoked by various other elements. The harvest of grapes is thrown "into the great wine press of the wrath of God" (14:19). That this is a judgment theme is confirmed by its biblical background in Is 63:1ff, in which God is described after the execution of his judgment upon his enemies as a wine-presser, who comes out of the press with his clothes covered in new wine. The discourse of the Apocalypse changes, however, as out of the press flows, not new wine, but blood which covers all the surrounding area, to a symbolic extension of one thousand six hundred stadia, which indicate the face of the earth. This scene is often incorrectly interpreted. It is not about the bloody end of the evil ones, but is the application of another messianic prophecy, from Isaiah, to the death of Christ. This prophecy will be explicitly taken up in 19:13, in the "robe dipped in blood" which clothes the Logos. We will see there that it refers to the passion and death of Jesus, which has broken all wicked authority.

Moreover, in ch. 19 the idea of the death of Christ which determines the destruction of the enemies will be described in a clear succession of events: first the Logos with the symbol of his death (the cloak soaked in blood) and his authority to judge (the two-edged sword). Then comes the battle against the enemies gathered in Armageddon (see 19:19; 16:16). In the scene of the wine press of ch. 14, however, all this is still implicit in the vague sign and a little ambiguous in the symbols used. Only the death of Christ is indicated with the clear sign of the wine press which "was trodden *outside the city*" (14:20), clearly Jerusalem. That this death brings the judgment of God is indicated by the expression: "the great wine press of the wrath of God" (14:19). The ambiguity lies in the fact that the blood could be read as that of the evil people crushed by the divine anger, but it refers, in fact, to the blood of Christ and its spreading over all the earth. This is paradoxically a positive thing: the spreading of the beneficial effects of the redemption to the whole of the physical and human reality.

The negative aspect of the pouring out of the blood, that which implies the destruction of the evil forces, is put forward in a forceful way through the detail which concludes the whole description with a horrible vision: the blood which reaches as high as a horse's bridle (14:20). The horses, as John has indicated in the fifth and the sixth trumpet, are a symbol of the spreading of diabolic influence over the earth. The blood which reaches their nostrils stops their advance. This detail of the horses is also a point which anticipates the great battle of ch. 19.

Perhaps the scene described here has an even wider symbolism. In the sea of blood which blocks and drowns the horses there could also be a reference to the Red Sea where the horses of the Egyptians had the same experience, as they pursued the Hebrews. That John has this in mind could be confirmed by the opening section of the next chapter, where the theme of the Exodus is taken up and further developed (see 15:2ff). In fact, many commentators have seen close parallels between the plagues which preceded the liberation of the Hebrews from Egypt and the punishments which accompany the pouring out of the seven bowls.

The scenes which follow the appearance of the Son of man on the white cloud thus develop as follows: after having recalled the messianic prophecy of Daniel (Son of man coming on the clouds) in his particular way as a pre-announcing of the death of Christ, John then links it with a series of other Old Testament messianic passages (from Joel, Isaiah and Exodus) tying them in with his meaning of the messianic prophecy in Daniel. The death of Christ, therefore, appears as the judgment of God on the world in its dual aspect: the gathering of the elect (reaping) and the condemnation and destruction of the evil forces (the vintage and the pressing of the grapes). The recalling of the Hebrew Exodus which concludes the account presents the death of Christ as a new Exodus which no longer frees only a small part of humanity, but the whole of humanity itself in so far as it is freed from diabolic persecution, foreshadowed in the Pharaoh's persecution of the chosen people. Christ is the new Moses who frees the new people of God, formed now from the whole of humanity, as John already indicated in the sixth seal. This blood is the new Red Sea through which the new people pass, obtaining their definitive salvation, and in which their persecutors, the diabolic oppressors of humanity, with the human agents, find their destruction.

At this point, one could ask why John gives the angels such an important role in all this. The reply lies in the fact that in the Apocalypse, the angels are the representatives of the Old Economy, the mediators of the old alliance, the Old Testament revelation. John has a deep conviction that the value of the Old Economy lay in the fact that it announced and prefigured the new, which was perfected in the coming and in the death of Christ. In this way the angels, who have been agents in the realisation of the Old Economy, have become, both in the old and new, the collaborators of Christ in the realisation of the divine plan of salvation. This helps us to understand the two-fold division of the groups of angels around the Son of man on the white cloud. The second group is used in close association with the messianic prophecies to speak of the vintaging of the earth. In fact, the vintaging is done by an angel (v. 19) while the reaping is done directly by the Son of man (v. 16). The difference is probably that, while the reaping is basically a positive symbol (gathering of the elect), the vintaging (especially with the consequent pressing of the grapes) carries with it more precisely the idea of judgment and the destruction of the evil forces. This is an image which is more closely linked to the idea of the divinity in the Old Testament, of which the angels are the representatives. Whatever might be the explanation of this particular, it is clear that the angels of the second group are the representatives of the witness rendered to Christ in the prophecies of the Old Testament.

What of the angels of the first group? They do not work. Their task is to proclaim absolute and immutable truths. The first angel is presented spectacularly: he flies "in mid-heaven," carrying "an eternal gospel" to announce to men, and he calls all to fear, glorify and adore God, the creator of heaven, of the earth, of the sea and of the fountains of water" (vv. 6-7). The second announces the fall of Babylon (v. 8). The third proclaims the tremendous and eternal punishments which await those who adore the beast (vv. 9-11).

In the message of the first angel is condensed what John has already presented elsewhere, for example, in the vision of chs. 4 and 10 (see 4:11 and 10:5-7) as the essence of the old revelation: there is only one God and he is the creator of all that exists. From this flows the necessity to give him alone all forms of respect and homage. This idea was already expressed, in the vision of ch. 4, by the perennial angelic liturgy (4:8) but which here, in the words of the first angel, assumes the character of a law proposed for the observance of the whole of humanity. In these words, in fact, are the first and most important commandment of the Law, given by God (Exod 20:2), as John believed, through the angels.

The terrible end of those who refuse to obey such a commandment is described in the messages of the second and third angels, in which is concentrated also the first and essential duty of every creature. The fall of Babylon is indicated in the rebellion and the expulsion of Satan from heaven. He is the first to violate the fundamental commandment. Even more, he dares to challenge the divinity, to make himself its equal and even to replace it in its lordship over creation and the homage which comes from creatures. The adoration of the beast is the supreme form of idolatry; it is the continuation on earth in history of the rebellion against God attempted by Satan in the beginning of all things. In the words of the third angel, therefore, is found the condemnation of every idolatrous cult, the other fundamental commandment of the Old Law (Exod 20:3ff).

The three angels of the first group, therefore, are representation of the old Law, just as the three which follow represent the messianic message of the ancient Prophets. On each side of the Son of man are the Law and the Prophets who re-announced and rendered testimony to the death of Jesus as the final and definitive fulfilment of the divine plan for salvation. This is a concept which John, in ch. 11, had already conveyed through the two witnesses, both killed on account of their witnessing. Chapter 14 takes up again that episode and symbol. In the first part (the Lamb with the one hundred and forty-four thousand on Mt. Sion), the concept of the salvation reserved for the slain "witnesses" is carried further. In the second part (the two groups of angels flanking the Son of man), the actual significance of the witnessing is deepened: a witnessing to the death of Christ.

We have already seen when dealing with the reaping and the vintaging, how John applies the witness of the Prophets to the death of Christ, but in what way is the Law a pre-announcing and a witnessing to the death of Christ? In the sense that the Law already also implied a judgment of God upon the world. On the basis of this, in fact, John thinks that sin, a rebellion against God, had already received its condemnation and its punishment, and justice has already been rewarded, even though only exceptionally, and through the sacrifice of one's life. The expulsion of Satan from heaven by the angels and the victory which the ancient martyrs had over him were obtained "by the blood of the Lamb" (see 12:10-11). In this way, while they were already an anticipated effect of the judgment which took place in the death of Jesus, they were also a pre-announcing and a pre-figuring of it.

For this reason John can say that the first angel carries "an eternal Gospel" (14:6). This message, though it refers only to the old Law, is already "Gospel," i.e., "good news" because it already speaks of the judgment of God upon the world, the condemnation of the wicked and recompense for the just ones. This "good news" of the judgment of God announced in the Law prefigures the judgment of God perfected in the death of Christ.

"BLESSED ARE THE DEAD WHO DIE IN THE LORD HENCEFORTH" (V. 13)

In the light of the considerations which we have just concluded, we can better understand the meaning of vv. 12-13 which have always presented difficulties for interpreters. Their very position between the first group of angels and the appearance of the Son of man on the white cloud, followed by the second group of angels appears to break up the whole structure, and some have suggested that they do not belong here. It is suggested that they should follow 13:10, for obvious reasons: there is a repetition of the theme of the "endurance of the saints." There are many similarities besides this expression. The contexts are similar, as both references to the endurance of the saints follow an invocation of the violence and persecution which comes from the beast: the "saints" evidently are those who oppose the pretensions of the beast to receive divine honours, and for this reason are slain.

The similarity goes further. In ch. 13, the reference to the "endurance of the saints" follows the mention of the "book of life of the Lamb who was slain from the foundation of the world" (13:8). We saw then that the eternal validity of the sacrifice of Christ gives sense to the "endurance of the saints," and rewards the sacrifices of their lives, as they oppose the pretensions of the beast. Ch. 14 takes up and develops this concept. In the first part we find the Lamb in the company of the one hundred and forty-four thousand upon Mt. Sion, and this is a clearer way of speaking of the relationship that links the sacrifice of Christ and the "witnesses" who went before him. In the second part we find the Son of man between two groups of angels who represent respectively the witness of the Law and the Prophets to the death of Christ. Between them we find this reference to the "endurance of the saints." It is an evident and explicit recalling of ch. 13 and the persecution of the beast against the "saints." Now, however, these "saints" are clearly identified with the one hundred and forty-four thousand mentioned at the beginning of the chapter. In fact, all of vv. 12-13 are to be understood as referring specifically to the spiritual reality which they symbolise.

The call to endurance is only an introduction. The text goes on with a definition of the "saints" as those "who keep the commandments of God and the faith in Jesus" (14:12). In this definition is reproduced the usual double testimony to the Law and the coming of the Messiah which we have met so often, and especially in reference to the slain of the fifth seal (6:9), to the descendants of the woman (12:17). John will apply it again to the martyrs admitted to participation in the reign of a thousand years (20:4). For John, it is this double testimony which expresses itself through martyrdom in the Old Economy. The proof of this claim is given in ch. 14. Here the double witness is firstly recalled indirectly through the name of the Lamb and his Father which the one hundred and forty-four thousand bear written on their foreheads (14:1), and then explicitly cited in the formula of v. 12. The placing of the same citation at this stage of development of the book is significant. It follows the first group of angels who represent the Law, and precedes the appearance of the Son of man on the white cloud, which introduces the second group of angels who represent the messianic prophecies. It serves as a sort of swivel between the two witnesses of the Law and the Prophets to the coming and the death of Christ.

The significance of vv. 12-13 however is not exhausted by this function. Because it is situated between these two allegorical groups, the formula is now a precise reference, without any further ambiguity, to the Old Economy. These "saints" who have rendered testimony come before Christ, exactly as did the Law and the Prophets, to which they render practical witness, sealing that witness with their own blood. With this in mind, we can resolve the perennially difficult v. 13. John hears a voice which says:

> "Write this: Blessed are the dead who die in the Lord henceforth."

This is then solemnly sealed by the voice of the Spirit who adds:

> "Blessed indeed, that they may rest from their labours, for their deeds follow them" (14:13).

There is a great deal of discussion over what is meant by the expression "henceforth." Putting aside for a moment that discussion, the general meaning of the passage is very clear: John simply affirms that the just ones (the dead who die in the Lord) obtain immediately after death (from now), blessedness, eternal life.

This is an obvious truth for the Christian, so why is John so emphatic about it? The explanation normally given is that John intends, in this way, to assure the faithful (all or a part of them) that they will be admitted to eternal life before the final coming of Christ. The key is the expression "from now." He is anxious to show that there is no delay. At this stage scholars differ. Some, mostly Catholics, argue that it refers to all the faithful who die before the parousia, while others see it as referring only to the martyrs. This all presupposes the post-Christ period awaiting his second coming. We are questioning that presupposition. Clearly "the saints" are those referred to in v. 12: "those who keep the commandments of God and the faith of Jesus," and we have argued that the reference is to the martyrs of the Old Economy.

Here, in ch. 14, John's argument has been expressed first symbolically in the scene of the one hundred and forty-four thousand who surround the Lamb on Mt. Sion, and then announced in an explicit and systematic way in vv. 12-13. The mention of the "endurance of the saints" which opens vv. 12-13 serves to evoke the idea of persecution. The definition of the "saints" as those who "keep the commandments of God and the faith of Jesus" links the group clearly with those slain in the scene of the fifth seal. After this John has their eternal salvation proclaimed by a voice which comes directly from heaven to which the seal of the Holy Spirit is added.

Such a solemn procedure indicates that what is being said

here may not be self-evident. In fact, if, as I believe, here and in the analogous passages the message is of a salvation given directly to a certain category of just ones (martyrs for the Law and the messianic promises) who lived before Christ, the Apocalypse is the only document in the New Testament to make such a point. Nevertheless, John appears convinced that he has found this doctrine in the revealed scriptures. The situation which he describes (voice from heaven, command to write, presence of the Spirit) is the same as the one he described in his inaugural vision (see 1:10ff), as typical of the transmission of divine revelation.

John had no difficulty in finding ample biblical support for such an idea. The Wisdom books are very concerned with the question of the ultimate retribution of the persecuted just ones on the other side of death. There had to be an answer to the apparent suffering of these people during their human existence. The idea of a new life and a divine reward as being especially linked with the ultimate sacrifice of self in martyrdom for the faith begins to emerge very strongly in the literature which came into existence during the domination and persecution of Antiochus IV of Syria: the book of Daniel (see Dan 12:1ff) and the books of the Maccabees (see Mac 3:9-14, 23-36; 12:43-45).

John's particular concentration upon the martyrs of the Old Economy, for whom he reserves the exceptional admission to final salvation, flows from his way of understanding the messianic significance of the death of Jesus upon the cross. The sacrifice of these "witnesses" is not simply an anticipation of Jesus' death, but in every sense a part of it, as, in John's view, the slaying of the Lamb can be understood as already being effective "from the foundation of the world" (13:8).

THE SEVEN BOWLS: THE THIRD "SIGN" (15:1—22:5)

The Pouring out of the Bowls: The Death of Christ as Judgment upon the Consequences of the Original Fall (Chs. 15-16)

15 ¹Then I saw another portent in heaven, great and wonderful, seven angels with seven plagues, which are the last, for with them the wrath of God is ended.
²And I saw what appeared to be a sea of glass mingled with fire, and those who had conquered the beast and its image and the number of its name, standing beside the sea of glass with harps of God in their hands.
³And they sing the song of Moses, the servant of God, and the song of the Lamb, saying,

"Great and wonderful are thy deeds,
O Lord God the Almighty!
Just and true are thy ways,
O King of the ages!
⁴ Who shall not fear and glorify thy name, O Lord?
For thou alone art holy.
All nations shall come and worship thee,

for thy judgments have been
revealed."

⁵After this I looked, and the temple of the tent of witness in heaven was opened,

⁶and out of the temple came the seven angels with the seven plagues, robed in pure bright linen, and their breasts girded with golden girdles.

⁷And one of the four living creatures gave the seven angels seven golden bowls full of the wrath of God who lives for ever and ever;

⁸and the temple was filled with smoke from the glory of God and from his power, and no one could enter the temple until the seven plagues of the seven angels were ended.

16¹Then I heard a loud voice from the temple telling the seven angels, "Go and pour out on the earth the seven bowls of the wrath of God."

²So the first angel went and poured his bowl on the earth, and foul and evil sores came upon the men who bore the mark of the beast and worshiped its image.

³The second angel poured his bowl into the sea, and it became like the blood of a dead man, and every living thing died that was in the sea.

⁴The third angel poured his bowl into the rivers and the fountains of water, and they became blood.

⁵And I heard the angel of water say,

"Just art thou in these thy
judgments,
thou who art and wast, O Holy One.
⁶ For men have shed the blood of
saints and prophets,
and thou hast given them blood to
drink.
It is their due!"

⁷And I heard the altar cry,

"Yea, Lord God the Almighty,
true and just are thy judgments!"

⁸The fourth angel poured his bowl on the sun, and it was

allowed to scorch men with fire;
⁹men were scorched by the fierce heat, and they cursed the name of God who had power over these plagues, and they did not repent and give him glory.

¹⁰The fifth angel poured his bowl on the throne of the beast, and its kingdom was in darkness; men gnawed their tongues in anguish

¹¹and cursed the God of heaven for their pain and sores, and did not repent of their deeds.

¹²The sixth angel poured his bowl on the great river Euphrates, and its water was dried up, to prepare the way for the kings from the east.

¹³And I saw, issuing from the mouth of the dragon and from the mouth of the beast and from the mouth of the false prophet, three foul spirits like frogs;

¹⁴for they are demonic spirits, performing signs, who go abroad to the kings of the whole world, to assemble them for battle on the great day of God the Almighty.

¹⁵("Lo, I am coming like a thief! Blessed is he who is awake, keeping his garments that he may not go naked and be seen exposed!")

¹⁶And they assembled them at the place which is called in Hebrew Armageddon.

¹⁷The seventh angel poured his bowl into the air, and a loud voice came out of the temple, from the throne, saying, "It is done!"

¹⁸And there were flashes of lightning, voices, peals of thunder, and a great earthquake such as had never been since men were on the earth, so great was that earthquake.

¹⁹The great city was split into three parts, and the cities of the nations fell, and God remembered great Babylon, to make her drain the cup of the fury of his wrath.

²⁰And every island fled away, and no mountains were to be found;

²¹and great hailstones, heavy as a hundred-weight, dropped on men from heaven, till men cursed God for the plague of the hail, so fearful was that plague.

STRUCTURE AND GENERAL THEME

Chapters 15-16 make up the central nucleus of the "seven" of the bowls which, as we have seen, forms the whole of the second part of the Apocalypse, from ch. 12 till the epilogue. Two chapters describe first the handing over and then the pouring out of the bowls at the hand of seven angels. The descriptive-narrative material of ch. 15 presents a preparatory phase, while ch. 16 describes the actual pouring out of the bowls.

Ch. 15 is made up of a series of visions which evidently take place in heaven. There is, at the beginning of the chapter, the vision "in heaven" of "another great and wonderful sign" (15:1). There follows the vision of those who have conquered the beast who "sing the song of Moses, the servant of God, and the song of the Lamb" (15:2-3). They are *standing* upon the sea of glass which is evidently the same as the one before the throne of the divinity in ch. 4 (see 4:6).

Then there is another group of visions which have the temple as their point of reference, "the temple of God which is in heaven" also mentioned elsewhere, e.g., at the end of the seventh trumpet (see 11:19). In fact, there is a clear recalling of that circumstance, because here also the Temple opens (15:5) and from it come out angels who receive bowls full of the anger of God so that they can pour them out over the land, the sea, etc., as will be described in ch. 16.

Considering the two chapters as a unit, we can see reproduced here the scheme which we noticed in ch. 14: two groups of scenes, the first of which is rather static and the second full of movement. To the vision of the Lamb surrounded by the one hundred and forty-four thousand on Mt. Sion (14:1) corresponds the vision of the conquerors of the beast upon the sea of glass. Corresponding to the scene full of movement in ch. 14, culminating in the vintage, is the exit of the angels from the heavenly temple to receive the bowls, with the command to pour them over the various elements of creation. In this case the analogy between the two is stressed by the fact that both the angels of the vintage and the angels of the bowls came out from the Temple (14:15ff; 15:5ff).

Again we find a typically Johannine repetition which carries the argument further and deeper. He is looking back to the final parts of the trumpets, the seals and even the letters. Chapter 15 begins with the vision of "another sign in heaven, great and wonderful" (15:1): the angels with seven plagues (v. 8). This recalls the two "signs in heaven" of the woman and the dragon, which began ch. 12.

Another linking element is the Temple of God in heaven. This goes back to the previous chapter and the reaping and vintaging, solicited or actually performed by angels who came out from the Temple. The Temple is seen as "opened" (v. 5). This goes back even further, literally to the conclusion of the seventh trumpet: "Then God's temple in heaven was opened, and the ark of his covenant was seen within"(11:9). This opening of the Temple and appearance of the ark of the covenant is the culmination of the promise of the "mystery of God" which had ben made by the "strong angel" in 10:7:

> "In the days of the trumpet call to be sounded by the seventh angel, the mystery of God, as he announced to his servants the prophets, should be fulfilled."

In this mystery of God there were two fundamental aspects: the coming of the messianic kingdom, stressed by the angelic submission (11:15-16) and the divine judgment upon the world (11:17-18).

Also in the seventh trumpet, the opening of the Temple of God which is in heaven is followed by "flashes of lightning, loud noises, peals of thunder, an earthquake and heavy hail" (11:19). All of this reappears at the end of ch. 16, after the pouring out of the last bowl, with great stress being given to the elements of the earthquake and the hail (16:18-21). This is also clearly intentional. We can now draw a very important conclusion concerning the scheme behind chs. 15 and 16: all the happenings described in the two chapters, from the moment in which the temple opens and the angels come out until the pouring out of the last cup, i.e., up to the end of ch. 16, are nothing else but a taking up and a further development of the seventh trumpet. In other words, the whole "seven" of the bowls is a development of the trumpet in which is perfected "the mystery of God."

The fulfilment of the "mystery of God" described in the seventh trumpet involves, however, the coming of the messianic kingdom and the inauguration of the universal judgment of God. These two aspects, in opposite order, have been taken up by John in the following chapters up till the epilogue of the book: judgment of God as the destruction of the wicked forces (chs. 17-20), the coming of the messianic kingdom (21-22). What he describes in chs. 15-16 is something more limited, something which happens between the opening of the Temple and the phenomena which accompany it. This is a period which cannot be measured in time, and thus, while here there are successive events, in the seventh trumpet it was all one event.

The event which is at the centre of this period between the opening of the Temple and the following is made clear in the fact that the death of Christ is already included in the two symbols which more or less frame the account: opening of the Temple, and the phenomena, especially the earthquake, both symbols of the death of Christ.

The succession of the pouring out of the bowls is a literary procedure. It is used to show various aspects of the one event, the death of Christ, especially judgment and the condemnation of the wicked powers. This explains why, in the first place, the pouring out of the bowls retraces, point by point, the succession of the trumpets. If they represent, as we have insisted, the perversion and the fall of the angels and the spreading of their influence in the world and in human events, the pouring out of the bowls, in so far as it repeats the stages of perversion, signifies the divine judgment which falls upon such perversion, condemning it and destroying its roots and wicked effects in the physical and human world.

It also explains another aspect, generally noticed by all commentators, in John's description of the successive pouring out of the bowls, largely upon the plagues which struck the Egyptians before the departure of the Hebrews. The meaning of this allusion is clear: the death of Christ represents a new Exodus, the liberation of humanity from diabolic oppression. This fresh and most explicit reference to the Hebrew Exodus does not come unexpectedly. We have already found it at the end of ch. 14 (the horses drowning in the blood from the wine-press) and a more evident one in ch. 15 (the victors over the beast who sing the canticle of Moses and the Lamb on the "sea of glass mingled with fire").

The contact with the Exodus reaches back even further: to the seven seals, and especially the fifth and sixth. Especially in the sixth seal there is an allusion to the Exodus in the seal on the foreheads of the one hundred and forty-four thousand, but they have already been recalled in 14:1, around the Lamb in Mt. Sion. The same people are involved in the opening of ch. 15 (vv. 2-3) singing the song of Moses. They are also the group of the slain of the fifth seal who received rest and eternal life under the altar (6:9-10).

The link with the sixth seal is not limited to recalling the Exodus. There is in the seal on the foreheads of the elect, a reference to a restraint placed upon hostile powers (the four winds held back by the four angels in the four zones of the earth) (see 7:1ff). In the sixth trumpet, this reference is taken up in the opposite direction: the hostile forces are let loose and they leave from the river Euphrates (9:14ff). We saw in this an allegory on the breaking forth of wars of domination, the worst consequence of original sin in history. The pouring out of the sixth bowl will take up this motif in 16:21ff, but in a quite different fashion.

Less apparent is the link with the sixth seal. It comes through the motif of the opening of the Temple of God in heaven, a motif which, as we have seen, sends us to the conclusion of the seventh trumpet. This opening of the Temple alludes to the perfection of revelation, the unveiling of the "mystery of God" communicated to mankind, making real the dwelling of God in its midst. This necessarily brings with it the end of the Old Economy in which "mystery of God" was wrapped in a curtain of silence and shadow, symbolised in ancient Jewish cult by the curtain which separated the people from the vision of the ark of the covenant (see Exod 40:1ff). The opening of the Temple also signifies the end of the ancient cult, a feature which has been referred to by the "silence for about a half an hour" which followed the opening of the seventh seal (see 8:1).

From this whole series of interlacing themes we can see how John has a concentrated summary of a great deal of the earlier part of the book in his description of the pouring out of the seven bowls. His intention is clear: the death of Christ brings to final perfection the divine salvific intervention of God, and sums up in itself all the greatness of the achievements of the Old Economy. It is, therefore, not the continuation but the replacement of the Old Economy; it confirms it on a spiritual level, but destroys it on a material, historical level.

THE SIGN IN THE SKY

Ch. 15 begins with the vision of a sign in the sky. It is connected, as the third in a series, to the two "signs" which opened ch. 12, that of the woman and of the dragon (see 12:1-4). The succession of the three signs constitutes a basic structural element which is the basis of the unity of the section from ch. 12 to the appearance of this third "sign" at the beginning of ch. 15.

We now know the significance of these three "signs." The first, that of the woman, represents the creation of humanity, in a stage of innocence and privilege within the universe. The second, that of the dragon, represents the first phase of the divine salvific intervention. This phase still has a negative aspect, the satanic rebellion which spreads among men. God protects the woman (humanity) from the persecution of the dragon, driving Satan from heaven through the action of angels, and giving to humanity, again through angels, the Law and the messianic promises of the Prophets. The explanation of the second "sign" occupies a large part of ch. 12 (the casting out of Satan from heaven) and the successive chs. 13 (the diabolic persecution represented historically by the union between the two beasts) and 14 (the choice of the elect, the giving of the Law and the confirmation of the messianic promises of liberation). The third "sign" is the death of Christ, which is the perfection of the messianic promise, the destruction of the enemies of the human race and the liberation of humanity from their yoke. Of the three "signs" this one is, for John, the most important; in fact, only this sign is called "great and wonderful" (15:1).

In chs. 15-16 the third "sign" is illustrated as taking place, especially in its judging aspects, understood as the condemnation of sin and of sinners. This illustration will go on until ch. 20. Chs. 21-22 will be dedicated to an indication of the positive aspects of the judgment of God, i.e., the gathering of the elect, beyond the Red Sea, beyond the desert, on the "great high mountain" of the new Jerusalem.

Understood in this way, the three "signs in heaven" correspond to the three "woes" announced by the great eagle before the sounding of the fifth trumpet (8:13), and which coincide with the final three trumpets. The three "woes," in fact, refer respectively to the fall of man (fifth trumpet), the giving of the Law and prophecy (sixth trumpet) and to the death of Christ (seventh trumpet). All three of these events, however, were seen in the trumpets from the point of view of the diabolic intervention which attempts to turn upside down all meaning, and to obtain results which are completely different from those willed by God. The creature man, giving in to the temptation which rises from the bottomless pit, falls into a condition of material and spiritual misery (first woe, the fifth trumpet). The witness of the Law and the Prophets is stamped upon and suffocated by the "beast which rises from the bottomless pit," the "holy city" is so profaned and corrupted that it becomes the residence of Satan (second "woe," sixth trumpet). The death of Christ therefore is seen only from a negative point of view: the profanation of the Temple and the end of Judaism (third "woe," seventh trumpet).

THE CONQUERORS OF THE BEAST

Ch. 14 concluded with the scene of the wine-pressing of the gathered grapes "in the great wine press of the wrath of God" from which issues blood to flood the earth and stop the advance of the horses (14:19-20). We saw in this a reference to the Exodus (see Exod 14:23). The scene which opens ch. 15 confirms that interpretation. John sees "what appeared to be a sea of glass mingled with fire."

> Those who had conquered the beast came forward upon it *standing* and singing "the song of Moses, the servant of God, and the song of the Lamb" (15:2-3).

The reference to the Exodus here is evident, and noticed by all commentators. It is normally understood as a model of the victory won by Christians or Christian martyrs over Satan. It appears to me that these conquerors of the beast are to be identified with the one hundred and forty-four thousand who stand on Mt. Sion with the Lamb (14:1ff) and, through them, to the one hundred and forty-four thousand of the sixth seal (7:1ff) and then to the slain ones of the fifth seal (6:9-10). It is clearly a question of martyrs, because the beast slays all those who oppose his absolutist and idolatrous pretensions (13:15). The fact that they are called conquerors indicates however that they are among those for whom being slain was a motive for their retribution, their receiving eternal life. In this they are conquerors. John presents them as "standing," a feature which is applied both to the Lamb (5:6; 14:1) and to the two "witnesses" (11:11) indicating in both cases a victory over the violent death they have suffered.

The scene of the conquerors of the beast "standing upon the sea of glass" takes up yet again John's repeated insistence, a message of the salvation given, within the context of the Old Economy, to those who have given witness, with the sacrifice of their lives, to the Law of God and the coming of Jesus Christ. This double witness is the characteristic of the slain of the fifth seal. It is concentrated into the name of God and of the Lamb with the one hundred and forty-four thousand on Mt. Sion borne on their foreheads (14:1). For the conquerors of the beast, this double witness is expressed through their "song of Moses, the servant of God" and the "song of the Lamb" (15:3).

The song of the conquerors contains another allusion to the Hebrew Exodus: the song which Moses and the Hebrews sang after the crossing of the Red Sea (see Exod 15:1ff). In reality, the reference is only to the circumstance because the song in the Apocalypse has no contact with Exodus. There are two themes:

(a) The exaltation of the power and majesty of God, seen especially in his intervention in history as judge, and an invitation to fear and glorify him. This is fairly close to the message of the three angels in ch. 14 (14:6-11) in which we saw a presentation of the divine Law and its judgment upon men.

(b) An explicit reference to the reign of God over the whole of humanity, i.e., to the coming of the messianic kingdom.

Again we find an echo of the double witnessing: the Law and the prophecies about the coming of Jesus Christ, i.e., the characteristic feature of the just ones of the Old Economy.

In this way is explained the fact that they sing not only the song of Moses, but also that of the Lamb. The conquerors of the beast have given witness, not only to the Law given by God to Moses, but also to the coming of Jesus Christ, in which the liberation promised and the Law would have their fulfilment. To sing "the song of the Lamb" means that these conquerors of the beast, like the one hundred and forty-four thousand on Mt. Sion, have a special relationship to the Lamb in two ways:

— Like him, they have given witness through the sacrifice of their own lives.
— Because of this, they have obtained, in anticipation, the benefits of the sacrifice of the Lamb.

The first of these confirms the idea that these conquerors of the beast are martyrs. The second clarifies further the significance of this scene, taking up yet again the theme of the salvation of the just ones in the Old Economy. That they are redeemed comes clear from the expression "standing," i.e., given a new life after death. The standing upon a sea of glass also indicates this. The "sea of glass" is evidently the same as the one in the vision of the throne in ch. 4:6, though here it is described as "mingled with fire." The explanation of this detail we can perhaps find by remembering what happened in the first four trumpets (8:7ff). There the rebellion and the fall of the angels was described as a throwing down of fire from heaven upon the sea and upon the land, i.e., upon the world of sea and land which was symbolised in ch. 4 by a "sea of glass like crystal." The fire which is now mixed with this sea is, in general, the influence of Satan, the moral and physical corruption which he has introduced. In a more specific sense, it represents the corruption of political authority (the sea) through which, in fact, the persecution against the saints, i.e., "those who observe the commandments of God and bear testimony to Jesus" (12:17), actually takes place.

Upon this "sea of glass mingled with fire" the saved of ch. 15 *stand*, i.e., doubly victorious. They have overcome persecution (conquerors of the beast) and they have broken the death-bringing power of Satan upon humanity caused by original sin, by already participating in the sacrifice of Christ, even before his coming. It is not impossible even to see in this sea of glass mingled with fire an allusion to the Red Sea, through which the Hebrews were saved from the oppression of Pharaoh. John is not interested in the historical detail of the story, but in its profound spiritual significance: the salvation and life which God promised to mankind, right from the start of history. For John, this comes to its perfection in Jesus Christ, but it has also had its "first fruits" (14:4) in the Old Economy, and the liberation of the Hebrew people from the slavery of Egypt was its material, visible symbol.

PLAGUES AND BOWLS

The "sign" in heaven which appears to John consists of seven angels who have in their hands "seven plagues, which are the last, for with them the wrath of God is ended" (15:1). It is natural to think that these seven plagues are the effects produced when the bowls are poured out, but it is clear that John wants to distinguish between the "plagues" and the "bowls." The "plagues," in fact, are already in the hands of the angels from the moment they appear, while the "bowls" are given to them by one of the four living creatures as they come forth from the Temple which is opened. Moreover, at that second stage, John again indicates that they already have the "seven plagues" in their hands (15:6-7).

John is a careful author, and this distinction is for a purpose. It is best found by looking at the description of the bowls. They are "bowls full of the wrath of God who lives for ever and ever" (15:7). Now the "wrath of God," like the wrath of God and of the Lamb which was mentioned in the sixth seal (16:7) and also in the "great wine press of the wrath of God" into which the grapes were thrown in 14:19, is simply an expression used to speak of the judgment of God, which also means condemnation and destruction for his enemies. In this sense, the contents of the bowls, when they are poured out, coincide with the plagues which the angels hold in their hands already. We can explain it in this way: for the judgment of God, in so far as it means condemnation and destruction for the wicked, the Law and its representatives, the angels, are sufficient. A similar explanation has already been suggested in the distinction between the reaping and the vintaging.

The judgment of God has, however, especially to the eyes of John, a positive aspect: the giving of salvation to the just ones, to the "servants of God" (see v. 3) in the judgment which happens at the death of Christ. Its positive aspect consists in the redemption, i.e., in the offer of salvation to all men. This task can be done only by Jesus Christ (see 5:2-7), who accomplishes it through the sacrifice of his own life. This is the probable reason for the distinction between the plagues and the bowls upon which John seems to insist.

THE PROFANATION OF THE TEMPLE AND THE END OF JEWISH CULT

The scenes which take place in the second part of ch. 15 have the Temple of God as their point of reference. It is found in heaven, but it is to be seen as representing the affairs of the history of the Jewish Temple, of which the heavenly Temple is its model. This is the succession of scenes: the Temple is opened; seven angels carrying seven plagues come out from it; one of the four living creatures hands them "seven golden bowls full of the wrath of God"; the Temple, now empty and into which no-one can enter until the cups have been poured out, becomes filled with the presence of the divinity (15:5-8).

The final scene, as can be seen from its biblical reminiscences (see Exod 40:34; I Kgs 8:10; Ezek 44:4), represents a consecration of the Temple by the divinity. Why is the Temple consecrated? We must notice what precedes. The Temple is now open. We know the value of this symbolic scene: it means a much wider divine revelation, open to all, but also the end of a certain form of cult. There have been repeated references to it: the silence in the sky of the seventh seal (8:1); the angel's pouring out the fire from the altar onto the ground (8:5); opening of the Temple at the conclusion of the seventh trumpet (11:19).

In his accumulation of these symbols, we see John indicating an interruption and an end. The death of Christ makes an end of the ancient Jewish cult. This is already in the Synoptic Gospels (see Matt 27:51; Mk 15:38; Lk 23:45) but John goes beyond them. He gives the reason why this happened. The slaying of Christ at the instigation of the High Priests has profaned the Temple and thus no one can enter the Temple until all the bowls have been poured out, i.e., for all the time during which Jesus is left at the mercy of death.

In all this John saw fulfilled the prophecy of Daniel on the profanation of the Temple and the interruption of the cult for a half a week (see Dan 9:27) which was to precede the final coming of the messianic kingdom. Daniel, of course, was thinking of the slaying of the High Priest Onias III by

Antiochus IV and the introduction of the statue of Zeus into the Temple. This was only a repetition of what Nabuchadnezzar had done when he destroyed Jerusalem and its Temple, taking off all the sacred vessels as booty (Dan 1:2), to be used by Balthassar in his famous banquet (Dan 5:1ff).

Despite the seriousness of those events, they were for John only a symbol of the further profanation and destruction of the Temple which would take place in the slaying of Christ. It is in this sense that the symbols of profanation, despoiling and material destruction of the Temple in ancient times are recalled. The bowls, in fact, an all-embracing symbol of the sacred vessels of the Temple, are now taken out from the Temple. The Temple, therefore, has been violated (it is opened) and despoiled of its goods. Further, John indicates that one of the four living creatures gives them to the angels. What does this mean? The four living creatures, we have seen are put forward to govern human history and, therefore, all the four empires which followed one another in the course of that history. Not even the work of the oppressors of the chosen people, the destroyers and the profaners, is removed from their authority. These evil ones may well be the instruments of Satan in inflicting his wicked rule upon mankind, but they are also the instruments through which God has gradually exercised his judgment upon the world.

The bowls are not only a symbol of the sacred vessels of the Temple, but are also "full of the anger of God." They therefore symbolise his judgment, following a biblical tradition (see Is 51:17; Jer 25:15ff). For John, this judgment of God upon the world is perfectly acted out in the death of Christ, of which the bowl (Greek *phiale*) and the chalice (Greek *poterion*) are a continual symbol in the New Testament and in the Christian literature of the first centuries. Still, even in this sense, in which they symbolise the judgment of God which happens in the death of Christ, the bowls are under the jurisdiction of the four living creatures. In fact, in the slaying of Christ the political authority, incarnated in the Roman Empire, has a decisive role, even if the responsibility for the deicide does not fall upon it alone, but also upon the religious authority represented by the Jewish synagogue. This is what John will illustrate for us shortly, in ch. 17, with the allegory of the prostitute seated upon the beast (see 17:3).

THE OPENING OF THE TEMPLE

We must return for a moment to the opening of the Temple, the handing over of the bowls which happens outside the Temple. We have seen here the symbolic representation of the profanation suffered by the Jewish Temple, first on a material level (despoiling, destruction, the introduction of impure and idolatrous elements) and finally on a spiritual level with the slaying of Jesus. This final profanation has marked the end of the Jewish cult.

Something similar appears to be found in earlier symbolic scenes. Among these, the opening of the Temple described at the end of the seventh trumpet (11:19). We have already remarked on a correspondence between the conclusion of the seventh trumpet and that of the angelic liturgy which serves as a preface to the "seven" of the trumpets, when the angel officiating at the cult takes fire from the altar, fills up the censer and pours it out upon the ground (8:5). Even this is a clear reference to the end of the ancient cult and, at the same time, to the divine judgment which falls upon the world. What happens in chs. 15-16 with the opening of the Temple, the handing over of the bowls and their being poured out over the earth, the sea, etc., is a variation of what was described in that angelic liturgy. Here also there is something taken from the Temple and then poured out through the hand of an angel upon the world. Here also it is a question of the judgment of God, but through the symbol of the bowls, this judgment is now more precisely identified with the death of Christ.

The opening of the Temple in ch. 15 looks back to the seventh trumpet, but this repetition, as usual, is not without important variations. In the first place, the Temple is no longer called "the Temple of God which is in heaven" (11:19) but "the Temple of the tent of witness" (15:5). We will attempt to explain this below. In ch. 11 the opening of the Temple revealed the ark of the covenant, and here it is not mentioned. It is possible to explain the difference by supposing that, in the first case, John alludes to an opening of the veil which separated the faithful in the Temple from the "Holy of Holies" where the ark was reserved, while in the second case (ch. 15) it is an actual opening up of the Temple itself which, in Exodus (see 40:1ff) is described as a large tent. The absence of a reference to the ark is better explained however by insisting that ch. 15 is concentrating on the devastation and profanation of the Temple. The ark is no longer there.

THE SEVEN ANGELS AND THE SON OF MAN

What follows the opening of the Temple of God in ch. 15 confirms the double significance, of judgment and salvation, of the end of something yet the beginning of something involved in that event. From the open Temple emerge seven angels with the seven plagues in hand. They are avengers, instruments of judgment and punishment. We must notice their dress. They are "robed in pure bright linen, and their breasts girded with golden girdles" (15:6). Their appearance recalls that of the man seen by Daniel on the shore of the river Tigris (see Dan 10:5), a figure which John has identified with the Son of man in the vision of ch. 1 (see 1:13).

These seven angels recall the symbol of the Son of man described in ch. 14, seated upon a white cloud with a golden crown upon his head. But the golden girdle girding their breasts, as we have already seen in ch. 1, is a more precise indication of the historical event of the incarnation, of the union of the divine and the human in Jesus Christ. The same can possibly be said also of the shifting of the colour "white" from the cloud to the clothing, which is again always used in the Apocalypse to refer to the new reality connected with redemption. In particular, the clothing of the angels anticipates the clothing of the heavenly army which accompanies the Logos on the white horse in ch. 19 (see 19:14). Above all, it anticipates the clothing of the spouse ready for the marriage with the Lamb:

> "It was granted to her to be clothed with fine linen, bright and pure – for the fine linen is the righteous deeds of the saints" (19:8).

The figure of the seven angels summarises the double significance of the death of Christ, as it puts into effect judgment and punishment for sin (the seven plagues) and makes possible the redemption of the new people of God (golden girdles, linen clothes). The bowls also given to them as they come out of the Temple have this double significance. In this and the following chapters, however, only the one aspect of the bowls appears, the destruction of evil, of which the judgment and the ruination of Babylon (chs. 17-18) are a grandiose representation.

The positive aspect, that of the redemption, will be described later in the allegory of the heavenly Jerusalem, but before arriving there, John will again take up the theme of the coming of the Son of man in the vision of the Logos in 19:11ff. This vision will take up, not only aspects of the Son of man from ch. 14, but also scenes from chs. 15-16. The events from the opening of the Temple to the pouring out of the bowls is repeated: the opening of heaven (opening of the Temple), the descent of the Logos on the white horse, accompanied by a heavenly army (the seven angels in pure linen, girded with gold) and the battle of Armageddon (the pouring out of the bowls).

THE "CONSECRATION" OF THE TEMPLE

The exit of the angels from the Temple and the handing over of the bowls are followed by another scene which still has the heavenly Temple as its point of reference. In fact, John says: "And the Temple was filled with smoke from the glory of God and from his power, and no one could enter the Temple until the seven plagues of the seven angels were ended" (15:8). John makes reference once more to the Temple of Moses and to its consecration by God when it was finally constructed (see Exod 40:32-36).

Between the two circumstances, however, there exist important differences. In the Apocalypse, the divine presence fills the Temple after it has been opened, which is the exact opposite to what happened in the Exodus. Moreover, the divine presence in the Mosaic Temple is described as occasional, and the prohibition of entry is tied strictly to the divine presence (see Exod 40:33ff). Here, instead, it appears that there is more than a prohibition because of the presence of the divine; it is impossible to enter until some external event happens, i.e., the pouring out of the bowls. It should also be noticed that the ark, the ideal centre of the Mosaic Temple, is no longer mentioned in ch. 15. These differences become even more significant if one remembers the fact that the heavenly Temple described here, contrary to the earlier cases, recalls much more precisely the Temple of Moses described in the *Exodus*. John, in fact, names it with an unusual expression: "The Temple of the tent of witness" (15:5). The Temple in *Exodus* is essentially a tent (see Exod 26:1ff). It is a tent where God descends to speak to Moses (see Exod 33:7ff). It is called "the tent of the meeting," a name which is given also to the most sacred part of the Mosaic Temple.

By calling the Temple a "tent," John takes away all the trimmings and brings it back to its original function: a sacred place for the divine presence, a place for the divinity to dwell. In this sacred place, as in the ideal Temple described in the final chapters of the book of Ezekiel, the ark is no longer necessary. It is now no less than the venerated place of custody for the "witness," i.e., the tablets of the Law, a symbol of the covenant between God and the chosen people, of his presence among them. Any material symbol is, of its very nature, subject to despoiling and destruction, as has happened to the Temple. From now on the Law will be represented and witnessed to be a presence which is not occasional, but stable, just as Ezekiel has prophesied about the future Temple (Ezek 43:9).

It appears, therefore, that we can now understand clearly

why John takes up the motif of the Temple in the culminating moment in which "the mystery of God" is perfected, i.e., the death of Christ. The heavenly Temple opens: a sign of the most complete revelation, and the end of a certain type of cult. It is now empty of all the sacred objects of the cult (the ark and the bowls which are handed over outside the Temple), and no-one can enter, not even the angels. The angelic liturgy and therefore, the ancient cult of which they are the representatives, ceases. It is the "silence in heaven for about a half an hour," announced in the seventh seal (8:1), the interruption of the angelic liturgy, foreshadowed in the scene of the pouring out of the fire taken from the altar (8:5).

The Temple, now reduced to a "tent," i.e., purified and taken back to its original function as the house of God, of his word and of his Law ("witness"), is "consecrated," i.e., filled with the presence of God in his glory and power. This presence, as in the Temple spoken of by Ezekiel (Ezek 43:9) is now stable, and permanent. It will no longer be necessary to enter there, not even after the pouring out of the bowls. When they are poured out, therefore, the mystery of God will be perfected, the redemption of the whole of mankind, and the "tent" full of the divine presence, will descend from heaven to earth. It is the "new Jerusalem" which descends from heaven, coming from God. This, in fact, is none other than "the tent of God with men. He will dwell with them, and they shall be his people, and God himself will be with them" (21:2-3). It is in this sense that John will be able to say that the new Jerusalem no longer has any Temple "for its Temple is the Lord God the Almighty and the Lamb" (21:22). The presence of the divinity in it makes the whole of it into a Temple. For this reason, while in the past the prophets measured the Temple as a place within whose borders God and his adorers dwelt (see 11:1-2), later there will be measuring of the new Jerusalem (see 21:15ff); it will be, in fact, all a "tent," the dwelling place of God among men (21:3).

THE POURING OUT OF THE BOWLS

The order in which the bowls are poured out upon creation by the angels repeats the trumpets: land, sea, rivers and fountains of water, the sun and the stars, "the throne of the beast" (the bottomless pit) and the Euphrates. Only the seventh trumpet and the seventh bowl lack a perfect correspondence, but this is easily explained when ones sees that, even though the seven bowls summarised all the preceding "sevens," the actual pouring out of the bowls is, in fact, a full development of all the implications of the seventh trumpet. It takes place between the opening of the Temple of God (15:5) and the lightning, sounds, thunder, earthquake, etc., which follow the pouring out of the final bowl (16:18ff), two phenomena which happen together in the seventh trumpet (11:19).

It is true that the pouring out of the bowls follows the order of the trumpets, but the effects which they produce are different. While the plagues, at least as regards the first four trumpets, strike directly on the physical world, and only indirectly strike humanity itself, here in the bowls all are directed against living beings and particularly against men. Another change of direction can be seen in the last three bowls. In the trumpets, humanity was struck by the three "woes" which corresponded with the final three trumpets. Here, though the plagues still strike men, their real objective goes further than mankind, into the profound root which has caused their deception, their physical and moral wickedness: the dragon and his two agents in history, the two beasts (corrupt political and religious authority).

The way in which the plagues spread appears also to be different. In the trumpets, the evils which first strike the physical world and then the human are not provoked by the angels. The angels sound the trumpets, but then something either falls from heaven (flame) or rises from the pit (locusts) to corrupt, to destroy, to torment and to kill. In the cups, it is the angels themselves who produce the evils, as they pour out the contents of the bowls one after the other.

There are, therefore, between the two "sevens" similarities and differences which appear to be intentional. Both can be explained by remembering that in the two different "sevens" John is representing two phases in the intervention of God in human history. The intervention always brings judgment and salvation, but they have different forms and levels. The phase of the trumpets has a defensive and provisional character: God limits himself to the driving out of heaven of Satan and his followers, to protecting the descendants of the woman, giving the Law and confirming, through the Prophets, his promise of liberation. In practice, however, this phase sees a widening of the attempt of Satan to dominate both the world and humanity, helped by political and religious authority which he has corrupted. This explains the sombre and dramatic conclusion (the three "woes") to the "seven" of the trumpets. It also explains why there is no direct link between the sounding of the trumpet by the angel and the actual evil which is produced. The ancient Law (the sound of the Trumpet) can reveal the presence of sin, but it cannot remedy it. It is therefore a partial and limited judgment of God.

The true and definitive judgment of God is represented here in the bowls, which symbolise the death of Christ. The plagues produced by the bowls are the revelation of the state of corruption and sin in which creation and mankind finds itself as a result of the original fall. John begins again, as in the trumpets, from the corruption of the physical world, but by now he has made clear to his readers that this is the effect of the sin of rebellion, firstly by the angels and then by humans. For this reason, the physical evils described here automatically become images of the misery and of the spiritual ruin into which humanity has fallen.

THE FIRST FOUR BOWLS

First bowl (upon the earth): the corruption of human nature and the loss of the original privileges through original sin (the evil sores: 16:2). *Second bowl* (in the sea, which becomes "like the blood of a dead man": 16:3): the corruption of political authority (the sea), based upon violence which brings destruction and death. *Third bowl* (into the rivers and the fountains of water which become blood: 16:4): the corruption of that which should have given strength and spiritual life, i.e., the perversion of Judaism to such a point that it came to kill those sent by God and also the Prophets (16:6: "For men have shed the blood of saints and prophets"). *Fourth bowl* (on the sun: 16:8): the high point of human pride which, in initiation of Satan, attempts to challenge heaven and the divinity, is severely punished, but never changes its ways (rebellion of Adam, tower of Babel, Sodom and Gomorrha, etc. up to the murderous attempt against the Son of God).

The first four bowls are, therefore, a great allegory of the disastrous effects of original sin, exactly as were the first four seals and the first four trumpets. Nevertheless, while the effects of the fall are illustrated largely in an external, material fashion (seals: miserable situation of man after the fall: war, famine, death; trumpets: the cursing of creation following the fall), here, instead, the divine judgment throws the spiritual aspect into relief in a special way. In the description of this aspect, as already in the two previous cases, we can see a similar *crescendo*, not so much in the succession of the punishments as in the growing blindness and hardness of heart among men. In no way persuaded by the punishment received after the first fall with the loss of his original condition ("foul and evil sores"), man perseveres in his attitude of challenging God, obtaining and building with his own hands even further evils and suffering. Not even here does he surrender. Instead of reflecting upon his actions and repenting, he rages against God, cursing him and blaspheming against him, as if God were the author of the evils (16:9).

THE FIFTH BOWL

With the fifth bowl the objective of the judgment of God changes. The angel, says John, "poured his bowl on the throne of the beast, and its kingdom was in darkness" (16:10). Where is the "throne of the beast"? Rome or Jerusalem have been suggested. But "beast" here has to be understood as Satan, and this throne must therefore be "the bottomless pit," in close parallel with the fifth trumpet (9:1ff). From there, in fact, come out the smoke which darkened the sun and the air. The fifth bowl carries on the work of the fourth which had freed the sun from the attack of the smoke arising from the bottomless pit. The fifth bowl, therefore, drives back the smoke into the bottomless pit, the kingdom of Satan, which becomes a kingdom of darkness.

It could be an image: darkness meaning error, spiritual blindness, or it could be a material darkness, as in the analogous plague in Egypt (see Exod 10:21) to which John is explicitly referring. Neither of these explanations, however, explains why "men gnawed their tongues in anguish and cursed the God of heaven" (vv. 10b-11a). It is probable that this darkness represents eternal perdition, parallel to the "exterior darkness" which Matthew often mentions (see Matt 8:12; 22:13; 25:30) or of the "night" into which Judas passes, as he takes his definitive leave of Jesus in the Fourth Gospel (see Jn 13:27-30).

In this way the fifth bowl is really the completion of the fourth. Human pride which dared to challenge heaven has not only been severely driven back by the divine power, but now, giving absolutely no sign of repentance, is driven away forever into that place where the diabolic temptations had their origin. From there they continue to blaspheme against God. The death of Christ is also judgment of God in this way: it makes final, for the proud one who knows no repentance, the loss of divine and eternal life which has been temporarily taken away from man by the original fall. In the same way, the judgment which takes place in the death of Christ gave life to those just ones who lived before Christ but who, because they were not martyrs, were not granted eternal life in anticipation.

These ideas will be systematically presented by John in ch. 20, when he speaks of the second judgment, when all the dead who are on the earth, in the sea and in hell are called

(20:12ff). In the fifth bowl John anticipates one aspect of the judgment which took place at the death of Christ: the definitive and eternal ratification of the condemnation reserved for the sin which knows no turning back or repentance.

THE SIXTH BOWL

In the sixth bowl the memory of the sixth trumpet is even more powerful than in the preceding parallels. The "great river Euphrates" is common to both (16:12 and 9:14). On the banks of that river John sees, at the beginning of the sixth trumpet, four bound angels who are then set free. There follows the invasion of the cavalry which slays one third of humanity (9:13ff). We have seen it as an allegory of warfare, the first and gravest consequence of original sin. In the east, in fact, and precisely in the lands washed by the Euphrates, according to the ancients, all the great conquering empires had their beginnings.

This is all taken up in the sixth bowl: the angel pours out his bowl into the Euphrates which dries up to leave the way open for "the kings from the east" (16:12). The description of what follows appears to shift from what was reported in the sixth trumpet. At the head of the Army which crosses the river to begin its invasion, we suddenly find three strange commanders: the dragon, the beast and the false prophet. From their mouths came out "three foul spirits, like frogs" (16:13). John explains that they are demons who spread out over the whole world to set up a great alliance against the divinity (16:13-14). The assembly point of this terrible army is Armageddon (16:16).

On closer observation, however, this is not as new or unexpected as one might believe, nor is it so very different from what was described in the sixth trumpet. There also, John is looking at the disastrous spiritual result of the plague of warfare rather than its more material aspect. The horror which rises from the contemplation of the carnage of war looks clearly in the direction of another, even more horrible place of death. There also at the head of that terrible army stands "the angel from the bottomless pit" whose name in Greek is *Apollyon*, i.e., "the destroyer," "the exterminator." The destruction sown by this being is not only of a material and physical nature. John, like the other Christians, is not aware of the warning of Jesus: "Do not fear those who kill the body and after that have no more that they can do. But I will warn you whom to fear: fear him who, after he has killed, has power to cast you into hell; yes, I tell you, fear him!" (Lk 12:4-5). To the Greek term *Apollyon*, which indicates a person, John has a corresponding Hebrew word *Abaddon*, which indicates a place where the dead reside, Sheol, Hades. The pair of words therefore reproduce another pain, already met in the fourth horseman: Death and Hades (see 6:8).

A similar thing can be said for the army (horses and horsemen) of the sixth trumpet, led by this fearful "angel from the bottomless pit." They are also clear demonic symbols. The three-fold colours (bright red, deep blue and greenish) of the shields of the horsemen and the corresponding substances which come out of the horses' mouths (fire, smoke and sulphur) point in this direction. We saw then a relationship with the colours of the second, third, and fourth horsemen. We can now put them in relation to the "three foul spirits, like frogs" which here in the sixth bowl come out of the mouths of the dragon, the beast and the false prophet. We can try to apply to these spirits the significance which we believe to have traced behind the substances vomited out by the horses: the demonic influences which drive man to violent murder (fire), pride (smoke) and the refusal of eternal life for eternal death (sulphur).

The "foul spirits" are three, but their action is described as one. We can observe now, in contrast to the hierarchy of people who send them out, the common action of the three spirits is described with aspects of the beast from the earth, who here is called the false prophet. Like the beast from the earth (13:13ff), these spirits perform miracles and works of propaganda. In the activity of corruption exercised by the dragon, by the beast (beast from the sea) and the false prophet (beast from the earth), John considers the last of the three the most dangerous and the most serious.

This can perhaps be explained by considering that the seduction worked by these spirits has as its scope the gathering of the powerful ones of the earth with all their forces, in Armageddon, where the decisive battle against the Logos will take place. This will be described in ch. 19. There, this battle is seen as a symbol of the death of Christ. The sixth bowl describes the preparations for it. It is well known that the earliest Christians saw the Jews as the schemers and plotters of this event, especially their spiritual leaders. This is what John is representing first as the beast from the land, and then as the false prophet.

THE SEVENTH BOWL

The seventh angel pours out his bowl "into the air" (16:17). This is new, when compared with the seventh trumpet, but the latter is indirectly recalled in the effects produced by the pouring out of the seventh bowl. Once again the heavenly Temple is at the centre of interest. From there "a great voice" comes out and announces: "It is done!" Then follow, as in the seventh trumpet, lightning, loud noises, thunder, an earthquake without equal in the history of mankind and a fearful hailstorm.

The voice which comes out of the Temple is God's voice, as the Temple is now filled only with God's presence (15:8) and John specifies that the voice comes "from the throne." The words announced by the voice evidently allude to the completion of "the mystery of God" which the "strong angel" of ch. 10 pre-announced for the seventh trumpet (10:7), but the Greek verb used here by John indicates something which has been fulfilled, now in a much more restricted and specific sense. It refers to the death of Christ which forms the object of the whole of the seven of the bowls, presented here as an actual historical event.

In fact, the description of what happens in the seventh

bowl is quite close to the description of the death of Christ as it is found in the Gospels: cosmic catastrophes (the darkening of the sun, etc.), the earthquake which shakes the city of Jerusalem, especially stressed by Matthew (Matt 27:51ff), the tearing apart of the veil of the Temple, and the words "It is finished!" on the lips of Jesus in Jn 19:30.

We need not be reminded that the Apocalypse is not a history book. Even points which clearly have their roots in some historical event are reinterpreted in a symbolic way. The bowl poured out "into the air" by the angel could be an imaginative way of speaking of the realistic event of the lifting up of Jesus on a cross, but this is immediately transferred to a symbolic place. This lifting up as the symbol of the messianic revelation of Jesus Christ on the Cross, follows a current idea, central to the fourth Gospel (see Jn 3:14-15; 8:28; 12:32) which the Apocalypse has expressed through the continual use of the prophecy of the Son of man coming on the clouds from Daniel. This is coupled with the symbol of the Lamb "upon Mt. Sion" (14:1) and with the encounter between the Logos and his adversaries at Armageddon which is to be understood, as we will see, as "the mountain of Megidelo."

The cosmic disturbances, only touched upon in the Gospel stories of the death of Christ, are also given a symbolic significance here: the fulfilment of the judgment of God which happens in that moment. John limits himself to stating briefly: "And every island fled away, and no mountains were to be found" (16:20). This is a repetition of a whole series of messianic prophecies which John had already developed in the sixth seal (6:12-17).

John takes up two of the cosmic catastrophes with greater concentration: the earthquake and the hail. They form part of the complex of phenomena (lightning, thunder, loud sound, etc.) which symbolically indicate in the Apocalypse a particular presence of the divinity and his intervention in history. As the book unfolds there is a gradual widening of these formulae which indicate the divine presence: from ch. 4 (the scene of the throne) where there are only "lightning, sounds and thunder" (4:5) up to the end of ch. 11 (seventh trumpet) where the formula is complete (11:19). Two elements, the earthquake and the hail were added here in ch. 11 to the earliest series of phenomena which marked the presence of the divinity.

The hailstorm described by John at the conclusion of the seventh bowl is remarkable: hailstones, heavy as a hundredweight, fall upon the earth, and men blaspheme God because of this unsupportable plague (v. 21). To understand the significance of this scene, it is opportune to recall that a falling of "hail and fire mixed with blood" opened the series of the trumpets. We understood it as an allegory upon the fall of Satan and the rebellious angels. We must see it in the same light here. What was described in the first trumpet was the divine judgment which, in the beginning, fell upon Satan and his angels. Their falling from heaven upon the earth, the effect of that judgment, is also seen as the sorrowful source of all the evils which break forth in the physical and human sphere.

What is described in the seventh bowl is rather the judgment of God upon the effects which the fall of Satan has provoked in humanity. He has caught up man with him in his rebellion against God, and man has been punished. God has taken away from him his original condition of privilege for a further period of trial, as he waits for his final liberation. In this trial, as John indicates in ch. 12, the persecution of Satan plays a part. He has been driven out of heaven, but not definitively closed in his prison, and so he works in humanity, firstly through his agents (the two beasts) and then in person coming up from the bottomless pit. The correct way to overcome this trial is to resist the diabolic temptation which, basing itself on pride, appears to exalt man but in reality, aims at making him a slave of the satanic domination and the power of death. It is quite possible to resist, and to give witness to the absolute sovereignty of God (his Law) and to remain firm in the promises of liberation (the coming of Jesus Christ). The way of error is to give in to the diabolic temptation, attributing to God the blame for the terrible effects which this erroneous choice brings to humanity (blasphemy).

The description of the earthquake is to be understood in a similar fashion. It is also a symbol of the judgment of God which strikes human pride, inspired and sustained by demonic pride, as it attempts to reach up to take over heaven. "And there were flashes of lightning, loud noises, peals of thunder, and a great earthquake such as had never been seen since men were on the earth, so great was that earthquake. The great city was split into three parts, and the cities of the nations fell" (16:18-19).

Yet while the hail represents only the negative aspect of the judgment of God, i.e., the punishment inflicted upon pride, the earthquake also contains something positive, touching upon the salvation and the divine life granted to the just ones. The earthquake, in fact, in the Gospel tradition carried by Matthew, is connected not only with the death of Jesus, but also with his resurrection, his victory over death (see Matt 28:2).

The same thing can be said for the Apocalypse, as we can gather from the episode of the two "witnesses," in whom is already foreshadowed the death and resurrection of Jesus. In fact, three and a half days after their slaying by the beast who rose from the bottomless pit, they return to life because of a spirit of life which comes from God, and they are taken up into heaven: "And at that moment there was a great earthquake, and a tenth of the city fell; seven thousand people were killed in the earthquake." (11:13).

The earthquake which follows the pouring out of the seventh bowl is clearly a repetition of that which followed the death and resurrection of the two witnesses, and the city which suffers because of it is also the same. There it was "the great city" which is allegorically called Sodom and Egypt, where their Lord was crucified (11:5), i.e., Jerusalem. Here the city is "great Babylon" (16:19). This latter term is a wider symbol, indicating the earthly city dominated by Satan. Nevertheless, Jerusalem is also included, a Judaism corrupted by an alliance with political authority, as John will show in ch. 17 with his allegory of the prostitute seated upon the beast. That allegory represents the resurrection of Satan, his complete resurgence from the bottomless pit through the union between religious and political authority, what John calls "Babylon." It is reserved, in a particular way, to "the great prostitute" (17:1), i.e., a Judaism which has become worldly, Jerusalem, and the measure of its responsibility in assisting Satan in his attack against the "seed" of the woman, i.e., "on those who keep the commandments of God and hear testimony to Jesus" (12:17). This process has been going on through the whole of human history, but it reaches its culminating point in the slaying of Jesus, which is being described in the "seven" of the bowls.

THE NEW EXODUS

In speaking of the contents of chs. 15-16 we have already noticed the correspondence which exists between this section of the Apocalypse and the events of the liberation of the Hebrew people from the slavery of Egypt, as it is told in the *Exodus*. There is a clear recalling of it in the initial vision of ch. 15: the conquerors of the beast upon the sea of glass who sing the song of Moses and the Lamb (15:2-3). Equally clear, and noticed by all the commentators, are the correspondences between certain plagues provoked by the pouring out of the bowls and the so-called "plagues of Egypt" which preceded the liberation of the Hebrews.

There were ten plagues of Egypt in the following order: water changed into blood, frogs, mosquitoes, flies, disease of the animals, foul sores, hail, locusts, darkness and finally the death of the firstborn (see Exod 7-10; 12:29ff). John takes up explicitly only five of these in the pouring out of the bowls: the foul sores (1st bowl); changing of water into blood (2nd and 3rd bowls); darkness (5th bowl); frogs (6th bowl); hail (7th bowl). It should be noticed that reference to the plagues of Egypt are also found in the "seven" of the trumpets: hail and fire mixed with blood (1st trumpet); changing of water into blood (2nd trumpet); darkness (4th and 5th trumpet); locusts (6th trumpet); great hail (7th trumpet).

The plagues recalled by John in the trumpets only partially correspond however to those used in the bowls, but the number used is always the same: five. Perhaps this number is not mere chance, and it might have something to do with the "five months" during which the locusts inflicted pain upon men in 9:5. The "five months" could even reflect the apocalyptic idea of the five millennia of the diabolic domination which precedes the messianic coming. If that suggestion has any foundation, the explanation of the fact that John uses five of the plagues of Egypt in both the trumpets and the bowls may lie along the same lines. The five months would indicate (naturally, in a symbolic form) the *duration* of Satan's dominion over humanity before Christ, while the five plagues would indicate the terrible *quality* of that domination.

THE TENTH PLAGUE: THE DEATH OF THE FIRSTBORN

Among the plagues not mentioned is the most serious affliction of the Egyptians: the death of the firstborn (Exod 12:29ff). It is an obvious absence. We have already said that the effects of the pouring out of the bowls described here are more fully illustrated in the chapters which follow. In particular, in ch. 19 we find the description of the battle between the Logos and his adversaries which is prepared and announced during the pouring out of the sixth bowl. Before that battle an angel invites the birds of the sky to a horrible banquet: the beast of humanity (kings, captains, mighty men, horses and riders, all men both free and slave, both small and great) will be wiped out and given to the birds to eat (19:18).

This will be the destruction of the first born. But it is not only this which John has in mind. We must not forget that the battle, is in reality, an allegory of the death of Christ. This is also the slaying of a firstborn. In fact, this is the deepest reality prefigured by the last and most serious plague. It was the decisive plague, the one which definitively saw to the liberation of the Hebrews. There also innocents were slain or, at least, those least guilty were the ones who procured the blessing of the liberation, and another innocent victim, the slain Lamb, whose blood was placed on their doorposts, preserved the Hebrews as the exterminating angel passed by.

In the death of Christ, described here in the "seven" of the bowls, John sees a profound realisation of what was foreshadowed in the last plague which freed the Hebrew people. There is, however, a reversal of roles. In so far as he is the firstborn who is slain, Jesus does not belong to the oppressors, but to those who suffer from injustice and violence: he is Son of God, firstborn of humanity subjected to death (1:5). In so far as he is also Lamb, he is not immolated by the oppressed ones as they stand ready to depart; he is slain by the oppressors who believe that, by doing so, they are making themselves secure against the divine anger which awaits them.

In that death there was not only a reversal of roles, but also a reversal of effects: death is transformed into life, defeat into victory. It constitutes the judgment of God upon the world, a consequence of which is that the powers of evil, and especially their infernal and terrestrial leaders (firstborn in that sense?) are destroyed and the new people of God are freed.

"LO, I AM COMING LIKE A THIEF!" (16:15)

In the sixth bowl, the formation of the alliance against God is described under the direction of the three leaders (the dragon, the beast and the false prophet), through the instigation of the three impure spirits which come out of their mouths, representing the wicked influence which they exercise over humanity. This alliance takes place at Armageddon (16:13-16). The earth and Hades, men and demons gather for a general and decisive assault against the divinity. And then, upon "the mountain of Megiddo" (the probable meaning of the word "Armageddon"), the Logos of God descends upon his white horse, accompanied by a heavenly army to confront the alliance against God (19:11ff). He will be the new Josiah, also vowed, like the holy King of Judah, to death in a new battle of Megiddo (see II Kgs 23:29). But his death, unlike that of the King of Judah, is to victory for himself and his followers, defeat and annihilation to his adversaries.

In the sixth bowl, the great encounter is described only in its preparatory stages: the gathering of the frightful army. Then comes the seventh bowl, with the allusion to the circumstances of Jesus' death (the voice which comes out from the Temple, from the throne: "It is done!" (16:17). It is as if between the facts described in the two bowls there was absolutely no connection. John goes ahead with rapid allusions to facts and personalities which are successively taken up again, each time at a deeper level in his description of their nature, their meaning and their mutual interrelationship.

Included in this way of going ahead in leaps, through allusion and anticipations which apparently have no connection, is found the strange v. 15: "Lo, I am coming like a thief! Blessed is he who is awake, keeping his garments that he may not go naked and be seen exposed." They are evidently words pronounced by Jesus, and for this reason commentators see them as quite out of place, breaking in between the action of seduction exercised by the three spirits on the kings of the earth (16:14) and the effects of this action, the gathering at Armageddon (16:16).

Not all commentators, however, see them as out of place. Some suggest that it is John speaking to persecuted Christians, warning them of the need for constant vigilance in the presence of so many dangers. This is certainly a better solution, but I would like to link v. 15, not with the second coming of Christ, but with the first. What is described in the sixth bowl, the three wicked leaders (dragon, beast and false prophet) and their representatives (three impure spirits) who corrupt the inhabitants of earth "to assemble them for battle on the great day of God the almighty" (16:14), is not an isolated fact which has happened only once in history. This succinct description refers to all the seductions and corruption worked by Satan, through his historical agents (corrupt political and religious authority), which has been going on since the beginning of time. Only the gathering of the army against God at Armageddon alludes to a precise circumstance: the assault against the divinity which took place in the slaying of Jesus Christ.

Thus we can explain the insertion of v. 15 (Lo, I am coming like a thief!) between the description of Satan's diabolic seduction (v. 14) and the gathering at Armageddon (v. 16). In fact, as v. 14 describes the corrupting action of Satan which continues through all of the period of the messianic waiting, from the fall up to Christ, the words of v. 15 represent the renewal of the promise of liberation which God, by means of the prophets, had made through the period of the ancient revelation. The promise is put directly on the lips of Jesus, because for John he is the real author of that revelation.

The gathering at Armageddon is thus presented as the point of meeting and clash between two contrasting actions, that of Satan which corrupts humanity and that of Christ who nourishes the hope of his coming. In this way, the tone and the form of the words which Jesus Christ uses is also explained, as he exhorts vigilance. The exhortation of Christ to vigilance and to waiting for his coming is close to the exhortations of all the letters to the churches of Asia. In particular, the expression "as a thief" and the reference to keeping their garments are found in the letter to Sardis (3:3-4). Nudity, complete spiritual destitution as a consequence of the loss of one's garments, which Christ warns will be the destiny of those who do not watch, is also his word of warning, in the seventh letter, to the community at Laodicea (3:17-18).

The Death of Christ as Judgment upon History: The Destruction of Babylon (17:1—19:10)

> 17 ¹Then one of the seven angels who had the seven bowls came and said to me, "Come, I will show you the judgment of the great harlot who is seated upon many waters, ²with whom the kings of the earth have committed forni-

cation, and with the wine of whose fornication the dwellers on earth have become drunk."

³And he carried me away in the Spirit into a wilderness, and I saw a woman sitting on a scarlet beast which was full of blasphemous names, and it had seven heads and ten horns.

⁴The woman was arrayed in purple and scarlet, and bedecked with gold and jewels and pearls, holding in her hand a golden cup full of abominations and the impurities of her fornication;

⁵and on her forehead was written the name of mystery: "Babylon the great, mother of harlots and of earth's abominations."

⁶And I saw the woman, drunk with the blood of the saints and the blood of the martyrs of Jesus. When I saw her I marveled greatly.

⁷But the angel said to me, "Why marvel? I will tell you the mystery of the woman, and of the beast with seven heads and ten horns that carries her.

⁸The beast that you saw was, and is not, and is to ascend from the bottomless pit and go to perdition; and the dwellers on earth whose names have not been written in the book of life from the foundations of the world, will marvel to behold the beast, because it was and is not and is to come.

⁹This calls for a mind with wisdom: the seven heads are seven mountains on which the woman is seated;

¹⁰they are also seven kings, five of whom have fallen, one is, the other has not yet come, and when he comes he must remain only a little while.

¹¹As for the beast that was and is not, it is an eighth but it belongs to the seven, and it goes to perdition.

¹²And the ten horns that you saw are ten kings who have not yet received royal power, but they are to receive authority as kings for one hour, together with the beast.

¹³These are of one mind and give over their power and authority to the beast;

¹⁴they will make war on the Lamb, and the Lamb will

conquer them, for he is Lord of lords and King of kings, and those with him are called and chosen and faithful."
¹⁵And he said to me, "The waters that you saw, where the harlot is seated, are peoples and multitudes and nations and tongues.
¹⁶And the ten horns that you saw, they and the beast will hate the harlot; they will make her desolate and naked, and devour her flesh and burn her up with fire.
¹⁷for God has put it into their hearts to carry out his purpose by being of one mind and giving over their royal power to the beast, until the words of God shall be fulfilled.
¹⁸And the woman that you saw is the great city which has dominion over the kings of the earth."

18 ¹After this I saw another angel coming down from heaven, having great authority; and the earth was made bright with his splendor.
²And he called out with a mighty voice,
"Fallen, fallen is Babylon the great!
It has become a dwelling place of
demons,
a haunt of every foul spirit,
a haunt of every foul and hateful
bird;
³ for all nations have drunk the wine
of her impure passion,
and the kings of the earth have
committed fornication with her,
and the merchants of the earth have
grown rich with the wealth of
her wantonness."
⁴Then I heard another voice from heaven saying,
"Come out of her, my people,
lest you take part in her sins,
lest you share in her plagues;
⁵ for her sins are heaped high as
heaven,
and God has remembered her
iniquities.

> 6 Render to her as she herself has rendered,
> and repay her double for her deeds;
> mix a double draught for her in the cup she mixed.
> 7 As she glorified herself and played the wanton,
> so give her a like measure of torment and mourning.
> Since in her heart she says, 'A queen I sit,
> I am no widow, mourning I shall never see,'
> 8 so shall her plagues come in a single day,
> pestilence and mourning and famine,
> and she shall be burned with fire;
> for mighty is the Lord God who judges her."

9 And the kings of the earth, who committed fornication and were wanton with her, will weep and wail over her when they see the smoke of her burning; 10 they will stand far off, in fear of her torment and say,

> "Alas! alas! thou great city,
> thou mighty city, Babylon!
> In one hour has thy judgment come."

11 And the merchants of the earth weep and mourn for her, since no one buys their cargo any more, 12 cargo of gold, silver, jewels and pearls, fine linen, purple, silk and scarlet, all kinds of scented wood, all articles of ivory, all articles of costly wood, bronze, iron and marble, 13 cinnamon, spice, incense, myrrh, frankincense, wine, oil, fine flour and wheat, cattle and sheep, horses and chariots, and slaves, that is, human souls.

> 14 "The fruit for which thy soul longed has gone from thee,
> and all thy dainties and thy splendor

are lost to thee, never to be
found again!"
[15]The merchants of these wares, who gained wealth from her, will stand far off, in fear of her torment, weeping and mourning aloud,

[16] "Alas, alas, for the great city
that was clothed in fine linen, in
purple and scarlet,
bedecked with gold, with jewels, and
with pearls!
[17] In one hour all this wealth has been
laid waste."

And all shipmasters and seafaring men, sailors and all whose trade is on the sea, stood far off
[18]and cried out as they saw the smoke of her burning,
"What city was like the great city?"
[19]And they threw dust on their heads, as they wept and mourned, crying out,
"Alas, alas, for the great city
where all who had ships at sea
grew rich by her wealth!
In one hour she has been laid waste.
[20] Rejoice over her, O heaven,
O saints and apostles and prophets,
for God has given judgment for you
against her!"
[21]Then a mighty angel took up a stone like a great millstone and threw it into the sea, saying,
"So shall Babylon the great city be
thrown down with violence,
and shall be found no more;
[22] and the sound of harpers and
minstrels, of flute players and
trumpeters,
shall be heard in thee no more;
and a craftsman of any craft
shall be found in thee no more;
and the sound of the millstone
shall be heard in thee no more;

²³ and the light of a lamp
shall shine in thee no more;
and the voice of bridegroom and
bride
shall be heard in thee no more;
for thy merchants were the great
men of the earth,
and all nations were deceived by
thy sorcery.
²⁴ And in her was found the blood of
prophets and of saints,
and of all who have been slain on
earth."

19 ¹After this I heard what seemed to be the loud voice of a great multitude in heaven, crying,
Hallelujah! Salvation and glory and
power belong to our God,
² for his judgments are true and just;
he has judged the great harlot who
corrupted the earth with her
fornication,
and he has avenged on her the blood
of his servants."
³ Once more they cried,
"Hallelujah! The smoke from her
goes up for ever and ever."
⁴And the twenty-four elders and the four living creatures fell down and worshiped God who is seated on the throne, saying, "Amen. Hallelujah!"
⁵And from the throne came a voice crying,
"Praise our God, all you his servants,
you who fear him, small and great."
⁶Then I heard what seemed to be the voice of a great multitude, like the sound of many waters and like the sound of mighty thunderpeals, crying,
Hallelujah! For the Lord our God
the Almighty reigns.
⁷ Let us rejoice and exult and give
him the glory,

for the marriage of the Lamb has
come,
and his Bride has made herself
ready'
⁸ it was granted her to be clothed with
fine linen, bright and pure" —
for the fine linen is the righteous deeds of the saints.
⁹And the angel said to me, "Write this: Blessed are those who are invited to the marriage supper of the Lamb." And he said to me, "These are true words of God."
¹⁰Then I fell down at his feet to worship him, but he said to me, "You must not do that! I am a fellow servant with you and your brethren who hold the testimony of Jesus. Worship God." For the testimony of Jesus is the spirit of prophecy.

THE PERVERSIONS AND FALL OF THE EARTHLY JERUSALEM

The concluding section of the book, which runs from ch. 17-22 has caused great discussion and a variety of interpretations, because here are found all the great themes which have made the Apocalypse a famous Christian book: the destruction of Babylon (chs. 17-18), the battle of Christ against the coalition of his enemies (ch. 19), the binding of Satan and the thousand year reign of Christ, the liberation of Satan and the final battle against Gog and Magog (ch. 20), the creation of a new heaven and a new earth and the descent of the new Jerusalem from heaven (chs. 21-22).

These themes have been used in discussions which ranged well outside the area of specialised interpretation into a whole system of interpretation of religious, political and social history which has often departed a considerable distance from the original design and idea of the author. Even today interpretations vary between literal and symbolic, historical and spiritual, often with serious contradictions. This had led to a great number of suggestions about the re-ordering of the text, reconstructions and corrections.

Ch. 17, dedicated to the explanation of the "mystery" of Babylon, is introduced by the presence of an angel, "one of the seven angels who had the seven bowls" (17:1). Towards the end of the section, in ch. 21, another angel, also "one of the seven angels who had the seven bowls" introduces John to the contemplation of the "spouse of the Lamb," of the new Jerusalem which descends from heaven (21:9ff). Therefore the section opens and closes with two scenes which correspond antithetically, as has been noticed by all the commentators. What has not been noticed, however, is that these two angels are the first and the last of a series of six, subdivided into two groups of three by the descent of the Logos in ch. 19. The first group appears in chs. 17-18 (see 17:1; 18:1; 18:21) and is connected with the fall of Babylon. The second group comes after the descent of the Logos and is connected with the battle of Armageddon (19:17), the binding of Satan for a thousand years (20:1ff) and the descent of the heavenly Jerusalem (21:9ff).

This series repeats the same sort of structure as the series of visions in the second part of ch. 14. We can draw from this a first conclusion of great importance: the final section of the book is taking up and developing what was synthetically anticipated in ch. 14. There we saw two great scenes, at the centre of which stood first the Lamb (14:1) and then the Son of man seated on a white cloud (14:14), two symbols which refer to the death of Christ, understood as his messianic revelation, already anticipated in the prologue (1:7) and in ch. 5 (see 5:6ff).

Corresponding with what is in ch. 14, we find in the final section of the book, at the centre of the series, the descent of the Logos on a white horse (19:11), clearly parallel with the vision of the Son of man seated on a white cloud in 14:14. This means that the descent of the Logos and the consequent battle between him and his enemies at Armageddon is also connected with the messianic revelation involved in his death.

In the final section of the book, and at the heart of its message is "the revelation of Jesus Christ" announced as the general theme from the very first words of the prologue. The culminating point of this revelation is, in fact, the death of Christ, which reveals him as the Messiah, at the one time judge and redeemer of mankind and of the cosmos. Not without reason does the Logos, who stands at the centre of the series which directs this section, come down from heaven, "clad in a robe dipped in blood" (19:13), and not without reason is the section opened and closed by two of the angels who had the seven bowls. In using the angels from the "seven" of the bowls, which, as we have seen, refers to the death of Christ, at the opening and closing of the final section, we have an indication that also here there is a further development of the same theme: the death of Christ which brings to perfection "the mystery of God" (see 10:7).

THE "MYSTERY" OF BABYLON

Chs. 17-18 are devoted to the destruction of Babylon. In fact, the actual destruction is not described. Ch. 17 illustrates the nature of the reality (Babylon) which is judged and condemned, while in ch. 18 it appears to be already destroyed, as one can see from the words of those who lament its fate. The destruction of the city, therefore, is what took place during the earthquake produced by the seventh bowl (16:18ff). This is a further indication that the contents of these two chapters are a repetition and a development of the seventh cup.

An angel, one of those "who had the seven bowls" (17:1), introduces John to the vision of the judgment and the condemnation of "the great harlot." The visionary is carried away "in the spirit" by the angel, into the desert (wilderness). This "in the spirit" reference indicates a prophetic situation. He is under a particular illumination of the Spirit about some aspect of the "revelation of Jesus Christ."

"In the desert" John sees a woman clearly dressed as a prostitute (v. 4). She is seated upon a monstrous being, with seven heads and seven horns, i.e.: like the dragon of ch. 12 and the beast from the sea in ch. 13. This is a famous vision, again subject to many interpretations. From the 3rd century onwards, the woman has chiefly been seen as an allegory of the imperial Rome, her moral corruption and her cruel and rapacious domination. In the internal struggles of the Church (African Donatism in the 4th-5th centuries, the Jacobites, Spirituali, etc., of the middle ages and especially during the protestant reformation) however, the Roman Church has been identified with the figure of the prostitute. Nowadays the identification with imperial Rome is largely taken for granted.

If one reads this passage *within its context*, however, it appears clear that the identification of the prostitute with Rome presents such serious obstacles that it becomes difficult to support. In the first place, the identification means that the woman and the beast upon which she sits represent *one thing*. Those who hold this refer all the characteristics to Rome: moral corruption, luxury, cruelty against the saints and the witnesses of Christ, idolatry (from the woman), the seven heads as the hills of Rome or seven empires, the ten horns, Rome's vassals (from the beast).

THE SEVEN HEADS

It is important to ease this confusion by distinguishing between the woman and the beast, even if they are united in a monstrous intimacy. The beast which supports the prostitute is, clearly, the dragon of ch. 12 and the beast from the sea in ch. 13. That means that it represents, at the one time, both Satan (the dragon) plus one of its historical manifestations: corrupt political power. In this case it will be the corrupt political authority of Rome.

This explains why, in ch. 17, the representation of the beast oscillates between that used for Satan (dragon of ch. 12) and that which can clearly apply to Rome (the beast from the sea of ch. 13). It is only to the diabolical being himself that one can apply the expression: "The beast... was, and is not, and is to ascend from the bottomless pit, and go to perdition" (17:8). These words have no sense if applied to Rome. Applied to Satan, they refer to his original state as the most perfect creature, his rebellion and dismissal from heaven, his relegation to the abyss, his brief return for the "great persecution" (see 7:14) which has Christ as its victim. Following this Satan is definitively defeated as he is thrown into the lake of sulphur (see 20:10).

On the other hand, its external presentation: seven heads and ten horns, as also its scarlet colour, can be read on two levels: referring to both Satan and Rome. The reference to the "scarlet beast" (v. 3) seems to take up the bright red colour of the dragon of ch. 12 (12:3), but is also connected with the colour of the clothes of the prostitute in the very next verse (v. 4). There it is a symbol (along with purple) of worldly authority.

The seven heads are explained by the angel to John: "The seven heads are seven hills on which the woman is seated" (v. 9). The reference to Rome seems explicit and detailed, but the message cannot be understood simply through historical identification. This is clear from the never-ending discussion over the exact Emperors who are the seven kings hinted at by the seven heads. Commentators argue whether the list should begin with Julius Caesar or Augustus, whether the Emperors of 69 A.D.: Galba, Otto and Vitellius should be included and whether one should conclude with Vespasian (79 A.D.), Domitian (96 A.D.) or Nerva (98 A.D.).

All this is greatly confused by v. 10: "They are also seven kings, five of whom have fallen, one is, the other has not yet come, and when he comes he must remain only a little while." What then follows is even more enigmatic: "As for the beast that was and is not, it is an eighth but it belongs to the seven, and it goes to perdition" (v. 11). The myriads of solutions which have been suggested show that it is impossible to understand the Apocalypse purely against a historical and temporal background.

It is more than probable that the beast is connected with Rome, but not to the point where Rome, and only Rome, coincides with the demonic reality which stood behind the Empire and used it for his tool in his battle against the divinity and his faithful upon earth. It is possible that John knew of the legend of Nero *redivivus* and this touches the meaning of the beast which was, is not, and which is to ascend from the abyss (v. 8). Nevertheless, his words refer first of all to Satan and his activity.

If this is the case, then it is not impossible that the seven kings referred to by the seven heads of the beast are to be seen, as Hippolytus of Rome already suggested in the 3rd century, as seven demons. This identification does not oppose the equivalence of seven heads = seven hills. The term "hill/mountain" as a spiritual entity opposed to God, of pride which rises up and attempts to take complete sovereignty, was current in Jewish tradition. In fact, in the second trumpet the Apocalypse described the fall of Satan as that of "a great mountain, burning with fire, thrown into the sea" (8:8). Again it was Hippolytus who saw in these seven hills, seven kings, the symbol of further wicked demons prepared to rule over the seven millennia which form history, according to the idea of the "cosmic week" current in apocalyptic literature, also widely used by John. In this scheme, the coming of the Messiah is placed at the end of the sixth millennium, and the messianic reign inaugurates the seventh.

In the light of this interpretation, Hippolytus gave a good explanation for the words: "five of whom have fallen, one is, the other has not yet come" (v. 10). The five who have fallen are the demons put forward for the five millennia which precede the coming of Christ; that one "who is" would represent the "king" of the sixth millennium, in the course of which (for Hippolytus, at the half way mark of the millennium) Christ would come; that which "has not yet come" would be the "king" of the seventh millennium. This final king was destined to "remain only a little while" because, for Hippolytus, his presence coincided with the beginning of the reign of Christ. He, however, then went on to make definite chronological calculations on the basis of this suggestion.

These calculations do not help us much, as we have already seen that the Apocalypse has no interest in a literal use of chronology, times and dates. Nevertheless, the idea that behind this enigmatic symbol of the seven heads hides an allusion to the "cosmic week" deserves our utmost attention. We have seen that John uses this, and his use of "sevens" indicates it most clearly. Even though his use of the scheme is not chronological, but rather symbolic and literary, he nevertheless keeps the order of the scheme in the succession of events. For example, he always places the salvific intervention in the sixth event of the series (e.g.: especially the seals and the trumpets), and he places at the beginning of the final seventh event, the culminating and all-resolving moment, i.e., the death of Christ.

Thus, even if he is not concerned about chronology, he knows how to use its "order of events" to place the whole of universal history in relation to the death of Christ as the coming of the messianic era. We have already seen that the use of the dragon with seven heads and ten horns is related to the scheme of seventy weeks from Dan 9:24ff, which precede the coming of the Messiah. The presentation of the dragon, therefore, is a symbol representing the period of waiting, extended by John to the whole of history before Jesus, seen as a gradual extension of the dominion of Satan over humanity. Even here, as originally in Daniel, the seven heads and ten horns are connected with chronological calculations.

In conclusion, the symbol of the seven heads is probably an indication of the domination exercised by the totality (seven) of evil spirits on the human and physical sphere. This domination is worked out on the historical plane, indicated by the ten horns, i.e.: the earthly sovereigns who are the vassals and the continuation of the authority of the other kings.

On the basis of this solution we can perhaps understand the eighth king. The angel explains: "As for the beast that was and is not, it is an eighth but it belongs to the seven, and it goes to perdition" (v. 11). To apply this, historically, to Nero or Domitian is too complicated. If, however, we apply it to Satan, it is not quite so difficult. Satan is "the eighth king" and he "belongs to the seven" in the sense that of all the evil and rebellious spirits who have dominated the world, he is the consummate expression. The fact that his reign is indicated as the eighth in a series possibly indicates that it extends, beyond the series which was concluded by the death of Christ, into the eternity of the punishment, in the lake of fire and sulphur, in which Satan and his followers are finally enclosed (see 20:10, 15).

THE TEN HORNS

The ten horns of the beast who carries the prostitute are explained by the angel as "ten kings" (7:12). It is a question of different kings, inferior to the former seven. In fact, the angel makes clear that they "have not yet received royal power"; they are not real kings, but "they are to receive royal authority as kings for one hour, together with the beast." The current interpretation which sees these lesser kings as the collaborators with Rome from the occupied territories is not impossible, but it leaves many questions to be answered.

The vassals of Rome were indeed inferior in dignity and authority to the Roman Emperors, and the authority was more apparent than real, before the authority of the Emperor. But what is meant by their receiving authority as kings for an hour? It is not as if the emperors had long reigns; in fact, between 68-70 A.D., there had been no less than four of them.

The difference between these two categories of king is better explained if one understands the first group as spiritual beings, i.e., angelic beings gifted by God with regal qualities by nature, and the others as mortal beings, men to whom authoritative positions are conceded for a short time. That the angels exercised authority over the created, human and physical world is a widespread idea in antiquity, both in biblical and non-biblical background. The Apocalypse shares this idea (see 4:4; 16:5; etc.). The rebellion against God which divided the angelic world into two groups had an influence on the authority exercised by the angels over the world, as some or all of it passed under the diabolic domination. As we can gather from the "seven" of the trumpets, the Apocalypse believes that only *part* of the physical world is dominated by demons (see 8:7ff).

In the seven heads of the beast we could therefore see the representation of the satanic rule over the world in its spiritual aspect, and in the ten horns we have the historical and human agents of the diabolic. They are the symbol of the human sovereigns who deliberately place themselves at the service of the beast by their use of authority. In fact, John explains: "These are of one mind and give over their power and authority to the beast" (v. 13). If this refers only to the vassals of Rome it is somewhat superfluous. It has a profound religious significance if it is applied to human rulers in general. The authority which they possess, even if it is passing, is given to them by God, as also is that of the demons: but the use of this authority depends upon them, upon the intention of their "minds" and these are "all of one mind."

In the ten horns of the beast we can see, in all probability, a representation of the series of human sovereigns who abuse their authority, objectively placing it at the service of Satan, and in opposition to the Lamb, i.e., to Christ. He will finally conquer them "for he is Lord of lords and King of kings" (17:14).

This expression is a further indication that we are dealing with *all* rulers, and not just the vassals of Rome. It says that Christ, overcoming Satan, destroys at the same time the source and foundation of wicked earthly authority. This, in fact, as the series of horsemen in 6:1ff shows, has the destruction and death of mankind as its object. While before Christ the death and destruction which Satan and his satellites bring to man is total, after Christ has conquered death, the authority of the wicked powers is limited to the physical area, to the killing of the body, as Jesus reports in the Gospels (see Matt 10:28; Lk 12:4ff). Certainly, even after the coming of Christ, Satan "after he has killed, has power to cast into hell" (Lk 12:5), because while Christ has given back to man access to eternal life, he himself has the power to withdraw and, by his own choice, return to diabolic domination.

The presentation of the beast with the seven heads and the ten horns represents, therefore, an all-assuming symbol of human history in so far as it is under the sign of the domination of sin and of Satan. It covers with this symbol the whole period of the messianic expectation, from the fall to the coming of Christ. It is probable that behind this image is the Danielic prophecy about the seventy weeks of waiting (see Dan 9:24ff). In fact the number of the heads multiplied by the horns comes to seventy. The symbolism is clear: the united forces of the wicked spirits and wicked men which rule the world make up the historical incarnation of Satan, his revelation which lasts and grows during the whole period of the expectation, from the fall to the coming of Jesus.

This, the probable meaning of the monster is all that holds up the prostitute: it represents Satan in his guise as "lord of the world," a lordship which is both physical and spiritual, religious and political. This interpretation does not *exclude* other more precise identifications with historical persons, places and times; nevertheless, the search for these details must not let us lose sight of the fact that the overall perspective of the Apocalypse cannot be contained within those limits, as it is a theological interpretation of the whole of religious history.

THE BEAST AND THE PROSTITUTE

In any case, whatever interpretation one gives to the beast, it is important to see it as a reality distinct from the prostitute. They are so distinct that John will describe, at the end of ch. 17, an implacable and murderous hatred between the two of them. In fact, the angel says: "And the ten horns that you saw, they and the beast will hate the harlot; they will make her desolate and naked, and drown her flesh and burn her up with fire" (17:16).

These words are nowadays still read as a prophecy about the destruction of Rome and its empire. This is a logical interpretation when prostitute and beast are identified with Rome, but the difficulty is that it means that Rome destroys herself. This leads to further theories about internecine strife and revolt. Some return to the idea of a Nero *redivivus* returning to destroy Rome at the head of the Parthians, which complicates the matter even further, as the beast has to be then explained as Nero. Some scholars, seeing all these difficulties, have decided that this passage is out of place or interpolated. Maybe none of this is required, as long as there is no confusion between the distinct entities of beast and prostitute. The latter seems to be a city, as the description of the devastation, looting, burning and even cannibalism are all pointing in that direction.

If the distinction is kept, the city cannot be Rome, which is represented, in some way, by the symbol of the beast and the ten horns. The city which falls to the savage aggression from the demoniacal powers and their satellites on earth is Jerusalem. In the destruction which is mentioned here we have a summary of a whole series of destructions of Jerusalem throughout her troubled history. In 11:2 John says the pagan peoples trampled on her for forty months – i.e., the whole of her existence, which is the same period as the preaching of the two witnesses (Law and Prophets) (11:3); of the authority of the beast from the sea (political authority) (13:5) and of the presence of the woman (Israel) in the desert (12:14).

But the destruction mentioned in this passage is different from those preceding. The city which is destroyed is no longer the "holy city": it is a "prostitute," nay, "the great harlot," "Babylon, the great, mother of harlots and of earth's abominations" (17:1 and 5). This, however, should not surprise us, in so far as this terrible metamorphosis has been anticipated in ch. 11, when John told us that the bodies of the two "witnesses," slain by the beast "who rises from the bottomless pit," lay unburied "in the street of the city, that great city, which is called, spiritually Sodom and Egypt, where also their Lord was crucified" (11:8).

Therefore, if the destruction to which the passage alludes is to be understood in a literal and material sense, it can only refer to the destruction of Jerusalem by the Romans in 70 A.D. Only then, in fact, after the slaying of Jesus Christ, did Jerusalem become, in the eyes of John and the early Christians, the definitive "prostitute," the opposite of the "holy city" which it had once been. The allusion to that historical event, however, is useful for John only to help him identify the reality (Jerusalem) hidden under the symbol of the "prostitute."

THE GREAT HARLOT

The distinction between the two elements, the beast and the prostitute, upon which my analysis of ch. 17 depends, is probably sufficient argument to prove that the prostitute refers to Jerusalem. This conclusion, as it is so paradoxical, may surprise, but so was John surprised, before the inspiration of the Spirit (see 17:6: "I marvelled greatly").

It should be said that an objective and continuous reading of the whole section which leads up to ch. 17 makes the identification of the prostitute with Jerusalem and Judaism neither surprising nor unexpected. It is a prelude to the story of the end of Judaism, the Old Economy, which has been indicated throughout the whole of the book. We have seen the repeated hint through the submission of the angels, the mediators of the Old Economy. Then there were further hints in the final parts of the four "sevens":
— the seventh letter (3:15ff).
— the sixth and seventh seal and the sixth and seventh trumpet: earthquake and destruction of "the great city" (11:8, 13), clearly Jerusalem.
— the seventh cup, where the earthquake strikes the great city: Babylon (16:19).

Despite some apparently different details, we are dealing with the same event. In both cases we have the earthquake which is used in the Apocalypse as a sign of the salvific intervention of Christ, an allusion to his death and resurrection. We have stressed how the unfolding of the events described in the bowls takes place, structurally, as a further deepening and spelling out of what had already been provided by the seventh trumpet. Thus "the great city," i.e., Babylon, which is destroyed by the earthquake of the seventh bowl is the same city as the one whose destruction is told and celebrated in the sixth trumpet, i.e., Jerusalem.

THE BEAST FROM THE EARTH, THE FALSE PROPHET, THE PROSTITUTE

We can come to the same conclusion from an examination of the internal elements of ch. 17. If we maintain the important distinction between the prostitute and the beast, the situation described in this chapter appears to be a recapitulation and also a further continuation of what was argued in chs. 12 and 13.

In fact, the scene of ch. 17 takes place in the desert and has as its protagonists the beast and the prostitute. All this is clearly taking up what we saw in ch. 12 concerning the woman who fled into the desert, followed by the dragon. The two situations correspond, but now there is a serious difference. In the first case, the woman feared and fled from the dragon, while in the second she has a relationship and even an intimacy with him.

The parallel (antithetic though it may be) is certainly not casual. The reference to the desert is not for effect, but a clear reference, in ch. 17, to a situation already described in ch. 12. There, it will be remembered, we saw a figure representing first the whole of humanity, in so far as it was the object of the first salvific intervention of God in his plan of salvation (the first flight into the desert) and then, more specifically, representing Israel, the specific object of God's saving action in the Old Economy (second flight into the desert). The prostitute of ch. 17 takes up that symbol once more, especially in its second aspect: the representation of the chosen people of Israel.

The fact that the woman is here presented under the aspect of a prostitute indicates that, evidently, her spiritual attitude has changed: she no longer fears her old adversary, but now has such a closeness to him that she believes that she can overcome him and make him subject to her desires. This is a vain hope, as this monstrous union finishes with the beast's destruction of the prostitute.

All this is an allegory of the perversion of Judaism, a perversion which, to the early Christians and to John, was above all evidenced in the Jewish refusal to accept Jesus as the promised Messiah. The conviction which stands as a basis to the Apocalypse as the motivation for this refusal by the Jews is to be found in their temporal, political and material understanding of who the Messiah might be. The Jews expected a political Messiah who would give them material riches, power and political domination over all the peoples of the world. Against all of this John continually counterposes "the revelation of Jesus Christ" as a Lamb, i.e., as a Messiah who has his messianic revelation and his victory in defeat and death; his power and his domination above all and essentially in the spiritual order.

It is precisely the secularisation of the messianic hopes which the Apocalypse seems to see as the prostitution of Judaism. As is well known, the metaphor of prostitution is taken by John from the Old Testament, especially the prophets, where it is synonomous with idolatry and is applied both to pagan cities and peoples and to Jerusalem and the Hebrew people. It is especially applied to the latter, as they were bound in a special way to Yahweh, often through the image of wife-husband, and thus infidelity is seen as adultery (see Is 1:21; Ezek 16:15ff; Hos 2:1ff; 5:3; etc.).

The idolatry spoken of in the Apocalypse, however, has a quite precise and concrete character. It is not only false cult, but the adoration of Satan himself, the recognition and acceptance of his blasphemous attempt to make himself the supreme and absolute divinity. The incarnation of Satan is, first of all, the beast from the sea, political authority (see 13:1). Therefore, the primary form of idolatry is the adoration of political authority, the giving way before the demands of such authority to make itself the absolute, thus usurping the divinity. The beast from the land (13:11ff) shows its wicked nature in its attempt to force "the earth and its inhabitants worship the first beast" (13:12), i.e., political authority which gives "breath to the image of the beast so that the image of the beast should even speak, and to cause those who would not worship the image of the beast to be slain" (13:15). In other words, corrupt spiritual authority has the moral responsibility for the crimes and the blasphemous pretensions which characterise the behaviour of corrupt political authority.

As is clear, the adoration of the image, idolatry, is not simply a cult offered to an inanimate object: it signifies for the Apocalypse the acceptance and the glorification of the absolutist pretensions of corrupt political authority. This is what the beast from the land does, and thus shows its true nature as a false prophet, the name given to this entity after ch. 13 (see 16:13; 19:2; etc.). The function of the false prophet is also to endorse and bolster up the actions of the beast, in such a way that to all the commentators it has appeared clear that the pair, beast from the sea/beast from the land, is matched by the coupling of the beast/the false prophet in the final part of the book.

The beast-prostitute pair, however, represents another expression of the same reality. This pair constitutes a repetition of the two beasts of ch. 13, described here not only in their complementary aspect, but also in the complexity involved in the symbol. The beast which acts as a support for the prostitute is both the dragon (Satan) and the beast from the sea (political authority); the prostitute gathers in herself the characteristics of both, but, on her own account, she takes up the symbol of the beast from the land, a secularised and corrupt spiritual and religious authority.

The symbol of the prostitute, like the beast from the land/false prophet, also points towards Judaism. The symbol signifies Judaism's perversion, through the metaphor of prostitution. Prostitution means idolatry and Judaism has become idolatrous because it adores the beast and its statue, political authority. This is the case not because it accepts the political domination of the Romans. It certainly does not, but is proudly opposed to it, and sees it as a demonic presence. In its opposition to the Romans, however, Judaism adopts their mentality, their means and their goals. In fact, Judaism dreamed of a messianic rule which would be the exact opposite of their present situation, in which those ruled would be the rulers, and those who oppressed would become the oppressed ones.

All this was wrong on the moral plane, but Judaism made the even graver mistake of using the promise of God in the Law and the Prophets as their indication that such was their Messiah, and such was their destiny. In doing this, they destroyed the authentic and profound spiritual and religious sense of the Law and the Prophets, uniting themselves with "the beast who comes up from the bottomless pit" to slay the two "witnesses" (11:7). For this wickedness, Judaism is not only a participator, but it has moral responsibility, in so far as to Judaism has been entrusted the care and understanding of the divine promises. It has failed in this God-given mission.

THE PROSTITUTE CALLED "MYSTERY"

The prostitute of ch. 17 is presented as the one morally responsible for all the wickedness and corruption throughout the world. With her "the kings of the earth have committed fornication, and with the wine of whose fornication the dwellers of the earth have become drunk" (17:2) and she is "Babylon, the great mother of harlots and of earth's abominations" (17:5). A man like John, with his deep knowledge of the Scriptures, could not attribute to Rome nor to any other city this sort of spiritual and religious responsibility. They could certainly be prostitutes, but to none of them could be given the description: "the great mother of harlots and of earth's abominations" (v. 5).

Such wickedness, so great as to become the model and paradigm of all wickedness, John could only place in a perversion which had been formerly pure and holy. This was the case with Jerusalem which shifts from "holy city" to "Sodom and Egypt" in 11:2 and 8. Here she is called "Babylon," and this indicates that she has now reached the lowest point in her degradation, identifying herself with the last and worst of Israel's enemies, Babylon, which had made an end of the Kingdom of Judah.

On the other hand, it is clear that we are before a sacred reality which has been perverted from the mysterious name which the prostitute carries on her brow: "And on her forehead was written a name of mystery" (17:5). This is the true name of the prostitute. The other name, "Babylon the great, mother of harlots and of earth's abominations" appears to be an explanation of the first name, as the angel says to John: "Why marvel? I will tell you the mystery of the woman, and of the beast...that carries her" (17:7).

The word "mystery" in the language of the New Testament does not simply mean an enigmatic reality which is difficult to comprehend. It is a term closely associated with the divine plan of salvation, the Kingdom of God and the death of Christ. This is also its meaning in the Apocalypse in other places where it appears (see 1:20 and 10:7). Therefore, if the prostitute is called "mystery," that means that she, even in the moment in which she is judged and condemned, still forms an integral and important part in the divine plan of salvation. This cannot be the case for Rome or any other pagan city, but only for Jerusalem. Only she, and no other city, will be renewed and will descend from heaven upon Mt. Sion to celebrate a marriage with the Lamb (21:2, 10ff), because "in the days of the trumpet call to be sounded by the seventh angel, the mystery of God...should be fulfilled" (10:7).

The "mystery of God" which is fulfilled in the seventh trumpet is the death of Christ. It marks at the one time both the judgment and the end of the Old Economy, of Judaism, of the earthly Jerusalem, and the beginning of a New Economy, of the heavenly Jerusalem, of an authentic spiritual Judaism, of the Church.

SHE WHO IS SEATED UPON MANY WATERS (17:1)

In the light of what we have just argued, we can better understand certain descriptive passages used by John for the prostitute which are widely (and wrongly) attributed to Rome.

The prostitute is "seated upon many waters" (17:1). This expression comes from the Old Testament (Jer 57:13), where it indicates Babylon situated on the Euphrates and surrounded by many canals. Here, however, the words "many waters" have an allegorical meaning, as the angel explains: "The waters that you saw, where the harlot is seated, are people and multitudes and nations and tongues" (17:15). They are the pagan peoples. It is natural, therefore, to think of Rome and its universal empire.

The dominion exercised by the prostitute, however, as we have seen, is of a spiritual nature: she dominates by fornicating with the rulers and the pagan peoples, which means that she is giving their conduct a religious justification, thus making herself responsible for them before God. In this way she effectively reaches a universal domination and is really seated "upon many waters," in so far as she becomes the adviser, the spiritual guide, the false prophet of the beast, and from her perversion all peoples and their leaders draw example and justification.

Her spiritual and universal dominion, based on wickedness, is the perfect antithesis of the spiritual and universal dominion of Christ. It may be an accident, but the expression "many waters" appears in Apocalypse only in relationship to Christ and the new reality which he has inaugurated. In the initial vision of ch. 1, the voice of the Son of man is compared to "a voice of many waters" (1:15) and in ch. 19 the voice which sounds from heaven to celebrate the marriage of the Lamb and his spouse is also "like a voice of many waters" (19:6). As well as this, the "multitude which no man could number" which represents humanity saved by Christ with his own blood, is also spoken of in 7:9 with a formula very close to that used to speak of the wicked domination of the prostitute: "a great multitude which no man could number, from all tribes and peoples and tongues" (see 17:15).

"DRUNK WITH THE BLOOD OF THE SAINTS" (17:6)

Therefore, the prostitute also aspires to a universal domination, like that of Christ. Yet, even though she pretends to use spiritual weapons, abusing the Word of God, the advantages which she has from her dominion are not spiritual, but worldly and material: riches, luxury and self-exaltation (see 17:4). Here she again shows her affinity with the beast from the land in ch. 13, who appeared like the Lamb, but "spoke," i.e., behaved, like the dragon (13:11).

The parody of Christ on the part of the prostitute reaches its high point in a gesture which has the air of a demoniacal celebration of the memorial of his passion and death. The prostitute, in fact, holds a chalice in her hand, an immediate recall of the eucharist for John's readers, but the allusion becomes even more precise. The chalice is "full of abominations" (17:4). This expression appears here and in the explanation of the name which the prostitute has on her forehead (17:5), and it recalls an expression from Daniel: "the desolating abominations" (see Dan 9:27) which he uses to speak of the profanation of the Temple.

As we have already shown, the eschatological discourses in the Synoptic tradition seem to place this prophecy from Daniel in close relation to the death of Jesus, organised and executed by the Jewish high priests. The reference to Daniel which appears to be present in our text here could confirm, precisely because of its allusive nature, that this interpretation of Daniel was current in the primitive Christian communities.

In any case, the "abominations" of which the chalice is full consist essentially of the pouring out of the blood of the just and the innocent, as is made clear by what follows: "And I saw the woman drunk with the blood of the saints and the blood of the witnesses of Jesus" (17:6). This also leads scholars to see the woman as Rome, but the earliest Church did not see it that way. As late as 156 A.D. in the *Martyrdom of Polycarp* we find that the persecutors are still being seen primarily as the Jews. In my opinion, this is how John sees it.

Apart from these historical considerations the "saints" and the "witnesses of Jesus" who are slain by the woman are not the followers of Jesus, but the just ones and the prophets of the Old Testament, as we have shown in the slain of the fifth seal (6:9ff), the two "witnesses" of ch. 11 and the descendants of the woman who flee into the desert in 12:17.

The description of the prostitute as being marked with just and innocent blood also points in the direction of Jerusalem rather than Rome. We are already prepared for this conclusion by the slaying of the two "witnesses," slain and dishonoured in the streets of that city, which became "Sodom and Egypt" (11:8). In fact, even the Gospel tradition has prepared us for this in the hard words of Jesus against Jerusalem, the slayer of the prophets and those who stoned God's Sent ones (see Matt 23:37; Lk 13:34).

In his violent invective against official Judaism, Jesus declares that it is responsible for all the murders from the beginning of time (Matt 23:35). This can be seen only if one understands that Israel has been specially chosen as the place and guardian of his word and his promise. Thinking of that, then we can understand the full significance of the terrible words which close ch. 18, in the celebration of the destruction of Babylon: "And in her was found the blood of prophets and of saints, and of all who have been slain on earth" (18:24).

The chalice which the prostitute holds in her hand is, therefore, like the one that Jesus drinks, a symbol of a blood which is shed in sacrifice. The difference is that the blood poured out by the prostitute is not her own and it is not poured out for a good and holy cause. On the contrary, it is poured out in violence, in the search for authority and domination. The pouring out of blood certainly is connected with that of Jesus for the redemption of the whole of humanity (see 1:5; 5:9; 7:14; etc.). But the prostitute can have no part of this, as she has taken the opposite side. What she hopes for is different: "Since in her heart she says: 'A queen I sit. I am no widow, mourning I shall never see.' Because of this, in one day only her terrible punishments shall fall upon her: death, mourning and hunger, she will be burnt up in fire" (18:7-8).

THE END OF THE UTOPIC WORLDLY MESSIANISM

The words just quoted are only a part of the masterpiece of ch. 18, dedicated to the end of Babylon. In this chapter, heavenly and earthly voices, in dramatic alternation worthy of a chorus from a Greek tragedy, allude to the fall of "that great city."

Despite its literary beauty, this is a song of destruction and death. Understood literally, this section, along with the horrible description of the battle of Christ in 19:17ff, has contributed to the widespread idea that the Apocalypse is the work of a fanatical genius who hated all the beautiful things in life and anything which was the result of the human spirit, any tendency to better the quality of human existence. Coupled with this is the interpretation that the book is about the ultimate end of created order, and there is a short step between such a view and an approach to life and history which is escapist.

This cannot be so. How is it possible that while there is a readiness to interpret the rest of the Apocalypse in an allegorical and symbolic way, this section is taken literally? In fact, it is not too difficult to see in the description of ch. 18 (as also of the battle in ch. 19) as in perfect accord with the rest of the book, which aims to show that Jesus Christ is the Messiah who comes in the form of a slain Lamb and who conquers through death. This is generally missed because of the faulty identification of Babylon with Rome, a point we have already discussed in our interpretation of ch. 17.

John is not speaking of political and temporal realities, but of spiritual and religious ones; not of Rome but of Jerusalem. Why, then, does this chapter have so much insistence on material aspects, on prosperity and economic wealth, all of which is destroyed? John's attitude implies, in the first place, a moral judgment not so much upon these things *in themselves*, as if they were intrinsically evil, but rather upon the means used to get to these ends and he lists these means without any hesitation: corruption, oppression of the weak, violence, blood. This applies, evidently and in the first place, to Rome and its violent imperialism. In fact, Rome, in so far as it represents violent and oppressive political authority, does come first in the presentation of the incarnation of Satan.

For John, however, there was something worse than all that, an imperialism which pretended to base itself on the word and the promises of God in order to impose itself. He saw this sort of thing in the messianic expectations of a certain type of Judaism, based upon the utopic idea of a domination, of a political and temporal nature, of Israel over all peoples. Blinded by this dream of worldly greatness, the Hebrews had attempted to suffocate with violence the voices of the just ones and the prophets who spoke out for the spiritual character of the divine promises, and when this was fulfilled in the person of Jesus, they refused him with hatred and fury.

John sees that these Hebrews were behaving in exactly the same sort of worldly way as were the pagan peoples, whom they should have been opposing. Satan attempts to impose his rule on the pagans through the violent use of political authority, and now the Hebrews, with their political and temporal ideas of the Messiah, have become his allies. In fact, the slaying of Christ, which comes about through the alliance of the Synagogue and the imperial authority, shows the profound unity which has developed between the two: corrupt political authority (Rome) and corrupt religious authority (Jerusalem).

Therefore, the destruction of "that great city" and of the great economic, political and cultural system which it represents, not only does not refer to Rome and its Empire, but it is not to be read as a refusal and condemnation of the created and human realities which are caught up in the destruction. The divine judgment, which the Apocalypse is expressing through concrete and dramatic images, does not strike at material reality, but the wicked, perverse and demoniacal design which uses material reality for its own end and its own exaltation.

THE END OF BABYLON AND THE SUBMISSION OF THE ANGELS

The first 10 verses of ch. 19 belong to the message of chs. 17-18. Vv. 1-8 contain a triumphant hymn from the heavenly creatures over the fall of Babylon. It expresses the joy, the recognition of the just for what has happened, and is a perfect contrast to the expressions of sorrow and regret which came from the wicked allies of Babylon (kings, merchants and seamen) which fill ch. 18.

At the end of the triumphant hymn follows a symbolic scene. John attempts to adore the angel who has revealed the wicked nature and the destruction of Babylon, but is severely prohibited, as he is told of his duty to adore only God (19:10). This scene will return in the Epilogue in 22:8, 9. We will see the significance of the scene later, and the importance of its rapid repetition.

For the moment we must dwell on the hymn of triumph over the fall of Babylon. Even though the argument is logical, i.e., the expression of joy and thanks to God for the destruction of Babylon, the hymn appears to be clearly divided into two parts (19:1-3 and 19:6-8), separated by the insertion of a liturgical scene which takes place in heaven and which describes, yet again, the prostration of the heavenly court in adoration before God (19:4-5). It seems possible to see a difference between the chorus which sings the first part of the hymn and that of the second. In the first case John hears from heaven "what seemed to be the mighty voice of a great multitude" (19:1) while in the second, to the voice of "the great multitude" are added others: "like the sound of many waters and like the sound of mighty thunderpeals" (19:6).

What does all this mean? As we already know the important distinction which John makes between the two economies, it is not impossible to see this behind the division of the hymn into two parts. In the first part there is the celebration of the destruction of Babylon which is to be taken in the widest sense, as the destruction of Satan; in the second, it is the institution of the messianic rule, the wedding of the Lamb and his bride. The destruction of Satan is the preliminary effect of the putting into action of the divine salvific plan which John sees happening in two moments: first, through the economy of the Old Testament and then in the death and resurrection of Christ.

This division in two is an allegory of the fact that the divine plan is unique, but happens in two distinct moments. A decisive argument for this is the insertion of the prostration of the angels between the two parts of the hymn in v. 4. We have already explained that this gesture is not simply one of homage, but an act of authentic submission. We know that John links this submission of the angels to the death of Christ. In fact, it acts as a linchpin between the two events celebrated by the hymn: the destruction of Babylon (Satan) and the inauguration of the messianic rule. This means that the destruction of Babylon, begun by the angels, is perfected only in the death of Christ which, however, is not limited only to that, as it is also the beginning of the messianic rule.

This helps us to understand the greater complexity of the choir which intones the second part of the hymn. The "voice of many waters" which is added to that of "the crowd of great multitude" is an attribute which the Apocalypse generally applies only to Jesus Christ (1:15; 14:2). The "sound of mighty thunderpeals" generally accompanies the revelation of Yahweh in the Old Testament (see 10:3ff). Putting all these elements together in the celebration of the coming of the messianic rule over the fall of Babylon, both of which happen in the death of Christ, shows that we are dealing with a culminating event in "the revelation of Jesus Christ."

While discussing the various "voices" which sing the hymn of triumph over Babylon, it is opportune to pause a moment at the voice of the "crowd of great multitude" which is found in both choirs. It is clear that it represents the angels. The immensity of the numbers is one of its attributes (see 5:11). On the other hand, if the first part of the hymn is an allegory of the Old Economy, as we have suggested, we can explain that it is only the angels which sing ("the mighty voice of a great multitude"), as they were its mediators and representatives.

It is also true, however, that the expression "a great multitude" comes in another passage to indicate a very precise human reality: the new people of God, redeemed by Christ, "from every nation, from all tribes and peoples and tongues" (7:9). How can this now be applied to the angels? There are two reasons. The first is that the old revelation, represented by the angels, is never an end in itself but is directed and subordinated to a new reality which has to come. In the old revelation also, therefore, the "great multitude" of the new people of God is present, and, in some way, speaks through the voice of the angels. The other reason is that the hymn of triumph for the fall of Babylon, even though it reflects the two moments in that fall, basically refers to the second, that which takes place in the death of Christ. As well as the fall of Satan, this event also gives birth to the "great multitude" of the people of God.

A confirmation of this suggestion can be found by comparing this hymn with the one sung by the one hundred and forty-four thousand who stand with the Lamb on Mt. Sion in ch. 14. That is also a hymn of triumph, but those who sing it are the one hundred and forty-four thousand just-martyrs of the Old Economy. The introductory formula to the hymn partly coincides with that of ch. 19, at the beginning of the second part: "And I heard a voice from heaven like the sound of many waters and like the sound of loud thunder" (14:2), but the "great multitude," found twice in ch. 19, is not mentioned. This is no accident. We have seen that there are close links between ch. 14 and the end of the book. This explains the similarity. The omission shows that between ch. 14 (the hymn of the one hundred and forty-four thousand) and ch. 19 (the hymn of "the great multitude") there exists the same relationship and the same differences that exist between the sign of the foreheads of the one hundred and forty-four thousand and the arrival of the great multitude in the sixth seal (see 7:2-12).

In other words, what is described between the beginning of ch. 14 and ch. 19 is presented as a repetition and a developement of what was synthetically described in the sixth seal, with its succession of the one hundred and forty-four thousand and "the great multitude." As we have already seen, these two scenes represent the two moments in the actualisation of the divine salvific plan: that of the Jewish economy and that which took place with the coming of Christ. The "seven" of the trumpets and that of the bowls are a repetition of the two scenes of the sixth seal, a repetition which follows the common rule of the Apocalypse, that everything is in everything: the first moment refers to the second, and the second absorbs the first into itself.

With the destruction of Babylon (chs. 17:1—19:1-8) we are still in the "seven" of the bowls which is an allegory on the death of Christ, of which the judgment and condemnation of Babylon are the first effects. The second, positive result is the redemption, described in full in chs. 21-22. For the moment John limits himself to a brief and indirect hint: "the great multitude" which sings the hymn. Before going on to his description of the positive effects John will describe the battle of Armageddon in the rest of ch. 19. This is the great event of the death of Christ which is at the centre of the whole book, but the references to it have gradually become more and more precise: the symbol of the slain lamb, the seventh seal (silence in heaven), the seventh trumpet (the fulfilment of the "mystery of God"), the seventh bowl ("It is done!").

THE END OF JEWISH CULT AND OF THE OLD REVELATION

There are two consequences of great importance which flow from the destruction of Babylon: the end of the Jewish cult and the end of the Old Testament revelation. This does not surprise us, as we are well aware that John sees the death of Christ as producing this destruction which is also the judgment of God upon the world and the end of the whole of the preceding order.

The end of the Jewish cult is indirectly recalled here through the scene of the prostration of the angelic court which John inserts between the two sections of the hymn (vv. 4-5). It is clear that the prostration is connected with the

destruction celebrated in the hymn. It is also evident that it has something to do with the various previous references to the prostration of the angels in Apocalypse. This is the last of a series:
— the vision of the throne in 4:9-10 (the prostration is announced as yet to come)
— the book received by the Lamb from the hands of God (5:8-14)
— the appearance of the "great multitude" in the sixth seal (7:11)
— the sounding of the seventh trumpet (11:16).

Given the pregnant and definitive value of submission which the act of prostration signifies, it is clear that in these various events we do not have a series of separate moments, but they all allude to one and the same fact; the cessation of the mediating function which the angels exercised in the Old Economy, not only in revelation, but also in the cult.

This is a concept which the Apocalypse stresses elsewhere, in its own form of allegorical language:
— in the silence in heaven after the opening of the seventh seal (8:1)
— in the opening of the Temple of God in heaven after the sounding of the seventh trumpet (11:19)
— in the interruption to the angelic liturgy which opens the "seven" of the trumpets, when the officiating angel takes the fire from the altar and pours it out on the ground (8:5).

This end of angelic mediation also means the end of the Jewish cult, in so far as John understood it as being offered to God through the angels. It also meant the end of the Law and the Old Testament revelation, because they were also communicated to man through the angels. This is another point which Apocalypse has made consistently.
— the swallowing of the book and the order to prophesy once again (10:8-11)
— the vision of the Son of man in ch. 1, with the "loud voice" from behind and the face to face vision of the Son of man (1:10-16).

The basic idea of these scenes is that the ancient revelation is over and that it has been replaced by a superior and more open revelation.

In ch. 19 we find an analogous concept in the scene in which John attempts to adore the angel (19:10), a scene which is repeated in almost an identical form shortly afterwards (22:8-9). There have been various explanations of the scene and its repetition. I see both of these scenes as best explained in the light of the general idea of the mediating function of the angels. Clearly John's attempt to adore the angels comes at the end of the revelation of two great mysteries: Babylon and the new Jerusalem. The nature and the destiny of these two opposing realities are revealed by the death of Christ. John finds proof for his claims already in the inspired words of the Old Testament Scriptures. The description of both realities are, in fact, taken from here. It would have been easy to make of the angels, who were only the mediators of the Old Testament revelation, the source of that revelation, the divinity. It appears that this was going on in the world which produced the Apocalypse, and we can find indications of this from the Pauline letters to the Colossians and the Ephesians.

On both occasions John is severely prohibited in his attempt to adore the angel, and told to reserve this for God alone (19:10 and 22:9). This is a vigorous affirmation of monotheism and prohibition of idolatry, but it is more than that. The words of the angel in both cases explain the function of the angels: their absolute equality with the human agents of revelation, the prophets. In fact, in the second case the angel extends this equality to all the members of the Christian community. This indicates two things:

(a) The angels, even before the coming of Christ, were not the authors, but only the instruments of revelation in so far as even then, Christ was the real author.
(b) After the coming of Christ "the Spirit of prophecy" which is "the witness to Jesus" (19:10) no longer passes through privileged mediators, angels and prophets, but is communicated to all the faithful who form part of the Christian community.

The Death of Christ as the Definitive Destruction of All Evil Powers (19:11—20:15)

19 ¹¹Then I saw heaven opened, and behold, a white horse! He who sat upon it is called Faithful and True, and in righteousness he judges and makes war.

¹²His eyes are like a flame of fire, and on his head are many diadems; and he has a name inscribed which no one knows but himself.

¹³He is clad in a robe dipped in blood, and the name by which he is called is The Word of God.

¹⁴And the armies of heaven, arrayed in fine linen, white and pure, followed him on white horses.

¹⁵From his mouth issues a sharp sword with which to smite the nations, and he will rule them with a rod of iron; he will tread the wine press of the fury of the wrath of God the Almighty.

¹⁶On his robe and on his thigh he has a name inscribed, King of kings and Lord of lords.

¹⁷Then I saw an angel standing in the sun, and with a loud voice he called to all the birds that fly in midheaven, "Come, gather for the great supper of God,

¹⁸to eat the flesh of kings, the flesh of captains, the flesh of mighty men, the flesh of horses and their riders, and the flesh of all men, both free and slave, both small and great."

¹⁹And I saw the beast and the kings of the earth with their armies gathered to make war against him who sits upon the horse and against his army.

²⁰And the beast was captured, and with it the false prophet who in its presence had worked the signs by which he deceived those who had received the mark of the beast and those who worshiped its image. These two were thrown alive into the lake of fire that burns with sulphur.

²¹And the rest were slain by the sword of him who sits upon the horse, the sword that issues from his mouth; and all the birds were gorged with their flesh.

20 ¹Then I saw an angel coming down from heaven, holding in his hand the key of the bottomless pit and a great chain.

²And he seized the dragon, that ancient serpent, who is the Devil and Satan, and bound him for a thousand years,
³and threw him into the pit, and shut it and sealed it over him, that he should deceive the nations no more, till the thousand years were ended. After that he must be loosed for a little while.
⁴Then I saw thrones, and seated on them were those to whom judgment was committed. Also I saw the souls of those who had been beheaded for their testimony to Jesus and for the word of God, and who had not worshiped the beast or its image and had not received its mark on their foreheads or their hands. They came to life, and reigned with Christ a thousand years.
⁵The rest of the dead did not come to life until the thousand years were ended. This is the first resurrection.
⁶Blessed and holy is he who shares in the first resurrection! Over such the second death has no power, but they shall be priests of God and of Christ, and they shall reign with him a thousand years.
⁷And when the thousand years are ended, Satan will be loosed from his prison.
⁸and will come out to deceive the nations which are at the four corners of the earth, that is, Gog and Magog, to gather them for battle; their number is like the sand of the sea.
⁹And they marched up over the broad earth and surrounded the camp of the saints and the beloved city; but fire came down from heaven and consumed them,
¹⁰and the devil who had deceived them was thrown into the lake of fire and sulphur where the beast and the false prophet are also thrown, and they will be tormented day and night for ever and ever.
¹¹Then I saw a great white throne and him who sat upon it; from his presence earth and sky fled away, and no place was found for them.
¹²And I saw the dead, great and small, standing before the throne, and books were opened. Also another book was opened, which is the book of life. And the dead were

judged by what was written in the books, by what they had done.
¹³And the sea gave up the dead in it, Death and Hades gave up the dead in them, and all were judged by what they had done.
¹⁴Then Death and Hades were thrown into the lake of fire. This is the second death, the lake of fire;
¹⁵and if any one's name was not found written in the book of life, he was thrown into the lake of fire.

THE HEAVENS OPENED

The new vision, at the centre of which is found the final decisive battle between the Word (Jesus Christ) and the coalition of his opponents, begins with an indication that the heavens opened (19:11). This opening of heaven is certainly to be related to the "open door in heaven" which began the vision of ch. 4 (4:1). As we remarked there, the opening of heaven is a symbol of an intervention of God to offer man the truth (revelation) and salvation which are, after all, the same thing. We have also repeatedly stressed how for the Apocalypse the divine intervention is developed in two moments: the Old Testament economy (Judaism) and the coming of Christ. These two moments, even though forming a continuous line of action, are related to one another as the beginning and the end, the imperfect and the perfect.

The "open door in heaven" of 4:1 and the "heaven opened" in 19:11 correspond in the same fashion: revelation and salvation begun, or better, promised and foreshadowed in the Old Testament (the open door) now received their full and perfect actualisation (the open heaven). The divinity, which at first revealed only his existence, power and majesty, now reveals the totality of his love for man and for all creation. This love is so great that it has driven the Son of God to come down from heaven to become a man among men and to share their destiny.

The "open heaven" indicates, therefore, the final and definitive fulfilment of revelation and salvation which took place in the coming of the Messiah, according to the image which Isaiah and other prophets from the Old Testament had already used to announce this event (see Ps 18:10; 144:5; Is 63:19). The basic meaning of this image is that the relationship between heaven and earth, i.e., between divinity and humanity, has been re-established in the fulness of its original integrity. From the open heaven descends the "Logos of God." Following him, and as a consequence of his descent, John will see immediately afterwards the descent of "the holy city, the new Jerusalem" whose real significance consists in the fact that God has come to dwell in a definitive fashion among men (see 21:2-3).

THE HORSEMAN ON A WHITE HORSE

From the open heaven John sees a white horse come forth, mounted by a horseman who bears all the traits of Christ. The scene has parallels in two places: the appearance of the white horse at the beginning of the first seal (6:2) and the Son of man seated upon the "white cloud" which we met in 14:14.

The links with the first seal are limited to the presence of the white horse and the idea of victory which, in both cases, is to come to the one seated upon the horse. There is an important similarity, but as we said while discussing 6:2, there is not sufficient evidence to establish an identity between the two horsemen. In fact, they are described quite differently in each case. The common symbol, therefore, is that of the horse, and this has a basic meaning: the horse is a symbol of war, and the white colour in the Apocalypse has a positive meaning. From this one can say that the idea common to both scenes is that of a war which will be crowned with success. This applies to the horsemen of the first seal, and also to the Logos of God who descends from heaven.

To go beyond this basic meaning depends, evidently, on how one further explains the symbol of the horse. In the succession of horses described in the first four seals we claimed to find an allegorical representation of the consequences for humanity which come from original sin, and especially the most serious of these: war. In the first horseman, therefore, we saw a symbol which resumed the human experience of the history of salvation: man comes forth "victorious" (i.e.: perfect: "the crown," "the bow") from the creating hand of God; he loses his prerogatives, but finally acquires them once more through the intervention of Christ (6:2: "he went out conquering and to conquer").

This could explain the repetition of the symbol of the white horse in ch. 19. Seated upon this horse, the Logos descends from heaven to combat his enemies. It is clear enough that we have an allegory of the incarnation here: the white horse symbolises the original condition of perfection which Christ has once again made possible for man by the very fact that he has taken on human nature. Guided by him, which means, taken up in his person, human nature will be victorious over the wicked and hostile powers which made him fall and which have robbed him of his original privileges. That will happen in a final and complete way in the battle which Christ is preparing to fight against his enemies, ranged against him at Armageddon.

We will see how this battle is an allegory of the death of Jesus on the Cross. For the moment we will limit ourselves to the observation that to describe Christ seated upon the horse, the Apocalypse, for the first and only time, uses the term "Logos" (Word) which appears, as is well known, in the Johannine Prologue. This needs investigation, but for the moment it is sufficient to notice how both passages use the term for the same purpose: to show the pre-existence and the divine nature of Jesus Christ. Both texts ultimately stress the incarnation of the Son of God. The scene of ch. 19 is really a dramatic presentation of Jn 1:14: "And the Word became flesh and dwelt among us."

THE ROBE DIPPED IN BLOOD

The person who descends from heaven has, as well as the divine nature, all the royal attributes: He carries "on his head many diadems" (19:12) and he is destined to govern the peoples "with a rod of iron" (19:15); "on his thigh he has a name inscribed, King of kings and Lord of lords (19:16) and he is "called Faithful and True and in righteousness he judges and makes war" (19:11).

It is furthermore a question of attributes which we have already met during the course of the book, especially in the vision of the Son of man in ch. 1. These indicate the nature of the messianic prerogatives of Jesus Christ. It appears that the priestly character of Christ, which was put into the foreground in ch. 1, is missing here. We must remember that the vision of ch. 19 is placed, logically and chronologically, before that of ch. 1, where Christ appears to John in his condition of the already risen one.

Our scene is placed before the death of Christ and thus he has not achieved his messianic revelation which, for John, takes place in his death. Even the name which he bears, especially "Logos of God," but also all the others, is not known by anyone except himself (19:12). The august reality of his person is still wrapped in symbol and mystery, awaiting its revelation. The divine horseman, in fact, despite the many sublime attributes given him is "clad in a robe dipped in blood" (19:13).

As all recognise, this comes from a famous passage in Isaiah where God is presented, after a terrible punishment of his enemies, likened to a warrior who returns from the battle covered with the blood of his enemies, or like a wine presser who climbs out of the press with his clothes dripping with the new wine (Is 63:1ff). Perhaps, however, this very passage of Isaiah has led many commentators to see the blood as that of the enemies which he has wiped out. This is a cruel vision which has also helped to make the Apocalypse into a message of a future ferocious revenge. Others, more correctly, have thought of the blood of Christ on the Cross, but as they also see the battle as some future event, the blood of Jesus still has to be understood as some sort of threat, a sorrowful memory which is the very incentive for revenge.

It is better to see that here, as in other places which we have already examined, John refers to the passage from Isaiah to give it a new significance in the light of the messianic event of Jesus Christ as he saw it: redemption and liberation for mankind. Thus in the cloak dipped in blood John sees, like the prophet, an allusion to the destruction of the wicked forces, hostile to God and to humanity. The destruction which he has in mind, however, takes place on a spiritual plane. For John, the only blood that ever flowed in this destruction was the blood of Christ, as we know from the very beginning of the book (1:5) and then from the dominant symbol of the slain lamb.

The vision of the Logos clad in a cloak dipped in blood who comes down from heaven upon the white horse therefore appears to be a further development of the vision of the Son of man seated on the white cloud in 14:14. We have already shown how the two scenes are structurally parallel, in so far as both form the central piece of two groups of angelic appearances. Basing our interpretation on this parallel, we can see in the vision of the Logos on the white horse the final and most explicit repetition of the prophecy of Daniel about the Son of man coming on the clouds (Dan 7:13), which forms one of the keys for an understanding of the Apocalypse. From this last use of the passage, it appears quite clear that John wants to explain the coming on the clouds as the supreme act of the messianic revelation of Jesus Christ, and he situates this act in his death on the Cross.

THE BATTLE OF ARMAGEDDON

In ch. 14 the apparition of the Son of man on the white cloud is followed by the apparition of three angels whose function it is to set about the task of the harvesting and the vintaging of the earth (14:15ff). We see in that an allegory of the death of Christ in its double aspect of the gathering of the elect and judgment. What the Apocalypse describes as subsequent to the appearance of the Logos on the white horse is, as we have already said, a repetition and a deepening of the same themes. Three narrative blocks follow one another, each one introduced by an angel: the battle of

Armageddon (19:17-21), the judgment and destruction of the Satanic rule (20:1-15), the gathering of the elect (21:1—22:5).

One could ask why these three blocks of events which largely are concerned with the New Economy are nonetheless introduced by angelic figures who, as we know, represent the Old Economy. The reply to this query is found by looking at the method used constantly by John to define the content of the new reality through a spiritual interpretation of the old. For the fundamental and constitutive event of the New Economy, the death of Christ and its effects (judgment and the gathering of the elect), he is convinced that we are to find its prefiguration and its pre-announcement in the facts, the personalities and the Scriptures of the Old Testament. In particular, in this final section, his attention concentrates on moments and themes which are drawn from that dramatic period which ran from the destruction of the kingdom of Judah and of Jerusalem up to the Babylonian exile and the hopes of a return and restoration which are found in the voices of Jeremiah, Ezekiel, Zechariah and Daniel (whom John would have seen as living during the Babylonian exile). In the destruction of Jerusalem and its Temple by Nabuchadnezzar and in the prophecies on the resurrection of Israel and the rebuilding of Jerusalem, John sees the prefiguring and the pre-announcing of all that happened in the moment of the messianic revelation of Jesus in his death and resurrection.

If we take account of this, we can give an explanation to the enigma of the name of the place in which the battle took place between the Logos and his enemies: Armageddon. In fact, in ch. 19 the name does not appear. The text says simply: "And I saw the beast and the kings of the earth with their armies gathered to make war against him who sits upon the horse" (19:19). It is clear that this is a repetition of what was narrated in the sixth bowl: the angel pours his bowl into the river Euphrates which dries to allow passage for "the kings from the east." Thus, from the mouth of the dragon, the beast and the false prophet come out impure spirits which "go abroad to the kings of the whole world to assemble them for battle on the great day of the Almighty ... And they assembled them at the place which is called in Hebrew Armageddon" (16:12-16).

There have been many attempts to explain this name. According to the majority the literal meaning would be "the mountain of Megiddo." Almost all the commentators agree that there is an allusion to the city of Megiddo, situated on the plain of Esdrelon, near which took place two of the great battles which were decisive for the history of Israel: Barak defeated the Canaanites, freeing the Hebrews from 20 years of slavery (Judges 5:19ff) and Josiah was defeated and killed there by the Egyptian king Necao (II Kgs 23:29). The victory of Barak is at the beginning of a Hebrew state in Palestine, while the defeat and death of Josiah virtually marks its end. Nabuchadnezzar's Babylonian invasion follows shortly after.

Commentators see problems in the relationship between these events and the Apocalypse. Even more difficult is the use of "mountain" because the city is on a plain. This enigma is possibly solved if the reference is seen as a battle, not in the events of the end time, but as an allegory of the death of Christ. This is the new and true Megiddo which takes into itself both the battle of Barak and the battle of Josiah. Like Josiah, the just and holy king who was slain, the innocent Jesus also falls victim of a coalition of evil powers. His death does not, however, signify defeat and destruction, as it did in the case of Josiah. On the contrary, it is precisely this event which forms the decisive element for victory because Jesus Christ is not simply a man like Josiah, but the "Logos of God" descended from heaven. Thus in his person can be repeated in a perfect way what the Scriptures said of Barak, that the powers of heaven had intervened to give him a powerful arm (see Judges 5:20).

If we are correct in interpreting the battle of Armageddon as an allegory of the death of Jesus, then the mention of a "mountain" is no surprise. The crucifixion of Jesus in all the Synoptics (see Matt 27:33; Mk 15:22; etc.) took place outside Jerusalem on a hill, Golgatha, which Christian tradition rapidly saw as a mountain. But perhaps, even more simply, the mention made of the "mountain of Megiddo" in reference to the death of Christ indicates that this is the event which will found the new Jerusalem "upon a great, high mountain" (21:10).

In any case, it is outside discussion that the battle between the Logos on the white horse and his united enemies at Armageddon is not only not to be understood in a literal sense, as the physical destruction of his adversaries, but it must not be interpreted as an end-time event. It symbolises. instead, the death of Christ, through a typological reading of events, facts and personalities of the Old Testament Scriptures. In this regard, it is useful to notice how the reference to the death of Josiah and the destruction of the kingdom of Judah, implied in Armageddon, is made here by John for yet another purpose. Very often we have seen his insistence that the death of Christ marks the end of Judaism. It should not be discounted that John, in evoking the memory of Megiddo, wanted to set up a sort of parallelism between the material destruction of the Jewish rule, consequent to the death of Josiah, and the spiritual end of Judaism, an effect of the death of Christ.

THE BATTLES OF ARMAGEDDON AND AGAINST GOG AND MAGOG

The majority of commentators maintain that the battle described in ch. 19 is the same as the one announced in ch. 16, during the sixth bowl. But in ch. 20, after the famous and much discussed thousand year reign of Christ, the Apocalypse presents us with another grandiose and definitive battle between the forces of good and evil: that inspired by Satan, freed from his thousand years' imprisonment, with the support of all the peoples of the earth, and of Gog and Magog. The text reads:

> "And when the thousand years are ended, Satan will be loosed from his prison and will come out to deceive the nations which are at the four corners of the earth, that is Gog and Magog, to gather them for battle; their number

is like the sand of the sea. And they marched over the broad earth and surrounded the camp of the saints and the beloved city, but fire came down out of heaven from God and consumed them" (20:7-9).

There has always been unanimity among commentators that this battle is a different battle from that of Armageddon, described in 19:17-21. In fact, between them there is the thousand year reign of Christ and that has always been understood as an event which took place as a consequence of the victory of the Logos at Armageddon. According to current interpretation, there is in the final section of the book a series of events presented in chronological order: the victory of the Logos at Armageddon, the chaining of Satan and the thousand year reign of Christ, the freeing of Satan and the battle against Gog and Magog, the final judgment and the descent of the new Jerusalem from heaven.

Several commentators, however, have found difficulty in accepting this chronological succession. It is quite clear that there are two parallel series: two battles, two judgments, two deaths, two resurrections. Perhaps ch. 20, like many others which we have seen (e.g., ch. 12) is a repetition, a summary of events already described, so that the author can further deepen his reflections on the profound significance of these events. Let us look closely at the events described in this chapter. An angel descends from heaven and binds Satan in the bottomless pit. Then follows a first judgment and a first resurrection, the reign of a thousand years. After this we have the freeing of Satan who sets about deceiving all the nations of the earth, Gog and Magog, for the final battle against God; the battle and the destruction of the forces of evil and finally a further judgment and resurrection. This time, however, it touches the whole of humanity, after which there is a second death, which means being wiped out from the book of life (20:14-15) and a second resurrection which means the inclusion within the heavenly Jerusalem (21:27).

It is clear that the battle against Gog and Magog forms a link between the two series which correspond perfectly in a parallel series of events in which it is not too difficult to see a familiar theme of the Apocalypse: the two stages of the working out of the divine plan for salvation, that which took place in the Old Economy, imperfect, partial and provisional, and that which took place in a full and definitive way in the coming of Christ.

If such is the case, then the battle against Gog and Magog of ch. 20 is a repetition, in a different form, of the battle of Armageddon, in which we have seen an allegory of the death of Christ. In fact, in ch. 20 the battle against Gog and Magog also serves as the deciding element between the two moments in the working out of God's salvific plan; we know that John sees this as the death of Christ. The battle against Gog and Magog is the same as the battle between the Logos and his enemies at Armageddon, and it has the same significance.

The identification between the two battles presents, at first, some difficulties. At the level of the unfolding of the events, only the preparation for the encounter is described in an analogous manner in both cases: an inspiration coming from Satan gathers all the people of the earth for a universal war against God and his people (16:14; 19:19; 20:8). But the way in which this satanic seduction is exercised in each case is described quite differently. In the case of Armageddon, the work of seduction is attributed to the dragon (Satan) and to his human representatives, the beast and the false prophet, working together (19:20), while in the battle against Gog and Magog only Satan seems to work in the first person, directly (20:7). This impression seems to be enforced by the fact that, in the battle of Armageddon, the beast and the false prophet are spoken of as being captured (19:20), while in the battle against Gog and Magog, only of Satan is it said that he "was thrown into the lake of fire and brimstone."

According to these externals, therefore, it looks as if there are two events: first the helpers of Satan are eliminated (battle of Armageddon) and then Satan himself (battle against Gog and ·Magog). But, when we remember that at Armageddon the Logos of God fights in person, how can it be said that the effects of his victory do not extend to the dragon (Satan) who is present in the battle? On the other hand, are the beast and the false prophet absent from ch. 20? It is true that, at the conclusion, when Satan is thrown into the lake of fire and brimstone, John adds "where the beast and the false prophet were" (20:10), but these words (if from John and not a zealous reader) need not necessarily be understood in the usual way: that the devil is thrown into a place where they *already* are. In the original Greek text there is no verb, and the phrase could also be understood as saying that the devil is thrown into the lake, where the beast and the false prophet *are also thrown*.

It is more than probable that the two assistants of Satan are present in ch. 20. John, in fact, speaks of a satanic seduction worked upon the nations of the earth. We know by now that this seduction is worked through these two agents. It is true that the text says that Satan seduces the people himself, but this is to reveal to us the profound meaning of the events, and not the way in which they actually happened. It will be recalled that, in the slaying of the two "witnesses" in ch. 11, John claims that they are slain directly by the "beast who comes up from the bottomless pit," Satan in person (11:7). In all the chapters which follow we see that all this happens because of two historical powers, worldly and corrupt political and religious authority, acting under the perverse inspiration of Satan.

But perhaps it is possible to go beyond these considerations, and to document even more precisely the presence of the beast and the false prophet in the battle of ch. 20. John says that Satan, freed from his prison, "will come out to deceive the nations which are at the four corners of the earth, that is, Gog and Magog" (20:8). Who are Gog and Magog? Most commentators see these names as coming from Ezekiel 38:1ff, and this is correct. John indicates that the people whom he mentions immediately before the names come from "the four corners of the earth": Germans, Huns, Arabs, Turks, etc. Contemporary commentators see the text as alluding to some dark, barbaric horde who will, at the end of time, fall to the light of reason and order.

All of this is fantasy. With the expression "four corners of the earth" John does not wish to indicate mysterious far-flung regions of the earth, but simply the totality of the face of the earth, which he sees as divided into four geographic-political sections. We have already seen this in the giving of authority over the earth to the four horsemen (6:8).

The peoples whom Satan seeks to deceive for a war against God are, therefore, all the peoples who are on the face of the earth. In the work of deception which he operates, we must also see his evil working through the coming and going of the four empires already used in various ways throughout the Apocalypse.

If this is the case, then Gog and Magog could be the collective name which John gives to the peoples of the earth, in so far as their history is worked out under the influence of Satan. The choice of these names is probably due to the fact that John wishes to stress the culminating moment of Satan's influence, the wicked violence against Jesus Christ, the promises and expected Messiah. Gog and Magog, in fact, perhaps already in Ezekiel, but especially in the later apocalyptic literature, were connected with the coming of the Messiah: they stood for the final, furious attack against the setting up of the messianic kingdom. We know that John continually applies Old Testament messianic prophecies to Jesus. Among these, the final part of the book of Ezekiel is one of the most famous, especially because of its vision of the resurrection of Israel and the reconstruction of the Temple. It is not casual that this part of Ezekiel is consistently present in the final section of the Apocalypse. There should be little wonder that John, after having seen the death of Christ prefigured in other events, personalities and prophecies of the Old Testament, sees it now pre-announced in the prophecy of Ezekiel on Gog and Magog. The battle of Armageddon is therefore the same as the battle against Gog and Magog. John shows this indirectly. In the battle of Armageddon, the words of the angel which invite the voracious birds to eat the flesh of the enemies of the Logos (19:17-18) are taken almost word for word from the prophecy of Ezekiel against Gog and Magog (Ezek 39:17ff).

Once we admit that the battle of Armageddon is the same as that against Gog and Magog, then the presence of the beast and the false prophet in the latter has no need of proof and it is not impossible that these two lieutenants of Satan are indicated precisely in the names of Gog and Magog. We have seen that they do not represent distinct nations, but the whole complex of humanity, especially in its political and military organisation. It is exactly something along these lines which the Apocalypse presents in the use of the two names Balaam and Balak in 2:14, the beast and the false prophet in 16:13 (and elsewhere), the beast and the prostitute in 17:1ff and especially in the beast from the sea and the beast from the land in 13:11f. These "couples," we have seen are different representations of the same reality: the collusion between political and religious authority to achieve worldly goals, dominion, power and glory. The search for these goals leads, ultimately, to the subjugation of humanity and aims at the elimination of the lordship of God over the world.

STRUCTURE OF CH. 20

Ch. 20 is certainly the most enigmatic section of the Apocalypse. It is enough to see the many attempts over the centuries to explain the thousand year reign of Christ (20:4-6) to have some idea of the complexity of the problems here. We will attempt to cut through the general line of argument on many of these thorny questions.

In this chapter, in fact, we do not see the description of a series of events which will happen at the end of time, but a further repetition of situations which the author has already dealt with. As in other cases we have already met (e.g., in ch. 12), this repetition also is not simply to fix the ideas firmly in the mind of the listener. The summary of the history of salvation, from the fall of the angels up to the death of Christ, contained here, repeats the general lines of ch. 12. The idea which dominates here is no longer, however, as in ch. 12, the announcement that the time for the fulfilment of the messianic promise is at hand. In ch. 20 the messianic event has already taken place in death and victory (the battle of Armageddon). The author now attempts to explain the significance of this event, the death of Christ: i.e., the judgment of the wicked powers and the salvation of the chosen ones.

Ch. 20 gives most attention to the judgment aspect of the death of Christ, understood as the condemnation and destruction of the forces hostile to God. In fact, at the centre of the chapter stands Satan. He is a negative hero, obviously, and not only because he represents destruction and death, but also because he is destined to succumb before the might of the forces of goodness and life. His defeat, as it is presented in this chapter, takes place in two moments. In a first moment he is defeated, bound and thrown into the bottomless pit by an angel for a certain period of time, a thousand years. During this time there is the rule of Christ and his witnesses. Then Satan is freed; he comes out of his prison, organises a general assault against the divinity and his people, but is definitively beaten and thrown into the lake of fire and brimstone forever. This defeat of Satan is accompanied by the beginning of another rule, this time not for a thousand years, but eternal; it is the reign of Christ over humanity. The description of this reign, through various images (new heaven and new earth, the marriage of the Lamb, the heavenly Jerusalem), is given by the author in chs. 21-22.

As we have already observed, the two moments of the defeat of Satan make up two series of perfectly corresponding events, with an identical scheme of development: defeat of Satan, judgment, the reign of the Godhead. Nevertheless, even though they correspond, the two series are antithetically related to one another in so far as one is provisional and the other definitive, one is temporal and the other eternal, one is limited the other universal. It is the type of contrast which we have seen throughout the Apocalypse which exists between the Old and the New Economy, between the new and the old covenant.

THE CHAINING OF SATAN

The chapter opens with the vision of an angel who descends from heaven armed with a "great chain." He binds Satan and closes him up in the bottomless pit for a thousand years. This sort of image, as scholars have shown, can be found in many peoples and cultures. John, as usual, has no need to go beyond the biblical tradition to find it. Something similar is found in the description of the judgment of Isaiah: the earthly and heavenly opponents of Yahweh are taken and thrown into a great pit to await judgment (Is 24:21ff). In Ezekiel, the idea that God will make his enemies fall into the abyss of Sheol is common (see Ezek 28:8; 31:15ff; and esp. 32:17ff).

The important point, evidently, is not to discover the source from which John may have drawn the idea of the chaining of Satan or the reign of a thousand years, but to understand what he is trying to say through the veil of these symbolic representations. To do this, it is essential to establish, first of all, *when* the events described actually take place. In this regard, the answers concerning the reign of a thousand years, from antiquity to our own time, are always linked to events of the end time. There has also been a spiritual interpretation, also from antiquity, which explains the reign of a thousand years as the period of the Church, from the death of Christ till the end of the world.

Our understanding of Apocalypse brings us to exclude *both* of these interpretations. In John's vision, the divine plan of salvation has its culminating and definitive moment in the coming of Christ, and especially in his death followed by his resurrection. Thus, when he speaks of events which follow one another, of before and after, it is clear that we are still in a phase which is previous to that central culminating point. This is especially important in ch. 20.

It is not only these considerations, however, which lead us to such a conclusion. The analysis of the elements which John uses for his description of the facts is equally enlightening. Notice, for example, the chaining of Satan. The author indicates very clearly that an angel performs this task. It has sometimes been pointed out that this angel appears as a representative or a symbol of Christ. After all that we have said on the function of angels in the Apocalypse, such a suggestion is clearly impossible. For John, the angels represent the mediators of the Old Economy and thus, if he insists here that it is one angel who binds Satan, then the event is somehow to be connected with that economy.

There are further indications that the chaining of Satan and the reign of a thousand years are events which precede the coming of Christ. The angel which comes down from heaven holds in his hand, as well as the chain, the key to close the door of the bottomless pit. In the fifth trumpet it is said that the key of the bottomless pit is given to Satan as he fell from heaven to earth (9:1ff). Yet again, in the vision of ch. 1 Christ solemnly affirms that he has the keys of Death and Hades (1:18). Is there a link between these facts, and if so, what is that link?

These questions can only be answered if we claim that the book is not the result of chance, but the careful construction of a skilful author, working with his own precise logic. According to this logic, it is clear that the situation described in ch. 1, i.e., the risen Christ holding the keys of Death and Hades is a portrait of the final and definitive situation. It is impossible for the keys to pass from his hands to others, because he is the one "who has the key of David, who opens and no one shall shut, who shuts and no one opens" (3:7). Now, on the contrary, the door of the bottomless pit which the angel closes on Satan is due to be reopened so that Satan can come out again from his prison (see 20:3, 7). The situation described in ch. 20, an angel who binds Satan and locks him in the bottomless pit, is clearly that initial situation. The liberation of Satan, whose beginning phase is described in the fifth trumpet (9:1ff) is found half way through the work, between chs. 20 and 1, when Christ is proclaimed as risen and victorious.

The scene of the chaining of Satan has still further aspects which need attention. It does not, in fact, come upon us as a surprise, because it has already been prefigured and announced in earlier, analogous scenes. In ch. 14, the announcement of the three angels which preceded the coming of the Son of man on a white cloud is centred upon the judgment of God which brings about the fall of Babylon (14:7ff). The fact that Babylon is fallen is proclaimed by another angel at the beginning of ch. 18 (18:1ff), before the choir who lament and weep over the destruction of "that great city." The announcement of these angels, as we have said in our analysis, refers to the great final victory which Jesus Christ, the Messiah will have against the forces of evil (the dragon and the two beasts) in coalition against him. It is also evident that the words of the angels refer to something which has already happened, to a fall of Babylon which has already taken place.

Moreover, the angel which descends from heaven in ch. 18 (notice another analogy between this angel who binds Satan) to announce the fall of Babylon is clearly a conqueror, as all the surrounding divine attributes indicate. There is another angel in the Apocalypse who descends from heaven: in ch. 10 one descends carrying the small open book (10:1ff). This angel is surrounded by divine attributes and places, as a tangible sign of victory and dominion, his feet upon both land and sea (10:5). It is not absurd that these various scenes are linked between themselves and also with ch. 20 by a single symbolic meaning. All, in fact, allude to a victory over Satan, a victory for which, in some way, the angels are responsible.

The explanation for all this is found in the book itself, in ch. 12, where the great battle which took place in heaven between the good and the bad angels is described: "Now war arose in heaven, Michael and his angels fighting against the dragon; and the dragon and his angels fought, but they were defeated and there was no longer any place for them in heaven. And the great dragon was thrown down, that ancient serpent, who is called the Devil and Satan, the deceiver of the whole world – he was thrown down to earth" (12:7-9). This is the victory of the angels over Satan which is celebrated in the scenes just mentioned, and which the chaining of Satan at the beginning of ch. 20 again presents in a dramatic fashion. This last scene, among other things, seems to contain an explicit reference to ch. 12: in both cases Satan is indicated with the same turn of phrase: "the ancient serpent, who is the Devil and Satan" (see 12:9 and 20:2).

The scene of ch. 12 also seems to have striking differences from ch. 20. While in the latter Satan is bound and closed in the bottomless pit, in ch. 12 he is cast down to earth. The difference, however, is at the level of expression and not of substance. Even after being cast from heaven (ch. 12) Satan appears to be incapacitated, and in a certain sense, "chained." At the end of the chapter, John describes him: "He stood on the sand of the sea" (12:18). We saw this as Satan's standing upon the dividing line between sea and land and as indicating that he no longer has a dwelling in either place, and he can no longer work directly. He uses his agents, the two beasts, the beast from the sea and the beast from the land (13:1ff). As well as this, the description of the fall of Satan from heaven to earth which appears in the symbolic scenes of the first five trumpets, seems to allude again to a certain powerlessness in his condition. In the fifth trumpet he has power only to open "the shaft of the bottomless pit" to allow the exit of the evils which come to torment humanity (9:1ff). It is through these that Satan, at least in a first moment, exercises his authority of destruction and death. In summary, everything happens as if he himself were, for the moment, chained and closed within the bottomless pit.

There is another more important explanation of the apparent difference between the two situations of chs. 12 and 20. The chaining of Satan described in the latter is in function of the thousand years' reign which is immediately described. As we shall see, the thousand years' reign is the allegorical representation of the salvation obtained by some just ones within the context of the Old Economy. It is on account of the thousand years' reign, i.e., on account of those just ones, who, despite Satan, are saved, that Satan is chained, rendered impotent. This activity, his only desire after his rebellion against God, is to spread his rebellion among all men, "to deceive the whole world." But God opposes this murderous project with his salvific plan whose working out is presented by the Apocalypse in two great stages: one of which has the angels as heroes and mediators, the other being realised by Christ. Even the first, which is certainly provisional and leads to the second, gives salvation to men, but only within certain limits and conditions. This is what John is indicating through his allegory of the chaining of Satan by hand of an angel.

In this way the analogies between the binding of Satan at the opening of ch. 20 and similar "angel" scenes are to be explained. The angel who descends from heaven to bind Satan is certainly to be linked with the angel at the beginning of ch. 18 who descends to announce that Babylon has fallen (18:1ff) and with that of ch. 10 who brings from heaven to earth the small open book. They are always symbols of the initial victory over Satan won by the angels, driving him from heaven and continuing their victory over him by their mediation in the communication to men of the Law and the revelation contained in the Old Economy.

The Old Economy, while certainly the fruit of a victory of the faithful angels over Satan, does produce a certain form of salvation, but this, John indicates, is already linked to the death of Christ. He does this by setting the allegorical scene of the chaining (which is a symbol of the positive value of the Old Economy) immediately after the description of the battle of Armageddon (symbol of the death of Christ), as if one was the product and prolongation of the other. Placing the two facts side by side and establishing between them a relationship of cause and effect, he wished to make us understand that the first victory won by the angels over Satan was only a prefiguration of the complete and definitive victory which Christ would win with his sacrifice, and it was already in some way the fruit and the anticipated effect of that sacrifice.

Even this is not new to us. The celestial hymn of ch. 12 celebrates the victory won by Michael and his companions saying: "And they have conquered him by the blood of the

Lamb" (12:11). It is in this direction which John's affirmation in 13:8 must be translated and interpreted: the lamb was slain "before the foundation of the world."

THE LIBERATION OF SATAN

The chaining of Satan by the angel is not, however, definitive. It will last for a long time, a thousand years, says John, using that number with an indefinite value of a long period of time. But at the end he will be freed, indeed "he *must* be loosed for a little while" (20:3). In the Apocalypse one speaks of "necessity" to indicate the infallible and inevitable way in which the plans of God are fulfilled, and especially, his plan of salvation. (See the repeated use of "the things which *must* take place": 1:1; 4:1; etc.).

If, therefore, it is "necessary" that Satan be freed, that means not only that the liberation happens because of a divine plan, but also that, somehow, it fits into the divine plan for salvation. He must be freed so that the divine salvific plan can take place. The idea of necessity which accompanies the freeing of Satan is explained in two ways:
1. He must be freed in so far as his chaining has been performed by angels, whose nature and dignity is the same as his. This cannot be a definitive defeat.
2. More importantly, the victory which the angels had over him at the beginning of the world has already taken place "by the blood of the Lamb" (12:11), i.e., in reference to the sacrifice of Christ. This event, in the divine vision of things, has been present from all time, even though in Christ it happened at a definite point of time. From the point of view of *history*, however, the first victory must be subordinated to the historical working out of the sacrifice of Christ.

In order for the sacrifice of Christ to take place *it is necessary* for Satan to be freed. Only he, in fact, can have the audacity and wickedness to carry an attack against the divinity itself, present on earth in the person of Jesus Christ. In this case, we have seen, he also uses the services of his two lieutenants, worldly political and religious authority, Rome and the Synagogue. While before the coming of Christ his agents limited themselves to the persecution and slaying of the witnesses to the word of God and to Jesus, when the divinity intervenes directly in the person of Jesus Christ, Satan himself is forced to rise from his place in the bottomless pit, as his whole plan for dominion over mankind is threatened. In order to attain the opposite goal, the liberation of mankind, God disposes that Satan be freed and come forth from his prison.

THE REIGN OF A THOUSAND YEARS

During the period in which Satan is bound and closed in the bottomless pit, there is the reign of a thousand years of Christ in the midst of his witnesses. As specialised studies indicate, the history of the origins of this notion is obscure and complex. Nevertheless, even here John finds it in the biblical and prophetic literature, and especially in the apocalyptic literature. Whatever the source, we can be quite sure that the idea was widely known and used in the world in which he lived and worked.

After all that I have said concerning the chaining of Satan and its meaning, it is not necessary to give a great amount of space to showing that the thousand year reign also refers to the Old Economy and it is an allegory on the salvation obtained through it. We should rather ask why John chooses such a complex and risky, misunderstood symbol to speak of this reality. Perhaps the answer is to be found precisely in the difficult and various interpretations and uses of the symbol. It is possible that John was led to choose this symbol because of the spread of millenarian ideas in the Christian community. Generally speaking, the opposite opinion is argued: millenarian ideas came into Christianity via the Apocalypse, which had taken them from Jewish apocalyptic. This has to be proved. It is possible to show that the opposite was the case. Millenarianism found its way into the early Chruch from many sources, quite independent of the Apocalypse, and earlier than this book. Thus, taking into account how John uses the symbol of the reign of a thousand years, the general thesis can be reversed, arguing that the Apocalypse did not introduce millenarianism but represents a reaction *against* such theories.

Such a hypothesis is possible, of course, only if one admits that John is using the thousand years as a symbol to represent the Old Economy. He is thus attempting to correct the idea of a thousand years which had become a part of the messianic expectation. This came into the early Church largely from Jewish apocalyptic, and was widespread, in various forms, in many movements and authors of the early centuries. Typical of these ideas is that which declares that the messianic rule will come at the end of time and will close all history. Another common trait is that this rule is not the decisive rule of God, but a sort of prelude and anticipation of it. In John's way of seeing things, history is essentially a history of salvation, a gradual working through of the divine salvific plan. The characteristics which John's contemporaries give to the reign of a thousand years belongs, for John, to the period of the Old Economy, the Jewish economy. That period is, in his eyes, the last period of history which comes before the definitive intervention of the reign of God, for which it is a preparation and an anticipation. In the scene of the angel who comes down from heaven in ch. 10 we traced a symbol representing the Jewish economy. John writes:

> "He lifted up his right hand to heaven and swore by him who lives for ever and ever... There should be no more delay, but in the days of the trumpet call to be sounded by the seventh angel, the mystery of God, as he announced to his servants the prophets, should be fulfilled" (10:5-7).

The "time" which will be concluded at the sound of the seventh trumpet, i.e., at the death of Christ, is the time of the messianic expectation, the time of preparation, the period of the Old Economy. Identifying this period with the current idea of the reign of a thousand years, John cuts short any danger for the Christians which might come from the insinuations of Jewish apocalyptic, that the Messiah is still to come. This would be to fall back into the ways of Judaism. John, however, perfectly coherent in his central argument that the death and resurrection of Jesus had already set up the reign and the dwelling of the divinity among men (see 21:3ff), picks up the Jewish idea of a reign of a thousand years, but applies it to the Old Economy.

By identifying the reign of a thousand years with the Old Economy, John has obtained a close bond between the two economies, the old and the new, binding them both to the person of Jesus Christ. Both make sense because of him. One of them, the old, has its sense from the hope and the waiting for the "mystery of God." It pre-announces and gives witness to this fulfilment which must come. Because of this the only ones who actually participate in the rule of a thousand years are the witnesses to Jesus and to the word of God.

We will come back later to this aspect of the reign of a thousand years as a moment of witness. Now, in conclusion to my considerations of the reasons why John used the ideas of millenarianism, we can add a brief reflection on the actual "thousand year" duration of this reign. In the apocalyptic tradition, both Jewish and Christian, the indication of the duration of this intermediary messianic rule varies. In Christian circles the "thousand years" prevails. This is influenced by the Apocalypse (with most Christian authors who follow millenarianism) or is linked (e.g., Letter of Barnabas) to the speculations on the "cosmic week" which fixed the duration of the world at seven thousand years. In Christian millenarianism the seventh thousand, corresponding to the seventh day, the repose of God, is that during which the thousand year rule of Christ is present, after which eternity begins, corresponding to a spiritual "eighth day."

It is quite possible that John took his use of "a thousand years" from the cosmic week theory with which he is very familiar. Naturally all idea of actual "chronology" is to be excluded. The number "a thousand" along with its multiples in the Apocalypse (see for example 5:11; 17:12) indicates a quantity or, as in this case, a duration which is indefinite. More important for John than a fixing of the precise duration of an intermediate reign is his desire to indicate its provisional character, destined to come to an end, no matter how long it may actually prove to be.

THE REIGN OF THE WITNESSES

Only a restricted number of the elect participate in the reign of a thousand years. Only they have a share in what John calls "the first resurrection" (20:5-6) whose content is described as having life, participating in the reign and the priesthood of Christ. "The rest of the dead" (some readings: "the rest of men") have no part in it.

If we observe the context of this first resurrection, the substance of participation in the thousand years' reign, we will notice that it is the same as Christ's provision for all his faithful ones by his death and resurrection: life, rule and priesthood (see 1:5-6). To participate in the reign of a thousand years means to participate already in the realities which Christ gives to mankind. This is sufficient to eliminate the opinion of some scholars who place this reign at the end of time. If we then add to this the fact that, according to the text, the participants are a very small number, we ought to conclude that this reign of a thousand years belongs to the period before Christ, in the Old Economy, limited and partial as it is, both in its character and as regards the number of those saved.

Let us pause for a moment to consider those admitted to the reign of the thousand years. John says:

> "I saw the souls of those who had been beheaded for their testimony to Jesus and for the word of God, and who had not worshipped the beast or its image and had not received its mark on their foreheads or their hands. They came to life and reigned with Christ a thousand years" (20:4).

There are many difficult questions which arise here. Are there one or two distinct groups or categories who participate in the reign? If one accepts that there are two categories, are not the second group, those who did not worship the beast or his statue also martyrs? Why is that not said? Many scholars see a second group, not as martyrs, but people obedient to the commandments. These problems arise out of an understanding of the reign of a thousand years as coming at the end of time, and thus speaking of the special place accorded to martyrs, or through its identification with the history of the Church, and thus the identifying a second group who are faithful to the law of God.

This latter position certainly does not do justice to the text. It is quite clear that those who will not worship the beast or his image are also martyrs, i.e., slain for religious motives. John has already told us this in 13:15 when he said that anyone who would not adore the statue of the beast was slain. Is it correct, therefore simply to identify the two groups? Care is needed, as the text must be respected, especially in the light of the message of the rest of the book.

Notice the first expression: "I saw the souls of those who had been beheaded for their testimony to Jesus and for the word of God" (20:4). With slight variations, this expression occurs several times in the Apocalypse, especially in the fifth seal (6:9) and in the section on the descendants of the woman persecuted by the dragon (12:17). The repetition of the same words clearly links the various situations. The descendants of the woman whom the dragon persecutes because they "keep the commandments of God and bear testimony to Jesus" (12:17) are certainly connected with "the souls of those who had been slain for the word of God and for the witness they had borne" (6:9) whom John sees under the altar at the opening of the fifth seal. These are also the ones whom John sees participating in the reign of a thousand years. Even the reward given in both cases is the same. The souls of the just who participate in the reign of a thousand years have life, rule and priesthood in Christ. Those of the fifth seal live and have their rest under the altar which is a symbol of Christ, and they receive "white garments" which, in the Apocalypse, symbolise the salvific reality brought by Christ (see 3:4; 7:9; etc.).

The rule of a thousand years of ch. 20 is therefore the

repetition and summary of the various earlier situations and its meaning is always the same: to explain for whom and under what conditions the salvation procured by the Old Economy was valid. It is granted to those who gave witness to the future coming of the redeemer of mankind and to the laws, given by God for that period of expectation, and who carried witness to the point of the sacrifice of their lives (see 12:11). The witness, joined to martyrdom, allowed access to the reign of a thousand years, i.e.: it gained for them, even before the historical arrival of Jesus, the salvation of Christ.

The witness, therefore, is two-fold: to the promise of God that he would send a saviour; and to his "word," his expressed will in his Law. There are also two categories of just-martyrs who are admitted to the rule of a thousand years. Do those who do not worship the statue and do not bear the mark of the beast make yet another category? No. It is clearly a further spelling out of the two former categories, especially the second: those who were faithful to the "word," the Law. In fact, the first and most urgent of laws was to fear and adore the unique God who had created heaven and earth (see 14:7). Now the pretension of the beast to force mankind to adore and worship him, imposing in this way his lordship, was an attempt to take the place of the one and only God. To give into such a pretension was to abandon oneself to idolatry, and this was condemned by the Law of God as the most serious of all sins.

To resist idolatry, therefore, represents the other side of the coin to giving witness to the Law of God, whose first commandment was a prohibition of idolatry (see Exod 20:2ff). It is this absolute prohibition of idolatry which the Apocalypse calls to "not worship the beast and its image and not receive its mark."

WITNESS AND MARTYRDOM

There are, therefore, two categories of the just ones who are admitted to the reign of a thousand years: those who announce and give witness to the coming of Christ and those who observe the word, the law of God, adoring him alone and refusing all forms of idolatry, whose worst form, according to the Apocalypse, is submission to political authority and its blasphemous pretensions. All this, we repeat, belonged to the period of the Old Economy, of the Law and the Prophets, the two witnesses who looked and moved towards the coming of Jesus Christ. It is not by chance, therefore, that the characteristics of the participants in the thousand years' reign correspond, point by point, to the announcement of the three angels who preceded the coming of the Son of man on the white cloud in the vision of ch. 14. The first angel carried "an eternal gospel to proclaim to those who dwell on earth, to every nation and tongue and tribe and people" (14:6). This is the promise of the universal redemption which will take place at the coming of Christ (the "witness of Jesus"). The angel adds: "Fear God and give him glory, for the hour of his judgment has come; and worship him who made heaven and earth, the sea and the fountains of water" (14:7). This is the "word," the Law of God. The second angel proclaims the driving out of Satan from heaven: "Fallen, fallen is Babylon the great" (14:8) and the third warns against his attempts to re-establish his authority by taking the place of God upon earth: "If anyone worships the beast and its image, and receives a mark on his forehead or on his hand, he also shall drink the wine of God's wrath" (14:9-10).

In the succession of these three angels we have seen an allegory of the Old Testament revelation and its content. The first part of ch. 20, which goes from the chaining of Satan to the description of the reign of a thousand years, picks up the same theme, spelling it out in a dramatic narrative form, but while it recalls earlier hints, it adds the theme of the salvation possible within the Old Economy, and summarises John's position.

1st Conclusion:
Salvation, which is always the effect of the "revelation" of Jesus Christ, was already possible during the period of the Old Economy. This is shown through the allegory of the chaining of Satan, which alludes not so much to his

inactivity in history, but to an interruption of his power to produce spiritual death, a power which he acquired by leading humanity into a rebellion against God.

2nd Conclusion:
Before the historical coming of Christ salvation was only possible under the conditions of the two-fold witnessing, to the coming of Christ and to the law, sealed with the sacrifice of one's life (martyrdom). This point has been stressed several times throughout the Apocalypse, especially in the fifth seal (see 6:9ff) and in the episode of the two "witnesses" (see 11:7ff).

The most consistent symbol of the just ones from the Old Economy who have been saved is, however, that of the one hundred and forty four thousand marked on their forehead and mentioned during the course of the opening of the sixth seal (7:3ff), and again in ch. 14, where they are described as in the company of the Lamb "standing upon Mt. Sion" (14:1ff). The identification of these with those admitted to the reign of a thousand years comes from various elements. The seal which is on their foreheads (7:3) is, explains John, the name of the Lamb and the name of his Father (14:1). This means that they have given witness to Jesus (the Lamb) and to the Law (his Father); it also indicates that they have never given in to the claims of the beast and never adored his image or placed his name on their foreheads. This refusal on their part has led to their death, so that the one hundred and forty four thousand are also martyrs.

This is not simply a question of deduction. Concerning the one hundred and forty four thousand, John, still in ch. 14, says that they "are chaste" and they "have not defiled themselves with women" (14:4). This means that they have not given themselves to idolatry, to the blasphemous claims of the beast. They are certainly to be identified with those conquerors of the beast, of his statue, and of the number which indicates his name, of which John speaks in the following chapter (see 15:2ff). They are "standing" upon "a sea of glass mingled with fire" and they sing "the Song of Moses, the servant of God and the Song of the Lamb." It is clear in all of this, as also for the marking of the foreheads of the one hundred and forty four thousand (see 7:2ff) that there is a reference to the freeing of the Hebrew people from the slavery of Egypt. It is also evident that, in both cases, the Exodus from Egypt becomes a symbol of the salvation worked by God within the context of the Old Economy. For the chosen ones of ch. 14 salvation also comes through the witness given to the Law (Song of Moses) and to the coming of Christ (Song of the Lamb). This is the "new song" which the one hundred and forty four thousand, and only they, sing in ch. 14, following "the Lamb wherever he goes" (14:3-4).

The "chosen ones" of ch. 15 are described by John as "standing" upon "a sea of glass mingled with fire" (see 15:2). This is again a reference to the Hebrew Exodus, to the passing through the Red Sea, but the "sea of glass mingled with fire" contains a clear reference also to the fall of Satan (see 8:8) and to the persecution of the just ones which he exercises by means of political authority (beast from the sea). On the other hand, these chosen ones are described not only as conquerors, but also as "standing," an expression which the Apocalypse uses to indicate the overcoming of the violent death inflicted by persecutors, as is clear from the Lamb (see 5:6; 14:1) and the two "witnesses" (11:11).

THE FIRST AND THE SECOND RESURRECTION

Witness and martyrdom are, therefore, the conditions for access to the reign of a thousand years, which means they are the conditions necessary to obtain salvation within the context of the Old Economy. Only these can take part, to the exclusion of the rest of humanity. Their experience is described as: "This is the first resurrection" (20:5-6).

We have tried to show that all this indicates the salvation obtained from the Old Economy, and the conditions necessary for it. But what does it mean, in so far as only a few obtain it while the rest are excluded? The text tells us quite clearly. After having said that these are the ones admitted to participate in the reign of a thousand years, John affirms:

"They came to life and reigned with Christ a thousand years" (20:4). A little further on he adds: "Blessed and holy is he who shares in the first resurrection! Over such the second death has no power, but they shall be priests of God and of Christ, and they shall reign with him for a thousand years" (20:6).

We have earlier stressed how the benefits of those who participate in the reign of a thousand years substantially coincide with those which Christ gives to mankind with his coming and his redemptive act. In other words, this means that "the witnesses to Jesus and to the word of God" who carry their witnessing to the point of sacrificing their own lives are admitted to all the benefits of the redemption even before this act has happened historically. Applying to them in anticipation the effects of the redemption worked by Christ, the exclusion of men from divine life by the divine plan of things after the fall is broken. They, in fact, unlike the rest of humanity, are welcomed into paradise immediately after their death, without having to wait for the opening of all doors which happened with the death and resurrection of Christ.

This is what John wants to say with his allegory of the reign of a thousand years and the "first resurrection." He has said it often through the Apocalypse: the one hundred and forty four thousand who stand on Mt. Sion with the Lamb in ch. 14 (14:1-4); the two "witnesses" (11:11ff); the souls under the altar in the fifth seal (5:9-11). This is the meaning also of the blessedness which closes the series of the first three angelic apparitions of ch. 14. They symbolise, as we have seen, the meaning and the content of the Old Testament revelation. The blessedness is preceded by a solemn affirmation which stresses again the value of faithfulness to the Law and to the coming of Christ in the Old Economy: "Here is a call for the endurance of the saints, those who keep the commandments of God and the faith of Jesus" (14:12). Then John hears a voice which sounds from heaven saying: "Write this: 'Blessed are the dead who die in the Lord henceforth.' 'Blessed indeed' says the Spirit, 'that they may rest from their labours, for their deeds follow them'" (14:13). If the blessedness granted to the souls of the just consists in the divine life, the rule and the priesthood of Christ, the expression "henceforth" would have no sense if it meant those who died *after* Christ. In that period, these gifts were already given to all the members of the Christian community in history, while they were alive. The just ones, who, according to the words of the beatitude, receive "henceforth" their reward from their death onward necessarily belong to the Old Economy.

It is this reward – eternal life, rule and priesthood with Christ – which John calls "the first resurrection." It is useless to debate the sense of the term, as it is clear from all that we have seen that John uses it in a purely spiritual fashion. The resurrection spoken of here is not only an eschatological reality but has already taken place, even before the coming of Christ. John never uses the word "to rise" to speak of those who participate in the reign of a thousand years, nor of the two "witnesses." He speaks rather of "having life." In the case of the witnesses, it is a spirit of life from God which enters them (11:11). The idea is one of a new form of life rather than a taking up of life once again.

The rule of a thousand years, therefore, means that certain people, under certain conditions, are given eternal life already in the period of the Old Economy, before the redemptive act of Christ. Given the conditions which we have seen at length, this salvation is granted to very few. And what of the others? "The rest of the dead did not come to life" (20:5). Does this mean that they were damned? No. It simply means that they are not admitted to blessedness "henceforth." It means that the exception made for the witnesses-martyrs is not made for them. Their destiny must wait, to be finally resolved, for the fulfilment of the "mystery of God," when the second resurrection and the second judgment will take place. This happens in the death of Christ.

THE FIRST AND SECOND JUDGMENT

Ch. 20 spoke of two "resurrections": one as a prelude to

the reign of a thousand years (20:4ff); the other as a conclusion of the wiping out of Satan and his allies Gog and Magog (20:12ff). The first is partial and touches only those who participate in the reign of a thousand years; the second is universal, and is applied to all the dead without exception.

Corresponding to these two resurrections there are also two judgments, the first partial, and the second, universal. Between the two judgments, as between the two resurrections, John establishes the same contraposition which exists between the two economies, between the first and the second period of the working out of God's plan of salvation. The first resurrection and the first judgment correspond to the first period, the second resurrection and the second judgment represent the total and definitive character of the all-fulfilling second period in Jesus Christ.

This is the reason for the distinction between the two moments which John introduces into the concepts of resurrection and judgment. Such a distinction was perhaps already current within Jewish apocalyptic where, however, it was always a question of two moments connected with the coming of the Messiah and the end of the world. The coming of the messianic kingdom, according to some Jewish ideas, would have brought a resurrection (bodily and spiritual) and a judgment concerning Israel alone, and then a resurrection and a judgment of the whole of humanity. All in all, this is basically what the Apocalypse is saying, but the authentic spiritual resurrection and judgment, linked with the eschatological moment, is now tied to the messianic coming of Jesus Christ.

In the Apocalypse, the first resurrection and the first judgment are applied to Israel or, better, to the Old Economy of which Israel was the constitutive and representative element. We have already seen this in regard to the participants in "the first resurrection," the reign of a thousand years, where we argued that they were the just ones of the ancient Jewish economy, the witnesses to the Law and to messianic prophetism. This interpretation is further proved by the way in which the first judgment takes place. John speaks of it as he opens his discourse on the reign of a thousand years, even before he mentions those who participate in the reign, the souls of the martyrs.

John says: "Then I saw thrones, and seated on them were those to whom judgment was committed" (20:4). The expression is vague and has caused a variety of interpretations. Who are these judges? Judgment is the right of the divinity, but it is clear that it is not only the divinity who exercises this function. Who are those who assist him? Not the souls of the martyrs, as many would argue: they are mentioned later and appear rather to be the object of the judgment.

A reply to these questions can perhaps be given if we keep in mind the model which inspires John here: the Son of man who comes on the clouds from Daniel (Dan 7:9ff). The vision, as we have seen elsewhere, is divided into two parts, of which the first is given to the description of the divine judgment and the second has an allegory on the triumph of the Messiah. We have already stressed the importance of this vision for the general structure of the Apocalypse which has in its two parts a symbolic representation of the two economies. It has been clear since the visions of chs. 4 and 5. Now in the vision of Daniel, judgment is exercised by people seated upon thrones in the presence of Yahweh (the Ancient of Days). The vision of Daniel is spelt out by John in ch. 4 of Apocalypse, in the sense that he gives a very clear description of the personalities seated on thrones beside Yahweh: they are angelic beings who look to the governing of the universe. We saw there an allegory of the understanding of the divinity and the angelic mediation which is characteristic of the Old Testament revelation.

The court of ch. 20 which is seated upon "thrones" to judge is, therefore, the same court as John presents in ch. 4 and it also comes from the description of Daniel 7. In Daniel also, this court pronounces judgment and sees that justice is done to the saints and the four beasts (the four Empires), especially the last, who is slain. John describes exactly the same scene as a prelude to the rule of a thousand years which has already beeen anticipated, in another fashion, in the scene of the fifth seal.

What we have said can be indirectly confirmed by the description which John gives shortly after the second judgment (see 20:11ff). There the judge is clearly one only, the divinity. The throne of God is alone and isolated, quite different from the scene in ch. 4. This is not the only difference. This throne is "great" and "white," two adjectives which indicate power and victory. The white colour, in particular, refers to the great victory won by Christ over the wicked forces (white horse, white garments, white cloud). The judgment which comes now is, therefore, to be linked with the victory of Christ: it is the consequence of his death and resurrection. There is a rapid allusion, indeed, to the death of Jesus in the allusion to cosmic catastrophes of 20:11 ("earth and sky fled away"), whose significance we now know quite well.

This explains why both the resurrection and the judgment which now take place have a universal character. In fact, in the working out of the divine salvific plan, the effect of the death of Christ is universal, both as regards judgment and salvation. Now the judgment can really have a universal character, because beside the "books" which contain the works of each single person is opened "another book... which is the book of life" (20:12). This is a symbol of eternal life which man had lost with original sin and which Christ gave back to the whole of humanity with his sacrifice, exactly as had been anticipated in the vision of ch. 5.

The second judgment also concerns all the dead. John says: "And I saw the dead, great and small, standing before the throne, and books were opened. Another book was opened, too, which is the book of life, and the dead were judged by what was written in the books, by what they had done. And the sea gave up the dead in it, Death and Hades gave up the dead in them, and all were judged by what they had done" (20:12-13). In the light of these words it has been natural to think of the final resurrection and judgment which, according to traditional belief, will take place at the end of time with the return of Christ.

These words do not, however, refer to that circumstance. It must be noticed that there is no reference to resurrection here. If all the dead are spoken of, it is only in reference to all of them being judged. Nothing is said of "new life" or "return to life," except indirectly, and in connection with the theme of judgment. In fact, "the book of life" is mentioned, in which are written, apparently, the names of those who, after judgment, are considered worthy.

Further, "the sea" and "Death and Hades" are the only ones to give up their dead. These expressions must not be taken in a physical sense. Clearly "the sea" and "Death and Hades" are symbolic expressions to indicate the wicked powers which live in those places, and which move to torment, subjugate and slay the men who live on the earth (see 6:8; 9:1ff; 13:1ff). To say that "the sea," "Death and Hades" are now forced to give up their dead means that the judgment now in action touches the souls even in their power.

The meaning of this symbolic scene which concerns the second judgment and the second resurrection is clear. If we hold that the judgment taking place is the effect of the death of Christ (battle of Armageddon, battle against Gog and Magog), in the scene described here we can see the representation in a dramatic form of a powerful belief of early Christianity (see I Peter 3:19). There was a belief that the salvific effects of the death of Christ extended, even in the first place, to all those who lived and died before the coming of Christ. This is what primitive Christian confession means by the expression of Jesus' descent into hell after his death. The Letter of Peter is very explicit on this, and it adds that he went to announce there to the men of old who, unlike the few just ones of that period (symbolised by Noah and his family) did not have faith and were not saved (I Peter 3:19-20).

The truth which I Peter passingly refers to has been amply developed in the Apocalypse through the allegory of the first judgment (first resurrection, reign of a thousand years) and the second judgment (second resurrection). It adds, however, that only a few from the old economy are saved by their faith. More than this, the Apocalypse makes clear that this faith, to obtain salvation, must be accompanied by martyrdom. This probably indicates that even in the Old

Economy, the old salvation was still the fruit of the death of Christ, of whose death the martyrdom of those just ones was a prefiguring.

With the exception of these few just ones, the rest of humanity was not saved. John says, "The rest of the dead did not come to life" (20:5). But their destiny, rather than the result of a definitive judgment, was the effect of the original sin which prohibited man from entering divine life. Such an exclusion was not definitive in so far as the fault and its consequences, according to the promise of God, would be overcome. The redemption worked by Christ with his death was this victory. Consequently, entry into the divine life was now possible for mankind (20:12: "Another book was opened, which is the book of life"). Only now is that object removed, and each man can go into the divine life, after a judgment "by what they had done" and "by what was written in the books," i.e.: in the light of the Law of God. Now access to the divine life is objectively possible because of the redemptive action of Christ.

The second judgment described by John in ch. 20 refers to the universal, conclusive and definitive character of the coming of Christ, and especially his death, as it finalises the divine plan of salvation (the book of life) and the condemnation (the second death) which it brings cannot be modified. This is not the case with the first judgment. The condemnation here consists in not having life, in being subjected to the domination of death, of Satan. This domination, however, is only provisional: in the moment of judgment, i.e.: the death of Christ, Satan ("the sea," "Death and Hades") are forced to give up their dead so that they may be judged "according to their works."

Even the life granted to the participants in the rule of a thousand years was, however, in some way, provisional and tied to the fulfilment of divine judgment. In fact, even if the second judgment will not be able to have a negative effect on them ("second death": 20:6), their blessedness is not yet perfect because the intervention of God to render justice to them is not yet perfected (see 6:10).

The second judgment also has a definitive character for

Satan and the other rebellious angels. Their destiny, certainly, has been indicated from the moment of their rebellion and their being driven from heaven. Still, they are not reduced to impotence. In the interval between their fall and the final judgment (death of Christ) they are allowed the authority to torment mankind (9:1ff). In fact, their leader, Satan, at the end of this interval is freed and is able to carry out his last frantic attempt against the divinity (20:7ff). Once the second judgment has taken place, however, Satan and his wicked allies are condemned to the "second death" (20:14): their destiny is definitive and their impotence total.

The Death of Christ as the Basis for the Gathering of the Chosen Ones in the Messianic Kingdom (Heavenly Jerusalem) (21:1—22:5)

> 21 ¹Then I sew a new heaven and a new earth; for the first heaven and the first earth had passed away, and the sea was no more.
> ²And I saw the holy city, new Jerusalem, coming down out of heaven from God, prepared as a bride adorned for her husband;
> ³and I heard a loud voice from the throne saying, "Behold, the dwelling place of God is with men. He will dwell with them, and they shall be his people, and God himself will be with them,
> ⁴he will wipe away every tear from their eyes, and death shall be no more, neither shall there be mourning nor crying nor pain any more, for the former things have passed away."
> ⁵And he who sat upon the throne said, "Behold, I make all things new." Also he said, "Write this, for these words are trustworthy and true."
> ⁶And he said to me, "It is done! I am the Alpha and the Omega, the beginning and the end. To the thirsty I will give from the fountain of the water of life without payment.

⁷He who conquers shall have this heritage, and I will be his God and he shall be my son.

⁸But as for the cowardly, the faithless, the polluted, as for murderers, fornicators, sorcerers, idolaters, and all liars, their lot shall be in the lake that burns with fire and sulphur, which is the second death."

⁹Then came one of the seven angels who had the seven bowls full of the seven last plagues, and spoke to me, saying, "Come, I will show you the Bride, the wife of the Lamb."

¹⁰And in the Spirit he carried me away to a great, high mountain, and showed me the holy city Jerusalem coming down out of heaven from God,

¹¹having the glory of God, its radiance like a most rare jewel, like a jasper, clear as crystal.

¹²It had a great, high wall, with twelve gates, and at the gates twelve angels, and on the gates the names of the twelve tribes of the sons of Israel were inscribed;

¹³on the east three gates, on the north three gates, on the south three gates, and on the west three gates.

¹⁴And the wall of the city had twelve foundations, and on them the twelve names of the twelve apostles of the Lamb.

¹⁵And he who talked to me had a measuring rod of gold to measure the city and its gates and walls.

¹⁶The city lies foursquare, its length the same as its breadth; and he measured the city with his rod, twelve thousand stadia; its length and breadth and height are equal.

¹⁷He also measured its wall, a hundred and forty-four cubits by a man's measure, that is, an angel's.

¹⁸The wall was built of jasper, while the city was pure gold, clear as glass.

¹⁹The foundations of the wall of the city were adorned with every jewel; the first was jasper, the second sapphire, the third agate, the fourth emerald,

²⁰the fifth onyx, the sixth carnelian, the seventh chrysolite, the eighth beryl, the ninth topaz, the tenth chrysoprase, the eleventh jacinth, the twelfth amethyst.

²¹And the twelve gates were twelve pearls, each of the gates made of a single pearl, and the street of the city was pure gold, transparent as glass.
²²And I saw no temple in the city, for its temple is the Lord God the Almighty and the Lamb.
²³And the city has no need of sun or moon to shine upon it, for the glory of God is its light, and its lamp is the Lamb.
²⁴By its light shall the nations walk; and the kings of the earth shall bring their glory into it,
²⁵and its gates shall never be shut by day – and there shall be no night there;
²⁶they shall bring into it the glory and the honor of the nations.
²⁷But nothing unclean shall enter it, nor any one who practices abomination or falsehood, but only those who are written in the Lamb's book of life.
22¹Then he showed me the river of the water of life, bright as crystal, flowing from the throne of God and of the Lamb ²through the middle of the street of the city; also, on either side of the river, the tree of life with its twelve kinds of fruit, yielding its fruit each month; and the leaves of the tree were for the healing of the nations.
³There shall no more be anything accursed, but the throne of God and of the Lamb shall be in it, and his servants shall worship him;
⁴they shall see his face, and his name shall be on their foreheads.
⁵And night shall be no more; they need no light of lamp or sun, for the Lord God will be their light, and they shall reign for ever and ever.

STRUCTURE OF CHS. 21 AND 22

The division into our present chapters, which took place in the Middle Ages, is arbitrary here. This final part of the book is dedicated to the description of the heavenly Jerusalem and it fills the whole of ch. 21 and the first five verses of ch. 22. Ch. 22:6-20 then form the epilogue, a conclusion both to this section and to the whole book.

The content of the final section is the description of the new reality, the new order, new creation which takes the place of all that has gone before and is now destroyed. There are basically two questions which have always arisen over this section:

(a) Is the description to be taken in a realistic way, or is it symbolic?
(b) Does this reality form part of history or is it beyond history, in eternity?

Obviously one's whole approach to the Apocalypse will determine the answers given to these questions. I do not see the new reality described here as either the conclusion or the arrival point of a series of events, set out in chronological order. In the final section, centred upon the vision of the new Jerusalem, I see simply the taking up and further development of a theme which has already been dealt with: the symbolic description of the positive effects produced by the death of Jesus Christ. Up till now John has been stressing its effects as the judgment of God upon the world.

The basic positive effects which the death of Christ has produced are, for John, the redemption, the elimination of the consequences of original sin, the restoration of the interrupted relationship between God and man, giving back to man the possibility to enter into the eternal divine life. This is the "good news" which Jesus Christ came to bring and to realise, and its preaching in the early Church produced the New Testament.

To explain this message, John chose a rather special means, the apocalyptic literary genre, which he understood as a continuation of Hebrew prophetism, especially messianic prophecy. Linked with this, John saw in the person and in the work of Jesus Christ the fulfilment of all that had been announced in that prophetic tradition. One of the main features of Hebrew messianic prophecy, especially after the Babylonian exile, was the return and the restoration of Israel, the reconstruction of Jerusalem and of its Temple.

Little by little this hope also became a part of the messianic expectations.

Little wonder that John, in presenting Jesus Christ as the promised and expected Messiah, also saw the restoration of Israel and the reconstruction of Jerusalem as its culminating moment. It is hardly necessary to recall that John uses this in an entirely spiritual sense, and is in no way interested in the political and temporal restoration of Israel and Jerusalem. His vision knows no barriers of race or territory, but applies to the whole of humanity. This does not mean that the new reality is totally divorced from the old. John establishes a powerful line of continuity between them both, even though the continuation into the second sees the overcoming and abolition of the first.

This explains, for example, how the new Jerusalem presupposes the destruction of the old (which had become Babylon) but nevertheless reproduces it, in all its aspects, even though now on a spiritual plane. In fact, it is clear that John's portrait of the new Jerusalem comes entirely from his reflections on the old prophecies of the restoration of Israel and Jerusalem, especially upon the last part of the prophecy of Ezekiel and the book of Zechariah. This fact must not be explained simply in terms of literary dependence. As always, John is using the old Scriptures as authentic "citations" for the double purpose of having behind him the authority of the word of God, and then of making his own specific interpretation of it, applying it to Jesus Christ and to his saving action.

The biblical references which John uses in this section do not only come from the period of the exile and of the return to Israel. Beyond these one can sense a constant reference to the circumstances of the beginnings of mankind described in the book of Genesis: the creation of the world, the creation of man and the condition of mankind in the garden of Eden. The new reality which John describes is not only the full and perfect realisation of the promises about the restoration of Israel; the restoration spoken of here is something far greater and deeper than that. It is the return of humanity to the original conditions of life in which it was created by God.

The new reality, therefore, does not simply mean the overcoming of a condition of exile for Israel, as a Jewish mentality might be tempted to think. The condition of exile, as John had indicated with the allegory of the woman in ch. 12, touches the whole of humanity, bereft of all its privileges and its glorious future because it listened to the deceitful promises of the murderous dragon. The exile of Israel and the persecution to which she is subjected are only a symbol of a condition under which the whole of humanity is living. It is this condition of the whole of humanity which Christ has come to heal. The new Jerusalem represents the coming out of the desert where Israel has been a pilgrim people; it also represents the coming out of that other desert where the whole of humanity has been in pilgrimage since being driven out of the garden of Eden.

Thus we must interpret the two-fold series of scriptural references which are the basis of this allegory which closes the Apocalypse: in the redemption of Israel, announced in the messianic prophecies, John sees the symbol and, indeed, the "first fruits" of the redemption of the whole of humanity worked by Jesus Christ. In the same direction we must understand the links between this final section and the rest of the book. As the new Jersalem is to be linked to the old and to return to the garden of Eden, so also is "the bride of the Lamb" (see 21:2 and 9) clearly linked with the woman of ch. 12 in her two-fold meaning: a symbol of Israel and of the whole of humanity. The description of the beauty and splendour of this heavenly Jerusalem repeats point by point the "promises to the conqueror" which are found in the "seven" of the Letters to the Churches of Asia, but they, in their turn, referred to the whole of the history of salvation which, through the experience of Israel, goes back to the origins of humanity.

The final part of the Apocalypse symbolically represents, therefore, the glorious conclusion, the final and perfect putting into action, of the divine salvific plan. The new Jerusalem is the symbol of the reconciliation established between humanity and God, of the new covenant, now eternal and definitive, of the new people of God, chosen no longer from one nation but from "every nation, from all tribes and peoples and tongues" (7:9). In this sense, it is a figure of the Church which, on the one hand, is the continuation of ancient Israel (see 1:20) but now gathers into herself and saves all peoples (see 21:25-26; 22:2).

THE "NEW HEAVEN" AND "NEW EARTH"

After all that I have just said, it is not necessary to demonstrate that the new creation is not to be understood literally, as referring to some sort of restoration from the ashes of a univeral catastrophe. We now know the meaning of the "universal catastrophe" which often appears in the Apocalypse: it is a symbol of the destruction of a spiritual world which has been upset by the rebellion of both angelic and human agents, a destruction which takes place in the death of Christ. It is the judgment of God which separates the good from the evil, the just from the unjust and places each one in his rightful place.

Heaven and earth are also renewed, and recreated as an effect of this judgment of God. In fact, they represent, respectively, the dwelling places given by God to the angels and to men. In both places, first in one and then the other, Satan has attempted to install himself with his plan of rebellion against God, and this has meant destruction and death for the inhabitants of both places. But he is driven out of both places: first from heaven by hand of the angels, and secondly from earth through the action of Jesus Christ. Now he has no dwelling, not even the bottomless pit. He is now fixed forever in his condition of spiritual death, "the second death," "the lake that burns with fire and brimstone" (20:10, 14).

The new creation of the heaven and earth corresponds to the story told in Gen 1:1ff as a prelude to the creation of man. In the Apocalypse, moreover, the creation of the heaven and the earth is only a first moment in the divine intervention which reaches out to the whole of reality: "And he who sat upon the throne said, 'Behold, I make all things new'" (21:5). In this case also, the creation of the universe serves the new creation of man (see 21:6-7). What is spoken of here is not in opposition to the creation of Genesis, or the destruction of it to replace it with something quite different; it is rather the continuation, the perfection of that first creation. It touches, not the physical world, but the spiritual. In it, in fact, is said: "The sea was no more" (21:1). Clearly this is not the physical sea, but that sea which earlier was forced to give up its dead (20:13), that from which had moved the first historical incarnation of Satan (ch. 13).

In this new universe, the "glory of God" and the "lamp which is the Lamb" (21:23) are substituted for the light and the moon and the sun. Even the vegetation which fills it and the river which waters it (22:1-2) are symbols of spiritual realities.

"UPON A GREAT HIGH MOUNTAIN"

The new Jerusalem is not gradually built up by the hand of man. She descends, perfect and prepared like a bride "from heaven," and she comes "from God" (21:2). This means that the redemption of humanity, this new and perfect creation, can be brought about only by the divinity. This is a concept which John has frequently stressed; e.g.: the scene of the sealed book which no one could open: "No one in heaven or on earth or under the earth was able to open the scroll or to look into it" (5:3).

The descent of the new Jerusalem from heaven is described in a scene which recalls the judgment of the great prostitute (17:1ff): "Then came one of the seven angels who had the seven bowls full of the last seven plagues, and spoke to me, saying, 'Come, I will show you the Bride, the wife of the Lamb.' And in the spirit he carried me away to a great, high mountain, and showed me the holy city Jerusalem coming down out of heaven from God, having the glory of

God" (21:9-11). The analogy between the two situations is based on the presence of an angel who is, in both cases, one of those "who had the seven bowls." As we have earlier attempted to explain, these two angels, who illustrate to John the nature and the destiny of the two opposing cities, are respectively the first and the last in the series of the bowls. Since the "seven" of the bowls is an allegory on the death of Christ, in the opposing destinies of the two cities one can see the reflection of the two-fold effect which that death produces: judgment and gathering of the elect; condemnation and salvation.

The link, and at the same time, the contrast between the two situations is then stressed by John with another quite significant detail. In the first case the visionary is taken by the angel "in the Spirit into a wilderness" (17:3) while here he is carried "in the Spirit...to a great high mountain" (21:10). In the first case the mention of the wilderness/desert sends us back to the situation described in ch. 12, of the woman who flees the dragon: an allusion to the human condition, sinful but aided by God with the promise of redemption and an allusion, in particular, to the chosen people (Jerusalem) especially in the desert, pursued by the furious Pharaoh. The mention of "the great high mountain" which we find in the second case is also a recalling of Jerusalem, built on an elevated place, on Mt. Sion. It is clear, however, that John contrasts "desert" and "mountain" on a symbolic level. At this level, while "the great high mountain" is an indication of inaccessibility and therefore of absolute security, the "desert" is an ambiguous sign: it can be a refuge, but it is also a place of trial and temptation. In fact, the prostitute of ch. 17 is the same woman as that of ch. 12 who has now succumbed to the temptations of the dragon who follows her.

Still on a symbolic plane, between the situation of the prostitute in ch. 17 and that of the "Bride" in ch. 21, there exists another contrast. They are placed, as we have seen, "in the desert" and "on a great high mountain," respectively. The prostitute, as well as being in the desert, is seated upon a monstrous beast, which is a sign of both political authority and Satan. Even Satan and that which he represents constitutes an imposing reality; even Satan is "a great mountain" but it is not "high" any longer, because he has been thrown down (see 8:8ff). The prostitute, therefore, has also attempted to escape from her precarious position and to establish herself on a mountain, but she has done it by depending upon Satan, i.e.: taking on his instruments and his plans of glory and human dominion. Thus, she is upon "a great mountain," but it is a mountain which has been thrown down from heaven to earth and from earth "into the lake of fire and brimstone," in eternal spiritual death.

"The Bride, the wife of the Lamb," on the other hand, has been taken away forever from the situation represented through the symbol of "the desert." She, in fact, comes down "from heaven" and is the direct creation of God. The "great high mountain" upon which she is placed assures her of a continual protection from the temptations and the persecutions of the pain and loneliness of "the desert." The mountain upon which she is placed is the same as the one upon which Christ wins his battle of Megiddo (16:16: Armageddon: the mountain of Megiddo!), and victoriously drives back the assault of Satan, Gog and Magog who arise from below towards the camp of God and the saints (see 20:9). On that mountain, the spiritual Mt. Sion, have already ascended, before Christ, all those who, like him, have given witness with the sacrifice of their lives, their faith in the word of God and their trust in the messianic prophecies (see 14:1). On this spiritual Mt. Sion, as well, Isaiah had also predicted the foundation and the centre of the messianic kingdom (Is 2:1ff), understood as a renewal of the cult and of the covenant with God.

"THE TENT OF GOD AMONG HIS PEOPLE" (21:3)

The profundity of the new reality which is called the "new Jerusalem" is found in the fact that here the divinity comes to dwell among men. In the light of this affirmation (v. 3) all other suggestions about the heavenly Jerusalem seem to falter, as they argue whether it is to be found as a part of history, or some sort of eschatological reality. We repeat that John's way of seeing things is not chronological in the sense usual in apocalyptic, where present and future are opposed to one another. His vision is theological and has as its centre the conclusion of the divine salvific plan in the coming of Jesus Christ. If one must speak of a *before* and of an *after* or rather, following a current expression, of a *now* and a *not yet*, one can only speak of it in relation to the *conclusion* which takes place in the death and resurrection of Jesus.

What interests John, in his vision of the putting into action of the salvific plan, is to affirm that with the coming of Christ the situation of humanity in its relationship with God is radically changed. *Before*, the relationship is broken, and man does not have access to divine life. *After*, the relationship has been set up once again, and man can participate in the divine life. This participation is possible, not only after death, as was the case for an exceptional group before Christ, but also during one's human life. For mankind, God has become "God with them" (21:3); he set up his tent among them, and they have become "his people" (21:3).

This is the substance of the new reality inaugurated by Christ. To indicate the intensity and the intimacy of this renewed relationship between God and humanity, John uses the image of a "marriage," of the union between a man and a woman (see 19:9) also common in other New Testament documents. In fact, in the Apocalypse this image is what one would today call an archetype. From this image comes, for example, the symbol of the "woman" which plays such an important part in the symbolic structure of the book. At the basis of this symbol stands the relationship between God and man understood as the relationship which unites a man to a woman, and all the other related ideas which come with it: faithfulness, unfaithfulness, betrothal, marriage, wedding feast, life together. It is not an accident, therefore, that female marriage symbols abound in this concluding part of the book (betrothed, bride, wedding, tent). It celebrates, in fact, the reconciliation and the restoration of the relationship between God and humanity.

"I SAW NO TEMPLE IN THE CITY" (21:22)

The new Jerusalem has no Temple "for its Temple is the Lord God almighty and the Lamb" (21:22). This detail has led almost all the commentators to think that the reality described here refers to something on the other side of history, in eternity. To understand John's affirmation, it is necessary to recall, yet again, the contrast which he establishes between the Old and the New Economy, between Judaism and the Christian message. For Judaism, only the Jerusalem Temple was the authentic place of divine cult. Against this way of seeing things, first Jesus and then his followers protested, in the name of an authentic spiritual cult, that this could not be limited to privileged places. A famous passage from the Fourth Gospel, the dialogue between Jesus and the Samaritan Woman (see Jn 4:19ff) spells this out very clearly.

To this polemic between Christians and Jews, which really was the same as the ancient prophetic preaching (see, for example, Is 58:1ff; 66:1ff; Jer 7:1ff), there are joined other motifs. The first and most important of these is the problem of the continuation of the cult and practices of Judaism in the new religion. In the end the attitude of distancing and eventual abandoning the old forms prevails, though not without difficulty, as we can see from the Acts of the Apostles, the Pauline Letters and the Gospels.

The Apocalypse builds upon this position of breach and separation, with considerable energy. We have seen indirect traces of this in John's idea of the role and function of angels and in the conclusion of the "sevens" of the seals and the trumpets. An explicit affirmation about the end of the Jewish cult and its substitution by a universal, spiritual cult appears to be behind the allegorical scene of ch. 8 where the angel takes the coals from the altar and pours them out upon the earth (8:5).

What John says here about the absence of a Temple in the new Jerusalem also comes into this polemic against Jewish cult, which he accuses of superficiality and above all, of the exclusion of all other peoples, as appears to be indicated in the allegorical scene of the measuring of the Temple (11:1ff). To recall that scene is not arbitrary, as John himself establishes, not by chance, a link between that scene and the measuring of the new Jerusalem which takes place in 21:15ff. The very fact that it is not the Temple which is measured, but the whole city, hints of an extension and of a universalisation of cult.

"The Lord God the almighty and the Lamb" (21:22) are the Temple and the new Jerusalem, and since they are now "God with them" (see 21:3), the divinity which dwells among men, the whole city and all its inhabitants are a Temple of God. The faithful, in fact, are not only a people of God (21:3): they have become "kings and priests," according to the promise made to Moses (see 1:6; Exod 19:6). Wherever they are, God is with them, and they worship him "in spirit and in truth," and not in the Temple of an earthly Jerusalem (see Jer 4:23ff). In this way one can explain the fact that the description of the new Jerusalem is based upon what the prophets Ezekiel and Zechariah make of the Temple which the Hebrew people must reconstruct on their return from the exile (Ezek 40-48; Zech 2:1ff). John sees the fulfilment of those prophecies, not in the material reconstruction of the Temple of Jerusalem, but in the beginning of the new economy, in the new covenant in which the dwelling of the divinity among men has rendered superfluous any material building as a privileged and exclusive *place* for the presence of God.

THE RIVER AND THE TREE OF LIFE

In the description of the new Jerusalem, the Temple-City parallel which John keeps making, following the Prophets, is found again in the presence of the river which flows through the city, "flowing from the throne of God and of the Lamb" (22:1-2). This river is found in both Ezekiel and Zechariah, and is used to represent the spiritual renewal which will spread through the whole earth as an effect of the

Jewish renewal of cult. In Ezekiel, in fact, the source of this immense river is under the Temple (Ezek 47:1ff), while in Zechariah it is Jerusalem (Zech 14:8ff).

The variation introduced by John, which has the river flowing directly from God and from Christ, is yet again to be understood as an interpretation of those prophecies, which are also messianic, in an anti-Jewish sense. The universal character of the renewed divine cult which would come from the advent of the Messiah does not take place through the universal imposition of the cult of Israel. Its universality will come from God's communication of himself to the whole of humanity, without any distinction of nation or race.

John, taking up his prophetic models of the river symbol, first uses them in a spiritual sense, detaching them completely from any of the practical cultic or ritual implications found in the prophets. The river which flows directly from the divinity and flows across the new Jerusalem becomes a very clear symbol of the divine life which is communicated directly to the whole of humanity, now that Christ has re-established the relationship between God and man through his sacrifice of self (see Jn 7:37-39). Thus the symbol of the river used here by John goes well beyond the prophetic models from which it is derived, probably reaching back to the ultimate origin of the symbol, even for those prophets: the description of Eden as it is found in Genesis.

According to the Genesis account of the creation, all the water which flows on the earth comes from one great river which arises in Eden (Gen 2:10ff). From this point it is not difficult to see the river as a symbol of the fulness of the spiritual life which spreads over the earth, especially when man's presence in Eden is seen as a symbol of the full and perfect relationship between God and humanity.

It appears clear John intends to recall the situation of Eden here from the mention which he immediately makes of "the tree of life" (22:29. See Gen 2:9). John also goes back here to Genesis rather indirectly, passing through a quotation from Ezekiel. In fact, the placing of this "tree of life" (literally: "wood of life") on the bank of the river, its extraordinary yielding of fruit and luxuriance and the universal enjoyment of the fruits, all go back directly to Ezekiel (Ezek 14:7 and 12). The term "tree" or "wood of life," however, not only eliminates any purely physical understanding of such a wonderful tree, but also takes us back to the situation of Eden. In other words, John quoted Ezekiel, and sees in his words a recalling and a spiritual reinterpretation of the Genesis account.

This is a typical example of how John uses the Old Testament. He is anxious to show that there is continuation which reaches its perfection in the person and the event of Jesus Christ. The new covenant, the new Jerusalem, the new people of God founded by him all reach back through the Jewish economy, to the very origins of humanity. The river and the spiritual trees which Christ places in this new creation, in this new Eden, are the full realisation of the wonders already contained in those same elements placed by God in the first Eden: they signify the abundance, the never ending and fruitful giving of life which the divinity now bestows upon mankind.

Thus: a return to the origins. But it is more than that, since all that was in the stage of promise and trial, as the allegory of the pregnant woman in ch. 12 indicated. The divine promises were linked to the son who still had to be born, and which will certainly be realised in Jesus Christ. But for the woman (humanity at its beginnings) the son is still in gestation and is exposed to the aggression of the dragon to such an extent that as soon as he is born, he is taken away from the woman and placed next to God in the security of heaven (see 12:2-5). The divine promises, because of diabolic temptation and human weakness, are not realised.

The redemption worked by Christ, however, takes humanity back to its original condition, but adds to that condition the full and definitive actualisation of what was, at the beginning, only a promise.

In the conclusion of this event, as related in the Apocalypse, we see a use of similar symbols and images to describe the perfection of something hitherto imperfect, broadening these symbols and their application without breaking from the original. We can now understand, for example, how the horseman of the first seal could be at the one time a symbol of a positive and a negative reality and could come out "conquering and to conquer" (6:1-2). We can understand how the woman-mother of ch. 12 could become, on the one hand, the great prostitute, yet on the other, the Bride of the Lamb. We must not wonder that in the closing scene of the great drama of Apocalypse we see re-appear the fearful sign of the tree of life, so closely linked with the sad fall of man at the beginning of his story of sorrow and pain.

The symbol which does not change is, however, completely transformed as regards its content. In Gen 2:9 it was a symbol of "the knowledge of good and evil." This aspect seems to be ignored and John speaks only of "life." But it may not be quite the case. In the distinction between the two trees in Genesis, John probably saw a reflection of the precariousness of the situation of man at the beginning. Now, however, after Christ has finally revealed the mystery of God, the tree of "knowledge" is identified with that of "life": to taste one means to taste the other; Christ communicates divine life and in fact makes true the claim of the tempter in Genesis: man now does become "like unto God" (see Gen 3:5 and 22). The redemption worked by Christ making man like God, has made an end of prohibitions and trials which were necessary then for admission to the divine life.

NUMERICAL AND MINERALOGICAL SYMBOLS

In contrast to the measuring of the Temple in ch. 11 which is general, and negative (11:2: "Do not measure the court outside the Temple; leave that out"), the measuring of the new Jerusalem takes place with great care and the smallest detail of the measurements and the materials of the city are described.

As regards the measurements, the basic number seems to be "twelve" and its multiples: twelve gates (21:12), twelve foundations (v. 14), a wall one hundred and forty four cubits (v. 17) and the overall measurement of the city is twelve thousand stadia (v. 16). The symbolism of this number is quite clear, as it calls upon the idea of the twelve tribes which formed Israel, to speak of the new reality which both continues and surpasses the old.

The use of the number "twelve" in this description could also indicate, always at a symbolic level, an implication of cosmological character. It appears as the multiplication of four by three: the structure of the city is a square (21:16), with three doors on each side (21:13). We have seen already that, in Apocalypse, "four" is the number which symbolises the cosmos, and, more precisely, the four corners of the earth. The number "three" is the "spiritual" number, non-cosmic, of divine nature or simply angelic. The addition of these two numbers gives "seven" which is the number at the basis of the whole of the development of Apocalypse, but which, not without reason, is found nowhere in this closing description.

The absence of "seven" should perhaps be explained, as I earlier suggested, on the basis of the symbolic meaning of the sum of two numbers (four and three) which indicate the two areas of reality, the visible and the invisible. This could mean that "seven" is a number which is complete in itself, but is not the ultimate perfection. It is a fact that the perfection is not achieved in the *sum* of the two numbers, but that number ("seven") disappears, and in its place we have the multiple of the two numbers: "twelve." Is it possible to push this way of reasoning to the point where we see here the empowering which the created reality (and especially man) has received from the contact with the divinity which makes of it a completely new creation?

Perhaps it is not necessary to use these risky interpretative speculations. Perhaps it was sufficient for John to notice that the number "twelve," as a number, not only of totality, but also of perfection, happens to coincide with the biblical revelation and certain cosmological speculations. The important thing for him is to stress that the effects of the work performed by Christ, the new creation, have a character and dimensions which are universal.

We must be even more prudent as regards the symbolism

of the materials which make up the city: gold, pearls, precious stones. There can be no doubt that there is a symbolic meaning behind them. It is extremely difficult, however, to analyse it, because very often the very material spoken of is difficult to identify even at a physical level.

There have been various directions of interpretations. Some link the precious stones with the zodiac and astrological speculations, while others look to the precious stones in the Ephod of the Hebrew High Priest, according to Exod 28:17ff; 39:10ff. John's constant practice of going back to biblical sources leads us to see the second suggestion more favourably. Could the new people of God founded by Jesus Christ be, perhaps, a people of kings and priests? Could the essence of the new covenant set up by his blood be, perhaps, the cult of God "in spirit and in truth" now extended to the whole of humanity? If this is the case, John may well have taken a symbol of prerogative from the old order and extended it to become a universal possibility in the new.

The possibility should not be excluded that John may have seen certain parallels between his biblical sources and the astrological speculations. They may have already been seen by the author of Exodus. However that may be, it appears clear that, whatever the specific meaning of each symbol, the very variety of the representation involved in the symbol indicates once again the comprehensive and universal character of the new reality.

THE MESSIANIC RULE

The new Jerusalem is described by John as the perfect realisation of the prophecies of the coming of the messianic rule. In fact, in the prophets, after the description of the negative effects which this event would bring (judgment of God, destruction of the enemies, destruction of the previous unjust systems) there follows a positive section, dedicated to an illustration of the new order of justice and peace which is to take the place of the old order. In this description we can distinguish, largely, two moments or aspects: one of a more spiritual nature which concerns the reform of a way of life and especially of the cult; the other giving more attention to the transformation of the material conditions of the world and of human reality.

In the great prophets of the classical Hebrew tradition the two aspects stand side by side, though in varying proportions. Isaiah and Jeremiah, and especially the former, are the most outstanding examples of this vision of a radical renewal of man and of the world on both levels, spiritual and material. In the successive developments of the Jewish prophetic traditions, especially after the Exile, there is a gradual separation of the two elements. In the prophetic line which was received into the Canon (especially Ezekiel, deutero-Isaiah and Zechariah), there is a greater insistence upon the reform of a way of life, the observance of the Law, the practice of cult. It is fairly probable that this was a type of messianism which grew in reaction to a form which accentuated the other more material aspect.

The position of the Apocalypse which we have attempted to illustrate is explained in the light of these precedents. The line which it takes in presenting the messianic rule is most decisively the spiritual one, the call for interior renewal. It is not possible to be otherwise, given John's desire to go back, particularly in the face of his Jewish opponents, to the authentic sources of their own revelation. In fact, he brings to a profoundly logical and coherent conclusion the spiritual tradition which he believes he has found in the Biblical tradition, freeing it from the remnants of material hopes and literal misinterpretations.

John's coherence along this line of spiritual interpretation touches also, as we have seen, the external and legal aspects of Jewish cult. He applies to the new Jerusalem, i.e., to the reality of the messianic rule inaugurated by Christ, the prophecies concerning the reconstruction of the Temple and the restoration of the cult (Ezekiel and Zechariah), but leaves out from them all that which concerned the external and the ritual. The people of the new messianic rule are truly a people of "kings and priests" or, as can also be translated, "a kingdom of priests" (see 1:6), but the cult which they offer is not exhausted in the careful and painful observance of rites and liturgical ceremonial.

What of the prophecies concerning the transformation of material conditions and the social and political situations of this world? This form of messianism was kept at the margins of official Judaism dominated by the priestly cast for a long time. However, it survived tenaciously, especially at a popular level, going more decisively in a political direction in the face of foreign occupation, first by the Hellenists of Syria and then by the Romans. In the period which preceded and follows the preaching of Jesus, messianic hopes are especially of this nature. It is especially on this political level that a union is eventually formed between the political messianism and that of official Judaism, leading to the Jewish rebellion of 68-70 A.D.

The disastrous result of that attempt, in which the Christian community plays no part, is not sufficient to discourage the Jewish nationalist faction from pursuing this line until a second revolt, under Bar Kochbah in 135, is finally defeated. When the Apocalypse was written towards the end of the first century, political messianism was, therefore, very much alive. This took place not only in Judaism. There was a variation of it, perhaps a little less political but nevertheless "temporal" in the idea of the reign of a thousand years (Millenarianism) which spread within the Christian community. As we have already suggested, the Apocalypse may be a reaction against both of these forms of messianism: Jewish and Christian.

The reaction is found in the way John interprets the ancient prophecies about the messianic rule. Perhaps it is not chance that precisely in this final part of the book there are many uses of Isaiah, the prophet who more than any other, portrayed the messianic era with vivid images of prosperity and material well-being. From him John receives, as well as the idea of the new Jerusalem (see Is 54:1ff; 62:1ff), the descriptive elements about the splendour and magnificence of renewed Israel and the universal character of its dominion over the peoples.

There is no need to show the symbolic character of this description which may have even been symbolic for Isaiah himself (see, for example, the glory of Yahweh illuminating the new Jerusalem in Is 60:19ff). The symbolic and spiritual value of the words of Isaiah is evident, and perhaps for this reason John recalls them twice in a very short space and with stress, in his description of the new Jerusalem (see 21:23-26; 22:5).

"AND THE NIGHT SHALL BE NO MORE" (22:5)

Continuing the theme of the spiritual character of the messianic rule described by John, the insistence of the author upon the elimination of the night and the darkness merits some consideration. It is not only referred to explicitly in two citations (21:5 and 22:5) but is inferred from the whole description of the city with an insistence upon elements of colour, light and transparence. The dominating feature of the description of the new Jerusalem is its splendour and light. Light is clearly a good thing, an indispensable condition for life in general and especially for the life of man, but it is a little strange that John uses only this aspect to speak of happiness and the satisfaction of all man's needs.

It is common opinion, with few exceptions, that this description (metals, precious stones, light, etc.) is to be understood allegorically. What must not be missed, however, is the *non-eschatological* character of the reality symbolised by the new Jerusalem. It is not a future life or eternity, but the new reality brought by Christ who has come to substitute and at the same time continue into perfection the old order. It is the spiritual Jerusalem which has come to realise what was announced and pre-figured in the old Jerusalem.

We claimed that it is a spiritual reality. Light imagery confirms this opinion. Light is the ancient and obvious symbol of life, especially of the spiritual life and the intellectual life. To be in light means to be able to see all things and the truth of all things: light is true knowledge.

To say that "the night shall be no more" is to say that all is unveiled and made known: and so it is, from the moment when "the mystery of God" is fulfilled (10:7) and "the revelation of Jesus Christ" has taken place.

LIGHT AND WATER: THE SYMBOLS OF THE DIVINE LIFE COMMUNICATED TO MAN

The new Jerusalem is surrounded and shot through with light, a symbol of the mystery brought to its completion, of the full and perfect revelation. A river crosses it: "bright as crystal, flowing from the throne of God and of the Lamb" (22:1). Even this river is symbolic, representing the communication of divine life to man, life which is not simply "existence" because even the water of the river is shot through with light: "bright as crystal," to show the moral and intellectual perfection of the new life.

Light and water, truth and life: these are the constitutive elements of the new Jerusalem, the messianic reign set up by Christ. From their combination that luxurious vegetation, the "tree of life" which covers the square of the city and the banks of the river, always bearing a great diversity of fruit draws its life and nourishment (22:2). This is also a symbol. It indicates the return of man to his original condition of innocence and, beyond that, the possibility that he will now taste the fruit of both trees, of life and of knowledge.

Light, water, fruits: to see, to drink, to eat. These basic needs of man are, of course, on a spiritual level, now satisfied. For John it is not a question of a variety of distinct values. Not only are they all complementary and inseparable, but they form that one and only absolute good, God himself, in the fact that now he dwells among men (21:3, 22; 22:3), and they worship him, contemplating his face and bearing his name on their foreheads (22:3-4) which means that they participate in his life. From the possession of this supreme good comes everything else and the exclusion of all evil. As there shall no longer be night (21:25; 22:5) so also "death shall be no more, neither shall there be mourning nor crying nor pain any more" (21:4).

In the evils, "death," "crying," "pain," there may be a

reference to the evils which came upon man when he originally fell: hard work for the man, the pain of birth for the woman and death for both (Gen 3:16-19). The condition which is eliminated in the messianic rule is that which follows original sin, an elimination, however, on a spiritual level.

The condition of the man, therefore, who enters the kingdom, is again that of man before the fall, but there is a fundamental difference. Then man was promised only immortality, if he could pass through a trial which tested his powers of renunciation; now life is given to him from this moment on, and now he has nothing to renounce, but a participation in the life of God himself to possess.

This is the essence, the very nature of the messianic kingdom which John is describing with such an abundance and skill in his use of images. We now know that this exuberant form of expression is not an end in itself, the uncontrolled manifestation of an extraordinary fantasy, but a most rational and controlled construction, in which every element has its part to play in the deepening and the communication of a very precise message. Nonetheless, what we have presented with such care here has already been anticipated in the earlier parts of the book.

One could recall what was described in the sixth seal. The whole event of the divine salvific plan, with its two phases, is summarised in two succeeding groups of saved: the one hundred and forty four thousand and "a great multitude which no man could number, from all tribes and peoples and tongues" (7:4-9). In this "great multitude" we have seen the new people of God which Christ, with the universally valid sacrifice of himself, has redeemed from the whole of humanity (see also 5:9). In the words with which one of the twenty four Elders presents the crowd to John are contained, in synthesis, all the motifs which return, fully developed, in the description of the new Jerusalem: adoration of the divinity forever in a perfect fashion, the developing of God among men, the abundance of spiritual food and drink, perpetual and unfailing spiritual light, the gaining of the source of life (7:15-17).

John succeeds in expressing the essence of this reality in even more concise terms, e.g.: "a kingdom of priests" (1:6), or through the symbol of the "white garments" (see 6:2; 6:11; 19:11, 14). For John "eternal life" is not something which happens on the other side of death; it is essentially a participation in the divine life. Because of this, the "white garments" are presented by Christ in the letters to the Churches of Asia as something which can be obtained, conserved or lost already in this life (see 3:4-5; 3:18).

THE LETTERS TO THE CHURCHES OF ASIA AND THE NEW JERUSALEM

Our mentioning the letters to the Churches of Asia and the "white garments" leads us to a point made earlier: the relationship between the "seven" of the letters and the description of the new Jerusalem. The links and internal references, implicit or explicit are frequent, and often noticed by the commentators. They are found, in the letters, especially in the final section, which I have called "the promises to the conqueror."

In the first letter, to Ephesus, the conqueror is promised that he will taste the fruits "of the tree of life which is in the paradise of God" (2:7. See 22:2). To the conquerors of the second letter, at Smyrna, is promised that they will not be struck "by the second death" (2:11. See 20:6, 14; 21:8). To the conquerors of the Church of Sardis, in the fifth letter, Christ promises, as well as the "white garments," that their names will not be cancelled "from the book of life" (3:5. See 20:12). It is above all in the promises made to the conquerors of Philadelphia, however, in the sixth letter, that the links between the two sections are so close that they are almost literal citations. Christ promises to the victor: "I will make him a pillar in the Temple of my God: never shall he go out of it, and I will write on him the name of the city of my God, the new Jerusalem which comes down from my God out of heaven, and my own new name" (3:12).

This passage not only establishes the link between the letters and the final description of the new Jerusalem, but also helps to define the nature of the latter. What is promised in the letters is presented as realised in the new Jerusalem. The promises of the letters do not primarily refer to a situation in eternity, on the other side of death; they allude to a radical renewal of human nature, its being and its activity, which begins "now" ("white garments"; "white stone"; "new name"). This renewal consists in a return to the original state of stability in that situation ("never shall he go out of it") and the real, not just promised, participation in the divine life ("I will write upon him the name of my God ...and my own new name"). The clearest manifestation of this radical transformation of human nature and its relationship to God is a parallel radical transformation of cult. Just as the new Jerusalem has no Temple because God and Christ are its Temple (21:22), so also in the letter to Philadelphia it is said that the spiritual material for the making of the Temple is the faithful, the members of the community: a symbol of the perfect union between the faithful and the divinity and, at the same time, of the priestly character of the new people of God.

A comparison of the promises of the letters and the new Jerusalem of the final part of the book shows, on the one hand, the realisation of the promises, and on the other, lends support to our interpretation of the letters. As regards the new Jerusalem, the letters reflect an earlier situation: of waiting, preparation and promise. Even though directed to contemporary Christian communities, they do not refer directly to their own concrete situation, but to that which has prepared it, through the announcement and the promise of the new reality which, in fact, the Churches are: the new people of God. The teaching which John wishes to give to the recipients of his document, who are the faithful of the whole Church (Seven Churches, i.e.: the totality of the Church), is not only a moral or practical exhortation. His message is of a theological nature. He wishes to convince them of a consoling truth ("good news," "*evangelion*"): they are the new Jerusalem; in them has been realised, in a concrete, full and definitive fashion, what had been only announced and promised to the old earthly Jerusalem.

This is what John is trying to do through the close linking of the letters and the final part of the book. Parallel to this, which has been very positive, John establishes another link of a more negative nature. As the promises to the conqueror are realised in the establishment of the new Jerusalem, so also the threats have their fulfilment in the dramatic judgment and destruction of Babylon. We saw there a symbolic representation of the condemnation and the repudiation on the part of God of the old Judaism, corrupt and worldly, now an ally of political authority and, along with it, an instrument of Satan in the assault against Jesus Christ.

The threats, like the promises, run through all the letters: a threat to remove the candelabra (2:5), to destroy that terrible form of idolatry which was prostitution to political authority (2:14: Balaam and Balak; 2:20ff: Jezebel and her lovers), to cancel from the book of life (3:5). All of these are allusions to the possible negative conclusion to the affairs of the ancient chosen people. In the seventh letter, to Laodicea (see 3:14ff) the warnings form a final sharp call, in which there appear to be precise allusions to the destruction of Babylon described in ch. 18. This is always on the spiritual level. To see it happen, one needs the communication of the Spirit of Jesus Christ, which he grants to those who believe in him. In the light of the Spirit one can see what the Jews, blinded by pride, are not able to see, that the heavenly Jerusalem, announced by Scripture, has been brought from heaven to earth by Christ. They have neither recognised nor accepted it and have thus remained outside, becoming "the synagogue of Satan" (see 2:9; 3:9).

THE EPILOGUE (22:6-21)

THEME: The "revelation of Jesus Christ" as his presence and the pouring out of the Spirit.

---

22 ⁶And he said to me, "These words are trustworthy and true. And the Lord, the God of the spirits of the prophets, has sent his angel to show his servants what must soon take place.
⁷And behold, I am coming soon."
Blessed is he who keeps the words of the prophecy of this book.
⁸I John am he who heard and saw these things. And when I heard and saw them, I fell down to worship at the feet of the angel who showed them to me;
⁹but he said to me, "You must not do that! I am a fellow servant with you and your brethren the prophets, and with those who keep the words of this book. Worship God."
¹⁰And he said to me, "Do not seal up the words of the prophecy of this book, for the time is near.
¹¹Let the evildoer still do evil, and the filthy still be filthy, and the righteous still do right, and the holy still be holy."

¹²"Behold, I am coming soon, bringing my recompense, to repay every one for what he has done. ¹³I am the Alpha and the Omega, the first and the last, the beginning and the end."
¹⁴Blessed are those who wash their robes, that they may have the right to the tree of life and that they may enter the city by the gates.
¹⁵Outside are the dogs and sorcerers and fornicators and murderers and idolaters, and every one who loves and practices falsehood.
¹⁶"I Jesus have sent my angel to you with this testimony for the churches. I am the root and the offspring of David, the bright morning star."
¹⁷The Spirit and the Bride say, "Come." And let him who hears say, "Come." And let him who is thirsty come, let him who desires take the water of life without price.
¹⁸I warn every one who hears the words of the prophecy of this book: if any one adds to them, God will add to him the plagues described in this book,
¹⁹and if any one takes away from the words of the book of this prophecy God will take away his share in the tree of life and in the holy city, which are described in this book.
²⁰He who testifies to these things says, "Surely I am coming soon." Amen. Come, Lord Jesus!
²¹The grace of the Lord Jesus be with all the saints. Amen.

EPILOGUE AND PROLOGUE: END AND BEGINNING

The second part of ch. 22 (vv. 6-21) is considered by almost all scholars as the conclusion or the "epilogue" of the Apocalypse. One could say that it is a conclusion well worthy of the rest of the book in its difficulty and obscurity; and for the differences of interpretation which it has caused. Many give it a passing glance, while others suggest that the text needs amending.

Of recent years there has been renewed interest in it because some scholars are discovering traces of a liturgical use here. If this is the case, the epilogue will be linked to the prologue which, as we saw, has a liturgical setting "on the Lord's day" (1:10). This has given rise to the suggestion that the whole book can be understood as a grandiose liturgy which closes in the epilogue.

While liturgical elements may certainly contribute to an understanding of the Apocalypse, they are not decisive; they do not provide the key to the reading of the document. In fact, it is fairly clear that those liturgical elements which some scholars identify (if such they really are) are also re-read in a symbolic fashion, becoming a part of the form of expression used by the whole book.

Without going any deeper into the various discussions of the concluding part of the book, I will attempt to explain it by looking at each of the constitutive parts, and examining them within the context of the whole book. I am doing this especially because the epilogue often seems to be considered as if it stands on its own, and has little to do with the rest of the book. The choice of the term "epilogue" is an indication of that tendency.

As this method did not work for the rest of the book, it does not work for the conclusion either. Here, as in the rest of the work, we will find that the process of the repetition and deepening of themes persists. The only difference from the earlier parts of the book is that it is not a question of an enlargement upon an earlier theme, but rather a clear cut and precise unveiling of the mysteries.

It is not, therefore, a true "epilogue," as we would understand one, a concluding summary of the whole work. In the final part of the book, it could appear ,that John's argument goes on without a final solution, but with an intensification of rhythm and pace to such an extent that one arrives at the end with the breathless waiting generally considered as characteristic of the whole book. This is not the case, as it has not been the case throughout the work. The ardent calling upon the coming of Jesus is still the echo of the long waiting which, in the past, preceded his revelation. This waiting is also present in the lives of those who, even now, are blinded by pride or simply by error and ignorance. As yet, they are not the beneficiaries of his revelation.

The end of Apocalypse in this way completes the theme of the "revelation of Jesus Christ" present since the prologue and developed throughout the whole book. This completion is not a conclusion, an end, but something which is still in active unfolding, in Christ and in humanity, in the "Spirit" and in the "Bride," in life and in light.

JESUS CHRIST, AUTHOR OF THE REVELATION OF THE OLD TESTAMENT

We have said that the final part of the Apocalypse is not really an epilogue, standing on its own, but rather the continuation of an argument which here develops into more frequent and precise formulae. The development of the work goes on, however, to the very end, like a spiral that always runs through the same orbit, but takes that orbit further. This procedure makes it quite difficult to be sure where the so-called epilogue, in fact, begins.

Normally vv. 6-9 are regarded as part of the epilogue. It is fairly clear, however, that they form a conclusion to the previous section, the description of the new Jerusalem. In fact there is a very close link between 22:6-9 and 19:9-10, which concludes the revelation of the nature and the destiny of Babylon. Here also there is first a solemn affirmation of the authenticity and the truth of the things revealed (22:6-7) and then an attempt by John, severely prohibited, to prostrate himself before the revealing angel (22:8-9).

The parallels between the two scenes force us to attribute the same function to them both. As well, as the first passage concludes the revelation concerning the earthly and infernal city, the second concludes the revelation concerning the heavenly city. This fact is important for the intervention of vv. 6-9. At least it clears away the many problems associated with their being read as a conclusion, not of a section, but of the whole book. Most of the problems, especially over who is speaking the words of vv. 6-7 (an angel or Jesus), come from the tendency to detach these verses from the preceding section.

It is, as we have claimed, a conclusion of the revelation

about the new Jerusalem. We must not forget that the illustration of this mystery, as also of Babylon, is done through an angel (see 17:1ff; 21:9ff). In the perspective of the Apocalypse, this fact has a precise significance: both of these mysteries, of perdition and of salvation, are already contained in the revelation of the Old Testament, which has angels as its mediators and representatives. This fact explains both why the angels illustrate the mysteries, and why there is so much use of the Old Testament in these passages.

Beyond this, it also explains why in both cases the angels conclude with a solemn affirmation of the fact that these are authentic words of God (see 19:9; 22:6). The angels are not the authors but only the instruments of the revelation. This concept is repeated, in both the symbolic scenes, where John attempts to adore the angel (see 19:10; 22:8-9). It appears, therefore, that in vv. 6-9 an angel, and not Jesus, is speaking. This is valid for v. 6: "These words are trustworthy and true," and, it appears to me, also for vv. 6-7: "And the Lord, the God of the Spirits of the prophets has sent his angel to show his servants what must soon take place. And behold I am coming soon. Blessed is he who keeps the words of the prophecy of this book."

With the exception of the affirmation, "And behold I am coming soon," it is clear that the rest of the words do not come from Jesus, but they refer to him. He is "the Lord, the God of the Spirits of the prophets" who "has sent his angel." This is shown by the parallel 19:10 and especially by the words of Jesus in 22:16: "I Jesus have sent my angel to you with this testimony for the Churches."

If it is the angel who pronounces these words, we can better understand their significance. They refer to the Old Testament revelation, they describe how it took place, and they also reveal its real author and, consequently, offer us the key to its correct interpretation. That revelation took place through the mediation and agency of the angels, but its real author was Jesus Christ. He, or better his salvific work, and the creation of the new people of God were the message of the Old Testament. This is what is clarified here:

the real object and ultimate goal of the Old Testament revelation was the foundation of the new people of God, the Church (see 22:16).

What, then, are we to make of the words, "I am coming soon"? They clearly belong to Jesus, but that does not mean that he has to be the one to pronounce them in this context. They are inserted into a central position, between the description of how the Old Testament revelation took place ("the Lord, the God of the Spirits of the prophets has sent his angel" - v. 6) and the invitation to observe "the words of the prophecy of this book" (v. 7). In the light of the argument of the whole book, the meaning of this central position is clear: it expresses the central character which, for John, the coming of Christ had at the heart of the Old Testament revelation. This has already been anticipated in v. 6: "what must soon take place." The words, "I am coming soon" are, on the one hand, an explanation of what has just been said and, on the other, a guarantee and a basis for the blessedness promised immediately after. In fact, the certainty of the blessedness which follows the observance of the words in the book is evidently linked to the certainty of the coming of Christ.

The direct speech, "I am coming soon" is what leads us to think of Jesus as actually saying these words. It is explained, however, by the fact that this is a fixed formula to announce the coming of Christ. It will be taken up again shortly (see 22:12 and 20) but also appears in the letters to the Churches of Asia (3:11. See also 2:5 and 16). It is possible that John, in tracing out this synthetic scheme of the Old Testament revelation, placed the messianic announcement directly on the lips of Jesus to stress that he was not only the author of that announcement, but also he who would bring it to its perfection with his coming. If, then, the Apocalypse has the liturgical elements which many would nowadays trace, this repetition of formulae in direct speech could well be explained as a fixed element of a responsorial.

"DO NOT SEAL UP THE WORDS OF THE PROPHECY OF THIS BOOK" (22:10)

Once the section on the revelation of the new Jerusalem is thus concluded, what follows from vv. 10-16 contains a direct discourse of considerable length which seems to come from Jesus Christ. This is made most clear in vv. 12 and 16, but vv. 10 and 11 should also probably be attributed to Christ. Only he, in fact, from among all the living can "open the scroll and break its seals" (5:2-3) and command John: "Do not seal up the words of the prophecy of this book" (v. 10).

The order received by John here is the antithesis of that which he received in ch. 10. There a voice from heaven commanded him to "seal," to "not write" what the seven thunders had said (10:4). We have already explained the value and meaning of that order: in the Old Testament revelation (proclaimed by the voice of an angel and carried by him in the "small open book") the word of the supreme divinity ("seven thunders") is "under seal," not even registered, it is so indirect and covered by symbol.

If John now, representing the human instrument of revelation, is ordered to "not seal up," this can only mean that the revelation is complete and the voice of the supreme divinity can be heard and understood. This has happened through the intervention of Christ who has given meaning, explanation and fulfilment to the ancient Scriptures, breaking open the seals.

Thus "the book of prophecy" whose seals John is asked to open is *not* the Apocalypse itself, as is widely believed, but the Scriptures, i.e., the Old Testament. Three times in a few verses "this book" is mentioned (vv. 7, 9, 10). It was natural to think that it referred to Apocalypse. The expression "this book," however, is pronounced on the first two occasions (vv. 7 and 9) by the angel, and therefore can refer only to that book which John (the human instrument of revelation) has interpreted by order of the angel (1:10-11), i.e. the Old Testament. On the third occasion (22:10), "the book" is mentioned by Christ who orders John not to seal it up: again it is the Old Testament, from which Christ has removed all obscurity and ambiguity.

In the third mentioning of "this book," the Apocalypse does come into the question. In fact, it explains "the revelation of Jesus Christ" (ch. 1) in so far as it illustrates the gradual revelation of Christ through the Ancient Economy and its history, and thus also contributes to the action of Christ, taking away the seals from the old revelation. It is a revelation which continues, now open and universal (see 10:11). It is the full realisation of the order of Christ: "Write what you see, what is and what is to take place hereafter" (1:19). The John who writes the Apocalypse is thus a real "brother" to the prophets (see 19:10; 22:9).

"I AM THE ALPHA AND THE OMEGA, THE FIRST AND THE LAST, THE BEGINNING AND THE END" (22:13)

The idea which dominates this final part of the book is still that which formed the basis of the prologue and the vision of ch. 1: the continuity between the two phases of the revelation which is centered upon the person and work of Jesus, forming a unique and constantly developing process, "the revelation of Jesus Christ, which God gave him" (1:1).

In Christ the difference and the qualitative step which certainly exists between the two phases is united in a harmonious continuity. Because of this, the "book of the prophecy" is always the same in so far as (be it written before or after Christ) he is always its author and object. It is no wonder then, that the same blessing: "Blessed is he who keeps the words of the prophecy of this book" is used by the angel in referring to the "book" carried and transmitted by him (the Old Testament: 22:7) and also by John in the prologue to indicate, specifically, the book which he writes and sends to his brothers in the faith (see 1:3).

There is only one book, because there is only one mission (the two commands to write the inaugural vision and the invitation to prophesy again in 10:11), there is only one human instrument (the prophets who, after the coming of Christ, are the same as the angels), one destination ("the Servants of God"). Above all, there is only one author and object: Jesus Christ. This explains why and in what way, both in the prologue and the inaugural vision and here at the end of the book, Christ insists on saying that he is "the Alpha and the Omega, the first and the last, the beginning and the end" (22:13. See also 1:8; 1:17f). This has been understood, and correctly understood, as referring to the whole of the divinity, in so far as it contains all things within itself. But for John it is true, essentially and in the first place, of Christ, and of his salvific action, because of which he really does stand at the "beginning" and at the "end" of the process of revelation and the putting into effect of the "mystery of God," i.e., the divine plan of salvation.

It is to this unique "book" of revelation, and not only to the Apocalypse, that the solemn warning never to add or remove anything is directed (22:18). The text indicates that Jesus and not John (as most think) is issuing this prohibition. Coming from him, it is to be applied to the whole "book" of which he is the author, speaking first through the angels (1:1; 22:6 and 16) and then through John (1:9). To think that the command came from John is a trivialising and a presumptuous act on the part of the author.

What is sought through this prohibition is much vaster. John wishes to prove that Jesus Christ is the Messiah. To arrive at this, he has used the Scriptures of the Old Testament. At the end of his attempt, John has Christ himself intervene, the author of the whole of revelation, to "witness" in person and with his authority, that this and only this is the meaning of the Scriptures.

The concern of John, therefore, is not only to avoid misunderstanding or to resist the ill-use of his book. The prohibition to add or take away is concerned, first of all, with the whole of the ancient Scriptures, whose author and object he has shown to be Jesus Christ.

"THE SPIRIT AND THE BRIDE SAY, 'COME'" (22:17)

John's attempt to link the conclusion of the book with what went before, and especially with the opening section is clear, and generally noticed by commentators. No one, it appears to me, has succeeded however in picking up the idea of continuity which this technique meant for the author: continuity in the revelation, which is essentially and in the fullest sense "revelation of Jesus Christ," not only between the old and new phases, but also, and above all, inside the new phase.

The popular idea that Apocalypse is the end of revelation, would have been foreign to the mind of the author. It comes from an approach which, as we have repeatedly seen, misses the author's intention. For him it is of first importance to stress how the coming of Jesus Christ into history brings to perfection, on a spiritual plane, all the promises of the coming of the Messiah. In particular, it brings that communication of the Spirit now to the whole of mankind, according to the prophetic prediction of Joel 3:1ff.

This is an important element in the preaching of the early Church (see esp. Acts 2:17-21), and it is basic to the Apocalypse. Here reference to the Spirit cannot be detached from the divinity, when the latter is put into relationship with creation and, especially, with humanity. One can think of the words of the prologue: "Grace to you and peace from him...who is to come...and from the seven spirits...and from Jesus Christ" (1:4-5) or the scene of the throne in ch. 4: "Before the throne burn seven torches of fire which are the seven spirits of God" (4:5). The Spirit, according to the messianic prophecies (see Is 11:2-3) is the prerogative of Jesus Christ, in so far as he is the Messiah. The Lamb, the symbol of Christ in so far as he performs the messianic work of redemption, possesses "seven horns and seven eyes, which are the Seven Spirits of God sent out into all the earth" (5:6).

It is not difficult to see in these words a reflection of the messianic prophecies on the pouring out of the Spirit. It is clear, therefore, that for John also the communication of the Spirit is an essential aspect of the work of Christ, in so far as it is a realisation of the promises attached to the messianic coming. The communication of the Spirit is a constitutive element in the reality of the Church in its twofold aspects of life and illumination, of faith and proclamation. This appears clearly in the letters to the Churches of Asia.

This Spirit, which is the Spirit of God (see 1:4; 4:5) which is offered to the new people of God coming from the whole of humanity, is a gift of Christ. In the Old Economy he sent it as "the Spirit of prophecy" which can be summarised as witness to the coming of Jesus Christ, and to the Law ("word") of God (see 19:10 and all that we said on the reign of a thousand years). This is the Spirit who speaks through the Scriptures of the Old Testament, revealing in them whatever speaks of the coming of Christ, the warnings and the promises associated with his coming, as we learn from the letters to the seven Churches: "He who has an ear, let him hear what the Spirit says to the Churches" (2:7, etc.).

The effective and universal communication of the Spirit happens only in the coming of Christ, as he is the Messiah who possesses the Spirit and has the mission to bring him to men, as the vision of the Lamb in ch. 5 indicates. This explains, therefore, the heartfelt invocation for the coming of Christ which closes the Apocalypse: "Come, Lord Jesus!" (22:20).

The invocation for the coming of Jesus at the end of the book is not for the actual coming of Jesus in itself, as is widely thought, as if it were a manifestation of impatience, of an anxious waiting for the end time, the consummation of all things. It merely expresses the conviction that the coming of Jesus is a good thing for man. We know how John sees the good of man: the communication of the divine life, of eternal life, of the Spirit. It is not chance that the symbols used for this reality – "the tree of life" and "the new Jerusalem" – return twice in this crowded conclusion (vv. 14 and 19). We also know that all this was made possible through the first coming of Christ, with his death and resurrection.

How are we to explain, therefore, all these invocations and promises of a "coming" which close the Apocalypse? They are to be understood, first of all, in relation to the present dimension, i.e., that spiritual and perennial "coming" of Jesus Christ in his Church and in the individual faithful, without which nothing of value and ultimate significance would take place on the historical plane. In fact, the coming of Christ is certainly, for John, a historical event which is unique and cannot be repeated, a given historical moment and an "event" (*kairos*) which the author purposely recalls in the prologue (1:3) and in the conclusion (22:10). Just as even before this "event" there has been a continuous "coming" of Christ in the promises and the witnessing to those promises and to the word of God, so also is there a continuous "coming" after the fulfilment of the promises, and in the participation of mankind in this fulfilment. Christ, in fact, is not only "He who will come," but also "He who is," and who always "is," in the past, in the present and in the future.

This meaning of the invocation for the coming of Christ stresses strongly the liturgical character of the prologue and conclusion to the Apocalypse. This is not only John's idea; all the New Testament expresses the belief that the coming of Christ in his faithful has its privileged place (although not the *only* place) in the liturgical assembly. In it, in the midst of those who are united in his name, Christ is really and concretely present. The liturgical character of the conclusion appears not only from the responsorial nature of some of the formulae, like "Come, Lord Jesus!" (22:20) but also from the reference to the "Spirit" and the "Bride"; from the invitation directed to "him who is thirsty" to come so that he might drink from the "water of life" (22:17).

The liturgical character of the passage also recalls the deep conviction of John that the present coming is nothing more or less than the continuation, or better, the full and perfect realisation of a "coming" which has always been going on. It was precisely in the liturgical gatherings where faith in the coming Christ searched for its roots and substance in the reading and mediation of the ancient Scriptures that this coming was announced and pre-figured.

Thus, seeing the Apocalypse as a reading of the Old Testament, interpreted in the light of the coming of Christ, we can explain not only its liturgical character, but also these invocations for the coming of Jesus. They refer, in the first place, to the invocation which was sounded in the period of waiting, witnessed to by the ancient Scriptures. The very fact that the cry of the Spirit and the cry of the Bride are distinct seems to indicate a moment of waiting, even though brief. The reference to the Bride is deliberate – a *promised* Bride (as in 19:7-8 and 21:2...while in 21:9 we find that the term "woman" – wife, is added).

As all this is situated in a liturgical context, it is clear that a continuity exists within the "revelation of Jesus Christ": that went before, the fulfilment of a promise of God. The same situation is found in the letters to the seven Churches of Asia: the words of Christ directed to the Jewish people are about "the Churches," i.e., the new people of God, as Christ himself explains at the conclusion of the book (22:16).

The past, therefore, is in the service of the present, says the Apocalypse. Is then the present in the service of the future? Certainly! There is this basic difference, however, at the level of the full realisation of the divine salvific plan: "It has been done!" (see 10:7; 16:17; 21:6). From now on the future is firmly committed to the hands of man.

BIBLIOGRAPHY

Commentaries:

Allo, E.-B., *Saint Jean. L'Apocalypse*, Etudes Bibliques (Paris, 1920).

Beasley-Murray, G. R., *The Book of Revelation*, New Century Bible (London, 1978).

Bonsirven, J., *L'Apocalypse de Saint Jean: Traduction et commentaire,* Verbum Salutis 16 (Paris, 1951).

Bousset, W., *Die Offenbarung Johannis*, Meyer Kommentar 16 (Göttingen, 1906).

Caird, G. B., *The Revelation of St. John the Divine*, Black's New Testament Commentaries (London, 1971).

Charles, R. H., *A Critical and Exegetical Commentary on the Revelation of St. John*, International Critical Commentary (Edinburgh, 1920), 2 Vols.

Collins, A. Y., *The Apocalypse*, New Testament Message 22 (Wilmington, 1979).

Kiddle, M., *The Revelation of St. John,* The Moffat New Testament Commentary (London, 1940).

Lohmeyer, E., *Die Offenbarung des Johannes*, Handbuch zum Neuen Testament 16 (Tübingen, 1926).

Loisy, A., *L'Apocalypse de Jean* (Paris, 1923).

Massyngberde, Ford J., *Revelation*, The Anchor Bible 38 (New York, Doubleday, 1975).

Sweet, J., *Revelation*, SCM Pelican Commentaries (London, 1979).

Zahn, T., *Die Offenbarung des Johannes* (Leipzig, 1924-26), 2 Vols.

For further bibliography:

Brütsch, C., *La Clarté de l'Apocalypse* (Genève, 1966⁵).

Feuillet, A., *L'Apocalypse. État de le question* (Paris-Bruges, 1963).

Vanni, U., *La struttura letteraria dell'Apocalisse*, Aloisiana 8a (Brescia, 1980²).

www.ingramcontent.com/pod-product-compliance
Lightning Source LLC
Chambersburg PA
CBHW071227290426
44108CB00013B/1316